Obstinate Hope

This engraved portrait of Nathaniel J. Wyeth (1802-1856), derived from a photograph of his death mask, is the only known likeness of him. OREGON HISTORICAL SOCIETY, #BB004327

Obstinate Hope
The Western Expeditions of
Nathaniel J. Wyeth

VOLUME ONE
1832-1833

BY JIM HARDEE

MUSEUM OF THE MOUNTAIN MAN
SUBLETTE COUNTY HISTORICAL SOCIETY

Obstinate Hope:
The Western Expeditions of Nathaniel J. Wyeth,
Volume One, 1832-1833
by Jim Hardee

Published by the Sublette County Historical Society
Museum of the Mountain Man
P.O. Box 909
Pinedale, WY 82941
www.MMMuseum.com

Printed in the United States of America.

ISBN-13: 978-0-9768113-7-4
ISBN-10: 0-9768113-7-5

Book design by Sommers Studio, Pinedale, Wyoming
www.sommstudio.com

FSC
www.fsc.org
MIX
Paper from
responsible sources
FSC® C014174

In memory of Sandy Boorman. I miss sitting quietly around the smoldering campfire with him, talking about life or just staring wordlessly into the glowing embers. Sandy instilled a confidence in me that made quiet an okay thing. Words cannot describe what times of solitude between two friends truly mean.

MAP 1 *Nathaniel Wyeth's First Western Expedition, 1832-33*

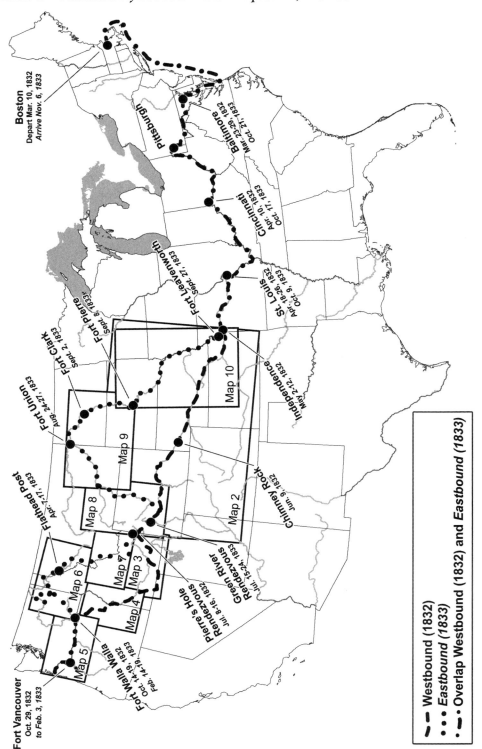

Boston
Depart Mar. 10, 1832
Arrive Nov. 6, 1833

Pittsburgh

Baltimore
Mar. 23-29, 1833
Oct. 21, 1833

Cincinnati
Apr. 10, 1833
Oct. 17, 1833

St. Louis 1832
Apr. 18-26, 1833
Oct. 9, 1833

Fort Leavenworth
Sept. 27, 1833

Fort Pierre
Sept. 8, 1833

Fort Clark
Sept. 2, 1833

Fort Union
Aug. 24-27, 1833

Flathead Post
Apr. 7-17, 1833

Fort Vancouver
Oct. 29, 1832
to Feb. 3, 1833

Fort Walla Walla
Oct. 14-19, 1832
Feb. 14-19, 1833

Independence
May 2-12, 1832

Chimney Rock
Jun. 9, 1832

Green River
Rendezvous
Jul. 15-24, 1833

Pierre's Hole
Rendezvous
Jul. 8-16, 1832

Map 10

Map 9

Map 8

Map 6

Map 5

Map 3

Map 4

Map 2

Westbound (1832)
Eastbound (1833)
Overlap Westbound (1832) and Eastbound (1833)

Contents

List of Illustrations

Maps

Acknowledgments

My examination of Nathaniel Wyeth's life began in the summer of 1992, when I spent ten days in the forests of the Sierra Nevada Mountains with Sandy Boorman as we led a program introducing mountain man practices to about thirty teenaged boys. During preparations for each meal, I would read Wyeth's journals aloud to anyone within earshot. What started out with just me and Sandy grew each day as a few more listeners seated themselves around the fire. By the end of the week, everyone in camp crowded around my stump, in rapt attention, as I regaled them with Wyeth's Rocky Mountain adventures. Hopefully, this current effort will be as stirring to the reader as the journals were to that earlier circle.

Many people played invaluable roles in the production of this book. I am grateful to the Sublette County Historical Society and the staff of the Museum of the Mountain Man. Without Director Laurie Hartwig's and Board President Clint Gilchrist's continued support and confidence in my ability as a historian, funding this project would not have been possible. Angie Thomas was key in tracking down images and assorted details. The editing skills and keen insight of Sue Sommers strengthened the story I wanted to tell. I thank all of you for your patience.

Various readers added immensely to the quality of the book, asking the right questions to send me digging for just a few more specifics to flesh out Wyeth's expeditions. Dr. Ken Zontek's academic review and scholarly advice was important in making sure the facts were in place. Mark Kelly and Carol Kuhn, always supportive of my literary endeavors, waded through the initial draft manuscript and offered many suggestions. Cliff and Melissa Tiffie and Scott Olsen, who have traveled horseback over much of the same ground as Wyeth, kept me on the right trail too. Dawn Ballou and Lea Hardee are credited with numerous improvements in the overall text.

I am indebted to Scott Walker and Clay Landry, who were always there when I needed particular information about resources or material culture. Bruce Belason, senior researcher and my "man on the ground" in Cambridge, was a tremendous help and relentless in his encouragement.

Several libraries and historical societies put up with my constant requests for documents and provided an abundance of assistance. My local Teton County Library never shied when I walked through the door. The Cambridge Historical Society, the Grand Rapids Public Library, and the Oregon Historical Society were always willing to steer me in a helpful direction. Countless regional museums, history associations and professionals seemed ever ready to answer e-mail inquiries, letters and telephone calls.

Obstinate Hope would not have been possible without the continued financial support of the Sublette County Museum Board and Sublette County Commissioners.

In spite of assistance from all corners, any mistakes are purely my own.

Introduction

Nathaniel Jarvis Wyeth (January 29, 1802 - August 31, 1856) is not numbered among America's greatest heroes. The success-ful Bostonian ice merchant is considered a failure in the fur trade. Yet Wyeth was a practical businessman with an adventurous Yankee spirit that led him twice across the continent and back, in 1832 and again in 1834, prior to the development of reliable maps or emigrant trails. Wyeth's contributions to westward expansion have been largely over-looked by historians.

Born and raised in Cambridge, Massachusetts, just across the Charles River from Boston, Wyeth found considerable and early suc-cess in New England's ice trade. His retentive mind, persistence in the face of failure, and keen curiosity enabled him to improve the effi-ciency and profitability of his business ventures. But behind Wyeth's restless and perpetual work ethic lay an unalloyed entrepreneurial ambition. The rising tide of information about the untamed Oregon country provided Wyeth's commercial objectives with a new target: the Pacific Coast. He collected the most up-to-date knowledge of the West and its fur trade by doggedly interviewing the finest minds in and around Boston, never imagining the scholars he consulted might possess flawed information.

Early Oregon immigrant Thomas J. Farnham rated the Bostonian's capability:

> *From what I saw and heard of Wyeth's management in Oregon, I was impressed with the belief that he was, beyond comparison, the most talented business-man from the States that ever established himself in the territory.*[1]

But Wyeth's timing was off. In 1832, the thirty-year-old greenhorn formed his own company, outfitted two dozen men, and trekked cross-country from one seaboard to the other with the intention of becoming a commercial pioneer. In fact, he was entering a highly competitive mar-ket in which three major companies were already contending for profits that had peaked and were beginning to wane. The American Fur, Rocky Mountain Fur and Hudson's Bay companies had dominated the beaver trade, leaving little room for newcomers. Yet Wyeth had jumped in with both feet, having correctly read the potential but missing the clues that he was too late to capitalize upon a boom/bust resource. Much like the modern rise and fall of the dot-com stock market frenzy of the 1990s, once a prospective investor realized it was a growing market in which to invest, the bubble had burst.

Wyeth's eventful 1832 westward odyssey made him the first American to cross the North American continent, ocean-to-ocean, within a calendar year. The eastern half of the journey, from Boston to St. Louis, began in March 1832 and involved a seagoing ship, primitive railroad, horseback and steamboat. Having arrived at the frontier town of Independence, Missouri, the New Englanders joined a supply caravan headed to the Rocky Mountains. Via pack train, horseback and afoot, Wyeth's crew reached the Columbia at the mouth of the Walla Walla River, then floated an HBC bateau downstream to Fort Vancouver. Paddling a canoe to the Pacific Ocean, Wyeth visited the West Coast at Cape Disappointment. The Bostonian arrived at the Pacific the second week of November 1832, eight months after departing his New England home.

Every one of Wyeth's men had deserted at various points along the way, and Wyeth's first venture dissolved with little fanfare. While wintering at Fort Vancouver, he attempted to work out an alliance with the Hudson's Bay Company and then, in the spring of 1833, initiated a trading agreement with Benjamin Bonneville. Neither proposition found favor. He made his way eastward to the 1833 fur trade rendezvous on Green River, then on to the States by way of the Yellowstone and Missouri rivers, accompanying a handful of trappers bringing their annual catch of beaver fur to market. During this trip, ever the entrepreneur, Wyeth clandestinely orchestrated a contract to supply a fur company with trade goods and provisions at the next summer's rendezvous.

In early November 1833, back in Boston once more, he set to work outfitting a second expedition. By early February 1834, Wyeth was again headed west, this time with an expanded business plan. He intended not only to compete in the mountain fur trade, but to also establish a salmon fishery on the Columbia and develop a farm in the

Oregon Country. However, these dreams and potential profits were later undercut when competitors beat Wyeth to that season's trapper gathering, deeply compromising the value of his supply contract. His alternate plan to rescue the venture resulted in the construction of Fort Hall, destined to be a major trading post along the emigrant trails to the Pacific – but not under Wyeth's tenure.

As 1834 waned, Wyeth continued to the Northwest and built another trading post, Fort William, near the mouth of the Willamette River. He tried his best to trap or trade for valuable beaver furs, catch and barrel salmon, and develop a farming operation – but each endeavor met with failure due to HBC competition, difficulty with employees and plain bad luck. Worn out, Wyeth returned home to Boston in 1836. Ill-fortune and harsh realities had overpowered the naïve expectations, obstinacy and hope that had driven him up until then. He had spent $20,000 (equivalent to over $500,000 today) and nearly five years of his life in the effort.[2]

Wyeth's failure in the dwindling Rocky Mountain fur trade, however, turned out to be secondary to his role as a key figure in the opening of the West. Several of the men who accompanied him settled in the Pacific Northwest, established farms, and eased the way for Americans still to come. Moreover, Wyeth's Fort Hall greatly enhanced the infrastructure of the Oregon/California Trail. Unwittingly or not, the trading post was located a short distance from where the main emigrant trail would fork, one branch to Oregon and the other to California.

The first American missionaries to the native populations beyond the Rocky Mountains, Jason and Daniel Lee, traveled with Wyeth's 1834 brigade, as did naturalists John Townsend and Thomas Nuttall. A catalog of over 100 plant specimens Wyeth himself collected on his first expedition was described by Nuttall and published by the Academy of Natural Sciences in 1834.[3] Wyeth's own familiarity with Indians of the Rocky Mountain region was solicited by Henry Schoolcraft to be published in a special section of a voluminous work on Native Americans.[4]

As evidence of his progressive nature, Wyeth's 1832 adventure was the first in the Rocky Mountains to record the use of firearms with the more modern percussion ignition system. Two years later, he was the first fur trade supplier to record the sale of items made from India

A plant specimen collected by Wyeth on the Flathead River in the spring of 1833 was named *Wyethia helianthoides* by naturalist Thomas Nuttall in honor of the intrepid explorer. The plant is more commonly known as white-rayed mule's ears. The illustration is from Nuttall's original 1834 publication, "A Catalogue of a Collection of Plants made Chiefly in the Valleys of the Rocky Mountains." ANSP LIBRARY & ARCHIVES, QH1.A16 PLATE V.

rubber, an early method of waterproofing. Though he never visited the West again, in 1839 Wyeth wrote a noteworthy memoir on Oregon for the House Committee on Foreign Affairs, familiarizing Easterners with events in the region and making it easier for Congress to support American interests in Oregon.[5] Wyeth lived to see Oregon become a territory of the United States in 1848.

Fortunately for history, Wyeth kept journals during these industrious years – 1832 throughout 1835 – which contain a wealth of information. Wyeth had been urged to publish his account soon after his return, but he would not consent to do so.[6] In 1899, the Oregon Historical Society finally published the journals, along with 245 letters written by Wyeth between August 1831 and September 1835. The diaries were then in the possession of Wyeth's niece, Mary J. Fish, of Taunton, Massachusetts.

The man who obtained permission to publish the diary was Frederic G. Young, a skilled historian, founder of the Oregon Historical Society and editor of its *Quarterly*. By the time Young received it, the book containing Nathaniel Wyeth's journal had been partially mutilated. At least four pages describing the earliest days of the journey seemed to have been removed; thus the exact date Wyeth began to log his account is unknown.[7] Consequently, events from March 1, 1832 (the day the New Englanders left Cambridge on their journey west), until Wyeth's first extant entry on June 6, 1832, have been reconstructed here primarily from Wyeth's letters and the recollections of expedition members John Wyeth and John Ball. Though Wyeth did not write every day, from the June 6 entry forward, the diary is intact and forms the underpinnings of this narrative.

This reassessment of Wyeth's fur trade incorporates writings by other men who accompanied or associated with Wyeth during his enterprise, adding dimension to Wyeth's story. His young cousin John Bound Wyeth deserted the 1832 expedition about half way to its destination. Once home, and with the liberal assistance of local physician/scientist Dr. Benjamin Waterhouse, John wrote a book about his exploits, often casting Nathaniel in a negative light.

Another point of view included in this volume is that of John Ball. A New York lawyer, Ball accompanied Wyeth all the way to Oregon on that first expedition and kept a journal, penning his own reminiscences some years later.[8]

As mentioned above, Wyeth's 1834 expedition included ornithologist John K. Townsend, who chronicled the journey to Fort Vancouver. Another member of this crew was future trapper Osborne Russell, whose *Journal of a Trapper*, spanning the years 1834-1842, is one of the finest primary accounts of life in the Rocky Mountains during the fur trade period. Isaac P. Rose also accompanied the 1834 caravan, and would tell his story to James B. Marsh, who in turn related Rose's tale in *Four Years in the Rockies*. Missionary Jason Lee used Wyeth essentially as an escort to the Pacific Northwest, and left a journal and several letters that lend perspective to the Bostonian's challenges. Lee's nephew Daniel would later team with J. H. Frost to publish *Ten Years in Oregon*, which mentions Lee's tour with Wyeth. Accompanying Lee's contingent was Cyrus Shepard, whose journals were used extensively in the preparation of his biography, *The Missionary Teacher: A Memorial of Cyrus Shepard*, which shed additional light on the 1834 westward excursion.[9]

Other primary accounts adding texture to Wyeth's story include the journals of William Marshall Anderson, who in 1834 accompanied William Sublette's rendezvous supply train – the one that scotched Wyeth's business plan. Washington Irving, while crafting *The Adventures Captain Bonneville,* accessed Benjamin Bonneville's journals, which included interactions between Wyeth and Bonneville. Irving fleshed these out through personal interviews with Wyeth himself.[10] Journals from contemporary trappers such as Alexander Ross, Warren Ferris and others also provide comparison adventures, helping to place Wyeth's experiences in context.

Regrettably, Nathaniel Wyeth's original journals have not resurfaced. It is hoped this new examination will alert the present owner, probably some distant descendant, to the need for revealing the whereabouts of Wyeth's diaries if they still exist. Meanwhile, this version of Wyeth's writings relies on Young's 1899 work. Young took pains to make only minor edits and added negligible supportive information. The Oregon historian's goal was to "reproduce the original faithfully to the letter." Yet, in describing Wyeth's manuscript, Young stated

From the conditions under which the record was made some parts are faint and mutilated but it is hoped that defects arising from this cause and from shortcomings in editing will not seriously impair the historical value of these documents.[11]

Since the original document is not available for examination, defects or shortcomings in Young's work will remain in this current examination of Wyeth's journals. Young often corrected what he perceived as the New Englander's nonstandard spelling. The bulk of these bracketed corrections have been deleted to present Wyeth's writing in its raw and original form. Where Young was unable to decipher Wyeth's handwriting, he placed a bracketed question mark, "[?]," within the text and these have been retained. Other bracketed notations have been added or retained where clarification seemed necessary. Wyeth frequently omitted periods at the ends of sentences, leaving an extra space instead. That space has been preserved so the reader may determine where a sentence ends.

Young included hundreds of Wyeth's letters from 1831 to 1835 in his volume. These are not reproduced here in their entirety but are excerpted occasionally to provide important details. Several previously unpublished letters from or to Wyeth have surfaced over the years; information gleaned from these is introduced as new source material, though not presented in full form.

This work is divided into two volumes, essentially one for each expedition. Volume One covers Wyeth's early days and the 1832-1833 expedition. Volume Two covers the 1834-1836 expedition and the subsequent years of Wyeth's life. Each of Wyeth's journal entries, from June 6, 1832 onward, is set within a grey box with month, day, year and location noted. No additional citation is provided since the source is the same for all of Nathaniel's entries: the original publication of Wyeth's journals by the Oregon Historical Society.

Commentary follows most of Wyeth's daily entries. This supplemental information clarifies or explains what is described in the day-to-day account and often compares the Bostonian's activities with those of contemporaries. Occasionally, Wyeth wrote at length, catching up on several days at a time. In these instances, the protracted entry is interrupted to allow accompanying commentary to keep pace. This hybrid style is intended to frame a more readable story while still maintaining a scholarly approach to the material.

A reasonably correct itinerary of Wyeth's travels is not easy to produce because Wyeth mentioned so few landmarks and often skewed the names of those he cited. Further complicating the task, many locations were unnamed at the time, or the place names he used have since changed. All too frequently, the only data Wyeth provided was a vague description such as "a small creek." What is presented here approximates the distances and directions entered for a day's travel. Ultimately, the route may have been quite different.

In late 1836, back in Boston and finished with the Rocky Mountains, Wyeth reentered the ice trade under his previous mentor and employer, Frederic Tudor. In future years, Wyeth would be instrumental in extending the Charleston Branch Railroad to Cambridge. He became a supporter of a growing local brick industry, and developed a profitable business shipping refrigerated produce from his own Massachusetts farm to the tropics. It was not surprising that when Nathaniel Wyeth died in 1856, he was praised as a "public benefactor." His success in the East far outweighed the misfortunes detailed in this book.[12]

Despite his evident self-confidence and ambition, Wyeth shrank from publicity. He would never consent to having a portrait or photograph made of himself; after his death, a photographic image was taken of his death-mask, and the only known image of Wyeth (see frontispiece) is a drawing based on this now-lost photo. Details about the death-mask or its whereabouts are unknown.[13]

Whatever paths Wyeth took, "he it was who, more directly than any other man, marked the way for the ox-teams which were so shortly to bring the Americanized civilization of Europe across the roadless continent."[14] Wyeth could never fit the mold of the classic mountain man as we understand it today, but his story is a fascinating one of perseverance and determination in America's Far West.

1.
The Early Years

Nathaniel Jarvis Wyeth seemed born to the cutting edge, whether on the borders of civilization or at the front lines of industrial progress. Perhaps Wyeth's liking for frontiers was a family trait. Led by Nicholas Wythe, the clan sailed from England to the New World in the mid-1600s and can be traced in early records as both "Wyeth" and "Wythe." George Wythe of the Virginia Commonwealth, a signer of the Declaration of Independence, was perhaps the best known of Nathaniel's early relations.[1]

The earliest recorded land purchases by Wyeth's ancestors lay on the fringes of Cambridge, Massachusetts, in the mid-1600s, and for over 200 years, the Wyeth family would own various parcels of land in the Cambridge area. The "Proprietors' Records" of early real estate transactions contain an entry of May 20, 1645, indicating Nicholas Wythe, a mason recently emigrated from England, purchased a "dwelling with outhouses, and about halfe an Acr. of Land" on the outskirts of the town's west end.[2] This parcel was marked "Wyeth" on maps of 1776 and 1830, and was located on present Garden Street, above Phillips Place.[3] Known as the Wyeth homestead, it descended from father to son for two centuries, passing from Nicholas to Ebenezer, to Jonathon, to Jonas, to Jonas II, to Job and finally to Jonas III, who sold the homestead property in 1850.[4]

On that May day back in 1645, Nicholas had also purchased a two-acre plot to the west, where he built a farmhouse that eventually contained Chippendale chairs and good silver, at least one piece being a genuine Revere.[5]

About one hundred years later, the Wyeth clan expanded a few miles farther into the country when Ebenezer, a brick-maker, bought a large farm that extended from the northwest portion of Mount Auburn to Fresh Pond. Directly across from their property was an area known as Stone's Wood or Sweet Auburn, destined to become Mount Auburn Cemetery. This area of Cambridge lay just west of the Tory estates that lined Brattle Street. Wyeth's new farmhouse was located at the corner of

WYETH FAMILY TREE

Ebenezer Wyeth & Susanna Hancock ----- Jonas
(1698 - 1754)   (1707 - 1789)

Ebenezer
Mary
Jonas
Joshua
William
Susanna

Ebenezer Wyeth, Jr. & Mary Winship ----- Jonas
Susanna
Mary
Noah Wyeth & Betty Fitch -----
Sarah

Gad
John
Elizabeth

Noah
Elizabeth

Jacob Wyeth & Elizabeth Jarvis ----- **Jacob Wyeth**
Nathaniel Jarvis Wyeth

Leonard
Charles

Anna

Job Wyeth & Lydia Convers -------- **John Bound Wyeth**
Andrew

Noah
Eliza
Abiel
Benjamin

Lydia
Dorcas
Isaac

Solomon Livermore & Abigail Jarvis ----- **Thomas Livermore**

Elizabeth
Mary

This segment of Wyeth genealogy shows the relationship of several Wyeths who played roles in Nathaniel's expeditions. Bolded names are family members who accompanied the Pacific Trading Company on its westbound 1832 journey.

modern Fresh Pond Parkway and Brattle Street. This pre-revolutionary dwelling was marked with small windows and two chimneys arranged symmetrically around the doorway.[6]

Today, the house has been moved to a different site altogether and much altered. It stands next to a historic manor, the former summer residence of wealthy Salem, Massachusetts, merchant William Gray. The Wyeth house was once attached as a service wing to Gray's mansion, built in 1804-1805 and known as "The Larches." The land immediately west of the Larches was Wyeth farmland, owned by the family until the mid-nineteenth century. Gray in fact purchased several acres in 1808.[7]

When America broke away from Great Britain, Jonas Wyeth, dressed in Indian garb, tossed chests of Bohea, Hyson and other teas into the harbor during the Boston Tea Party. Ebenezer Wyeth fought the Redcoats at Bunker Hill. Noah and four other Wyeths took up arms against His Majesty's army on April 19, 1775. Ebenezer's son, John, owned the *Harrisburg Advertiser*. During the Revolution, the newspaper supported George Washington's war effort, and when the fighting was over, John was awarded the postmaster position in Harrisburg, Pennsylvania.[8]

Nathaniel Wyeth's father, Jacob Wyeth, was Ebenezer's seventh child. He was born in 1764 and raised in Cambridge. Jacob graduated with distinction from Harvard College in 1792 and became a man of "high scholarly attainment" who was prominent in literary circles.[9] Jacob married Elizabeth Jarvis, the daughter of a leading English family, in November 1796.[10] Elizabeth was a descendant of another Declaration of Independence signer, John Hancock. Her girlhood home was located near Cambridge Common, where George Washington first gathered his Revolutionary troops on the old Lexington-Concord road. It was said that Elizabeth looked out the window of her home to see two British soldiers drink at their well while on their way to Concord. Harvard University would later purchase portions of the property for an athletic field and name it after the Jarvis family.[11] Both Jacob and Elizabeth lived long lives – Jacob died at 92 years of age and Elizabeth at 89.

Soon after graduating from college, Jacob purchased from his father eight acres bordering Fresh Pond. There, in 1796, he built a hotel on the wooded promontory "high on a bluff, shaded by trees, and looking out across the Pond into the west wind," in what is today Kingsley Park.[12]

Retail, by Messrs. No. 13, Cornhill, United States.

T, elegant MANSION street, No. 483, late ets, No. 63. Terms above.

given that the y appointed execu-

ROBINSON, f Norfolk, merchant, n herself that trust, lirects. All persons ite of the said de- t the same; and all state, are called upon

OBINSON, Ex'x.

TO BE LET,
At a moderate rent, a convenient four story brick House in Columbia-street, well calculated for a genteel family For particulars, apply to CHANDLER ROBBINS, Real Estate Broker, No. 12, Exchange-street, or to Mr. KUPFER, Short-street.   dec 29

INSTRUCTION AND BOARDING.
A LADY in the vicinity of Boston, is desirous of taking young children to board and instruct upon reasonable terms. Reference may be had on application at the Centinel Counting Room.
dec 15   7t

FRESH POND HOTEL.
THE subscriber being desirous of rendering the above situation a place of resort during the Winter as well as the Summer months, has provided such conveniences as, he hopes, will be deemed suitable for the accommodation of visitants.
Balls and large parties can be entertained upon a short notice, in as good style as elsewhere.
NATHANIEL I. WYETH.
Cambridge, Dec. 3   8sp

Goods are stored, lea and half Duck, Ravens Diaper, Drillings, Leat Old Sable Iron and c Also—A small invoice and Ravens Duck, and a age, assorted, from Cab to S. PARKMAN Jun.
dec 25

WASH L
S. H. PARKER, 12, . by the London WASH LEATHER, s Drawers, Toweling for &c. and for many oth sale cheap for cash, by sept 8

HARD
M. NEWELL, No. 2 . ceived by the lat a general assortment of WARE, which he offer terms, for cash or credit

Nathaniel Wyeth advertised the Fresh Pond Hotel in the *Columbian Centinel*, a Boston newspaper, on January 5, 1825. The understated text assured the reader that "large parties can be entertained upon a short notice, in as good style as elsewhere." The use of a capital "I" in place of a "J," as in Wyeth's middle initial, reflects the influence of Latin, a convention of the time. THE BOSTON ATHENAEUM

Lyman Willard took over the Fresh Pond Hotel around 1840. The advertisement above shows (left to right) boathouses, the stairway leading from the lake up to the hotel, games being played on the lawn, the family home of Jacob Wyeth, fruit orchards, horse stables, and a cage where ducks were kept and released for sport. CAMBRIDGE HISTORICAL SOCIETY, CHS IMAGE COLLECTION

The hotel was an easy buggy ride from town. Its long driveway led from the highway to stables and a large turn-around for carriages. The Fresh Pond Hotel was one of the region's best known landmarks until the railroad made New Hampshire more accessible and drew vacationers to the north. Wyeth's establishment was one of the most upscale resorts around Boston, complete with plate-glass windows and black walnut newel posts at the stairs. The inn was successful enough to pay off its construction loans within eighteen months.[13] Jacob earned a better-than-satisfactory living from it until he retired in the 1820s and left the hotel's operation to younger generations.[14]

In 1885, the hotel was bought by the Sisters of Joseph, who ran a Catholic girls' school and convent. It later became a roadhouse before being moved to the corner of Lake View Avenue and Worthington Street and converted into a tenement.[15]

Activities at the Wyeths' Fresh Pond Hotel included the typical fishing and fowling already available to the public along its shaded shores. Jacob Wyeth later provided swing sets, a bowling alley for games of nine pins on the lawn, and a number of small boats for sailing and rowing. Famous for its gourmet menu, the on-site restaurant boasted a wide range of wines and other alcoholic beverages. An in-house orchestra played a variety of music including college songs when well-to-do students from nearby Harvard came to dine. Frequently, the graduating class of seniors would retire to the Fresh Pond Hotel following commencement.

> *In the evening, preceded by the "Boston Brigade Band" we marched up to Fresh Pond Hotel where Mr. Wyeth (who will ever flourish in our recollections of College scenes) had provided a most superb supper. – Our wines, which were Claret, Champaigne, and Madeira, were ... the very best ... We broke up in pretty good order and returned to Cambridge without occurrence of any accident.*[16]

It was into such a dynamic environment that this story's central character entered the world. Nathaniel Jarvis Wyeth was born in the family home at the Fresh Pond Hotel on January 29, 1802, the fourth child and youngest son of Jacob and Elizabeth Wyeth.[17] He was named after his maternal grandfather, Nathaniel Jarvis.

The Fresh Pond Hotel property (pictured here circa 1888-92) was purchased by the Sisters of Joseph in 1885. The Mount St. Joseph Academy operated as a boarding school for young ladies, while the Jacob Wyeth house was made into a convent.

CAMBRIDGE HISTORICAL SOCIETY, CHS IMAGE COLLECTION, 1E.0006 CHS

Though little is known of Nathaniel Wyeth's early life, he no doubt spent his younger years exploring the borders of Fresh Pond and observing the activities of his older siblings. His oldest brother, Jacob, graduated from their father's alma mater, Harvard University, and eventually became a doctor. Another older sibling, Leonard, conducted an extensive trade in silk and lace. He was later joined by brother Charles in that business, then based in Baltimore, Maryland. Nathaniel may have been expected to attend Harvard as well, though he seems to have been content to join his father in managing the Fresh Pond Hotel, taking over in the 1820s.[18] Nothing else is known about Wyeth's education.

In 1824, on his twenty-second birthday, Nathaniel married his second cousin, Elizabeth Jarvis Stone, who was a couple of years his senior.[19] He built a new home on the family's acreage and planted a few fruit trees. During the hotel's shoulder season, he harvested winter ice from the surface of Fresh Pond to stock the hotel's thickly insulated ice house. By improving methods to cut the shifting ice, Nathaniel arrived at a series of inventions and patents for what became a lucrative career. Wyeth reduced the back-breaking labor of gathering and storing ice, which helped the commodity become a major export from Boston to the West Indies and the Far East.

In the early nineteenth century, ice was harvested with axes and shovels. Nearly two-thirds of the resulting misshapen chunks and slivers could melt away before being sold and delivered. Such a slow process was highly susceptible to dawdling employees, untimely thaws or snow storms – an entire year's ice crop could be quickly ruined.[20]

One of the ingenious devices Wyeth fabricated around 1825 was a horse-drawn ice cutter that scored and grooved the surface of the pond into uniform squares. These squares were then broken apart with cutting bars, resulting in smooth-sided blocks of uniform size. The blocks could be stored, shipped and delivered easily. This most basic of inventions cut the cost of harvesting ice from approximately thirty cents per ton to about ten cents per ton, according to some estimates. More importantly, this method promoted the sale of ice by weight rather than size.[21]

Nathaniel also recognized that above-ground ice houses would be more effective than the underground vaults then in use. He devised immense structures with double-layered walls that were packed with insulation, usually sawdust, which could preserve blocks of ice for a year or longer.

Frederic Tudor, the nation's pre-eminent ice dealer of the time, was already exporting ice to many parts of the world. He was impressed with the young prodigy and invited Wyeth to join his company on November 1, 1826, at a salary of $500 per year.[22] Wyeth was soon supplying Tudor with ice from Fresh Pond. Tudor was twenty-two years older than his developing protégé; his experience and influence may well have helped spur the younger Wyeth toward becoming a determined, driven businessman. Tudor's basic philosophy can be deduced from the creed hand-printed on the cover of his diary:

> *He who gives back at the first repulse, and without striking the second blow despairs of success, has never been, is not, and never will be a hero, either in war, love, or business.*[23]

Wyeth sold Fresh Pond's ice crop for the winter of 1826-27 to Tudor, and freighted it onto Tudor's outgoing ships at Boston. By 1827, Wyeth was managing the Fresh Pond ice-houses of the "Ice King," as Tudor was becoming known.[24] Tudor's diary consistently commends his young employee, describing him as "active & intelligent," and "just enough of a schemer & inventor to be valuable."[25]

The following winter, 1827-28, provided a stage on which Wyeth's tenacity and ambition could shine. The weather was fairer and warmer than usual, presenting myriad problems for the ice business. Though temperatures fluctuated, for most of December they stayed at or above 36 degrees and some days much higher. By the middle of the month, not a block of ice had yet been harvested. Looking ahead, Tudor conferred with Wyeth about his new, as yet untested invention: an iron and steel ice cutter that could cut consistently sized blocks. Wyeth also had an idea for an improved ice-loading machine, and Tudor had approved its construction.

On Christmas Eve, Wyeth found five-inch-thick ice on Fresh Pond. Shortly after New Year's Day, Wyeth began cutting ice for his own ice-house, even though it was only six inches thick. That thickness was fine for local use, but Tudor needed thicker blocks for export.[26] While in charge of Tudor's ice business, Wyeth was also harvesting ice for retail dealers in Boston. Moreover, others were working Fresh Pond too, and

Known as Boston's "Ice King," Frederic Tudor (1783-1864) employed Wyeth in the early years of his career in the ice trade. FRANCIS ALEXANDER CIRCA 1830; MUSEUM OF FINE ARTS, BOSTON, #SC197612

with unseasonably warm temperatures as mid-January approached, mud was getting thick around Fresh Pond. On January 13, 1828, Tudor found Wyeth wandering in the woods "in all the lonely perturbation of invention & contrivance," focused on how he could improve his earlier handiwork.[27]

On January 22, the mercury plummeted to two above zero and Tudor wrote in his journal, "The frost covers the windows, the wheels creak, the boys run, winter rules & $50,000 worth of ice now floats for me upon Fresh Pond."[28] The next day, with a modicum of success, Wyeth tested the new apparatus for hoisting blocks of ice onto wagons. Tudor commented that Wyeth

> *was on the pond without hat or coat. He had forgotten that the Therm. was at the freezing point. In his yet unsettled plans he found warmth and circulation from the calm-seeming but in fact vigorous action of his mind.*[29]

Ice Production in Nineteenth-Century America

Illustrations 1 through 3 are engravings of ice harvesting at Fresh Pond.
They appeared in *Scribner's Monthly Magazine*, August 1875.

SCRAPING

1. The first step in harvesting ice was to scrape the snow from the frozen surface of the pond. CORNELL UNIVERSITY LIBRARY, MAKING OF AMERICA DIGITAL COLLECTION

GROOVING.

2. Wyeth invented a horse-drawn plow with sharp teeth to score the surface of the ice in long grooves, marking the size of the blocks. CORNELL UNIVERSITY LIBRARY, MAKING OF AMERICA DIGITAL COLLECTION

SAWING, CALKING AND BREAKING OFF.

3. The blocks were further sawn as needed, maneuvered into open water, and guided to the ice house. CORNELL UNIVERSITY LIBRARY, MAKING OF AMERICA DIGITAL COLLECTION

4. *Gleason's Pictorial Drawing Room Companion* of February 1854 published this illustration of ice-cutting at Spy Pond in West Cambridge, Massachusetts. Here the cut ice is floated across open water in preparation for removal from the pond. Ice houses where the ice will be stored can be seen in the background at right, along the pond's edge. MASSACHUSETTS HISTORICAL SOCIETY

Due to the muddy roads, the wagons could not get close enough to the ice cutters on the frozen lake. Wyeth's fertile imagination then created a new method for getting the ice to the wagons. The work crew cut a canal through the ice, making a watery track from the work area to the icehouse's lifting apparatus. Then, the men floated blocks to the lift, drew them from the pond, and slid them along a path to the wagons.

Every time the temperature dipped below freezing, Wyeth had his men on the ice, sometimes throughout the night. If the sky was overcast, he cut ice even if the temperature rose. In between working for various vendors, Wyeth managed to deliver ice to Fresh Pond Hotel's icehouse, where his goal was to keep 200 cords, each stacked eight by four by four feet, readily available for hotel use.

On February 8, Wyeth reported to Tudor that the previous night, he had found nine-inch-thick ice on the south side of the pond where a steep hill shaded the area. The crew had managed to harvest forty cords. Most of the ice was being cut at night since the daytime temperatures were too warm by noon. Even then, it was slow – ten cords one night, maybe fifteen cords the next. The roads were sloppy; it had taken sixteen oxen and horses to drag ice blocks measuring only six feet in length.

That winter's below-average quantity of ice from Fresh Pond was soon stored. Other ponds were investigated for potential harvests. South of Cambridge, at Jamaica Pond, the ice was already gone. In West Cambridge, Spy Pond's ice was little better. Tudor and Wyeth inspected Spot Pond in Medford with no luck. Wyeth soon found Swain's Pond, a small body of water in nearby Malden, had been overlooked by other ice-cutters. The ice was nearly one foot thick. Wyeth and a dozen men started work there on February 17, hoping to take as much as 500 cords of ice from this pond, nestled in the foothills and protected from sun and wind.

Tudor sharpened Wyeth's determination by offering him one dollar additional commission for every cord over one hundred that Wyeth could load from this pond. Thus, when Wyeth and his crew arrived at the pond at 3 a.m. and found a large rock obstructing their way to the ice, they did not hesitate to blast it from the road with a charge of gunpowder. By dawn, Wyeth and his wagons had arrived at their destination, much to the chagrin of neighbors. By breakfast, the owner of the land had discovered what was going on. Through quick negotiations, Wyeth acquired the rights to harvest the ice.

But adversity dogged the Tudor Company. Wyeth planned to work the men through the night, sleeping only during the warmest parts of the afternoon, but it started raining shortly after dark. Come morning, the ice had thinned by a full two inches. The roads became so bad that Tudor's chaise fell into a rut and broke its springs. Installing 300 yards of sailcloth to shade the ice did little if any good and, to top off an already rotten day, a horse broke through the pond and had to be rescued.

Yet another source, Long Pond, had been identified, but the yield would be only fifteen cords at best. On February 21, Tudor went to check the progress at Swain's Pond only to find Wyeth and the men in their cups at Wait's Tavern. They had done as much as they could.

Soon after, Tudor asked Wyeth if he was willing to travel north until he found ice in decent enough condition to cut. Tudor's offer of an extra ten percent of the profit from any ice sold from the new region had Wyeth skittering off to Kennebec, Maine. Keeping the plan secret from competitors, Wyeth and his team of ice-cutters snuck out of Cambridge on February 26. Their goal was to cut 100 cords of ice per day until they had 1,200 cords.

Wyeth returned from Maine on March 24 declaring he had cut 1,132 cords of ice. He then proceeded to New York, Philadelphia, and Boston to peddle this commodity while the price soared. By winter's end, Wyeth had delivered the Tudor Company an ice yield and profits well ahead of the competition. As a result, Tudor increased Wyeth's salary to $1,200 per year.[30]

With the responsibilities and benefits from his work for Tudor, Wyeth soon resigned his Fresh Pond Hotel position, leaving his cousin Jonas to run the establishment. In 1829, Wyeth was granted a patent on his ice-cutting process. While Tudor sought to monopolize New England ice exports, Wyeth still hoped to increase the volume of his personal shipments during off-duty hours. The two men began experimenting with new ways to force ice to thicken earlier in the season. Selecting a patch of water in front of the icehouse on Fresh Pond, Tudor and Wyeth theorized that if they could confine the water with a wooden fence, the ice would form faster and thicker. They even picked a spot free of springs and weeds, but did not proceed for fear the competition would realize what they were doing before they could get the process patented.

The idea, however, had merit. In January, 1830, with the ice only three inches thick, Wyeth suggested trying to double it by "passing one sheet [of ice] under the other & cutting round so as to let it rise a little." The men tested the concept on the night of January 17. It worked so well that two days later, Wyeth tried it on a larger section of ice, fifty feet square. January 22 brought Wyeth's jubilant report that on a pond where the ice had been only four and half inches thick, he had produced a nine-inch block. Three days later, they were getting blocks twelve inches thick.[31]

Within a few years, Wyeth's new method would become the industry-wide standard. By the winter of 1833, pond ice five inches thick could be doubled and doubled again to produce blocks up to twenty-one inches thick.[32]

Meanwhile, Wyeth's employer had other industries in mind. During the summer of 1828, Tudor and E. R. Dorr had partnered to purchase the Ixion graphite mine near Sturbridge, Massachusetts. The mine tended to fill with water, and Tudor thought a windmill might keep the mine dryer than the pumps currently being used. Tudor turned to Wyeth, who had a windmill set up and working in short order. In May, Wyeth went to New York on personal business, and while he was there, Tudor had him consult with the sales firm of Atkinson and Rollins, to persuade more activity in marketing the mine's primary product: lead crucibles for melting other metals.[33]

The graphite mine sold crucibles of black lead, sometimes called plumbago, in large quantities to American brass foundries. In August 1829, Wyeth had gone to Martha's Vineyard to inspect clay specimens that might improve this product. Shortly after, he fell ill and production slowed nearly to a halt. When Wyeth finally recovered, his inventiveness did too. He improved the quality of the lead by extracting more quartz from the ore. He ground the quartz, then washed it with water, allowing the heavier impurities to sink and the fine lead to float free. Wyeth then compressed the purified lead, mixed with glue, into the pot's shape. After a few mis-steps, his experiments eventually yielded a stronger crucible.

In the fall of 1829, Tudor's mining partnership with Dorr fell apart, leaving him the sole owner. By October, Tudor had put Wyeth in charge of the mine operations in exchange for a quarter of its profits. Typical of

Wyeth, he found innovative ways to improve mining processes, increasing the yield of ore. However, he also reduced employee wages by twenty-five percent.

Between the ice business and his duties at the graphite mine, Wyeth's entrepreneurial mind kept churning. Everywhere he looked, there seemed to be yet another opportunity to make more money. Inevitably, he soon turned his eyes to the West.

2.
Oregon Beckons

Sometime in 1829, Wyeth attended lectures given by Hall J. Kelley, a former Boston teacher who promoted the settlement of the western territories. Kelley had read the journals of the Lewis and Clark Expedition soon after their publication in 1814 and became convinced that the undeveloped region of the Pacific Northwest was "the most valuable of all the unoccupied parts of the earth."[1] Kelley was obsessed with convincing Americans to colonize the Oregon country. Having unsuccessfully petitioned Congress for funds with which to encourage western settlement, Kelley began a movement to enlist Americans who could fund their own emigration. In 1829, he organized the Oregon Colonization Society, incorporated two years later as the American Society for Encouraging the Settlement of Oregon, under a special act of the Massachusetts legislature approved June 22, 1831. Wyeth borrowed books and documents about the West from Kelley and quickly signed on with the fellow Bostonian's expedition.[2]

From Kelley's material, Wyeth learned that when the War of 1812 concluded, a dispute had arisen between the United States and Great Britain over the boundary of Oregon country, with both nations claiming sovereignty. Diplomats from the two sides failed to establish borders, thus a compromise was forged while negotiators sorted out the issues. The ambiguous treaty, which sanctioned joint occupation, was called the "Convention Respecting the Fisheries, Boundary, and the Restoration of Slaves Between the United States of America and the United Kingdom of Great Britain." Often shortened to the "Anglo-American Convention of 1818," the document was signed October 20, 1818, and resulted in a sometimes bitter struggle for commercial control of the Oregon country.[3]

Since the treaty allowed for settlement, some Americans saw a golden opportunity. Hall J. Kelley became one of the more vocal proponents for the United States' possession of Oregon, and he soon convinced Wyeth of the commercial prospects in the Pacific Northwest. Kelley, and in all likelihood Wyeth as well, anticipated that when the

Hall Jackson Kelley (1790-1874), often called the "Prophet of Oregon," promoted a plan for Oregon settlement that drew Nathaniel Wyeth's attention to the Pacific Northwest.
OREGON HISTORICAL SOCIETY, #BB009711

issue was resolved, the region north of the Columbia River would go to the British and the districts to the south would become American lands. The perpetually entrepreneurial Wyeth could see an advantage in occupying the country prior to the dispute's settlement.

In June 1831, Kelley published the twenty-eight-page *Manual of the Oregon Expedition*. This work, also known as *A General Circular to all Persons of Good Character, who wish to Emigrate to the Oregon Territory*, outlined Kelley's proposal to establish two commercial and agricultural communities on the Columbia River. Each colony would be "a free and enlightened, but redundant population from the American Republic." Kelley endeavored to recruit 3,000 emigrants for his proposed settlement; Nathaniel Wyeth became one of thirty-seven agents listed in the circular, from whom information on the proposed migration could be obtained.[4]

Wyeth could not continue to juggle New England business interests and Oregon possibilities indefinitely. During the summer of 1831,
with the idea of Oregon simmering in his mind, Wyeth headed south in
search of new markets for the improved Ixion lead crucibles that were
finally beginning to sell. He reported to Tudor the potential of nearly
$10,000 a year in sales. At the time he returned to Cambridge, Wyeth
seemed completely committed to the Ixion product, suggesting Tudor
sell the mine to him. However, his enthusiasm waned rapidly. Wyeth
was growing more and more focused on the Oregon adventure.[5] Before
long Nathaniel, like Kelley, was obsessed with the Pacific Northwest.
His cousin John remarked,

> *Mr. Hall J. Kelly's writings operated like a match applied to the
> combustible matter accumulated in the mind of the energetic
> Nathaniel J. Wyeth, which reflected and multiplied the flattering
> glass held up to view by the ingenious and well disposed
> schoolmaster.*[6]

Wyeth wrote Kelley from Philadelphia that August, recommending
his older brother Jacob,

> *now practicing Medicine and Surgery in N. Jersey at Howell
> Furnance, [who] wished me to enter his name as an applicant for the
> birth of Surgeon in one of the companies of the first expedition, which
> scituation he is desirous of obtaining only in the event of a scituation
> being offered me which I shall accept, he not wishing to remove to
> that Country without me.*[7]

His mind made up, Wyeth informed his brother Charles of his Oregon initiative:

> *My plan is to go out there and carry with me what property I can
> spare after leaving support for my wife, and do what I can with it. It
> will perhaps not much more than get me there, and after finding what
> can be done in the fur trade, or other business, write to friends, whom
> I shall prepare before hand, to send me the means of doing business.*[8]

This expedition was to be led by Captain Benjamin L. E. Bonneville and Major Joshua Pilcher, two men with whom Wyeth would remain in contact throughout his western adventures. The quasi-military structure of the Kelley corps required that a captain be appointed for every fifty male adults; Wyeth was to be one of these officers. Each subscribing emigrant was to pay his own expenses to St. Louis, Missouri, where he would be assigned to a billet.[9] The men in this first expedition force were to be "soldiers," in Wyeth's words, and privates would receive 200 acres of land from the company.[10]

For a large part of 1831, Wyeth planned and worked under Kelley, with the initial expedition to Oregon set to leave Boston on the following January 1. To Wyeth's dismay, this first group of men and the later expeditionary force that included women and families had been combined under a Kelley-amended plan, delaying Kelley's departure date until spring 1832.[11] As early as November 1831, Wyeth hinted in letters to his brothers at a growing skepticism that Kelley would ever get out of Boston and his frank disapproval of including women and children on the first trip.

Meanwhile, Wyeth's home life was encountering problems that likely fed his impatience to head west. Elizabeth had grown dependent on alcohol. Wyeth confided to Tudor that he wished to be apart from his wife because of her "habit of drinking." Wyeth's boss recognized that his young protégé "had been a long while greatly distressed by this domestic trouble." Tudor noted in his diary that this issue with Elizabeth was the main reason Wyeth was so determined to go to Oregon.[12]

By December 4, Wyeth had separated from the group and organized a new company of his own. Wyeth was more interested in Oregon for trade and commerce than for settlement. Thus, he founded the Pacific Trading Company, a joint-stock business aiming to trade for furs on the Columbia River. A specific geographic destination for the PTC's first expedition, other than vague references to Oregon, does not appear in any of Wyeth's surviving records. Hall J. Kelley had drawn a map for a community at the confluence of the Columbia and Willamette rivers, so Wyeth may have kept that endpoint in mind. He may or may not have known that the Hudson's Bay Company's Fort Vancouver, a major destination for ocean-going trade vessels, was also in that locale.[13]

In a letter to his brother Jacob, Wyeth described his venture based on a string of trading posts as "a similar plan to the Hudson Bay and North West" companies.[14] Wyeth's plan called for a five-year mission into the West. He hoped to enlist fifty men who would each contribute $40 of their own money toward all expenses while pledging their implicit obedience to the organizer. Equipment, arms, transportation beyond St. Louis – all would be paid from this fund. Members would also share eighty percent of any profit realized. Wyeth calculated sixteen percent for his own risks and services. The remaining four percent was assigned to Wyeth's older brother, Jacob, who would serve as the company doctor.

Ideally, the emigrant party would consist of men "in the various branches of iron work manufacturing of arms and ammunition and a few to cultivate such articles of use."[15] Wyeth hoped to engage "Coopers, Blacksmiths, Founders, and ingenious persons of any trade" but wanted "nothing to do with any persons who are not industrious and temperate men and of good constitutions and peacible dispositions."[16] All of these men were to convene in Baltimore, Maryland, by March 10, 1832, to be armed and clothed by Wyeth – they could arrive "as scantily provided for clothes as possible" and only needed a "great coat which should be ample in order to sleep in it."[17]

By late December 1831, Wyeth had entered negotiations with Captain Dixie Wildes for a vessel laden with cargo to sail for the mouth of the Columbia River. He also wrote to the U.S. Representative from Massachusetts, Edward Everett, offering his "services to obtain information concerning that Country which in time would be useful" and requested copies of two treaties pertinent to the Oregon country "claimed by the U.S. on the Pacific Ocean, and made with G.B. somewhere about the years 1817 & 1828."[18] Everett would later become Secretary of State under President Millard Fillmore and would be the featured speaker at the dedication of the cemetery at Gettysburg in 1863, his two-hour oration preceding that of Abraham Lincoln. Everett was also a professor at Harvard University and a friend of up-and-coming naturalist Thomas Nuttall. One of Nuttall's closest neighbors was Nathaniel's uncle, Job Wyeth. As is ever the case, who one knew was as important as what one knew; when Nathaniel wrote to his Congressman, he included a letter of introduction from Nuttall, Everett's long-time associate.[19]

Wyeth studied the treaties supplied by Everett. Because the Pacific Trading Company would traverse various states of the Union as a uniformed body, each man carrying his own weapons, Wyeth worried that his men might be viewed as an unlawful armed force. Consequently, he asked Everett for further clarification and information about any permits he might need in order to legally execute his plans.[20]

The senator's response convinced Wyeth that the U.S. government had not yet extended its laws over the Oregon country. Wyeth concluded that the right to trade in the unsettled Pacific Northwest was implied by the government's public acts, such as U.S. protection of American trade vessels, and the demand for the return of Fort Astoria following the War of 1812. Wyeth had presumed that no license would be required to trade with Indians residing outside of bona fide U.S. territories. All in all, the Bostonian was confident his current plan was safe from government interference for "there could be no infraction of law where none exists."[21]

Former attorney John Ball, age thirty-eight, signed a pledge card joining Kelley's American Society for Encouraging the Settlement of the Oregon Territory on September 15, 1831.[22] Ball was a native of Hebron, New Hampshire. Born November 12, 1794, he was raised with a rigid Puritan outlook. John Ordway, who had accompanied Lewis and Clark, was Ball's childhood neighbor. Ball graduated from Dartmouth College in 1820, then practiced law in Lansingburgh, New York.

Ball had enlisted with Kelley just three months after the Society had been officially recognized by the government. Correspondence between Ball and Kelley indicated that Ball took an active part in promoting Kelley's work by printing and distributing Oregon propaganda throughout the region. Ball had received fifty pledge cards, like the one he had signed, for use in recruiting others to the movement. The relationship between the two men was significant enough that Kelley shared with Ball the details of meetings with co-leader Joshua Pilcher, delays in securing government funding, and a decision to defer the migration's departure for a month.[23]

Kelley's delays frustrated Ball, however; as a child he had listened to neighbor Ordway's tales of adventures in the West and was anxious to experience the frontier. While on business in New York City in the closing days of 1831, Ball met another would-be pioneer: New Yorker

Wyeth party member John Ball (1794-1884) commissioned this portrait in 1831, a year before he headed west to Oregon country.
OREGON HISTORICAL SOCIETY, #BB009690

Theophilus Bache, from whom he learned of Wyeth's plan to "cross the mountains to Oregon next season [and] wrote to him to inquire if [he] could join the party."[24] Ball thought of Wyeth as

> *an active business man, as great philosopher as I ever met, all learned by his own observation he goes ahead in everything, a good hunter, will mend a gun or wagon or anything else with a Jack Knife.*[25]

Closing out his business affairs, Ball bought basic supplies in Lansingburgh, New York, including a half-stocked percussion rifle with an

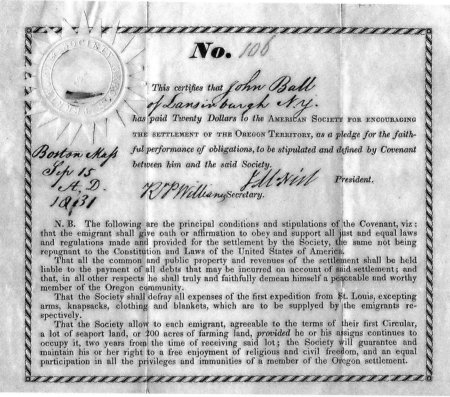

No. 106

This certifies that *John Ball*
of Lansingburgh N.Y.
has *paid* Twenty Dollars *to the* AMERICAN SOCIETY FOR ENCOURAGING
THE SETTLEMENT OF THE OREGON TERRITORY, *as a pledge for the faith-*
ful performance of obligations, to be stipulated and defined by Covenant
between him and the said Society.

Boston Mass
Sep 15
A.D.
1831

J.H. Neil President.
R.P. Williams Secretary.

N. B. The following are the principal conditions and stipulations of the Covenant, viz:
that the emigrant shall give oath or affirmation to obey and support all just and equal laws
and regulations made and provided for the settlement by the Society, the same not being
repugnant to the Constitution and Laws of the United States of America.
That all the common and public property and revenues of the settlement shall be held
liable to the payment of all debts that may be incurred on account of said settlement; and
that, in all other respects he shall truly and faithfully demean himself a peaceable and worthy
member of the Oregon community.
That the Society shall defray all expenses of the first expedition from St. Louis, excepting
arms, knapsacks, clothing and blankets, which are to be supplyed by the emigrants respectively.
That the Society allow to each emigrant, agreeable to the terms of their first Circular,
a lot of seaport land, or 200 acres of farming land, *provided* he or his assigns continues to
occupy it, two years from the time of receiving said lot; the Society will guarantee and
maintain his or her right to a free enjoyment of religious and civil freedom, and an equal
participation in all the privileges and immunities of a member of the Oregon settlement.

All members of the American Society for Encouraging the Settlement of
Oregon Territory, including John Ball, signed a pledge card agreeing to Hall J.
Kelley's terms. Ball received certificate no. 106 on September 15, 1831. GRAND
RAPIDS HISTORY AND SPECIAL COLLECTIONS, ARCHIVES, GRAND RAPIDS PUBLIC LIBRARY, GRAND RAPIDS, MICHIGAN.

extra barrel for shot, two canisters of gunpowder, a shot pouch and a
copper flask. Before leaving the state, he learned what he could from
Alfred Seton and Ramsay Crooks, who, while working under John
Jacob Astor in the Pacific Fur Company in 1812, had been in the very
country for which Ball was headed.[26]

At about the same time, Wyeth was approached by his young cousin
Thomas Livermore about signing on with the company. Because Thomas, not quite eighteen years old, was still a minor, Wyeth volunteered to
write the youth's family. Seeing himself in the prospective adventurer,
Wyeth explained his Oregon plans to Uncle Solomon, anticipating that

such a quest would be ideal for someone who had "arrived at that time of life at which a young man should have chosen some business to meet the wants of existence."[27]

Numerous letters from Wyeth to his brothers indicate a somewhat frantic quest for funds, but also seem to affirm his family's involvement in the western venture. In the first weeks of 1832, subscriptions from Charles, Jacob and Leonard Wyeth were mentioned in various letters detailing monetary arrangements for Nathaniel's blooming enterprise. Wyeth would eventually be forced to plead his case to his wife's family as well, who apparently did not approve of him going to Oregon.[28]

Wyeth contributed $3,000 of his own money to finance the venture, principally by liquidating many personal resources. He raised another $5000 by mortgaging property recently purchased from Harvard College. He negotiated loans from his brothers and from Frederic Tudor. As collateral to Tudor, Wyeth assigned the ice cutter patent and $800 worth of mortgage on his new house. An additional $5,000 was promised by these same men to cover the cost of a ship and cargo to be sent to the Columbia River. Henry Hall and the firm of Tucker and Williams would take care of shipping the following year, presuming Wyeth had a return cargo. The proceeds from this anticipated load would pay for the goods received and the freighting costs as well.

Tudor learned of Wyeth's imminent departure when, on Friday, January 6, 1832, Wyeth announced "his determination to leave my employ in consequence of his domestic inquietude. It is a great loss to me."[29] Tudor wrote a lengthy letter to Wyeth the following Sunday and tempted his protégé with offers of more money, but Wyeth's mind was made up.

Unfortunately, discussions with Captain Wildes concerning his vessel sailing to the Columbia had advanced at a snail's pace as January closed, and would eventually fail altogether. Wyeth continued forming detailed plans. He would purchase most of his trade goods in St. Louis, the "great mart of the Indian trade," but he was mindful that a little iron and steel could be obtained cheaper in New Orleans. Knowing that tobacco played a large role in Indian relations, and that it would ultimately be less expensive to grow his own in Oregon rather than transport it from the East, Wyeth instructed brother Charles in Maryland to obtain sufficient seed for a "considerable crop and have it well dried

Before leaving Lansingburgh, New York, to join Wyeth, Ball purchased some basic supplies from J. M. Caswell & Sons, including powder, a short-barreled percussion rifle, a few tools, a shot pouch and a copper powder flask. GRAND RAPIDS HISTORY AND SPECIAL COLLECTIONS, ARCHIVES, GRAND RAPIDS PUBLIC LIBRARY, GRAND RAPIDS, MICHIGAN.

and soldered up in tin cans" and to be on the lookout for a potential
Pacific Trading Company recruit competent to raise such a crop.[30] He
also asked Charles to ascertain the best mercantile houses in St. Louis.

On January 23, he answered a letter from Uncle Solomon regarding
young Thomas Livermore's desire to accompany the PTC. Wyeth suggested Thomas make himself a master of the bugle similar to Lewis and
Clark's "Tin blowing Trumpets."[31] He explained:

> *The bugle ... should be of the plainest kind and the most simple*
> *to use and the least liable to get out of repair or broken. It will be*
> *used chiefly as a signal for parties at a distance, and sometimes in*
> *marching a little music will enliven us. We propose that one should*
> *learn it well and then teach all the rest. We shall have as much as ten*
> *and to be used alternately so as not to be tedious to any one. I am*
> *uterly ignorant of all kinds and uses of music but have thought that*
> *we could march by a number of bugles but if we cannot they will at*
> *least do for signals which is in fact their only esential use.*[32]

At the end of January, Wyeth made a revealing reply to an inquiry
from I. P. Hughes, another Oregon prospect. The attitude and priorities
Wyeth set forth here, though prudent from a business standpoint, fore-
shadowed tensions that would hamstring the PTC on the long trail ahead:

> *each man gets as near as possible of 8-10 of a full and equal*
> *division of the profits and the other 2-10 go to pay me for my*
> *services as head of the Co. ... I am to be the sole director of the*
> *movements of the Co. and its agent in all transactions of business.*
> *I will come under no bonds to the Co. Conceiving that the fact*
> *of my carrying out with us 4000$ is bond enough ... if a bond is*
> *necessary anywhere it is from the men to me, that they shall not*
> *after my property is invested in this thing desert me which would*
> *occasion a sacrifice of all I am worth.*[33]

Wyeth explained to his brother Charles that this style of commitment from members of the company was advantageous because hired
men might desert and would not have the same spirit as men working for a share of the profits. Furthermore, paying wages would have

depleted the limited capital in the coffers; employees would have to be paid regardless of profit or loss.[34]

The fur trade focus of Wyeth's venture had been implied in several letters up to this point. As a practical businessman, Wyeth studied how the fur trade was being conducted in the West. The prime beaver habitats were along the borders of the continental divide – ultimately closer to the Pacific Ocean than the New England markets for which the hides were bound. In the cooler months of early spring and late fall, trappers plied their trade in the icy ponds and streams, harvesting the thick pelts of beaver, otter, muskrat and other valuable animal skins. Each summer, these brigades met at an agreed-upon location, called *rendezvous*, to sell their hard-earned harvest for needed supplies to see them through the next season. Besides gun powder, lead, tobacco and traps, the men bought coffee, sugar, trade goods and various necessaries.

St. Louis, Missouri, had become the center of the trade's distribution hub. Goods were freighted from there, often upriver by boat, to Westport or Independence, Missouri, jumping off points on the frontier. Caravans of pack animals then transported the supplies overland to the mountains. When the rendezvous wound down, the same mules were loaded with the furs to be carried back to Missouri for shipment to eastern cities or across the Atlantic to European markets.

Wyeth had done his homework. He instructed his brother Leonard to check out suitable traps in New York. He wanted forty dozen of the devices which "should weigh 5 lbs. double springs, Jaw without teeth and chain about 6 feet long with two swivels in it." Enough suitable traps may not have been available in New York, because Wyeth would have Charles checking for them in Baltimore a month later. He also wanted "the kind of gun used by the Amer. Fur Co." Another item of importance was "a certain kind of beads which is a kind of curency among the Indians."[35]

Wyeth wrote Charles of his attempt to arrange for "men already in the N.W. trade" to take his shipload of trade goods and supplies to Oregon country. Ever the entrepreneur, Wyeth hoped to piggyback on existing oceangoing trade in sea otter pelts, tallow, and other commodities between Boston and the Pacific Northwest. He postulated an advantage in sending his supplies on a ship already scheduled for such a venture: "they run no risque because if I never arrive there they have only to continue the voyage as an ordinary N.W. Coast voyage with just as good chance of profit as if expressly fitted out for that purpose."[36]

In keeping with his capitalistic approach to this West Coast project, Wyeth made inquiries about salmon and their abundance on the Columbia River. The Boston markets had been importing pickled salmon since the Colonial Period, most recently from Newfoundland. But in April 1831, the brig *Owyhee* arrived with fifty-three barrels of the preserved fish obtained on the Columbia River. This could not have escaped Wyeth's attention and must have spurred his thinking on ways to enter the trade. How are salmon taken? How are they smoked? How are they pickled? When do they go up and down the rivers? How do they keep?[37] Wyeth might merge the fur trade and the salmon trade into a profitable gamble. Interestingly, in light of the joint occupancy of Oregon country, the barrels of salmon were taxed by customs agents as "foreign caught fish."[38]

Wyeth foresaw a fortune to be made in the plush furs that could be acquired in the mountains and imagined a string of trading posts across the West, supplied by a warehouse at the mouth of the Columbia. Ships could make regular trips from Boston to the Columbia, bringing supplies and merchandise, then returning with bales of fur and barrels of cured salmon.

The concept of a trading post system throughout the Rocky Mountains was nothing new. In the late 1790s Sir Alexander MacKenzie, a Scot and a Northwest Company man, traveled across the North American continent to the Pacific Ocean and published an account of his trek soon after. MacKenzie suggested the opening of an intercourse between the Atlantic and Pacific oceans and the creation of trading posts throughout the interior and at both extremes. This, he averred, would command the entire fur trade of North America.[39] Not surprisingly, such a statement had drawn the attention of the United States government; MacKenzie's name appears regularly in President Thomas Jefferson's correspondence beginning as early as April 1803. Brash ideas such as those propounded by the NWC man prodded the President to organize an American expedition to the Pacific under the command of Meriwether Lewis and William Clark.[40]

That pair's successful Corps of Discovery returned from its epic exploration of the Louisiana Territory in September 1806 after nearly two and a half years' absence. The men were fêted in nearly every American town from St. Louis, Missouri to Washington, D.C. Amid the clamor, Lewis found time to write reports about the journey and send them to his superiors, chiefly President Jefferson. In his initial letter to the president, composed the day of his arrival in St. Louis, the captain stated:

> *The Missouri and all it's branches from the Chyenne upwards*
> *abound more in beaver and Common Otter, than any other streams*
> *on earth, particularly that proportion of them lying within the Rocky*
> *Mountains. The furs of all this immence tract of country including*
> *such as may be collected on the upper portion of the River St. Peters,*
> *Red river and the Assinniboin with the immence country watered*
> *by the Columbia, may be conveyed to the mouth of the Columbia by*
> *the 1ˢᵗ of August each year and from thence be shiped to, and arrive*
> *in Canton earlier than the furs at present shiped from Montreal*
> *annually arrive in London ... If the government will only aid, even*
> *in a very limited manner, the enterprise of her Citizens I am fully*
> *convinced that we shal shortly derive the benefits of a most lucrative*
> *trade from this source.*[41]

Meriwether Lewis had clearly recognized the important role the Columbia River drainage would eventually play not only in the fur trade, but as a driver of United States expansion and imperialism. One nearly immediate effect of Lewis and Clark's return was a stimulation of the fur trade on the upper Missouri River and into the Rockies.

This activity did not go unnoticed by America's first multi-millionaire and fur magnate, John Jacob Astor. In 1808, Astor devised a plan to

> *embrace in the course of 4 or 5 years the whole of the fur trade & to*
> *extend to the western ocean ... and to have a range of Posts or trading*
> *houses on the Rout made by Captain Lewis to the sea.*[42]

Astor considered an establishment at the mouth of the Columbia as

> *the emporium to an immense commerce; as a colony that would*
> *form the germ of a wide civilization; that would, in fact, carry the*
> *American population across the Rocky Mountains and spread it*
> *along the shores of the Pacific.*[43]

To accomplish this goal, in 1810 Astor sent the ill-fated brig *Ton-quin* around Cape Horn to the Columbia with a contingent of men to build the post that came to be known as Astoria. Meanwhile, an overland expedition led by Wilson Price Hunt departed St. Louis, headed west to rendezvous with the initial party. However, Astor's strategy was thwarted by the outbreak of the War of 1812. He lost his fort to the Northwest Company, and the model originally touted by MacKenzie was laid aside. The full story of Astor's attempt to monopolize the fur trade in the Pacific Northwest was told by Washington Irving in his 1836 publication, *Astoria or Anecdotes of an Enterprise Beyond the Rocky Mountains*. A personal friend of Astor's, Irving had access to company records and journals in the creation of his story.[44]

Like MacKenzie, Lewis, and Astor before him, Wyeth saw inherent advantages in the fur trade, and in a trading post system. But Wyeth also saw the existing Rocky Mountain fur trade as inefficient, and he thought he could profit by improving it. The high cost of freighting supplies overland from St. Louis severely compromised profits, and Wyeth believed this could be reduced by using sea lanes in both directions. New England ships sailing to the Pacific Northwest traditionally needed thirty months to make the voyage, because so much time was spent trading with Indians along the coast to gather a lucrative cargo of furs. If the fur cargo, collected instead in the Rocky Mountains, was waiting at the Columbia River, transport time could be cut in half. Vessels would merely sail to the Columbia River, drop the cargo of trade merchandise, collect bales of pelts and barrels of salmon, and then return to Boston after a short detour to the Hawaiian Islands.[45] Concurrently, Wyeth needed to advance the PTC mission on the ground by leading a contingent of men to collect furs in the Rocky Mountains and deliver them to the mouth of the Columbia.

Wyeth must have convinced others that his idea was viable, because by early February 1832, twenty-three men had paid their first installments toward the $40 assessment to the PTC. Though he had originally aimed to enlist fifty paying members, and would have enrolled more if possible, Wyeth deemed twenty-five men sufficient. Camp equipage was ordered and most of the arms were safely stowed in the armory, the rest contracted for delivery in about two weeks. Arrangements were made for pack horses and wagons to transport gear as far as Wheeling, West Virginia. Wyeth advanced his Oregon plans while he finalized arrangements to ship Mr. Tudor's ice.[46]

In contrast, Hall J. Kelley had by this time made little, if any, progress. Wyeth received a letter from Kelley in mid-February, to which he replied, "However well your affairs are going on at Washington matters little to me. Anything they can do will come too late for my purposes."[47] It was clear from his response that Wyeth had washed his hands of Kelley's flagging schemes. True to Wyeth's assessment, when hoped-for Congressional funding did not materialize, Kelley again postponed the exodus, this time until June 1832.[48]

Wyeth's finances were less than robust. This kept him maneuvering in order to stay solvent. He received financial backing through arrangements with numerous entities: Judah Touro of New Orleans; Norris and Company out of New York; Tucker, Hall and Williams from Boston; Davenport and Bryan of New York; Boston's Joseph Baker and Son; and assorted smaller investors. He continued to press various family members and even his former mentor Frederic Tudor.[49]

With a long absence in mind, and ever the pragmatist, Wyeth signed a power of attorney with James Brown, an attorney in Cambridge, to act on his behalf while he was away. Of particular interest, in a March 1832 letter to his brother Leonard, Wyeth declared he intended to keep a journal of his travels, and would send one copy to attorney James Brown, and one copy jointly to Leonard and Charles. They were instructed to "preserve with care" this diary of Wyeth's for future publication. Wyeth expressed concern that his journal should remain proprietary, believing that premature disclosure "would destroy one half of its [publication] value and it may be that I would not wish all the facts of the trade divulged before I am done with it."[50]

As plans progressed, another of Nathaniel's cousins, sixteen-year-old John Wyeth, became destined to head for Oregon as the youngest member of the Company. John, one of Uncle Job's five sons, reported that for many months prior to their eventual departure, the group had met at Nathaniel's house every Saturday night to

arrange and settle the plan of our future movements, and to make
every needful preparation; and such were his thoughtfulness and
vigilance, that it seemed to us nothing was forgotten and every thing
necessary provided.[51]

Ultimately, the shareholders agreed upon preparations to assemble at Baltimore in late March.

Meanwhile, John Ball had traveled by sleigh to Washington, D.C., where he met with Missouri Congressman William H. Ashley, who happened to be staying at Brown's Hotel at the same time.[52] Ashley had been active in the fur trade, beginning in 1822, when he and Andrew Henry led an expedition up the Missouri River, headed for the Rocky Mountains. Ashley had initiated the current rendezvous system of supply in the mountains. General Ashley answered Ball's many questions about the Rockies of the Far West, but informed Ball that "It would be as difficult to tell all ... that may occur or be needed on such a journey, as for a carpenter to tell every blow he had got to strike on commencing to erect a house."[53] Nevertheless, the former attorney soaked up every bit of information bestowed by the retired fur trader.

Ball spent several days in Washington. He attended the sessions of Congress and noted the presence of Vice-President John C. Calhoun, Henry Clay, Thomas Hart Benton, Daniel Webster, Rufus Choate and former president John Quincy Adams. He also paid an unannounced visit to President Andrew Jackson and listened to a decision from Chief Justice John Marshall regarding *Cherokee Nation vs. Georgia,* in which the Cherokee sought a federal injunction against laws passed by the State of Georgia depriving them of rights within its boundaries. The Supreme Court did not hear the case on its merits but ruled that it had no original jurisdiction in the matter, as the Cherokee were a dependent nation, with a relationship to the United States like that of a ward to its guardian.[54]

On February 20, shortly before leaving town, Ball purchased a sextant, compass, thermometer, tape measure and "mountain" (altitude) thermometer with which to make scientific observations while on the upcoming trek. Ball then moved on to Baltimore to await the arrival of Nathaniel Wyeth.[55] There, he was joined by John Sinclair, who had also learned about Wyeth's expedition from Theophilus Bache. Aware that

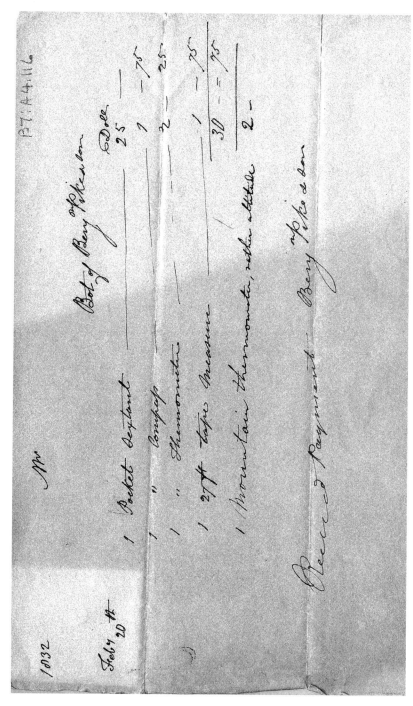

While in Washington, D.C., in early 1832, John Ball bought a sextant, compass, pocket thermometer, tape measure and altitude thermometer for making scientific observations during his western travels. GRAND RAPIDS HISTORY AND SPECIAL COLLECTIONS, ARCHIVES, GRAND RAPIDS PUBLIC LIBRARY, GRAND RAPIDS, MICHIGAN.

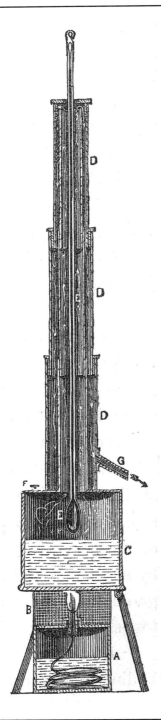

John Ball's mountain thermometer, similar to this 1864 model, measured altitude based on boiling point.

The device contained a thermometer with an elongated bulb, about a foot long. In the diagram, C is a copper boiler into which water is poured. This container is supported by a tripod stand to allow a lighted alcohol lamp, A, to be placed underneath.

The lamp's flame is surrounded by fine wire gauze, B, to protect it from wind. EEE is a three-section telescoping tube, proceeding from the boiler, and open at the top. Another tube, DDD, similarly constructed, envelopes this and is screwed to the top of the boiler. An opening at the top admits the thermometer, and another lower down, G, vents the steam.

As steam is generated, it rises in the inner tube until it attains a stationary point, which is the boiling temperature. The thermometer, sealed by an India-rubber washer, allows the level of the mercury to be visible in order to measure the water's boiling point. At sea level, water boils at 212 degrees. Because atmospheric pressure decreases with greater altitude, the variance between actual boiling point and 212 degrees can be used to measure elevation above sea level.

Each degree difference equates to about 550 feet of ascent. During a reading Ball would take in the Rocky Mountains, the water boiled at 196 degrees, a difference of 16 degrees. Although it appears large and cumbersome, the instrument could be disassembled and packed in a portable tin case for traveling.

SOURCE: HENRY NEGRETTI AND JOSEPH ZAMBRA, *A TREATISE ON METEOROLOGICAL INSTRUMENTS: THEIR SCIENTIFIC PRINCIPLES, METHODS OF CONSTRUCTION, AND PRACTICAL UTILITY* (LONDON: NEGRETTI AND ZAMBRA, 1864), 94-99. IMAGE COURTESY OF COLORADO STATE UNIVERSITY.

he was about to "go into camp life," Ball had dinner at Belsover's, which he reported to be "one of the best tables I ever sat at."[56]

Knowing they would start west in the morning, two of the younger members of the party, Thomas Livermore and William Bell, spent their last night out on the town before embarking on so great an adventure. They claimed they slept at a friend's house but Wyeth was aware of their subterfuge. Bell would end up with a dose of "clapp" that Wyeth attributed to this evening's indiscretion.[57]

Wyeth had finally secured a ship, contracting with owners of the brig *Sultana*, Joseph Baker and Son. The *Sultana* was captained by James L. Lambert.[58] The ship was already loaded with the supplies Wyeth thought necessary to advance his commercial enterprise in the Pacific Northwest, including 1,000 empty salmon barrels and a large quantity of salt for preserving green pelts acquired in their coastal trade.[59]

Diverging from his initial plan, Wyeth did not hire the *Sultana* to carry additional goods expressly for the PTC. Instead, he arranged to purchase any surplus goods that Baker's vessel might have on hand after completing its own trading ventures. The boat's owner provided Wyeth with a letter of credit allowing him to draw needed supplies at Boston prices from the ship's stores once they reunited on the coast.[60]

This agreement, though somewhat tenuous, was advantageous to both parties. The *Sultana* would not have to suffer the loss of carrying unsold, essentially useless goods back to its home port should Wyeth not succeed in reaching his Pacific goal; and if all went well, Wyeth would be able to purchase surplus goods at prearranged rates without paying freight charges. Though this equipment would not be accessible until the overland party reached the Pacific and met the ship, the goods would be available for their use at that time and for Wyeth's return trip to Boston.[61]

Lambert was thus sent on his way to sail around Cape Horn for a future rendezvous with Wyeth's overland party at or near the mouth of the Columbia River.

3.
Departure for the West

It must have seemed to Wyeth a long time coming. On the first of March, 1832, the Pacific Trading Company prepared to march out of Cambridge and on through neighboring Boston to spend ten days acclimating to camp life and hardening themselves for the journey ahead. According to Wyeth's journal and John Wyeth's published account, twenty-five men enlisted to go with Wyeth to Oregon, several of whom are known only by their surnames: Wiggin Abbott, William Bell, W. Breck, Stephen Burdett, Griswell, Kilham, Lane, Hamilton Law, Thomas Livermore, George More, William Nudd, Walter Palmer, G. Sargent, Solomon Howard Smith, Styles, Calvin Tibbetts, Guy Trumbull, R. C. Wakefield, Weeks, Whittier, John Woodman, Dr. Jacob Wyeth, and John Wyeth.

Additional members Theophilus Bache, John Ball and John Sinclair would be waiting to join them in Baltimore. If Wyeth made a roster of the men in the PTC, it has not surfaced. Rather than a separate member of the party, "Styles" may have been a nickname for Bache, accounting for the extra name gleaned from the records.[1]

Cousin John Wyeth, born in June 1815, was the youngest of the bunch – sixteen when the expedition set out – and like Thomas Livermore needed his father's consent to join.[2] Among this motley assortment of men and boys were a doctor, a gunsmith, a blacksmith, two carpenters and two fishermen; the rest were farmers and simple workmen.[3] Ball referred to this "hardy, rough illiterate set of fellows" as

laborers and loafers, such as [Wyeth] had picked up in and about Boston by high representation of the pleasures of the journey and the fortune-making result of the enterprise, none of them, as time shoed, at all understanding what they were going into.[4]

The Cambridge recruits now gathered in uniform dress before their Captain. Wyeth's invented rank was merely from his position as "leader of the Band of the Oregon adventurers, after having inspired twenty-one persons with his own high hopes and expectations."[5] John Wyeth assessed the company:

> *Each one wore a coarse woollen jacket and pantaloons, a striped cotton shirt, and cowhide boots: every man had a musket, most of them rifles, all of them bayonets in a broad belt, together with a large clasped knife for eating and common purposes. The Captain and one or two more added pistols; but every one had in his belt a small axe.*[6]

They carried "tents, camp-kettles, and the common utensils for cooking victuals" because their plan called for avoiding the added expense of inns and taverns as they made their way west.[7] The main camp equipage was transported in three conspicuous wagons, designed by Wyeth and built by the two company carpenters and Dexter Clapp, the village blacksmith.[8] Although innovations in the ice industry had been one of Wyeth's applauded talents, John Wyeth may not have been convinced of his cousin's gifts as a transportation engineer:

> *Our three vehicles, or wagons, if we may call by that name a <u>unique</u> contrivance, half boat, and half carriage, may be mentioned as an instance of our Captain's talents for snug contrivance. It was a boat of about thirteen feet long, and four feet wide, of a shape partly of a canoe, and partly of a gondola. It was not calked with tarred oakum, and payed with pitch, lest the rays of the sun should injure it while upon wheels; but it was nicely jointed, and dovetailed. The boat part was firmly connected with the lower, or axletree, or wheel part; – the whole was so constructed that the four wheels of it were to be taken off when we came to a river, and placed in the wagon, while the tongue or shaft was to be towed across by a rope. Every thing was as light as could be consistent with safety.*[9]

The citizenry of Cambridge was anything but enthusiastic about Wyeth's venture. Rather, they "considered it a hazardous enterprise, and considerably notional."[10] As the expedition left Cambridge, the local wags from Harvard described "a boat begot upon a wagon," comparing the transports to something like a mule – neither horse nor ass. As one of the wagons passed the crowd, a collegian called it "a thing *amphibious,* anatomically constructed like some equivocal animals, allowing it to crawl upon the land, or to swim on the water."[11] The wagon was soon dubbed an *amphibium*. This did not seem good enough to some onlookers, who felt surely the ingenious inventor of such a machine ought to have more credit. Thus, as the vehicles wheeled toward Baltimore, the name *Nat-wye-thium* was bestowed to acclamation and "good-humored raillery."[12]

Trade goods comprised the bulk of the freight. These included vermillion and other paints, glass beads, small looking-glasses, a gross of axes, and a number of trinkets such as cheap knives, buttons, nails, hammers and a "deal of those articles, on which young Indians of both sexes set a high value, and white men little or none."[13] Additionally, thirty-four pack animals had been purchased for the voyage. Nineteen were loaded with trade goods, leaving only fifteen available to ride, plus two privately owned, personal horses. Everyone knew going in that there would be ample time spent afoot.[14]

It is believed that among the buttons brought for trade was a style that modern collectors call "Phoenix buttons." Today these moderately scarce relics are occasionally recovered from sites throughout the Pacific Northwest. The buttons are embellished with an image of a phoenix, an imaginary bird that, according to legend, burns itself up only to arise from the ashes more beautiful than before.

Manufactured by Robert Bushby of London, three distinct designs have been found, each emblazoned with the French phrase, *Je Renais De Mes Cendres* ("I am reborn from my ashes"), and a regiment number. The buttons were originally made for Henri Christophe, a West Indian slave who rose to be king of Haiti and who played a major part in the uprising that liberated Haiti from European domination. He became King Henri in 1811 and ordered special buttons for his military's uniform coats, but upon his suicide in 1820, the buttons became surplus. As the story goes, Wyeth accepted a load of Christophe's uniform coats and buttons in exchange for ice during his former business in the West Indies. This fable may or may not be true, but it resonates with what is known of Wyeth's ingenuity and business sense.[15]

Encamped for ten days at Long Island Head in Boston Harbor's Quincy Bay, the men hoped to inure themselves to the rigors of camping and sleeping outdoors before boarding a ship for Baltimore. Such a

brief period, however, could never
have adequately acclimated them
for what lay ahead. In 1830, the
225-acre Long Island had been
described as the most pleasant
place in Boston Harbor and was
predicted to become a summer
resort. Although it was part of the
city of Boston, much of the narrow island was used for pasture.
A twenty-foot-high stone light-
house, built in 1819, stood on the
northernmost point of the island,
directing ships passing through

**Brass military buttons emblazoned
with a phoenix were thought to have
been brought west amongst Wyeth's
trade goods.** FORT VANCOUVER NATIONAL
HISTORIC SITE

Broad Sound, between Long and Deer islands, into the harbor. A luxury hotel, erected by the Long Island Company, was commodious and
convenient, though never mentioned in Wyeth's correspondence.[16] Just
how close Wyeth's men pitched their tents to the comforts of the inn
remains unknown.

While camped there, Wyeth was able to catch up on a little correspondence, including some last-minute financial arrangements. In a
letter to Hall J. Kelley, Wyeth chided him yet again for procrastinating:

> I am per[f]ectly well aware of the importance of cooperation of all
> the Americans who may go to that country but I am well convinced
> that this thing has been delayed too long already and that further
> delay will defeat my enterprise beside not being in the habit of setting
> two times to do one thing.[17]

Following its training period, the troop boarded the packet *Ida* on
March 10 and set sail for Baltimore, Maryland. When the sails were
hoisted, John Wyeth found himself on board a sea-going vessel for the
second time in his life. The young traveler literally weathered the journey of just under two weeks, "experiencing a snow-storm, severe cold,
and what the landsmen considered a hard gale"[18]

After rounding the tip of Cape Charles and entering Chesapeake
Bay, the brig put in at Point Comfort, Maryland. The ocean storms had

left many of the men seasick and they had eaten little, mostly bits of salted beef and pork. Wyeth went ashore with a half dozen men

> to procure some oysters, eggs &c. I ordered a supper for those with me and after supper I think two Bttles of Champagne and one of Madera were drank and I believe some ardent spirit. Afterward the landlord treated to some more I presume on acc. of the novelty of the Enterprise or some slight acquaintance with myself. Having got what stores I could for those on board and seeing the frolic had gone far enough I returned on board.[19]

Some of the men, Bell particularly, drank far too much alcohol that night. Intoxicated, Bell tossed a handkerchief full of raw eggs from the pier into the skiff before climbing in and setting off for the *Ida*. It was a foggy night but Wyeth managed to steer the launch three miles back to the mother ship with nothing but intermittent stars as a guide.[20]

They arrived in port at Baltimore about midnight on March 23. When the sun came up the amphibious carriages caused quite a stir, as did the whole company. Baltimore newspapers commended its form and discipline, citing a striking contrast to the parties of less-organized emigrant families who had passed through in the previous thirty years on their way to Ohio, Kentucky and other western territories. Consistent with the plan to avoid costly inns and taverns, the troop marched two miles outside the city and set up camp. Here they were joined by Bache, Ball and Sinclair.

Having finally set foot on the path that would lead to Oregon, Wyeth expressed tempered optimism in a letter to Leonard:

> I am determined to give up no more to melancholy feelings but rouse myself up to exertion and enterprise and forget the things that have been and all but what is before me. If I am successful there will be some comfort in it if otherwise I will have some serious and present misfortunes to keep me from brooding over more distant and metaphysical ones. If I fail in my enterprise it will be an undertaking that few men could even look at if successful it will be fame and wealth enough to keep me on a par and in standing with the best.[21]

Four days later, the Nat-wye-thiums were loaded onto horse-drawn rail cars on the newly established Baltimore and Ohio Railroad – the longest railroad in the country at the time. Constructed primarily so Baltimore could better compete with the Erie Canal in moving goods inland, the tracks had opened for travel only a few months earlier, on December 1, 1831. The rails extended just sixty miles west to the town of Frederick, Maryland, but that was sixty fewer miles for Wyeth and his company. Ball would later comment on this railroad's unique construction for its day. A flat iron strap, riveted onto granite blocks or stringers, served as the rail. "The winter frost had so displaced these blocks that it was very rough."[22]

The edition of the *Frederick Herald* published the following Saturday would supply details barely mentioned or omitted in other primary sources, describing the group as "accompanied by a physician, a mineralogist and a naturalist ... and four dogs of enormous size ... as trusty sentinels." The newspaper also noted that the Pacific Trading Company's "ultimate destination is Astoria at the mouth of the Columbia river."[23]

On March 29, the men started out from Frederick on foot, dragging the wagons by hand behind them as they traveled over the Allegheny Mountains. Ball described the return to camp life, sleeping in tents at night and cooking their "grub at a fire by the roadside."[24] The innkeepers in the region, when it was discovered the party was from New England, showed an unwillingness to accommodate Yankees. Their inhospitality rose to a degree "not met with among the savages," in John Wyeth's unschooled opinion. He would learn more about this later.[25]

> At one public house on the mountains near which we halted, the master of it, learning that we came from Boston, refused us any refreshment and lodging. He locked up his bar-room, put the key in his pocket, went out, and came back with four or five of his neighbours, when the disagreement ran so high, that the tavern-keeper and the Yankee Captain each seized his rifle.[26]

Wyeth pointed to the sign on the tavern door, demanding drinks and, in this instance, lodging for the night. He insisted that the innkeeper's license required provision of suitable bedding for travelers as well as stable and feed for horses and cattle. Wyeth prevailed in the dispute and spent the night in the house along with three others from the party – all well armed and determined to defend themselves should the need arise. The rest of the company bivouacked near the wagons "like veteran soldiers, in their tents."[27]

Trudging on for some days, they reached Cumberland, Maryland, where Ball visited the coal mines. They followed the National Cumberland Road, one of the first major routes to be improved at government expense. Continuing across the Alleghenies, by April 6 the company had arrived at Brownsville, Pennsylvania, a flourishing little town at the head of navigation on the Monongahela River. Boarding a steamboat in Brownsville, wagons and all, the men embarked on the two-day journey to Pittsburgh, at that time not much more than "a small village of smoke and dirt."[28]

Pittsburgh was then a principal point of departure for west-bound travelers. Two hundred thirty miles into their journey, Wyeth posted letters to his brothers, describing to them yet more financial dealings. He also wrote to Hall J. Kelley, apparently in answer to an earlier letter, reiterating that up to ten emigrants from Kelley's group, who wanted to join Wyeth, would be welcomed if they defrayed their own expenses and did not delay the PTC's progress. These additional travelers never appeared.[29]

In Pittsburgh, Wyeth purchased tickets for passage to St. Louis on the steamboat *Freedom*. The boilers were fired on April 8. Also on board was Reverend Lyman Beecher, about to become the first president of Lane Theological Seminary in Cincinnati. Beecher was an early proponent of renouncing ardent spirits and was co-founder of the American Temperance Society. He was also the father of abolitionist author Harriet Beecher Stowe. Narcissa Whitman would later describe him as "a small man, quite indifferent in his appearance."[30]

Ball related a humorous tale regarding Beecher:

One pleasant day, as we were smoothly gliding down the stream, [Beecher] and also Wyeth and myself were promenading the deck which had no bulwarks. We noticed that he turned many steps before he reached the stern of the boat, while we went so near that our next step would have been overboard. [Wyeth] remarked, "How is it that

Mr. Beecher is so much more cautious than we sinners?" Implying
that Mr. Beecher doubtless claimed that all would be right with him
should he be drowned, while with us we made no pretentions in that
direction.[31]

John Wyeth and John Ball both described the beauty of the surrounding hills that bordered the Ohio River. About one hundred miles
from Pittsburgh, Ball noted "Seneka Oil Creek" which would "blaze at
the application of a match."[32] The petroleum-laden waters of the river
have been well documented since the early 1700s. Seneca Indians gathered the oil by absorbing it into woolen blankets laid on the water's
surface, then wringing out the oil. Some ceremonies involved simply
lighting the viscous fluid which floated on the stream's surface; the oil
was also used for medicinal purposes. Euro-Americans bottled the ooze
and peddled it as "Seneca Oil," proclaiming it as a miraculous cure-all
for internal or external maladies of man or beast.[33]

As Wyeth's group descended the Ohio River, it passed through the
village of Wheeling, Ohio, on to Marietta, then finally stopped for a
day's layover in Cincinnati on Tuesday, April 10.[34] Three of the young
men, including John Wyeth, engaged in the tomfoolery of reckless
youth on an evening jaunt into the burgeoning city:

In the evening we went into a public house, where we treated
ourselves with that sort of refreshment which inspires fun, frolic, and
mischief. We remained on shore till so late an hour that every body
appeared to have gone to bed, when we set out to return to our steam-
boat. In our way to it we passed by a store, in the front of which stood
three barrels of lamp-oil, at the head of a fine sloping street. The evil
spirit of mischief put it into our heads to set them rolling down the
inclined plane to the river. No sooner hinted, than executed.[35]

Fortunately for the three hooligans, the barrels were found the
next morning, unscathed. The owners of the oil carted their property
back up the hill to the store without looking for the culprits. But had
they been caught, the boys had already schemed to blame it on unruly
Southerners since the Boston trio must necessarily be innocent, coming from the "land of steady habits and good principles."[36]

For the *Freedom's* Cincinnati-to-St.-Louis leg, Wyeth struck a deal with the steamboat captain to reduce costs. The company men were to assist in loading wood for the boilers when the vessel made its frequent stops along the route. Only Dr. Jacob Wyeth was excused from the wooding chore and though everyone saw the necessity of lending a hand, that did not prevent widespread complaining. This was the first sign of any discontent among the members of the PTC.

The *Freedom* powered through the Falls of the Ohio, a dramatic occasion which John Wyeth found "really terrific to an inexperienced farmer or mechanic" yet "sufficiently appalling to silence all grumbling."[37] After short stops in Louisville, Kentucky, and a few other minor ports, the steamboat entered the Mississippi River, at this time quite muddy and slow. The boat could not put in at Cairo, Illinois, according to Ball, because it "was all swamp about the mouth of the Ohio."[38]

On April 18, 1832, the *Freedom* arrived in St. Louis, Missouri. All of Wyeth's men were in high spirits; they had long looked forward to this town as a temporary resting place. They soon realized, however, that most of the information Wyeth had obtained in the East was of little use. Experienced hands who had traveled west quickly advised them that the Nat-wye-thiums would not withstand the rough roads, rapid streams, and eddies in the rivers ahead. Wyeth was constrained to sell the complicated wagons for less than half what they originally cost. It was painfully apparent that they were about to embark on a journey for which they were little prepared.

In St. Louis, Wyeth met Kenneth McKenzie of the American Fur Company (AFC), from whom he learned of the treachery of the Blackfoot tribe. The Bostonians also found out that William Sublette, agent for the Rocky Mountain Fur Company (RMFC), was preparing his own expedition to the mountains, set to depart on the first of May from Independence, Missouri, more than 250 river miles west of St. Louis. Fortunately, none of these veteran traders "felt any apprehensions or jealousy from the new comers from Boston; but treated them with friendship."[39] From the outset, Wyeth had hoped to induce some experienced mountaineer to guide the party west, and now determined to seek Sublette's aid.

Ball found St. Louis to be "then but a village, mostly consisting of old French buildings along the levee and a street near the river, but few good buildings in the place." He reported seeing a steamboat loaded with United States soldiers sent to the Illinois River to fight Black Hawk, who was overrunning the country near where Chicago stands today.[40]

Those with experience persuaded Wyeth to apply to Superintendent of Indian Affairs William Clark for a trading license. The permit issued to him on April 19, 1832, allowed him to trade at "Horse Prairie, and Quamash Flats; Lewis's forks of Columbia" with twenty-six men for two years. The license indicated the capital to be employed by Wyeth amounted to $726.90. Though he would be in competition with several other merchants, Wyeth had not only the smallest brigade but the least amount of capital invested. By comparison, American Fur Company, with 147 men, had nearly $61,000 in capital; Benjamin Bonneville, licensed with 100 men, had over $17,000 in capital; and William Sublette, with 39 men, had over $11,000 in capital. All three of these licenses listed the same trade locations as Wyeth's. Considering Wyeth's assets and inexperience, it is no wonder the St. Louis traders did not see the Pacific Trading Company as much of a threat.[41]

McKenzie's AFC steamboat, the *Otter* (Ball mistakenly called this the *Otto*), was departing up the Missouri River in about a week, bound for the town of Independence on the far western edge of the state. Wyeth's contingent put its goods and baggage on board and prepared to travel to this last bastion of frontier settlements. River travel was slow on account of the snags and other obstructions for which the Big Muddy was famous. Several of the men, including Ball and John Wyeth, occasionally disembarked and walked when the boat moved particularly slowly.

Ball commented on the condition of the available drinking water during their upstream voyage:

> *The bed of the Missouri is a quicksand, mixed with soil. The water is the color of well-creamed coffee. After drinking it and shutting the mouth one can feel the grit. But still thus it flows eternally on at four knots per hour.*[42]

A short distance above Jefferson, Missouri, a gravel bar extended across the entire river, making the water too shallow for the boat to proceed. Several men, Ball included, quit the boat and hiked overland to Lexington, Missouri: "five days through woods, mud, creeks & over prairies, in rain & shine."[43] Along the route they passed a tavern and were hospitably received. They were "lodged and fed in their best manner and at a very reasonable rate," according to Ball, who was introduced for the first time to a thin bread of wheat flour called johnny cake.[44]

Following that jaunt, the walkers reassembled with the main party at Lexington on April 29 and the *Otter* steamed upriver, finally arriving at Independence a few days later. It was here, many miles from home and on the brink of the frontier, that some of the men began to have serious doubts about their decision to head west. With a young man's slim understanding of human nature's inability to grasp what cannot be anticipated, John Wyeth opined that it "would have been wiser had we asked [questions] before we left Cambridge, and ruminated well on the answers."[45]

William Sublette, brother Andrew and about fifty men were camped at Independence, making final preparations to take a caravan of supply-laden pack mules to that year's rendezvous at Pierre's Hole in today's Teton Valley, Idaho. This contingent was soon joined by Robert Campbell, with a small five-man outfit of his own, and RMFC's Thomas Fitzpatrick, accompanied by four men. Ball reported that Sublette allowed Wyeth's group to join them, under the condition that the Easterners take their due part in guarding and defending the camp in case of Indian attack. The collective party now numbered about ninety men and nearly three hundred head of livestock.[46]

Sublette figured Wyeth's plan to develop a fur trade post near the mouth of the Columbia would not compete with his own business, having judged the New Englanders as men of theory, not of practice.[47] The experienced trapper/trader was willing to initiate the tenderfoot Wyeth to the methods of Rocky Mountain travel. He suggested they purchase two yoke of oxen and fifteen sheep to sustain themselves on the first part of the trip. Since none of these greenhorns had traveled into the West, they accepted Sublette's advice. The livestock supplemented other trail provisions Wyeth carried, including a chest of tea, pepper and salt, corn meal and 450 pounds of bacon.[48]

Sublette had brought a few head of cattle to provide meat for his own crew until it reached the buffalo country. In a May 12 letter to William Ashley, Sublette explained that finding enough pack horses had been difficult; he had been forced to purchase mostly mules, and those at higher prices than desirable. Sublette commented that two dozen Bostonians were going out with him "if they can keep up as they are on foot." Horses had been hard for Wyeth to come by as well.[49]

The combined parties stayed in camp at Independence for about ten days, getting ready for the push west. The day before departure, Wyeth assigned his cousin John to guard the livestock. John came into camp at dusk claiming the sheep had strayed and that he had tied up the oxen and gone after the sheep. While he was gone, the oxen had allegedly broken loose and could not be found. Wyeth suspected that

Thomas Fitzpatrick (1799-1854), a partner in the Rocky Mountain Fur Company, crossed trails with Wyeth several times. The two first met as they traveled to the 1832 rendezvous in Pierre's Hole. HISTORY COLORADO, SCAN #10027099

something was amiss in John's story and sent another man to the spot to check it out. That man reported to Wyeth that John could not show any place where the oxen had been bound and no tracks could be found.[50]

About this time, Thomas Livermore informed the Captain that John's guns were not in camp. Wyeth called all the men to arms and it was discovered that neither John nor Weeks were equipped for defense. Both were instructed to produce their weapons, which were Company property, but refused. Wyeth put the pair under guard and after a bit, Weeks offered to retrieve their guns which had been secretly stashed outside of camp as part of their plan to desert. Fortunately, another man accompanied him, because Weeks attempted to escape while out and about. Eventually, both rifles were produced and all the livestock were eventually rounded up.

On the morning of May 12, Wyeth called the Company together and related the episode from the prior evening.[51] Tracks had since been found indicating the oxen had been tied at a completely different location than John Wyeth had described. Nathaniel told his men he had no power to release John from the Company because his young cousin was under the age of majority and within his personal charge. Weeks, on the other hand, should be dismissed, provided he compensated the Company for expenses he had incurred, over and above what he had already contributed. A vote was taken per Company rules and recorded by the clerk: Weeks was discharged, with the requirement that he pay an additional $40 in order to keep the Company's clothes and equipment then in his possession.

Weeks refused to reimburse the PTC, so Wyeth threatened to tie him to the tail of a horse. This produced the desired effect. The guilty man paid up and was released. Wyeth reported that the Company felt "much insenced at this attemp at desertion" and fully seconded the punishment meted out by Wyeth. Nathaniel reaffirmed his expectation of complete obedience to orders and his determination to enforce his rule "at all hazards." Those who lagged would be put on guard duty.[52]

Later that same day, the entire party left Independence, with the New England group following Sublette's caravan. In strict military order, they marched in double file. Those who were mounted rode double file, Sublette in the lead, giving orders as needed. Campbell, as lieutenant, brought up the rear. The expedition was finally on the road, heading out of the frontier hamlet in a southwesterly direction on the Santa Fe Trail.

Before nightfall, Wyeth realized Kilham had deserted, accompanying the banished Weeks. John Wyeth later asserted that "whether they had any real cause of dissatisfaction with our Captain, or whether they only made that an excuse to quit the expedition and return home, it is not for me to say."[53] But if Wyeth's report is to be believed, John's dissatisfaction with the enterprise was abundantly evident the previous evening. The younger Wyeth had likely been aware of, if not involved in, the two men's plans to absent themselves.

During these initial days on the actual frontier, everyone seemed to test Wyeth's command. Even Doctor Jacob was once put on guard duty for avoiding work required in setting up camp. Teenaged Thomas Livermore complained that his feet hurt; Wyeth, now accustomed to being lied to, demanded an examination. Livermore refused to remove his boots and insisted that his word should be good enough. Disagreeing, Wyeth meted out the same duties to the youth as to the others.

Some members of the PTC were apprehensive about going any farther west, but at the same time were reluctant to turn back this far into the journey. Instead, they endeavored to spoil the expedition by ruining the few horses they had. Tin pots and picket pins were found under pack saddles, raising sores on the backs of many animals. It was not long before the men were all afoot except those who were sick, disabled or hunting.[54]

The last encampment before crossing what would become the Missouri State line was a small Mormon community in Jackson County known as Prairie Settlement. Located near the unorganized area that subsequently became Indian Territory, the Mormons at Prairie Settlement

Robert Campbell (1804-1879), pictured here in later life as a successful St. Louis entrepreneur, was a business partner of William Sublette during the Rocky Mountain fur trade. Campbell was one of many fur trade personalities Wyeth met during his first expedition.

CAMPBELL HOUSE MUSEUM, SAINT LOUIS, MO

were well positioned to sell goods and equipment to passing Santa Fe traders.[55] Ball reported procuring some milk from these Saints. After another seventy miles or so they reached an Indian village, probably the Kansa tribe, living near modern Topeka, Kansas. Along the way to that village, the party swam their horses across the Kansas River and visited briefly with a white man near today's Lawrence, Kansas. This settler acted as a gunsmith for the Indians. Ball claimed this man would be the last Caucasian they met outside of their own party.[56] Although not quite accurate (the group would encounter white trappers the very next month), the comment reflects Ball's sense of having left his own civilization far behind. He also noted they found honey in abundance, confirming that bees were moving farther west. Honey bees are not native to North America but were brought to this continent by European immigrants. Swarms advanced westward just ahead of the settlers.[57]

On leave from the U.S. Army, Benjamin
Bonneville (1796-1878) led a fur trade
expedition of his own at the same time
as Wyeth, becoming the first person to
take wagons across South Pass. DENVER
PUBLIC LIBRARY, WESTERN HISTORY COLLECTION, Z-8881

In late May, another one
hundred miles along, earlier
informant Thomas Livermore
deserted, along with Bell and
Griswell. It had been twelve
days since Kilham and Weeks's
departure.[58]

Wyeth had been out hunt-
ing on foot with Bache at
the time the trio absconded,
which apparently allowed
the three men to "effect their
intention, a thing they would
not have dared attemp had I
been in camp."[59] The men "taking French leave" stole three
horses and Wyeth ran another
horse into the ground trying to
overtake them, reducing the
number of available animals
for the remaining party by
four. The Pacific Trading Company had now shrunk by five, leaving a
total of twenty men.

Continuing their march up the Kansas River along the prairie at
the edge of the timber, they reached the Blue River on May 21.[60] At 208
miles from Independence, they forded what is known today as Rock
Creek in modern Jefferson County, Nebraska. Sometime between 1832
and 1842, however, this stream acquired the name Wyeth Creek. The
watercourse shows as "Wyeth's Run" on the map of John C. Fremont's
1842 expedition. It was on this creek that the Corps of Topographi-
cal Engineers officer and his guide Kit Carson carved their names on a
boulder during their midday break.[61]

Before long, the fur men overtook the party of Captain Benjamin Bonneville, who was driving wagons to the mountains on the
unmarked, unimproved road. On leave from the U.S. Army, Bonneville had mounted his own fur trading expedition headed for the Rocky
Mountains. Historians have consistently speculated that Bonneville's

temporary separation from the U.S. Army to conduct a trapping foray
in the West may have been secretly connected to American political and
military interests.[62]

William Sublette had taken wagons to the fur trade rendezvous on
the Wind River east of the Continental Divide in 1830, but no one had
brought them across the Continental Divide as Bonneville planned to
do.[63] There is no evidence that Wyeth and Bonneville ever consulted
each other prior to launching their separate plans, although they must
have been aware of each other as early supporters (indeed, Bonneville
was considered a leader) of Hall J. Kelley's Oregon settlement proposal.

After a quick salute, the Boston party traveled on and Bonneville's
wagon dust disappeared behind them. Continuing west, Wyeth's men
struck the Platte River near Grand Island and the future site of Fort
Kearny. The Platte, a wide but shallow watercourse, is often described as
"too thick to drink – too thin to plow." Its name (French for "flat"), was
bestowed by the Mallet brothers in 1739.[64] The trail continued up the
valley of the Platte to the junction of its North and South forks. Crossing the South Platte, Wyeth's group followed up the north bank, reaching the North Platte near Ash Hollow.

The Platte's north bank could also be designated as its left bank.
Proper determination of the right and left side of a stream is made while
facing downstream. Some editors denote shores as right and left because
that does not change as the river meanders. However, compass bearings
are used in this work to provide easier orientation for the general reader.

The route kept to the North Platte for nearly 400 miles.

MAP 2 *Independence, Missouri, to Pierre's Hole Rendezvous, 1832*

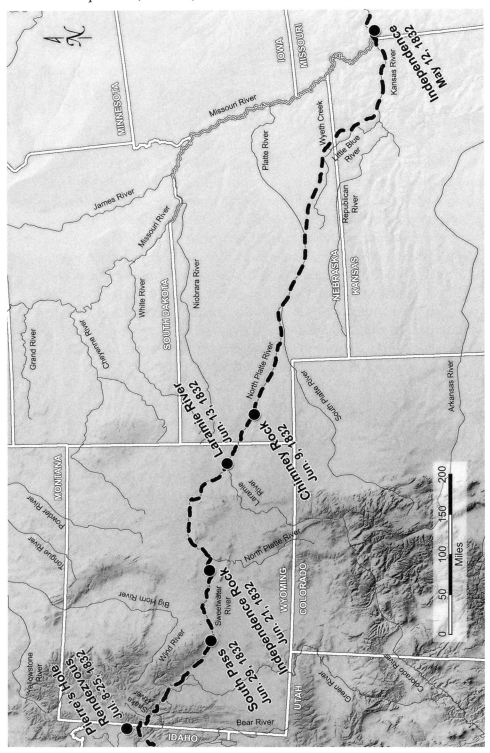

4.
Westward to the Continental Divide

By early June, provisions were near exhaustion. An occasional deer had been added to the larder, and the men expected to see buffalo any day, but for the most part, the caravan had depended on the sheep and oxen they had driven from Independence. About the first of June, a little rain shower improved the prairie grass for their livestock.

Day after day, the ninety or so men in the combined companies followed the north fork of the Platte westward. Sublette's authority kept order over the entire group; he had quickly established a routine for all the men to follow after "Halt!" was called each day. Guard duty was assigned and any sentry caught sleeping would be forced to walk the next day as punishment. Ball described a typical evening camp:

Mr. Sublette leading the band, always selected the ground, having reference in doing so to water, always encamping on the river or other stream, to feed for horses and safety of the place for defense in case of an attack, which he seemed to rather expect. And if such place was reached by that time, he usually ordered "halt" by the middle of the afternoon, so as to give the horses time to feed and make full preparation for night. The horses were unpacked and men or messes arranged in a manner to leave a large hollow square, the stream forming one side. And then the horses were immediately hoppled, four feet tied together, and turned out of camp and a guard placed beyond them, to keep them from straying too far or drive them if attacked. Then about sundown he would cry "ketch up, ketch up" always repeating his order. Then each man would bring in the horses he had charge of, keep them still hoppled and tie them to short stakes carried with us, driven close into the ground, giving each one as much room as could be without interfering with others, so that they could feed also during the night. Then a guard, changed every three hours, sat for the night. As soon as light in the morning the order would

be "turn out, turn out." And all would rise from their earthly beds,
turn the horses out to bite, get a hearty breakfast, then the horses
were saddled and packed and formed in line and the order given to
"march." And as a reward for their expedition, the first ready took
their place nearest to the commandant. In the middle of the day a
stop was made, the horses unpacked to rest them, but not turned out,
and a lunch taken by the men, if wished, of meat already cooked, and
in half an hour pack up and march on.[1]

With the pack horses carrying 180-pound loads, the animals were
not able to trot, according to Ball, but "they soon formed the habit of
walking fast."[2] Each morning, the men who were ready to go first were
privileged to take their place next to Sublette – a protocol repeated
every day. This appeared to be Sublette's standard operating procedure
on the trail; a remarkably similar description would be provided by
Henry Spalding a few years later. He reported a typical day's schedule:
"rise at half past three and turn out the horses, start at 6, turn out at 11,
start again at 1, campt at [five?] and picket the horses at 8. A guard was
kept night and day."[3]

From this point onward, the journal of Nathaniel Wyeth appears
in grey boxes throughout the text. Due to missing pages in the original journal, the first extant entry may not be complete, but may have
begun on a previous page.

JOURNAL OF CAPTAIN NATHANIEL J. WYETH'S EXPEDITION TO THE OREGON COUNTRY, 1832-33

June 6, 1832   **North Platte River**

gray and my face like a plumb pudding   the skin is entirely
bare[?] of skin is entirely off one of my ears   On the blufs the
ghnats are equally troublesome but they do not annoy us much
except in the day.   Geese appear here mated and I have seen
some broods of gooselings.   Some rain last night.   still barren
and grass bad   our horses about the same   our men troubled
with the relax   toward night found buffaloe   killed one which
made a scanty meal for all hands for supper   made 25 miles

Wyeth apparently had an allergic reaction to repeated insect bites which painfully transformed his face. The men began to suffer from "want of good and wholesome water" drinking from the North Platte's shallow, muddy stream.[4] Many of the men, including Dr. Wyeth, contracted diarrhea, Wyeth's "relax." Trappers referred to this condition as *mal de vache*, (French for "cow sickness"); it was thought to be caused by water with high alkali content. Fur trader Charles Larpenteur described it as a kind of dysentery, though he alleged the origin was "eating too much fat meat alone."[5]

Having slaughtered the last of their livestock, the travelers suffered the "sharp gnawing of hunger" before reaching the buffalo country. Once there, it would be a few days before they found any animals to hunt. John Wyeth complained that "after we killed them we had no wood or vegetables of any kind wherewith to kindle a fire for cooking."[6] Ball described using "dry buffalo droppings" for fuel, cooking the meat primarily by boiling it in camp kettles.[7]

June 7, 1832   *North Platte River*

7th   Started out hunting   killed two antelope   about 10 saw a herd of Buffaloe crossing the River   waited til they rose the Bank and commenced slaughter   killed 3 and wounded many more   these afforded a timely supply to the party and we ate hearty.   Saw today the first appearance of muskrat since leav the settlements also Pelicans.   Last night in cutting a tree for fuel caught two young grey Eagles one of which we ate and found it tender and good also a Badger   saw some rattlesnakes and some other kinds not known to me   the men appear a little better the men [horses?] about the same   Thr. 90 deg.   wind S.E.   my face so swelled from the musquitoes and ghnats that I can scarce see out of my eyes and aches like the tooth ache

At times, Wyeth's party went a day or two without seeing buffalo, then would see them in countless numbers. Ball noticed the same herd that Wyeth mentioned as it grazed across the river:

on the wide bottoms and the side bluffs beyond like a herd of cattle,
up and down the country on that side as far as we could see, and
continued the same during our twenty-five miles' march and no end
to them ahead, probably, 10,000 seen in that one day.[8]

Buffalo is a far leaner meat than beef to begin with and this early
in the year, the buffalo were leaner still from poor winter forage. The
men grew weak from eating such a limited diet. Quarrels broke out
over any part of the animal with tallow, even caul – the fat around the
internal organs such as the liver and kidneys.[9] John Wyeth voiced the
complaints and gripes of the other Bostonians, who found themselves
far out of their element: "that grumbling, discontent, and dejection
should spring up amongst us, was what no one can be surprised at
learning. We were at times very miserable, and our commander could
be no less so."[10]

The men soon learned the adage "meat is meat," meaning that all
sorts of animals would find their way into the stew pot including eagles
and badgers. The New Englanders found that mountaineers were not
picky when hungry. In fact, menus were often limited only by what a
man could catch or his waning prejudices might abide. "From buffalo
down to the rattlesnake, including every quadruped that runs, every
fowl that flies, and every reptile that creeps, nothing comes amiss to
the mountaineer," as George Ruxton put it.[11] Like Wyeth, trapper
Rufus Sage told of finding "a bald-eagle's nest, with two half-grown
fledglings. One of our party, ascending the tree, captured the young
ones, and we had a fine meal from their carcasses."[12] As for eating badgers, Sage also told a humorous tale of such a meal:

We had left the Fort without provisions, and I accordingly proceeded
a short distance in advance for the purpose of killing antelope. Riding
slowly on, I noticed a badger not far ahead, and dismounted to shoot
him. But the creature becoming alarmed sprang for his hole, and I
hastened to stop him. This I effected by tightly grasping his tail as
he was in the very act of entering his burrow. In the chase my rifle
had accidentally discharged itself, and here commenced a struggle

*between me and the badger, I to retain my hold while I unbelted
my pistol to dispatch him, and he to enforce his liberty. At length I
succeeded, and a choice supper was made from his carcase, which, to
all intents, was the fattest thing I ever saw.*[13]

John Wyeth described finding rattlesnakes, as well as grizzlies,
which he called "the largest and fiercest bears, – a very formidable
animal, which it is not prudent for a man to attack alone."[14] John Ball
reported seeing no spring, nor crossing a stream in hundreds of miles
up the North Platte, though the party crossed many dry creek beds
where "torrents must have run at the melting of the snow."[15] On June
8, the men could see an entire day's march across the plains ahead and
in the distance a "big castle" appeared, a "striking landmark in this prairie sea."[16] The next day, moving up the river, they approached the landmark, which in the years ahead would become well known to travelers
on the trail to the Rocky Mountains as Chimney Rock.

June 9, 1832   *North Platte River near Chimney Rock*

*9th   I date this the same on acc of a mistake of a day
heretofore   made 30 miles and yesterday 25   arrived at the
Chimney or Elk Brick the Indian name   this singular object
looks like a monument about 200 feet high and is composed
of layers of sand and lime stone in layers the sand blowing
out lets the lime rock fall down and this action has in time
reduced what was once a hill to a spire of nearly the same
dimensions at top and bottom   it looks like a work of art and
the layers like the ranges of stone   it is scituated about 3
miles from the river.   Rain and thunder at night wind strong
S. E. river as muddy as ever   the blufs for the last 20 miles
have occasionally a few stinted trees apparently Pitch pine and
cedar   the small streams that here empty into the Platte are
frequently dry near the river during the day while above they
are running free while at night there is running water entirely to
the river   Party in better order   Horses about the same   we
now judge ourselves within 4 days march of the Black Hills*

Alfred Jacob Miller painted this sketch of Chimney Rock in 1837. The formation, in modern Nebraska, was a well-known landmark on the overland trail to the Rocky Mountains. WALTERS ART MUSEUM, BALTIMORE, MD

Wyeth's innocuous reference to the Indian name for Chimney Rock may indicate either delicacy or humor. This formation had been described by other fur traders in slightly more graphic terms. William Drummond Stewart, in his novel *Edward Warren*, wrote that Indians called it *"Penus cervus"* and artist Alfred J. Miller included a French translation on his watercolor "Returning from Hunting Near *Puine du Cerf*" – both sly references to a deer penis. Zenas Leonard declared that Natives called it "Elk Peak" while William Marshall Anderson wrote "E. P., or Chimney Rock, a solitary shaft." Warren Ferris would contribute another moniker, "Nose Mountain."[17]

> **June 10, 1832**   *North Platte River*
>
>   *10th   28 miles,   2 Buffaloe*
>
> **June 11, 1832**
>
>   *11th   30 miles,   6 Buffaloe*

These brief entries likely report the number of bison killed on each day. In a letter to his brother, Robert Campbell had reported that the Black Hills came into view on June 11 and after that, they were never out of sight of snow. This particular mountain range is not the Black Hills in modern South Dakota; rather, it is today's Laramie Range in Wyoming.[18] Campbell reported frost every night for the past three weeks and that camp was made alongside snow banks on many an evening.[19]

> **June 12, 1832**   *North Platte River*
>
>   *12th   Nothing remarkeable   crossed Wild Horse Creek coming in from the S.*
>
> **June 13, 1832**   *mouth of Laramie River*
>
>   *13th   Came in sight of the Black hills and crossed Larrimee fork of the Platte   in getting over one of my rafts broke the tow line   the raft went down stream lodged on a snag and upset wetting most of the goods on it and loosing two Horse*

loads as it lodged in the middle of the river and the stream very rappid   the goods were with difficulty passed ashore   here an alarm was occasioned by the appearance of 4 men on the blufs behind us and an attack was expected every moment which would have been bad as our party was much scattered in crossing   They However proved to be a part of a party of 19 men in the employ of Gant & Blackwell.   They last winter lost all but 3 of their animals and in going to Santa Fee got enclosed by snow in the mountains and nearly starved to Death, and at first they were hard to tell from Indians or devils   they are now in good health having felt well for some time   all of them joined Mr. Fitzpatricks party and proceeded on foot with us to the mountains.   Killed an antelope

On June 13, the combined party halted on the banks of the Laramie River, named for Jacques LaRamee, a trapper killed on that river around 1818-19, according to Jim Bridger.[20] Snow could still be seen in the surrounding mountains and the spring runoff caused high water. The crossing required the construction of rafts to negotiate the nearly half-mile-wide turbulent current. Ball told of a few courageous men who mounted horses and swam them over as a lead to the other horses. Though reluctant, the livestock were driven across but got swept well downstream before making the opposite shore.[21]

Ball told of the men bursting into loud laughter at Sublette's bull boats and, in spite of the more experienced man's exhortation to build a similar craft, Wyeth was determined to make log rafts, with terrible results. Once across the river, they made camp with the Laramie Range as a scenic backdrop for the tired travelers.

The nineteen men who joined the party here, remnants of a Gantt and Blackwell brigade, had left St. Louis for the Rocky Mountains the previous spring, on April 24, 1831. Upon reaching the Laramie River, they had divided into three trapping parties while Blackwell returned east for more supplies. Blackwell encountered Fitzpatrick, who was also on his way east, and traveled on to St. Louis with him.

Now a year later, while on the way to rendezvous, Wyeth and Sublette found the Gantt and Blackwell men once again in the vicinity of the

Laramie. These trappers had not heard from Blackwell since they had separated from their boss the previous summer; however, they recognized Fitzpatrick. He told them their company was insolvent, though he may have said this only to recruit the trappers for the Rocky Mountain Fur Company. Alfred Stephens, leader of the brigade, sold the 120 beaver skins they had trapped to Fitzpatrick and agreed to accompany the supply train to Pierre's Hole. Fitzpatrick then cached the furs and raced ahead of the caravan to alert the trappers already waiting at the rendezvous that Sublette was on his way with supplies. The errand would turn out to be a harrowing experience for the solitary rider.[22]

In September 1832, the nineteen Gantt and Blackwell trappers would find a note from Gantt, telling them Blackwell had returned with supplies and the two leaders now planned to establish a trading post on the Arkansas River. It appears that Fitzpatrick blatantly lied to decrease competition in the field.

June 14, 1832   *North Platte River*

14th   started late and left the river at which we had encamped and proceeded 16 miles   killed one antelope and one elk

June 15, 1832

15th   went out for game   killed one antelope, 2 deer 2 Buffaloe   made this day 20 miles and passed the first of the Black hills   the country is now thinly wooded with Box Elder ash Pitch pine cedar and cotton wood and a variety of small shrubs among which are the cherry, currant and thorn   wild sage here almost covers the country and is a plant of many years groth   arrived in camp   found the company had killed plenty of Buffaloe and were encamped on a small stream coming in from the S.   20 miles.

The scenery began to change from the monotonous plain to a hilly, partially-wooded country. Both Wyeth and John Ball remarked on some of the plant life.[23] As they traveled into the Black Hills, John Wyeth reported some of the men were still not well and that the sicker men fell off their horses from weakness. An indignant John noted,

It was to me particularly grievous to think that he, who was to take care of the health of the company, was the first who was disabled from helping himself and others, and this one a blood relation. It required a man of a firmer make than Dr. Jacob Wyeth to go through such a mountainous region as the one we were in: a man seldom does a thing right the first time.[24]

John also contrasted the "dismal looking" Black Hills with the Rocky Mountains saying they, too, would be called mountains if they were not in such proximity to the Rockies, "whose peaks overtop everything, and elevate themselves into the region of everlasting frost and snow."[25]

June 16, 1832   *North Platte River*

16th   Warm in mng. cold and rainy in the afternoon   a little hard snow on the Peak of the Black hills   a white Bear was seen this day   Black ones for some days past.   The lime rock still continues   primitive pebles in the streams and on the knols   the hills pointed up very sharp from the same cause as the Chimney   the country appears desolate and dreary in the extreme   no one can conceive of the utter desolation of this region   nevertheless the earth is decorated with a variety of beautifull flowers and all unknown to me   hard travelling disenables our botanist to examine them   we have on the whole meat enough but the supply is too unsteady.   There are here two kinds of Rabbits the largest weighing about 15 lbs ears 6 inches long   plover and other marsh birds a[re] common and some 2 or 3 kinds of Gulls.   Struck the Platte river again   here about 100 yds wide the water high and rapid   we here find a small kind of Parsnip the blossom yellow root about 5 inches long 1/2 inch thick of more than one years groth   the men appear better   Horses about the same   made this day 20 miles

It is interesting to note the contrast in Wyeth's description of the countryside: "desolate and dreary in the extreme" in one breath and "a variety of beautiful flowers" in the next. Ball also noted the "pleasant change."[26] Wyeth had not identified a botanist in the party. Perhaps it was a coy reference to himself. Wyeth routinely noted many plants, minerals, and animals. For example, what he called a "white bear" was a common term in the mountains for a grizzly.

June 17, 1832   *North Platte River*

17th   Wind high N.W.   Ther 40   a drear and cheerless day   made 25 miles   killed 3 buffaloe 1 antelope 1 Deer crossed 2 small streams from the Black hills running into the Platte   saw some rabbits & white bears   Hops.

June 18, 1832

18   reached the place for fording the platt

June 19, 1832

19th   Passed over my goods during a severe wind without accident

June 20, 1832

20th   Mr. Subblettee passed over his goods and at night mooved on about 3 miles

It was likely that Sublette located his camp away from Wyeth's in order to find better forage for the livestock. More than 300 head of horses would require quite a bit of grass. This was the first occasion, however, that Wyeth remarked on the separation of camps.

They forded the North Platte on June 18 about three miles northeast of modern Casper, Wyoming. Fremont described it as

two hundred feet breadth of water ... the channels were generally three feet deep, and there were large angular rocks on the bottom, which made the ford in some places a little difficult ... this has always been used as the best ford.[27]

The prominent granite outcrop known as Independence Rock, sketched by Alfred Jacob Miller in 1837, was another familiar milestone for west-bound travelers, many of whom carved their names upon its surface. WALTERS ART MUSEUM, BALTIMORE, MD

June 21, 1832   *Independence Rock*

21st   Made a long march of 30 miles during which one of my Horses gave out   killed this day 3 Buffaloe and fired at a white bear   arrived at camp at 11 ock at night.   I have ommitted one day on the other side of the Platte   I date this right   we arrived at Rock Independence at noon after a march of 15 miles

Apparently without a calendar, Wyeth was having trouble keeping his dates correct. He had noted a mistake back on June 9. The day he omitted must have been June 8 but he corrected himself. Leaving the North Platte, the Sweetwater became their guide and the party arrived at Independence Rock, another famous landmark of the westward trail. This large granite monolith in today's southwestern Natrona County, Wyoming, covers about twenty-five acres. There are several versions of how it came to be named. Some say that Thomas Fitzpatrick was paddling down the Sweetwater in a bull boat loaded with the winter's harvest of furs and wrecked nearby on July 4, 1824. He cached the hides and named the rock in honor of the day. William Ashley has also been credited with christening the trail marker after spending July 4, 1825, camped in its shadow. Benjamin Bonneville has been recognized as naming the outcrop because it stands alone and sovereign on the prairie. Bonneville's naming was supposed to have occurred in 1832.[28] Since Wyeth was ahead of Bonneville and already knew the landmark's name, the latter story should be dismissed.

Camped at Independence Rock, Ball and John Wyeth both mentioned this historic landmark and both gave their versions of its history. Ball's story of a "prior party having stopped here and celebrated the 4th of July on it" has maintained its currency, but John's declaration that "the huge rock in the shape of a bowl upside down" was so named because it was "the resting place of Lewis and Clarke on the 4th of July" may have raised skeptical eyebrows even at the time. Lewis and Clark were never close to this isolated mass of granite.[29]

June 23, 1832   *Sweetwater River*
Written July 2

   *23   Yesterday we left the Platte and struck the Sweet water
   on which this rock stands   it is scituated in a gorge within 30
   feet of the stream and is granite   today is warm   last night
   frost and the two last days cold and disagreeable from this time
   to 2nd July frost each night and snow once   our course lay in
   various directions from S.W. to N.W. following the Sweet water
   and leaving the first snowy mountains on the right hand*

Wyeth wrote this, and the next several entries, during an attempt to catch up on July 2. The New Englanders had left the North Platte and on June 22 reached the Sweetwater, here flowing through the formidable Sweetwater Canyon. The Sweetwater was said to have been named by William Ashley in 1823 when, after the alkali-laden water the trappers had been drinking, this refreshing stream tasted sweet. While this might be true, the date is clearly wrong because Ashley did not go that far west in 1823. But David Thompson correctly labeled the stream on his map, drawn sometime between 1814 and 1824, casting a sour note on that legend. In 1830, Warren Ferris credited the accidental drowning there of a mule, its packs full of sugar, "some years since." However, Ashley himself inscribed the name in his 1825 diary, before he had ever seen the river and before any loads of sugar were likely to have reached its banks.[29] John Wyeth admitted the water was "cool, clear, and pleasant ... a good remedy for our sick, as their bowel complaints were brought on and aggravated by the muddy water" they had been forced to consume.[30]

Neither Captain Wyeth nor Ball made much mention of crossing the Sweetwater, but John Wyeth went into great detail over the difficulty of the ford. The following incident is so similar to the one John Ball and Wyeth described with the raft back on the Laramie River that it is possible John may have mistaken the event's location – or the Captain may have been so obstinate that he repeated the experience.[31]

The younger Wyeth's antagonism toward his cousin had evidently been increasing; this event probably hardened his attitude further. John described Sublette's party building a bull boat, and Sublette again suggesting, as he had at the Laramie River, that Wyeth do the same.

However, the former ice merchant again focused his attention on the construction of a log raft to transport his party's goods across the river. John reported that the bull boat was

> *capable of transporting man, horse, and goods over a pretty strong*
> *current. At the sight of it, we Yankees all burst out into a loud laugh,*
> *whether from surprise, or pleasure, or both, I know not. It certainly*
> *was not from ridicule; for we all acknowledged the contrivance would*
> *have done credit to old New-England. While Captain Sublet and his*
> *company were binding the gunwale of the boat with buffalo-sinews,*
> *to give it strength and due hardness, our Captain was by no means*
> *idle. He accordingly undertook to make a raft to transport our own*
> *goods across the river. Sublet expressed his opinion that it would*
> *not answer where the current was strong; but Captain Wyeth is a*
> *man not easily to be diverted from any of his notions, or liable to be*
> *influenced by the advice of others; so that while Sublet's men were*
> *employed on their Bull-boat, Wyeth and a chosen few were making*
> *a raft. When finished, we first placed our blacksmith's shop upon it,*
> *that is to say, our anvil, and large vice, and other valuable articles*
> *belonging to blacksmithery, bar-iron, and steel traps, and alas! a cask*
> *of powder, and a number of smaller, but valuable articles. We fixed a*
> *rope to our raft, and with some difficulty got the other end of it across*
> *the river to the opposite bank by a man swimming with a rope in*
> *his mouth, from some distance above the spot he aimed to reach. We*
> *took a turn of it round a tree. Captain Sublet gave it as his opinion*
> *that the line would not be sufficient to command the raft. But our*
> *Leader was confident that it would; but when they had pulled about*
> *half way over, the rope broke, and the raft caught under the limbs of*
> *a partly submerged tree, and tipped it on one side so that we lost our*
> *iron articles, and damaged our goods and a number of percussion*
> *caps. This was a very serious calamity and absolutely irreparable.*[32]

Sublette knew a bull boat's superior buoyancy and shallow draft was better suited to western rivers than a heavy log raft. Wyeth's Yankee stubbornness, which in Boston had secured his success, proved costly here. The loss of these goods would turn out to be a critical setback for the Pacific Trading Company.

Karl Bodmer included bull boats in his 1843-44 aquatint of a Mandan village. Wyeth learned the reliability of these native-made coracles in crossing the swift current of Rocky Mountain streams. These boats were typically made by stretching buffalo hides over a skeletal framework of willow branches.

WISCONSIN HISTORICAL SOCIETY, WHI-6337

Wyeth did not record this event, but a clue emerges in William Sublette's papers. Sublette would charge Wyeth ten dollars for transporting thirty traps by horseback from the Sweetwater to the rendezvous in Teton Valley, indicating that a shuffling of pack loads occurred here.[33]

Compounding the men's misery at this time were the mosquitoes during the night, and the gnats during the day. Wyeth had mentioned "ghnats" plaguing the daylight hours, to which his cousin added,

> *At this point of our journey we were sadly tormented by musquetoes, that prevented our sleep after the fatigues of the day. This little contemptible insect, which they call here a gnat, disturbed us more than bears, or wolves, or snakes.*[34]

Dispirited not just about the conditions of the moment, but also about future prospects, John wrote,

> *Here I, and others were entirely convinced that we were engaged in an expedition without being provided with the means to accomplish*

it. Our boats and wagons we had disposed of at St. Louis, and
here we were on the banks of a river without even a canoe ... Two
thirds of our company were sick, and that without any particular
disorder that we can name, but from fatigue, bad water, scanty food,
and eating flesh half raw. Add to this worry of mind, and serious
apprehensions about our fate when the worthy Captain Sublet
should leave us.[35]

June 29, 1832   **South Pass**
Written July 2

on the 29th we crossed on to the head waters of the Colorado
during all this time we found abundance of Buffalo   the
travelling good but the grass poor   the streams all fordable but
rapid   five streams have been crossed to this time and we are
now encamped on the 6th   all running into the Colorado   trout
are found here also some beaver   Some of my men talk
of turning back and I give them all free liberty   many of my
horses have given out and the rest are failing fast and unless
we soon come to better grass they will all die and leave me on
foot   the waters running into Lewis river are not more than 8
miles distant,   on the creek where we are there are pine trees
in shape lik a Balsam tree leaves like a pitch pine Bark rough
yellowish and scaly   The mountains in this region are not
conspicuous   are isolated and admitting free passage between
them in any direction   the creeks are sufficiently numerous for
watering but feed is poor

Though Wyeth did not mention it, the party had crossed the Continental Divide at South Pass on June 29. Reaching the waters of the Colorado was significant enough that two men recorded it: John Wyeth ("about the first of July"); and John Ball (who asserted it was June 28).[36] Wyeth's "head waters of the Colorado" denotes the Green River in today's western Wyoming. The Lewis River is better known as the Snake River today. Although there is no way to locate the men's camp with certainty, Wyeth's estimate of eight miles to the waters of the Lewis is incorrect or an error in transcription. Judging from Ball's itinerary, the distance would have been at least 30 and as much as 50 miles.

The company trudged on from the Sweetwater crossing and marched up its south bank, headed for the Green River Valley. Ball, writing with the advantage of retrospect, was able to supply historical context:

> We were at the celebrated South Pass of the Rocky Mountains, said by his political friends, when a candidate for President, though he was not there till ten years after, to have been discovered by General Fremont. And it was by no means then new to our fur traders. It has its name from Lewis and Clark and other early travelers always keeping on the main Missouri which led them to a crossing far north and more difficult.[37]

July 1, 1832   **New Fork River**
Written July 2

the 1st July we rested all the afternoon   a respite quite acceptable to our weary legs   Our average during these days about 20 miles but in some cases quite circuitous   White bears are seen but none have been killed.   Wolves and antelopes plenty,   King fishers   Our hunters have just brought part of 4 Buffaloe   At night encamped on the same creek that we passed this mng. and soon after were visited by 6 men from Dripps & Fontenelles concern who with 13 others are encamped 5 miles from this place.   This night at about 12 ock. we were attacked by Indians probably the Blackfoot.   They approached within 50 yds. and fired about 40 shots into the camp and some arrows   they wounded three animals got 5 from Mr. Subblette   One from an Independent hunter and 4 which I left out of camp for better feed   mine were all poor and sore backed and useless

Somewhere between the Sweetwater and the Green, John Wyeth spotted a number of men on horseback riding toward them at full speed. At first the riders were taken to be Indians and the camp was put on full alert, preparing for battle as everyone had practiced. It turned out to be a band of six trappers attached to the American Fur Company under the leadership of Andrew Drips and Lucien Fontenelle. These six men, plus thirteen more, were camped about five miles from where Wyeth set up for the night.[38] This AFC trapping party was making its way to the rendezvous in Pierre's Hole to reunite with its main brigade. John Wyeth reported that these trappers "kept company with us till we came to Pierre's Hole."[39]

On July 1, the Sublette-Wyeth party camped along the trail toward the Green River Valley, probably on the New Fork River just a few miles south of present-day Pinedale, Wyoming. At about midnight, Indians really did attack. The raid was carried out by Gros Ventres (rather than Wyeth's speculated "Blackfoot") on their way north, returning to their homelands after a lengthy visit with Arapaho relatives in southern Colorado. Sublette described this as a skirmish with three hundred Indians lasting almost an hour.[40]

After the attack, Ball found himself somewhat surprised at how readily he was able to go back to sleep. He speculated that it "showed how a man will become, in a measure, indifferent to danger. I felt some fears before getting where there were Indians, but felt little after."[41] Writing home a couple of weeks later, Wyeth told his brother Charles of "a most ludicras fight with the Blackfeet, no blood drawn, but I lost 4 horses." On the same date, a more carefully worded letter to his wife described merely "a bloodless skirmish."[42]

The adversary in this encounter, the Gros Ventre of the Prairie, were considered a band of the Blackfeet Confederacy. Sometimes called Atsina, the Gros Ventres referred to themselves as A'ani or "White Clay People" and did not use the Atsina designation.[43] The frequency of trapper conflicts with this tribe was astounding and, more often than not, when mountaineers described clashes with "Blackfeet," they were referring to Gros Ventres. Since the Gros Ventre language is difficult, they often spoke to strangers in the Blackfoot tongue, possibly obscuring their identity.[44]

Some Canadian tribes called this group the Falls or Rapids people due to the cascades on the Saskatchewan River where they lived. The French translation of *Gros Ventre* is Big Belly, a misinterpretation of tribal hand signs for the numerous waterfalls in their lands.[45] The A'ani, or Gros Ventre of the Prairie, should not be confused with the Gros Ventre of the River, better known as the Hidatsa who lived along the Missouri River.

L'other Side of the Rocky Mountains
July 14th 1832

Dear Wife In good health and spirits I have arrived here
two thirds to my journeys end. Livermore and two others
deserted me and stole two horses. if he calls please
treat him with the contempt he deserves 7 more have
deserted me since leaving me 12 men which is all
I want having got through all the dangerous Country
I have had a bloodless skirmish with the Black feet
Ind. by whom I lost 4 horses I have got so far with as little
difficulty as I expected. you will not hear from me again
for some time and this letter must be short as the posts
by whom it is sent must move on.

I am by affe. Husband

Nath. Wyeth

Wyeth wrote to his wife on July 14, 1832, noting what he called a "bloodless
skirmish with the Black feet" which had occurred on July 1. He also complained
about Thomas Livermore's earlier desertion, advising Elizabeth "if he calls
please treat him with the contempt he deserves." It appears that Wyeth had
not written much news to his wife in the preceding months, and did not plan
to write much more: "you will not hear from me again for some time." The
letter would be carried to St. Louis after rendezvous by William Sublette; it was
postmarked in that city on October 5. SUBLETTE COUNTY FUR TRADE PAPERS #2010.551.0096,
MUSEUM OF THE MOUNTAIN MAN, PINEDALE, WY

As for the Blackfeet Confederacy, there are three primary bands: Siksika (Blackfoot), Piikani (Piegan) and Kainai (Blood). "Blackfoot" is the English translation of the word "siksika" and can be confusing because this designation was applied to many tribes in fur trade documents. Today, some Blackfoot people are annoyed by the Anglicized plural "Blackfeet," because the word is not plural in the Blackfoot language, but most Blackfoot people generally accept either name. "Blackfoot" is more typically used in Canada, while "Blackfeet" is more common in the United States. Some authorities indicate "Blackfeet" represents the Confederacy of the assorted bands while "Blackfoot" represents only the Siksika band.[46]

July 3, 1832   *Green River*

3rd   Decamped and in company with the men above mentioned proceeded to their camp and passed on to our route which lay W.   This night encamped on the waters of the Colorado   25 miles

---

The Company traveled across the foothills of the northern Green River Valley, using the river as their guide. They stopped to visit the AFC trapper camp along the way. Then, they trekked upstream in a northerly direction, keeping to the Green River.

July 4, 1832   *Hoback River*

4th   Decamped and at noon crossed the divide and drank to my friends with mingled feelings from the waters of the Columbia mixed with alcohol and eat of a Buffaloe cow   made this day 30 miles and 25 yesterday   The snow clad mountains now entirely surround us   the streams this side increase rapidly.   One bear seen this day   the grass much better and some fertile land here   the earth in some places was frozen snow yesterday and today   Three of my men are sick and I have no spare animals for them.

Crossing the Hoback Rim, they descended into Little Jackson's Hole, in the vicinity of today's Bondurant, Wyoming. The waters here drain into the Hoback River, which in turn, enter the Snake, a major tributary of the Columbia River. The day's march took them part way into Hoback Canyon. The walls of the deep ravine shade terrain rarely invaded by the sun. Ball reported, "we reached a brook flowing into the Lewis river, which we pursued through a deep break in the mountain." He also recorded an hour or two of snowfall within the micro-climes of the gorge.[47] The party celebrated Independence Day with a toast, the first mention of alcohol since leaving Missouri.

The men also got their first glimpse of the "Trois Tetons" rising in the north, though it is not clear where such a view is possible. Ball wrote,

> *Large snowcapped mountains were seen in the north, which we afterwards learned were the "Trois Teton," fifteen thousand feet high. The only way I had to ascertain our altitude was by the temperature of boiling water by my thermometer, which I made, allowing five hundred and thirty feet to a degree, eight thousand four hundred and eighty feet.*[48]

Ball over-estimated the height of the mountains – the peak of the Grand Teton, largest in the range, is 13,722 feet above sea level.[49] Air pressure, which varies with weather conditions, affected the "mountain thermometer" Ball carried, so without a barometer, his projection of the party's elevation was likely inaccurate as well. Because the device calculated elevation from the boiling point of water, those calculations could also be affected by impurities in the water.[50]

July 5, 1832   *Hoback Canyon*

5th   We passed along a wooded River and through a very difficult road by its side so steep that one of my Horses loosing his foothold in the path was rooled down about 100 feet into the river   he was recovered but so much injured as we had to leave him shortly after.   Made this day 20 miles

Continuing through Hoback Canyon, Ball described the country as "more difficult than any we had experienced."[51] The treacherous trail crossed and re-crossed the river, zigged and zagged through the deep defile, and occasionally traversed almost perpendicular mountainsides. At times there was scarcely enough room for the horses' hooves. In 1811, one of Wilson Price Hunt's pack horses had rolled, load and all, "into the river from a height of nearly two hundred feet but was not hurt."[52] Warren Ferris described a trip through the same canyon when the men dismounted and led their animals over the most dangerous places. Still, three of the mounts lost their footing and fell sixty to seventy feet into the river below. Two were but slightly injured; one was killed instantly.[53]

John Wyeth described the precarious nature of Hoback Canyon in similar terms:

> *It is difficult to keep our feet on these highest parts of the mountains; some of the pack-horses slipped and rolled over and over, and yet were taken up alive. Those that did not fall were sadly bruised and lamed in their feet and joints ... One of our horses was killed by a fall down one of these precipices, and it is surprising that more of them did not share the like fate.*[54]

The younger Wyeth also advised his readers that the mule was "best calculated, as we experienced, for such difficult travelling."[55] Hoback Canyon was a difficult passage for any traveler, whether greenhorn from New England or seasoned mountaineer.

5.
Rendezvous at
Pierre's Hole: 1832

Wyeth appears to have let nearly three weeks pass without a journal entry, then on July 26 made a lengthy update – and indeed a lot had happened.

July 6, 1832   *Jackson Hole*
Written July 26

6th   We marched early and at 2 ock stoped on Lewis river and within 20 miles of the Trois Tetons three very conspicuous snow covered mountains visible in all this region   this river here runs nearly S. and is divided over a bottom about 2 miles and into 8 streams very rapid and difficult   these we forded which consumed the time until night and encamped after making 18 miles on the W. bank with no grass.

On July 6, the party made its way into Jackson's Big Hole. The possessive form "Jackson's Hole" was common usage during the fur trade, as was the adjective "big," to differentiate it from the lesser valley to the southeast. Named for trapper and brigade leader David Jackson, the apostrophe and "s" were later dropped and today, the valley is simply called Jackson Hole.[1]

The trail from Hoback Canyon left the river at Camp Creek, crossed northwest over the adjoining foothills, and rejoined the Snake River at Game Creek or Horse Creek before entering Jackson Hole. Either route avoided the steep canyon walls of the Snake River in the southern end of Jackson Hole and shaved distance off the trip. At the southern end of Jackson Hole, the Snake River flows from the west side of the valley directly over to the east side. The trail from Game Creek entered the valley further north, eliminating the extra river crossing by entering from the south.

The Teton Mountains were still visible directly north and the grandeur did not escape Wyeth. He had never seen such "conspicuous" mountains as these peaks jutting toward cerulean skies. The trail crossed over to the west side of the Hole, where the Snake would be forded. This traditional crossing place was adjacent to the mouth of Mosquito Creek.

John described the process of crossing to the west side of the river:

One man unloaded his horse, and swam across with him, leading two loaded ones, and unloading the two, brought them back, for two more, and as Sublet's company and our own made over a hundred and fifty, we were all day in passing the river.[2]

On John's return trip, his mule stepped on a round river rock and stumbled, throwing the young lad out of the saddle. The current was strong and promptly swept him downstream. He was able to grab a low-hanging bush to save himself from drowning.

July 7, 1832   *Teton Pass*
Written July 26

in the morning of the 7th we proceed up a small brook coming from a gap of the mountains due south of the Trois Tetons and passed the range of mountains of this range without much difficulty   it is a good pass for such a range and fresh animals would have no difficulty in passing through it   On the highest point we had snow accompanied with heavy thunder and being out of meat fed upon the inner bark of the Balsam trees   a tree similar if not the same with the Eastern Balsam   At Night we encamped at the foot of the pass on the western side and at the commencement of a large valley with several streams running through it into Lewis River surrounded with high and snow clad mountains   The weather is here warm in the day time but frost every night   the grass is good the land ordinary.

After horses, gear and men were across the Snake River, the party camped for the night. The next morning, July 7, they reloaded the pack animals and started up Mosquito Creek. The trail over Teton Pass in the nineteenth century followed creeks in the area; today's State Highway 22 is nearby but travels a different route. Wyeth did not mention that the previous evening Sublette had decreed that Jacob Wyeth, George More and Stephen Burdett, being too weak to walk, must be provided mounts for the trip over the mountain. According to John Wyeth, three horse-loads of PTC goods were consequently cached near the river-bank. Interestingly, nothing in Nathaniel's or John's journals confirms that this cache was ever retrieved.[3]

The path up Mosquito Creek was thickly timbered, but the trail was not terribly steep until near the top. All three of the weak men had difficulty staying in the saddle; with the ups and downs of the trail, George More slipped from his horse at one point. Sublette proceeded to the pass and waited for the sick riders and slower walkers to catch up. John admitted "at best, we could hardly keep up with his veteran company."[4] While all of the men may have felt the effects of the high altitude, the healthier men were able to travel faster.

While on the summit, Wyeth dined on the cambium layer of the balsam fir. Many parts of this tree are edible (though not necessarily palatable). The needle tips, and the pitch blisters that appear on its smooth trunk, can be eaten or made into tea. The soft inner bark can also be dried and ground into meal.[5]

The travelers' descent on the west side of the pass began on today's Mail Cabin Creek. According to Ball, as Sublette and the greenhorn Bostonians wound their way down the creek toward rendezvous, the men met a party of trappers who "appeared liberal in their expenditures for their new bought luxuries and who also seemed to be generally well satisfied with their wild life." Apparently, this was a group from rendezvous out for a jaunt or perhaps in search of Sublette.[5]

Descending Mail Cabin Creek, the party crossed the drainage to Coal Creek, followed that upstream and crossed the divide to Mesquite Creek, and trailed that down to Moose Creek, which brought them into Pierre's Hole, today's Teton Valley, Idaho. The end of this arduous day saw the men again camped at the foot of the Tetons – but this time on the western side. The campsite would have been in the extreme southern end of Pierre's Hole, probably near the junction of Moose and Trail creeks, where the trail over the Tetons enters the valley.

July 8, 1832   *Pierre's Hole Rendezvous*
Written July 26

On the 8th we proceed into the plain and after a march of 10 miles arrived at the rendezvous of the hunters of this region   here we found about 120 Lodges of the Nez Perces and about 80 of the Flatheads   a company of trappers of about 90 under Mr. Dripps of the firm of Dripps & Fontenelle connected with the American Fur Co.   Many independent Hunters and about 100 men of the Rocky Mountain Fur Co under Mess Milton Sublette and Mr. Frapp.

On July 8, the combined parties proceeded to almost the center of the valley. Here they found trappers of various fur companies waiting for them. They had reached the annual rendezvous. These summer gatherings had been initiated by William Ashley in 1825 to provide a way for trappers to turn in beaver hides and other valuable pelts collected during the previous year in exchange for supplies necessary to continue their business. Traders and trappers met at a location that was predetermined, but usually varied from summer to summer. This differed from other fur interests such as the Hudson's Bay Company, which transacted business at more or less permanent trading posts.

For this eighth annual rendezvous (and the second held in Pierre's Hole), mountaineers began converging in June, anxious to conduct business and celebrate. The rendezvous of 1832 would turn out to be a legendary Rocky Mountain fur trade extravaganza. With possibly the highest attendance of the summer gatherings, it ranks today as one of the most important rendezvous ever held.[6]

Due to the highly profitable market in beaver pelts, competition for fur in the Rockies had reached fever pitch. Rocky Mountain Fur Company had placed about one hundred men in the field this trapping season; American Fur Company boasted around ninety mountaineers. The disintegrating Gantt and Blackwell Company was represented by about twenty-two now-independent trappers. The Bean and Sinclair outfit numbered about fifteen. Wyeth led twenty rookies. William Sublette's supply train was staffed by around eighty men including those of

1832	distance	course	Place		1832	dis	Course	Place
May 12	10 mile	S.W.	Independence Mis.	June 15	20			On Plat, encamped
" 13	10	S.W.	cross line State	" 17	20			"
" 14	27	W.	On Santafee road	" 18	20			off Platte many...
" 15	12	N.W.	hilly	" 19	20	S.W.		Platte turns towards S.
" 16	10	N.W.	Kanzas river	" 20				cross the Platte
" 17	15	N.W.	up river	" 21	5	S.W.		up Platte
" 18	25	N.W.	over hills	" 22	25	S.W.		over hills towards Sweetwater
" 19	23	N.W.	"	" 23	20	W.		to & up Sweetwater
" 20	13	N.W.	quit river	" 24	20	W.		"
" 21	25	N.W.	rolling country	" 25	20	W.		very sandy
" 22	15	N.W.	"	" 26	20	W.		on branches
" 23	25	N.W.		" 27	20	W.N.W.		over main State to Mountain
" 24	20	N.W.	"	" 28	20	W.N.W.		cross the divide to Siskade
" 25	15	N.W.	"	" 29	20	W.N.W.		across creeks at foot mou
" 26	20	N.W.	"	30	15	W.N.W.		" "
" 27	20	N.W.	"	July 1	10	W.N.W.		" "
" 28	25	N.W.	to the Platte	" 2	5	N.		
" 29	15	W.	up Platte	" 3	25	N.W.		
" 30	20	W.	"	" 4	25	N.W.		cross divide to Lewis river
" 31	25	W.	"	" 5	20	N.W.		Bad defile
June 1	25	W.	"	" 6	15	N.W.		& cross Lewis branch
" 2	25	W.	"	" 7	20	W.N.		cross ridge
" 3	25	W.	"	" 8	10	N.W.		to Rendezvous
" 4	10	W.	on N. side S. branch					
" 5	20	N.W.	to N Branch...					
" 6	25		up N Branch Pl					
" 7	25							
" 8	25							
" 9	25							
" 10	25							
" 11	25							
" 12	25		Larenge's fork					
" 13								

Once on the trail from Independence, Missouri, John Ball kept a log of each day's mileage, direction and pertinent landmarks. This page tracks the beginning of his journey up until his arrival at the 1832 Rendezvous. GRAND

Campbell and Fitzpatrick. This made a total of about 330 non-native people in Teton Basin. With 120 lodges of Nez Perce and about 80 lodges of Flathead anxious to trade for the Americans' goods, the Indian presence far outnumbered the white – probably close to 1,500 native men, women and children.

Wyeth reported several contingents of Native American tribes and noted some fur company brigades in attendance. His journal was mostly business; unlike other first-person accounts, he spent little time describing the rousing, hair-raising escapades for which rendezvous was known.[7]

John Wyeth was more interested in what people were doing. He recorded that William Sublette had pointed out a place for the New Englanders to set up their camp. He also observed some of the differences between the enterprising veteran trader and his own group:

While Sublet was finishing his business with his Indian trappers, they delivering their peltry, and he remunerating them in his way with cloth, powder, ball, beads, knives, handkerchiefs, and all that gawdy trumpery which Indians admire, together with coffee, rice, and corn, also leather, and other articles, – we, being idle, had time to think, to reflect.[8]

Ball, meanwhile, besides providing such data as creekwater temperature (40 degrees), also revealed keen interest and insight into human behavior. He had

never witnessed such recuperation of men as during the two weeks we lay at our ease in this camp, feeding on the dried buffalo meat, and our drink the pure cool mountain creek, a branch of the Lewis river, on which we were encamped. And among us, a varied congregation of some two hundred white men and perhaps nearly as many Indians, there was quite a social time, and a great exchange of talk and interesting indeed, from the wide and varied experiences of the narrators. There were cultured men from city and country down to white men lower than the Indian himself. Men of high-toned morals, down to such as had left their country for its good, or perhaps rather personal safety.

Some made the season's trip from the miasmic air of the Mississippi and its city follies to recuperate their bodily and mental derangement. And it proved a grand specific. This mountain-pure air and ever-shining sun is a grand, helpful thing for both soul and body, especially when feeding on only meat and water.[9]

In a letter to his parents, Ball added,

Here they come from the states to trade with the indians & those that hunt beaver, no other fur is worth carrying so far, bring traps, arms & ammunition, beads & other trinkets, and all sorts of groceries, flower rice &c. flower & rice $1.50 pr. pound, sugar coffee ea. $2. all in proportion. A few yards of scarlet cloth, string of beads & paper of vermillion, awl, & fishhook will buy a horse. The indians have many. It is known before hand where the traders are to come & the indians & hunters assemble, there are in this place within five miles Seven or 8 thousand horses & mules, & one or two thousand whites & Indians.[10]

> **July 9 - 16, 1832**   ***Pierre's Hole Rendezvous***
> ***Written July 26***
>
> *I remained at this encampment until the 17th during which time all my men but 11 left me   to these I gave such articles as I could spare from the necesities of my own Party and let them go.   While here I obtained 18 Horses in exchange for those which were worn out and for a few toys such as Beads Bells red and Blue cloth, Powder and Balls fish hooks vermillion old Blanketts   We also supplied ourselves with Buffaloe robes   we have now a good outfit and here we found plenty of meat which can be had of the Indians for a trifle*

Perhaps the terse quality of Wyeth's narrative stemmed from the upheaval taking place within the Pacific Trading Company. His men were approaching open rebellion, but Wyeth would brook no debate. Each man knew when he signed on with the PTC that the Captain's rule was to be obeyed.

According to John Wyeth, the discord brewing among the Bostonians had come to a head in Pierre's Hole on July 10:

We had been dissatisfied for some time, but we had not leisure to communicate it and systematize our grievances. I, with others, had spoken with Captain Sublet, and him we found conversable and communicative. Myself and some others requested Captain Wyeth to call a meeting of his followers, to ask information, and to know what we were now to expect, seeing we had passed over as we supposed the greatest difficulties, and were now nearly four thousand miles from the Atlantic, and within four hundred miles of the Pacific Ocean, the end and aim of our laborious expedition, the field where we expected to reap our promised harvest. We wished to have what we had been used to at home, – a town meeting, – or a parish meeting, where every freeman has an equal right to speak his sentiments, and to vote thereon. But Captain Wyeth was by no means inclined to this democratical procedure. The most he seemed inclined to, was a caucus with a select few; of whom neither his own brother, though older than himself, nor myself, was to be of the number. After considerable altercation, he concluded to call a meeting of the whole, on business interesting and applicable to all. We accordingly met, Captain Wyeth in the chair, or on the stump, I forget which. Instead of every man speaking his own mind, or asking such questions as related to matters that lay heaviest on his mind, the Captain commenced the business by ordering the roll to be called; and as the names were called, the clerk asked the person if he would go on. The first name was Nathaniel J. Wyeth, whom we had dubbed Captain, who answered – "I shall go on." – The next was William Nud, who, before he answered, wished to know what the Captain's plan and intentions were, whether to try to commence a small colony, or to trap and trade for beaver? To which Captain Wyeth replied, that that was none of our business. Then Mr. Nud said, "I shall not go on;" and as the names of the rest were called, there appeared seven persons out of the twenty one, who were determined to return home. Of the number so determined was, besides myself, Dr. Jacob Wyeth, the Captain's brother, whose strength had never been equal to such a journey. His constitution forbade it.[11]

Wyeth's account omitted most of this, the deterioration of his dream. But John Wyeth detailed the group's shareholder meeting, ramrodded by the company founder in such a way that a vote of no confidence in Wyeth's leadership was virtually assured. Seven of the New Englanders wanted to return East. Four others would opt to join the ranks of the Rocky Mountain trappers, leaving less than half of Wyeth's original company.

> *But to return to our dismal list of grievances. Almost everyone of the company wished to go no farther; but they found themselves too feeble and exhausted to think of encountering the risk of a march on foot of three thousand five hundred miles through such a country as we came. We asked Captain Wyeth to let us have our muskets and a sufficiency of ammunition, which request he refused. Afterwards, he collected all the guns, and after selecting such as he and his companions preferred, he gave us the refuse; many of which were unfit for use. There were two tents belonging to the company, of which he gave us one; which we pitched about a quarter of a mile from his. George More expressed his determination of returning home, and asked for a horse, which after considerable difficulty he obtained ... The Captain likewise supplied his brother with a horse and a hundred dollars.*[12]

When the final tally was taken, Jacob and John Wyeth, Styles, Palmer, Law, and Bache elected to return east under the protective eye of William Sublette when the caravan of fur-laden pack mules headed out. Wakefield, Nudd, More, and Lane left the Company to become trappers. The eleven men choosing to continue to the Columbia with Wyeth were Abbott, Ball, Breck, Burdett, Sargent, Sinclair, Smith, Tibbetts, Trumbull, Whittier and Woodman.[13]

The men understood that their success thus far had been largely due to the providence of William Sublette. After departing Pierre's Hole, they would be on their own with no experienced mountaineer to guide them.

On July 12, Wyeth moved his tent half a mile from where the renegade Yankees had set up theirs. He may have been bitter, but in replacing his worn out horses with first-rate Indian mounts, Wyeth displayed characteristic resourcefulness. He had already begun salvaging his plan for commerce in the Pacific Northwest. John Ball, who remained faithful to the Company, wrote that "the full price of a pony was but a blanket and a cheap knife. So we supplied ourselves with all we needed."[14] Wyeth also bought a supply of buffalo robes and plenty of dried buffalo meat for the trip ahead.

July 17, 1832   *Pierre's Hole*
Written July 26

On the 17th we put out and stered S.E. in direction to a pass through the same mountains by which we entered the valley   these Mts. run E. & W. and the pass I refer to is the next E. of the one refered to and through it the waters of this valley reach Lewis River which is on the S. side of this range   at night we encamped within about 8 miles of the commencement of the pass

Wyeth must have recognized that without the generous guidance of William Sublette, the difficult trip to Pierre's Hole could have been a disaster. Watching the myriad trappers at rendezvous, he may have scouted the scene for another experienced mountaineer to lead him toward the Columbia. With no apparent hesitation, Wyeth approached Milton Sublette, brother of his former sponsor, for permission to accompany his brigade west when it left rendezvous for the fall trapping season.

Milton, a partner in the Rocky Mountain Fur Company, and another partner, Henry Fraeb (whom Wyeth identified as Frapp) led a party of about twenty men. Adding Wyeth's eleven, a handful of free trappers led by Alexander Sinclair, and a small brigade that included Zenas Leonard and George Nidever, the combined group numbered about forty. Some of the trappers were bound for the Humboldt, some to the Salmon, and Wyeth, of course, to the Columbia. On July 17, they headed out.

The band traveled to the southern end of Pierre's Hole, intending to cross modern-day Pine Creek Pass the following day on the westward route. They camped, according to Ball, "on a prairie near some timber on a little creek," which was likely Trail Creek, just west of today's Victor, Idaho.[15] What happened next would become a legendary milestone in fur trade history.

July 18-19, 1832   *Battle of Pierre's Hole*
Written July 26

On the 18th we did not leave camp   when near starting we observed 2 partys of Indians coming out of the pass about 200 in number with but few horses   after securing our camp our riders went out to meet them and soon found them to be Blackfeet   a little skirmish ensued   one of the Blackfeet was killed and his Blankett and robe brought into camp   on this the Indians made for the timber the women and children were seen flying to the mountains   at this time only 42 men being the party of Mess Milton Sublette & Frapp mine and a few Independent Hunters were in sight and the Indians were disposed to give us their usual treatment when they meet us in small bodies   but while the Indians we[re] making their preparations we sent an express to camp which soon brought out a smart force of Nez Perces Flatheads and whites   the Indians finding they were caught fortified themselves in a masterly manner in the wood.   We attacked them and continued the attack all day   there were probably about 20 of them killed and 32 horses were found dead   They decamped during the night leaving most of their utensials lodges &c and many of the dead   we have lost 3 whites killed 8 badly wounded among which is Mr Wm. Sublette who was extremely active in the battle   about 10 of the Indians were killed or mortally wounded of the Nez Perces and Flatheads   in the morning we visited their deserted fort   they had dug into the ground to reach water and to secure themselves from our shot   It was a sickening scene of confusion and Blood[s]head   one of our men who was killed inside ["inside" is crossed out and "near" written above it] their fort we found mutilated in a shocking manner   on the 19th we removed back to our former ground to be near our whole force and to recruit the wounded and bury the dead.   We think that 400 lodges or about 600 warriors of the Blackfeet are on the other side of the pass and if they come they must be met with our whole force in which case the contest will be a doubtful one.   We have mad[e] Horse pens and secured our camp in as good a manner as we can and wait the result   this affair will detain us some days.

The men Wyeth called "riders," whom Fraeb sent to meet the Indians, were Antoine Godin and a Flathead man. The "little skirmish" occurred when Godin and his companion realized the approaching Indians were Blackfoot. The chief came forward to parley, the two scouts quickly murdered him, and waving the fallen leader's blanket, they galloped back to camp. Thus began the Battle of Pierre's Hole.

Wyeth wrote to his brother Leonard the day after the battle. In terms of proximity to events, this letter is second only to one penned by Robert Campbell, who had started to write his brother Hugh the morning of the battle, dropped his pen to join the fight, then finished his note after the battle was over.[16] Wyeth, therefore, recorded one of the freshest accounts of the conflict.

Rocky Mts July 19th 1832
Bro Leonard
Another skirmish with the Blk-feet has delayed all the Party and give me an opportunity to write you further. I have given to Mr Sublette letters of Introduction to you & Charles he has assisted me much and I beg you to extend to him as much politeness as you possible can he is a person of great respectability in this business and has made a fortune in it which is an easy matter for anyone who will follow it provided he meets with no accidents it is not certain that he will go east with winter but should he my pride is much concerned in his reception. In the skirmish I alluded to above the killed and wounded on our side is about 20 the Black feet were completely defeated leaving about 20 horses dead on the ground and some of their dead (an unusual thing in Indian warfare they escaped in the night and their trail could be followed by their blood and the dead & dying. among the dead horses were found some of those taken in the first skirmish. they were in a fort which occasioned our severe loss. none of my twelve men were hurt, most of them being on camp guard at the time. we are detained by the wounded. Jacob has enough to do and earns some money by his skill this battle lasted from 8 oclock in the morning until dark and during the night the miserable remnant of about 100 warriors made their escape. most of them were wounded probably not 20 got away alive. I move down Lewis River on which

*I now am in Co with 42 men including my own and shall soon be
out of the Black foot country say in 200 miles more. Whiskey sells
here 2$ pr pint flour 2$ rice, sugar the same. Red & Blue cloth such
as you get for 1.50 for $10.00 pr yd. Blankets [account?]18$ a
piece $3. Guns at $40 Traps at 20$ and other things in proportion
and pay in Beaver at $4 pr lb but with all this chance I have saved
only enough to supply myself in Horses and food for the rout down
and subsistence there I think of stopping as soon as I get out of the
dangerous country and trapping this fall and next spring in order to
get the wherewith to bottom an order for goods upon $5000 will be
a plenty and I am in hopes to get this by that time barring accidents.
please communicate the contents of this to Charles as I have no time
to spare in writing give my best respects to your good wife etc
Aff your Bro
Nath'l Wyeth
P.S. Mr Sublette badly wounded*[17]

Counting Wyeth's letter as well as his journal, there are thirteen eye-witness accounts of this battle. Not surprisingly, the multiple accounts offer diverging, conflicting and confusing testimony.[18] Because the battle has been examined in detail in other sources, the perspective here will be that of the tenderfoot Bostonians.

The Indians were Gros Ventres – the same band that had attacked Sublette's camp a few weeks prior, enroute to the Green River Valley. Once their chief fell at the hands of Godin, the Indians opened fire and began pouring out of the pass. Milton Sublette then sent an express back to the main rendezvous camp to alert his brother and call for reinforcements. Wyeth contended that "about 200" Gros Ventres were headed toward them but the first hand reports contain a wide degree of variability in the number of Indian men, women and children. Regardless, the forty or so mountain men were badly outnumbered. Ball detailed the combatants' tactics:

*As we watched to see what they would do next, they seemed at first
to break up and scatter, but soon we saw that a large band, the
warriors, seemed coming directly towards us to make a fight. So we
immediately tied our horses to bushes near and put up our saddles as*

a kind of breastwork. But before they reached us, they turned off into
some timber on a stream, built a kind of fort of logs, bushes, their
saddles and blankets, as a shade, if we attacked them, and took their
horses into the fort with them.[19]

In nearly no time, William Sublette and a large contingent of trappers, Nez Perce, and Flathead warriors arrived on the scene. Little coordination took place between the mountain men and friendly tribes. Approaching in haphazard fashion, they could see only the fortification of the Gros Ventres, while those inside could easily view the approaching enemy. Several mountain men and their allies were shot as they snuck toward the fort. William Sublette sustained a serious shoulder wound which was treated by Dr. Jacob Wyeth.

Trappers laid siege to the barricaded Gros Ventres, surrounding their entrenched position and firing randomly and blindly into the stronghold. Some attempted to slip closer for a better shot, only to be repelled. Sublette suggested burning them out, but was dissuaded by the Flathead and Nez Perce, who protested that the valuable spoils of war would then be lost.

In the late afternoon, a Gros Ventre taunt was misinterpreted to mean that the main rendezvous camp was under attack by an even larger faction of the enemy. This caused the trappers to pull back and race north, thinking to protect the small party left to guard the trade goods and baled furs. When the contingent arrived, the false alarm became clear. By then it was too late in the evening to return to the battle:

When night came on we encamped in the best manner of defence
we could, and the next day expecting surely an attack from them,
built a high fence and strong pen for our horses in such case, and
a guard on the open prairie to run them in if attacked, and then
awaited the result.[20]

In the night, the Gros Ventres managed to steal away under cover of darkness, leaving most of their possessions behind. When trappers returned to the battleground and visited the fort the next morning, they found a number of dead horses, but the attackers had carried off the bodies of most of their dead. Wyeth estimated "about twenty" of the enemy were killed; numbers varied greatly among other accounts. On the trappers' side, six to eight mountaineers may have been killed and perhaps as many as twenty-five of their Indian allies.

After surveying the scene, the mountain men and their Indian allies returned to the rendezvous site for a few days, waiting to see if there would be any further hostilities. The men still feared that an even larger body of warriors was in the vicinity and that a fresh attack could be in the offing – but it turned out that the fighting in Pierre's Hole was finished.

As recently as 2001, during excavation for a subdivision just south of modern Driggs, Idaho, the remains of a male Native American were found. The construction site along Teton Creek was thought to have been the location of the main rendezvous camp. John Ball had reported that mortally wounded men from the battleground were brought into this main camp and other accounts describe the burial of men who had died of their injuries after the battle. It is quite likely that the recently discovered bones and artifacts were the grave of a man associated with the 1832 Battle of Pierre's Hole.[21]

Though Wyeth often used "we" in his description of the battle, his actual participation in the combat is uncertain. According to Joe Meek, Nathaniel Wyeth played a role that may have caused more harm than good.

> The mountaineers who followed Sublette, took up their station in the woods on one side of the fort, and the Nez Perces, under Wyeth, on the opposite side, which accidental arrangement, though it was fatal to many of the Blackfeet in the fort, was also the occasion of loss to themselves by the cross-fire.[22]

Ball explained his party's reluctance in the fight:

> We twelve Yankees felt that we had no men to spare to be killed or wounded, that we were not called upon to go out of the way to find danger, but had they attacked our camp, we should have taken our full part, to save ourselves and horses. But we readily assisted in taking care of the wounded and in other ways aid, as far as we felt belonged to us.[23]

John Wyeth asserted that

Captain Nathaniel J. Wyeth's party had no concern. He himself was in it a very short time, but retired from the contest doubtless for good reasons ... not one of those who had belonged to Captain Wyeth's company received any injury.[24]

July 24, 1832   *Pierre's Hole*
Written July 26

On 24th we again moved out of the valley in the same direction as at first viz about S.E. and encamped at night in the gorge of it   during the march I visited the scene of our conflict for the first time since the battle   the din of arms was now changed into the noise of the vulture and the howling of masterless dogs   the stench was extreme   most of the men in the fort must have perished   I soon retired from this scene of disgusting butchery

---

On July 24, Milton Sublette and Henry Fraeb led their party of trappers, including Wyeth and his men, south once again. They made but ten miles that first day and camped in the mouth of Pine Creek Pass. The group passed the battle site and inspected the aftermath of the carnage. Others had already poked around the empty Gros Ventre fort, but it was Wyeth's first visit. He did not stay long.

The same day, Alfred Stephens led a small contingent, including former PTC shareholder George More, out of the valley and heading east toward the Laramie River.[25] More was riding out in front as the band traveled through Hoback Canyon. Suddenly, as many as two dozen Gros Ventres jumped them. More, thrown from his horse, was shot. He and another man died in the short fracas. Stephens was seriously wounded in the leg and died several days later.[26]

MAP 3 *Pierre's Hole Rendezvous to Bruneau River, 1832*

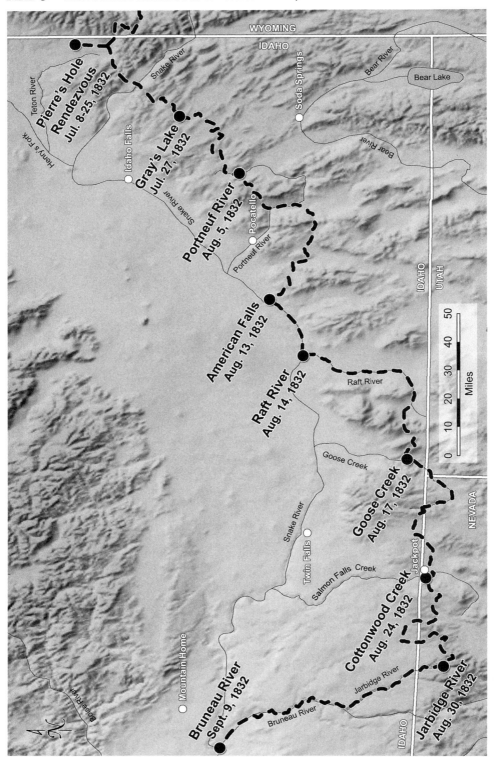

6.
Crossing the Snake River Plain

July 25-26, 1832   *Snake River*
Written July 26

On the 25th we proceeded through the pass which is tolerably good and in a direction of about S.W. by S. and encamped 15 miles on Lewis River (here concentrated into one rapid stream) and about 30 miles S. of where we crossed it in going into the valley   we are now employed in making bull boats in order to cross it   One Buffaloe and some antelope killed today

26th crossed the river in a bull boat without accident in 4 hours and moved on in a westerly direction about 4 miles when we struck into a deep ravine with a little water in it   this ravine is bordered by high presipices on each side and is small   3 miles up this we encamped for the night   this stream is called Muddy   as there is several of this name it is requisite to distinguish this by the cognomen of Muddy that falls into "Lewis"

In showery weather, Wyeth's men, together with the Rocky Mountain Fur Company, headed by Milton Sublette and Henry Fraeb, rode fifteen miles to the southwest, which brought them out of Pierre's Hole and to the Snake River. On this side of the mountains, the waters raced through Snake River Canyon, in contrast to the wide, braided stream Wyeth described in Jackson's Hole. Wyeth woefully underestimated the distance between the ford reached on July 6 and this crossing. The actual distance is nearly sixty miles. Even experienced travelers would have avoided Snake River Canyon and been unfamiliar with its geography; the New England greenhorn was likely not alone in his ignorance.

Having seen William Sublette's success using a bull boat to ferry goods, and having countenanced utter failure with his own river-crossing schemes, Wyeth opted to imitate his wilderness tutors. Wyeth recorded the construction of bull boats; Ball wrote that the RMFC trappers had "packed along, what they called a bull boat." After crossing the

Snake, a trio of free trappers left the party to pursue the trapping season on their own, headed for "the mountains to the left," which Ball declared to be Blackfoot territory.[1]

July 26, 1832   *Fall Creek*

26th   we moved up the Muddy until we found the forks of it then followed the Right hand say 3 miles then took a south direction and struck another stream (small) and running in the opposite direction   this we followed about 5 mil[e]s making 15 this day and encamped

This duplicate July 26 entry may indicate that Wyeth had lost a day in his reckoning. He would catch the error in August. The stream Wyeth called "Muddy" is known today as Fall Creek. Osborne Russell also referenced this creek when his trapping brigade traversed the same ground in later years. After leaving winter camp, Russell's party made its way to the Lewis (Snake) River

and ascended it SE to the mouth of Muddy Creek ... Here Mr. Bridger ordered a party of 12 trappers to branch off to the right and hunt the headwaters of the Grays and Blackfoot creeks ... We ascended Muddy and crossed the mountain on to Grays creek.[2]

Milton Sublette led the combined party three miles up into the Caribou Range before camping for the night.

The "right hand" fork retains the name Fall Creek on modern maps but was also known as Sulphur Creek.[3] Following upstream another three miles would have taken the travelers to Beaver Creek which enters Fall Creek from a perpendicular direction. Beaver Creek led them up onto Beaver Ridge, which they crossed about a mile to the north of Flag Knoll. The party then dropped down onto the North Fork of Lava Creek, spending the night near its junction with the main branch. During the day's travel, Ball related that while looking at the "blacksmith-cinder-like rocks" and volcanic bluffs, he was nearly bitten by a rattlesnake.[4]

July 27, 1832 *Gray's Creek*

27th. We moved down the stream until its junction with another called Grays creek which we crossed and assended a high bluff and travelled an average course of S.W. and encamped on a small creek making 15 miles this day 2 days since I first this side the mountain met with the prickly pear and since leaving the valley of the Rendezvous the fruit that was green one day is ripe the next. The nights are still frosty but the days are very warm as in N[ew] E[ngland] at this time fruits we have 3 kinds currants one of gooseberry all different from those of the U.S. and Service berrys all the first are sour the latter sweet the country through which we have travelled for these two days past has a strong volcanic appearance the streams occupy what appear to be but the craks of an over heated surface the rocks are blown up in blubbers like a smiths cinders some rocks ten feet through are but a shell being hollow. A substance abounds like bottle glass of about the same weight not so transparent about as brittle the fracture is smooth and glossy with the exception of the cracks as above the country is tolerably level for a mountainous country but excessively dry. During our first days march from Lewis River beside the ravine above mentioned we passed three craters of small volcanoes (as I suppose) and I am told there is a boiling spring near the same place We here find buffaloe plenty and fat and entirely different from those met with in the Spring on the Platte it is preferable to the best beef. Our party have taken lice from the Indians they are a great trouble as well as the Musquitoes these last trouble us in the day but the frost seals their wings at night when the first relieve them until morning.

Moving downstream, the party followed Lava Creek to its confluence with the outlet of Gray's Lake. Gray's Lake was named for Iroquois trapper John Gray whose Indian name was Ignace Hatchiorauquasha. Though relatively shallow, it is one of Idaho's largest lakes. On some post-fur trade maps, the lake is called John Day's Lake but it is consistently referred to as Gray's Lake throughout the fur trade.[5] Gray's Creek, named for the same man, appeared in the journals of several other trappers, most notably Osborne Russell and Warren Ferris.[6] The high bluff they ascended was likely Outlet Ridge, crossing over just north of Sugarloaf Mountain. The rest of the day's journey roughly paralleled Homer Creek before halting to camp on Reed Creek. Ball described the terrain as "a pleasantly rising country back from the river."[7] Like Wyeth, he noted the area's geology:

> After crossing the Lewis river, I observed the first strata of the igneous or volcanic rock in conglomerate. And ever after met with it and saw beautiful white and variegated marble bowlders, and lime and granite rock partially melted down, but still showing the original rock.[8]

The "boiling spring" Wyeth mentioned is Fall Creek Mineral Spring, about two miles upstream from the mouth of Wyeth's Muddy (Fall) Creek. Wyeth's report of "plenty and fat" buffalo matches that of Russell, who would hunt the region in January 1840:

> On the 15th we tried to cross the mountain to Gray's Valley but were compelled to turn back for the snow On the 20th made another trial and succeeded and encamped at the Forks of 'Gray's Creek' here the ground was bare along the stream ... I killed two Bulls which came in good time after living upon Dried meat all winter.[9]

Wyeth noticed that the bison he saw here were "entirely different from those met with in the Spring on the Platte." He had correctly distinguished the *Bison athabascae* – mountain buffalo, sometimes called wood buffalo – from the plains buffalo or *Bison bison*.[10] Washington Irving also pointed out the most obvious difference between the two species:

> the buffalo on the Pacific side of the Rocky Mountains are fleeter and more active than those on the Atlantic; those upon the plains of the Columbia can scarcely be overtaken by a horse that would outstrip the same animal in the neighborhood of the Platte.[11]

Modern scholarship does not distinguish between the two as sub-species but makes it more a matter of ecotype as opposed to genotype. In other words, put bison in the woods and they take on a different appearance. These mountain bison differed from the plains bison in some physical traits including darker pelage and taller height.[12]

July 28, 1832   *Meadow Creek*
Written July 29

On the 28 we moved in a direction about S.W. and during the march took the bearing of the Trois Tetons which was N.E. by E. and I think 75 miles   we made 7 miles and encamped on a little stream meandering through a valley of about 100 acres of fine Black land with the grass as good as the buffaloe and the cold weather could admit of.   Here we found plenty of cows and more Bulls   13 of the first were killed   they were fat and we stopped to make meat   these cows were killed by running them down which is a dangerous method   expensive in horses and Requiring much skill in Riding   We of course were obliged to employ help for none could be got by approaching while they were Running them

---

On this day's travel, Sublette's brigade and the Bostonians followed Reed Creek across Crane Flat, southwestward to the meanders of Meadow Creek. Wyeth took a compass bearing back toward the Tetons and guessed those mountains to be seventy-five miles away, probably overestimating by ten or twelve miles.

Here, they hunted buffalo in a manner that the experienced mountaineers had learned from Native Americans. Rudolph Friederich Kurz observed the techniques of the mounted hunters near Fort Union in 1851:

When running buffaloes the hunters do not use rifle-patches but take along several balls in their mouths. The projectile thus moistened sticks to the powder when put into the gun. In the first place, on buffalo hunts, they do not carry rifles, for the reason that they think the care required in loading them takes too much time unnecessarily when shooting at close range; and, furthermore, they find rifle balls too small. The hunter chases buffaloes at full gallop, discharges his gun, and reloads without slackening speed.

To accomplish this, he holds the weapon close within the bend of his left arm. Taking the powder horn in his right hand, with his teeth he draws out the stopper, which is fastened to the horn to prevent its being lost. He shakes the requisite amount of powder into his left palm and closes the powder horn. He grasps the gun with his right hand, holding it in a vertical position, pours the powder down the barrel, and gives the gun a sidelong thrust with the left hand, in order to shake the powder well through the priming hole into the touch pan (hunters at this place discard percussion caps as not practical).

Now he takes a bullet from his mouth and with his left hand puts it into the barrel, where, having been moistened by spittle, it adheres to the powder. He dares not hold his weapon horizontal – the position taken when firing – for fear that the ball may stick fast in its course, allowing sufficient air to intervene between powder and lead to cause an explosion and splinter the barrel. There is no danger so long as the ball rolls down freely. Hunters approach the buffaloes so closely that they do not take aim but, lifting the gun lightly with both hands, point in the direction of the animal's heart and fire. They are very often wounded in the hands and face by the bursting gun barrels, which – especially when the weather is extremely cold – shatter as easily as glass.

The hunters always aim at the heart of the larger beasts of the chase, the surest and simplest method, since the heart is an inevitably vulnerable part ... Buffalo chasers must not only have the enduring qualities of swift riders, but they must also be accustomed to the habits of the animals. A buffalo runner must be faultless in pressing close upon his quarry, and at the same time being alert to spring aside if a buffalo tosses his head. Otherwise, if he be only a passable horseman, he will immediately find himself upon the ground and may count himself happy if he is not trodden underfoot.[13]

Osborne Russell also wrote about the skilled horses employed in this method:

> The most general mode practiced by the Indians for killing Buffaloe is running upon horseback and shooting them with arrows but it requires a degree of experience for both man and horse to kill them in this manner with any degree of safety particularly in places where the ground is rocky and uneven. The horse that is well trained for this purpose not only watches the ground over which he is running and avoids the holes ditchs and rocks by shortening or extending his leaps but also the animal which he is pursuing in order to prevent being 'horned' when tis brot suddenly to bay which is done instantaneously and if the Buffaloe wheel to the right the horse passes as quick as thought to the left behind it and thereby avoids its horns but if the horse in close pursuit wheels on the same side with the Buffaloe he comes directly in contact with its horns and with one stroke the horses entrails are often torn out and his rider thrown headlong to the ground After the Buffaloe is brought to bay the trained horse will immediately commence describing a circle about 10 paces from the animal in which he moves continually in a slow gallop or trot which prevents the raging animal from making a direct bound at him by keeping it continually turning round until it is killed by the rider with arrows or bullets.[14]

None of the New Englanders had run buffalo before and all lacked the horsemanship and other requisite skills for such a dangerous yet exhilarating chase. The trappers, however, succeeded in killing thirteen cows. This obliged the party to make camp in order to dry the meat.

July 29-30, 1832   *Meadow Creek*

29th   We remained all day making meat with a hot sun   this morning sent 3 men down the creek fishing   they caught 21 Salmon Trout and returned at 10   this afternoon it rained hard and during the storm the squaw of one of the party was delivered of a Boy in the bushes whither she had retired for the purpose   it[s] head was thickly covered with Black hair   it was as white as is usual with the whites   in less than an hour afterwards the squaw made her appearance in camp as well and able for a days travel as usual   it continued raining all night and until 8 of the 30 on which acc. our march was defered for the day which was afterward fine and our meat dried well.   4 Beavers were caught from about 12 traps last night   during this day one of the party saw an indian which must have been a Blackfoot as otherwise he would have come to camp   yesterday and today we had Thunder & Hail as well as rain.

The Indian woman who had given birth was Henry Fraeb's wife. John Ball wrote,

> *One day we delayed our march, we knew not why, till after a time we heard an outcry for a few minutes from Frapp's wife, out to one side in some bushes. And we soon learned, the cause of our laying over, was to give her the opportunity to lay in, give birth to a child in camp and not on our day's march.*[15]

The damp weather eventually cleared, allowing the buffalo meat to continue drying satisfactorily, an act Ball called "a wise forethought."[16] Four beaver were caught on this day – the first mention Wyeth has made of traps being put out though it is not clear who set them. Ball had reported other "trappers stopping to set their traps for beaver on the branches, that showed signs of their residences in and on the same."[17] Most likely trapping was an ongoing activity pursued by all.

Fur companies typically followed trails that paralleled streams. Fresh indications of beaver activity near an evening camp triggered the trappers to action. Where a suitable place for a "set" was found, a trapper might place as many as six traps in the water. In the morning, before the brigade moved out, trappers checked their traps and skinned any beaver caught, returning to camp to pack their gear. These fresh hides were scraped and stretched by camp keepers once the party halted that evening.[18]

William Sublette, who had remained in Pierre's Hole to recuperate from his shoulder wound, had healed enough to ride, and on August 1 started the fur-laden caravan of pack mules out of Teton Valley on the journey back to St. Louis. Wyeth's deserters accompanied him homeward. They traveled over the pass, north into Jackson's Hole, then up the Gros Ventre River into Union Pass. From there, they dropped back down into the Green River Valley and followed the usual path to the eastern settlements. This out-of-the-way route was taken to avoid the Indians who had fought in the battle of Pierre's Hole and who were believed to still be in the area.[19]

August 1-11, 1832   *Portneuf River*
Written August 11

1st. Augt   I date this the 1st on acc. of having missed a day in the time past.   This day we made about 15 miles in a S.W. direction and most of the way in a deep valley and encamped on a small creek running into one called Blackfoot   this latter is the second stream we have passed which emties into S. fork of Lewis River   the first was called Grays River and is also small (this since crossing Lewis River)   Here we stopped until the 4th to make meat of which I made enough to eat and no more while the other two parties who had god buffaloe Riders and Horses made considerable   while her we lost one Horse while attempting to Run Buffaloe by throwing his Rider and Running among the Buffaloe and going off with them   I sent out a party to get fish of two men   they Returned with about a peck of craw fish and a dozen of trout   these average about 1 lb and are fine eating.   We have here the Sandhill Cranes in plenty.   On the 4th we moved due south and crossed Blackfoot and struck over to a stream emtying into the same as Blackfoot called Portneuf from a man killed near it   18 miles   here we found Buffalo in the bottom and the Hunters are now out Running them.   Here we remained this day and the 5th when the men I had sent out to hunt the horse returned   as I had expected them on the 4th I was much alarmed for their safty being in a dangerous country   while here we made 7 bales meat   On the 5th. we mooved S. down the valley 3 miles and encamped on a creek running into the valley   on the 7th we

*made 21 miles first down the N. side of the valley and taking
the first creek running out of the valley then in a S.W. direction
and encamped on it   from the valley above mentioned rises
Bear River running into the Big Salt Lake distant about S.E. 50
miles   Currants and service berrys are now ripe.   I have been
sick from indigestion for some days more so than I ever was
before.   We have here the Sandhill Crane Turtle dove Robbin
Blackbirds (Crow & Cow) Kingfishers Black & Mallard Ducks,
Gese.   We find meat making a tedious business.   On the
8th we moved S.W. 15 miles following the main Portneuf out
of the valley for about 12 miles then took one of its tributaries
for about 3 miles and encamped on the S.W. side of the valey
in which this branch runs   here we cached 6 Horse loads of
goods and remained on the 9th & 10th & 11th moved on in a
S.W. direction not following any stream but passing the ridge
bordering the valley in a low place near where a small run puts
into the valley from a very rugged pass.   We made this day 15
miles and encamped on a small run going into Portneuf.*

Wyeth began this catch-up entry by correcting the date. On August 1, with the thermometer at a chilly 20 degrees F, Wyeth's bunch moved on in a southwest direction, the country being "passed through zig-zag, as Milton Sublette ... and Frapp were after beaver, and went up and down the mountain streams hunting them."[20]

Leaving Meadow Creek, the party switch-backed its way up, over and around the Paradise Hills, ending the day in the vicinity of Brush Creek's headwaters. This stream emptied into the Blackfoot, a river named in 1819 by Donald McKenzie for the Indians his Northwest Company brigade encountered there. This band of the Blackfoot Nation called itself the Siksika.[21] John Ball reported that Fraeb's wife

*sat her newborn baby, feet down, into a deep basket that she hung
to the pummel of her saddle, mounted her horse and rode on in
the band as usual. And she had another child of two or three, who
had his own horse. He was sat on the saddle and blankets brought
around him so as to keep him erect, and his gentle pony went loose*

with the other pack horses, which kept along with those riding and never strayed from the common band.[22]

In one account Ball named "Mrs. Milton Sublette" rather than Mrs. Fraeb as the mother of the child, but Ball's initial report and that of Wyeth confirms it was the Fraebs who welcomed the newborn.[23]

While running buffalo, a horse threw its rider and ran off with the buffalo herd – saddle, tack and all. Wyeth promptly sent men after the wayward mount. Without waiting for their return, the party continued south and crossed the Blackfoot River. Eighteen miles later, they made the Portneuf River which empties into the Snake near modern Pocatello, Idaho, but they continued south, upstream on the Portneuf.

Peter Ogden recorded that the Portneuf River was named for a man called Portneuf who was the first to trap on it. There was a Joseph Portneuf at HBC's York Factory at the time, but it is not certain this is the same man. Warren Ferris, however, proclaimed "the river enters the plains, though a narrow opening in the mountains, somewhat resembling a huge gateway, hence it is called Porteneuf (New gate.)"[24]

While based in the Portneuf River Valley, Wyeth's men hunted buffalo, processing only what meat the Bostonians needed at the time, while Sublette's trappers "made considerable." Wyeth found "meat making a tedious business" perhaps due to the plentiful game birds and ripening berries here. His severe indigestion may have resulted from eating too many of the handpicked fruits. Ball recounted that wolves "make the nights hideous" in this vicinity.[25]

On August 7, Milton Sublette led the party along the north side of the valley, then veered off at the first creek – probably modern Topponce Creek or one of its branches. Traveling predominantly southwest, they probably hit North Rapid Creek and followed it to its confluence with the Portneuf, which they followed upstream for a few miles. This latter river flows south from the vicinity of their previous camp, turns west for a short distance, and then loops back to the north before bending west again, passing through a narrow gorge as it heads toward the Snake. The twenty-one-mile cross-country route taken by Sublette would not have saved much time or distance but they may have been trapping as they went.

Wyeth's comment about the Bear River rising in the "valley above mentioned" and this watercourse "running into the Big Salt Lake distant about S. E. 50 miles," begs clarification. The Bear passes through the southern end of the valley in which the party camped, but from that point to where the Bear enters Salt Lake is about eighty miles, as the crow flies.

The next morning, the brigade tracked up the Portneuf for about twelve miles, then turned up one of its tributaries for an additional three miles. This stream would have been near present Garden Creek. During several days at this camp, a storage pit was dug to cache the loads from a half-dozen pack animals. It is not clear why this cache was necessary or whether all of the cached goods belonged to Wyeth.

In his other writings, Wyeth would note a dramatic swing in temperatures throughout the day. At sunrise, the thermometer showed 18 degrees above zero, but by noon it had reached 92 degrees.[26]

When they moved out on August 11, the travelers did not follow any particular stream. They crossed the ridge that parallels the west side of the Portneuf River through a "very rugged pass," probably where West Arimo Road cuts through a dramatic breach in the range. Fifteen miles of travel placed their camp at the end of the day on or close to Rattlesnake Creek.

August 12, 1832   *Bannock Creek*

12th   We made in a S.W. direction about 6 miles not following any stream but encamped on a very small run with poor grass.

This day was a comparatively short trek of only six miles, ending on a small creek without much feed for the livestock, likely in the vicinity of Bannock Creek.

August 13, 1832   *American Falls*

13th   We made 24 miles in a west and by N. direction and met no water for this distance and encamped on a very small run issuing from a spring a few miles from Lewis River   we are here in sight of the River running through an extensive valley in a S.W. direction   here are the American falls   the place may be known by several high and detached hills arising from the plain   the falls at one place 22 feet and the Rapids extend a considerable distance down the River   We found here plenty of Buffaloe sign and the Pawnacks come here to winter often on account of the Buffaloe   we now find no buffaloe   there are here abundance of Service berrys now ripe   during a short walk from camp this mng. I saw a buff colored fox with a white tip on his tail.   Wolves here serenade us every night making more noise than 50 village dogs and better music for they keep in chord and display more science   yesterday we parted from 16 men bound out trapping.   We are now in a country which affords no small game and a precarious chance for Buffaloe

The sixteen men "bound out trapping" were the former Gantt and Blackwell brigade, now heading for the Humboldt River. George Nidever, one of these free trappers, recorded, "We parted with Wyatt's company about 100 miles from Pierre's Hole and with Frapp just north of Salt Lake."[27] Ball erroneously stated the men "left us on the Humboldt," but that was clearly not so. Perhaps he meant they left *for* the Humboldt.[28]

The distance traveled on August 13 made up for the previous day's brevity. Twenty-four miles in summer, with minimal water, must have constituted a long, dreary march. Traveling up Arbon Valley, Sublette and Fraeb picked their way across the rugged terrain of the Deer Creek Mountains. At day's end, they found a spring from which they could see the Snake River, just a few miles to the north. Ball lost his pocket thermometer somewhere on the trail.[29]

Today, American Falls is submerged beneath the reservoir formed when the river was dammed in the mid-1920s. The falls take their name from Americans at the site in the early 1820s. Wilson Price Hunt, leader of the overland Astorian party, described camping by the cascade on October 24, 1811, estimating it was "about thirty feet high." Some writers credit Hunt's expedition as the party for which the falls were named, citing the drowning of Antoine Clappine as the incident giving rise to its christening. While it may be the Astorians for whom the falls are memorialized, Clappine drowned when his dugout canoe capsized some eighty river miles downstream near modern Milner, Idaho, at the Cauldron Linn.[30] Though Hunt's brigade is often credited with inspiring the name, the following year, returning Astorian Robert Stuart would dub the location Portage Falls.[31] Yet another genesis story comes from Joel Palmer who was at the falls on August 11, 1845 and camped "within one mile of the American Falls ... at the springs," but whether this is the same spring where Wyeth camped is not clear. Palmer stated

> *A party of American trappers going down this stream in their canoes, not being aware of their proximity, were hurried along by the violence of the current; and passing over the falls, but one of the number survived.*[32]

Another source declared the disaster-stricken party to have been attached to the American Fur Company in 1829.[33]

In 1837, Irving would write about the view that greeted Bonneville upon reaching American Falls in autumn 1833:

> *The banks of the river, for a considerable distance, both above and below the falls, have a volcanic character: masses of basaltic rock are piled one upon another; the water makes its way through their broken chasms, boiling through narrow channels, or pitching in beautiful cascades over ridges of basaltic columns.*[34]

August 14, 1832   *Raft River*

14th   We made 30 miles in a S.W. direction and encamped on a creek called Casu River   it joins the main River below the Am. falls.   This days Ride was through an excessively barren country with no water between the two last camps   on the N. side of the Lewis River and about 50 miles distant from it is a range of snowy mounts.   also two or three points in the chain of this side with snow on them.

The Raft River was known by various names in earlier times. Here Wyeth called it "Casu," although in the original journal, according to Young's edits, he had written and crossed out "Ocassia." The river's name was said to derive from the peasant French word cajeaux, or "raft."[35] Ferris called it "Cassia," and Russell named it "Cozzu (Raft River)."[36] Jason Lee explained that the river "received its name from the circumstances that some of the traders were obliged to make a raft to cross it in high water."[37] The English name goes back to at least 1825 when Ogden sent men to "examine Raft River."[38] Robert Stuart referred to the stream as Trout Run during his 1812 trek.[39] Irving described Bonneville arriving at "a picturesque, but inconsiderable stream, called the "Cassie."[40]

Wyeth, keeping to the river's south side, was crossing the Snake River Plains, a largely volcanic, semi-arid region in southern Idaho covered in prickly pear and sagebrush. Wyeth's "range of snowy mounts" was Duncan Ridge. The few snow-covered "points" to the south may have been Mount Independence, Cache and Graham peaks, in the Albion Mountains along the present Idaho/Utah border. The headwaters of Raft River are in the Albion and Raft River mountains.

August 15, 1832   *Raft River*

15th   We made along the banks of the Ocassia about 25 miles and encamped on the west bank of it.   The valley of the Ocassia is about 4 miles wide and of a rich soil but the excessive cold and drouth of this country prevents vegetation from assuming a fertile character.   The air is so dry that percussion caps explode without striking and I am obliged to put the caps on and fire immediately except in the night when we consider it safe to keep the caps on the guns   we have in this country a large kind of black crickett 2 inches long said to be used as food by the Indians   they are in great numbers and roost on the sage at noonday   there are also in the streams abundance of craw-fish   we see antelope and old buffalo sign

---

Continuing up Raft River, Wyeth noted the potential for farming, but predicted a lack of water would hinder such development. In modern times, intense irrigation has reversed Wyeth's prediction but has reduced the Raft River to a trickle of what it was during the fur trade era. The day's travel would have put Wyeth's men in the vicinity of modern

Malta, Idaho. John Work's Hudson's Bay Brigade had followed a similar route a year prior, camping in nearly the same location on May 7, 1831. The HBC party was fortunate to find buffalo in the neighborhood.[41]

Percussion guns were new technology at the time; Wyeth had supplied his company with some of the first to be used in the Rocky Mountains.[42] In the percussion ignition system, a small metal cap containing a light explosive charge was placed over the end of a firing tube that directed flame to the main powder charge in the rifle's barrel. This cap, in effect, took the place of priming powder in the pan of a flintlock's ignition. The hot, dry air that would hamper future agriculture also played havoc with these rifles. Wyeth would write in 1848:

> The dryness of the atmosphere, at this time, was so great that on the Raft River, on the 15th of August, I could not discharge one barrel of my double percussion gun without causing the other to explode from the slightly increased heat. One man was wounded in this way, and guns several times exploded, and I was obliged to discontinue the practice of placing caps on the guns, in the day-time, until immediately wanted for use.[43]

Leaving the weapons unprimed left those carrying percussion rifles exposed to danger in the event of a surprise attack. Fortunately, Milton Sublette and many of the other men would have carried the older but trusted flintlock guns rather than relatively untested newer equipment. The experienced trappers of the Rocky Mountain Fur Company may well have looked askance at the practice of carrying an unprimed weapon.

Other trappers discussed large black crickets as a food source.[44] Joe Meek related that

> the people who lived in and who still inhabit this barren waste, were called Diggers, from their mode of obtaining their food – a few edible roots growing in low grounds, or marshy places. When these fail them they subsist as did our trappers, by hunting crickets and field mice. Nothing can be more abject than the appearance of the Digger Indian, in the fall, as he roams about, without food and without weapons, save perhaps a bow and arrows, with his eyes fixed upon the ground, looking for crickets![45]

Meek added:

> *In our extremity, the large black crickets which are found in this country were considered game. We used to take a kettle of hot water, catch the crickets and throw them in, and when they stopped kicking, eat them. That was not what we called* cant tickup ko hanch, *(good meat, my friend), but it kept us alive.*[46]

As for crawdads in this region, HBC's John Work identified a tributary of the Snake near Raft River as "Small Crawfish River," no doubt for the presence of this edible freshwater crustacean.[47]

August 16, 1832   *Raft River*

16th   We made 25 miles up the same side of the Ocassia then crossed it and followed S.W. 3 miles and encamped on a small mountain run making in all 28 miles in a W by S. direction   yesterdays march was in a direction W by S.

Farther upstream, Raft River runs along the foot of the Jim Sage Mountains. The party rode along the base of the range, then crossed the river where it made a decidedly southern turn. The "small mountain run" is Edwards Creek. Ball told of concocting a "good sauce to go with our dried meat" from berries they found on this day.[48]

August 17, 1832   *Goose Creek*

17th   We moved in a W. by S. direction about 15 miles to a creek putting into Lewis River on which we found no beaver of consequence having been traped out by the H.B.Co. some years before.

Entering a much rockier region than the previous few days, the brigade passed below Graham Peak, close to if not through what travelers on the Oregon Trail would call the City of Rocks. By day's end, they had negotiated Granite Pass and were camped on the waters of Goose Creek, which drains into the Snake River well over thirty miles north. Ogden called this the Riviere Charlo when he camped there on May 11, 1826. Goose Creek may have been named by this 1832 brigade of trappers under Milton Sublette, though Wyeth makes no mention of geese on the river.[49]

Wyeth's "H.B. Co." was, of course, the Hudson's Bay Company. British trapping brigades had been active in the Snake River country for many years, starting with Donald McKenzie's Northwest Company outfit in 1818. Michel Bourdon hunted the area with the Snake Country Brigade of 1822. Alexander Ross and Peter Skene Ogden were there in 1824, at which point Ross believed the area had been trapped out. Ogden, in his own quest for a profitable hunt, discovered Granite Pass two years later on June 11, 1826. John Work, mentioned above, took his trappers through the region in 1831.[50]

Milton Sublette and Fraeb probably explained to Wyeth that the region had already been trapped heavily by the HBC, thus their decision to travel to the Humboldt River, well to the west. HBC had been trying to eradicate beaver along the Snake River and its southern tributaries in order to create a fur desert – a buffer zone to keep American trappers from encroaching on the Pacific Northwest. HBC officials were confident that once the joint occupancy of Oregon country was settled, the regions north of the Columbia River would belong to Great Britain. It made sense to garner all the furs possible from regions that might soon be off limits, and save the northern regions for later trapping.[51]

August 18, 1832   *Goose Creek*

18th   We moved out up the creek about 8 miles and still found no beaver   saw one Pidgeon Woodpecker   this creek runs through what are called cut rocks otherwise volcanic   in this region I found one mountain of Mica Slate enclosing garnetts.   The Basaltic rock appears to be the same formerly and the remains of the Garnetts are in some cases to be seen.   also I have found here granite in small blocks   there is also much white sandstone compact   the clefts on each side creek are high and perpendicular but the bottom affords good

> *grass for this country.   There is no timber except willow and alder in the bottom and cedar on the hills   this days course about S. along the creek*

Wyeth indulged his interest in geology in this journal entry and in many to follow. There is no evidence that he had received any formal instruction in that discipline, but he may have gleaned some insights from John Ball. Trained in the sciences at Dartmouth College, Ball paid great attention to his environment, as his diary proves. He was "scrupulously exact in relating scientific truths, and a very accurate observer," according to one of his professors. Ball's geologic descriptions of the West would later be published in the *American Journal of Science and Arts*.[52]

"Cut rocks" is a phrase Wyeth used repeatedly in his diary to indicate a steep canyon, ravine or gulch, with sharp, precipitous walls. The garnets Wyeth referred to could have been star almandine garnets, Idaho's state gem. The day's route traversed three modern states – leaving modern Idaho, crossing the northwest corner of what is now Utah, and entering the northeastern portion of today's Nevada.

August 19-20, 1832   **Goose Creek**

19th   We moved up the creek about 12 miles in a S.W. direction   there was still little beaver   this afternoon I took 2 men and proceeded from camp about 8 miles about W. following the creek and slept there   at sunrise on the 20th we moved up about 12 miles in a W direction and while I was engaged in the brook setting a trap we found three Indians following us   the two men were on the bank and were seen but myself in the creek was unnoticed   when they crossed to go to the men I presented my pistol to the first one who made a precipitate retreat back while I made mine to my gun having got which I beconed them to come to me which they did   we then went to camp which we found had moved this day about 10 miles in same direction   these Indians were Snakes the first we had seen during the march   the party passed a hot spring   the country still volcanic.

Wyeth followed what would become a portion of the California Trail along this section of Goose Creek. He and a couple of men separated from the main camp in hopes of catching beaver. On this excursion, Wyeth learned a valuable lesson about where to keep his rifle while setting traps. Having left his gun lying on the bank, he waded into the creek. Wyeth had only his pistol at hand when three Indians approached his two companions on the shore. The handgun proved menacing enough to keep the Indians at bay until Wyeth could slosh back to his long gun.

Luckily, the Indians were Shoshone, often known as Snakes, named for the river upon which so many of them lived.[53] They accompanied the trappers back to the main camp which had moved in the meantime nearly ten miles closer.

Several hot springs lay along the course of travel. Not knowing the waters were thermal, John Ball was startled when he stooped to drink from one of them and found the water very hot – 100 degrees or more by his estimate.[54]

August 21, 1832   *Goose Creek*

21st   We followed the creek in a N.W. direction about 5 miles when we met a village of the Snakes of about 150 persons having about 75 Horses   they were poorly off for food and clothing but perfectly friendly   they are diminutive in person and lean.   We encamped to trade with them but did nothing except getting a few skins for moccasins   this morning caught my first Beaver a large one.

The party moved up Goose Creek until the men met the main Shoshone camp. The Shoshone were one of the first tribes to acquire horses, though the exact date is unknown. Having obtained them from the Comanche in the late 1600s or early 1700s, these mounts shifted the balance of power, giving great advantage to the Shoshone. However, by the time Lewis and Clark reached the Rockies in 1805, many Shoshone horses had been lost to tribes who had traded for firearms, again shifting the source of power.[55] Shoshone were typically considered less well off than other tribes; this band had few goods with which to trade. The highlight of the day was that Wyeth managed to finally trap a beaver!

August 22, 1832   *Goose Creek*

22nd   We followed the same creek about 2 mils and then struck into a ravine in a west direction and in about 6 miles came to a warm spring near a cold one which formed a run which we followed in a west by S. direction   this we followed about 2 miles and encamped making this day 18 miles

The farther up Goose Creek they went, the narrower the canyon became. Finally, perhaps a half mile south of its junction with Rattlesnake Creek, the party found a gorge that allowed passage out of the valley, onto and around Deadline Ridge. On the west side of this ridge, a number of hot springs can be found uphill from natural springs. A likely candidate for Wyeth's campsite is on South Hannahs Fork, two miles below where its cold stream mingles with the hot waters of Muddy Spring.

August 22, 1832   *Big Creek*

22nd   We proceed in a S.W. direction and struck the same stream on another branch about 2 mils from the junction   about 15 mils this day   these two streams unite and run in a N. direction through impassable cut rocks   this night caught 2 Beaver and slept out of camp.

Wyeth created a second entry dated August 22. The north and south branches of Hannahs Fork unite to the southwest of Wyeth's camp, then join Big Creek a few miles farther west. Turning north and going downstream on Big Creek would have taken them into a deep canyon, but from Wyeth's wording, the party did not take this route. Rather, they proceeded upstream, to the west of southwest for fifteen miles, following Big Creek toward its junction with Shoshone Creek. During the day, the party again crossed modern state boundaries between Idaho and Nevada.

The brigade must have made an early halt that gave Wyeth ample time to move away from the main base and find a separate place to camp. Enough evening light remained for Wyeth to get traps in the water and catch two beaver.

John Ball wrote frankly that "none of our company knew where we were," implying that even Milton Sublette and Fraeb were a bit turned around. Ball said they crossed a "Cat Creek" on August 23, but it was clearly not the modern stream of that name; that one is north of Snake River near Sun Valley, Idaho.[56]

August 24, 1832   *Shoshone Creek*

24th   Proceed up the creek in a S.W. by W. direction about 18 miles then in a W. by N. direction about 6 miles.   The last half of this days travel was through clefts of Scienite rock pretty well broke to pieces by heat apparently   we have here 2 kinds of Lizards the one like that of the United States as far as I could see   the other shorter and more sluggish   here we find the banks of the streams lined with Diggers Camps and Trails but they are shy and can seldom be spoken and then there is no one who could understand them and they appear to know little about the signs which afford other Indians a mode of intelligence   from this region specimens No. 1 are obtained.

Entry dates for Wyeth's journal became more problematic the further the party traveled from civilization. Dates were skipped, duplicated and sometimes "corrected" in such a way that the calendar became ever more confused.[57] This begs the question of how trappers kept track of dates throughout the year. Keeping a diary with regular, daily entries was by far the simplest method for calendar-keeping. However, few journals have come to light, leaving historians to conclude that few beaver hunters kept them. Richens Lacey "Uncle Dick" Wooten, Colorado mountain man and trapper, provided a good description of how his brigade tried to keep an accurate record of the days on an 1838 trek of nearly 5,000 miles:

We didn't know until we got back just how long we had been gone. Like the man who went around the world in eighty days, as the French novelist tells in the story, we lost our reckoning. When we got out in the mountains we found that nobody in the party had an almanac. A Frenchman named Charlefou agreed to act as timekeeper and recorder of the days, his calendar being a square stick upon which he cut a notch every day.

After we had been out some time and had entirely lost the run of dates, so that we couldn't have told to save our lives what day of the month it was without taking a look at Charlefou's stick and figuring it up, the Frenchman met with an accident and his calendar was lost. Then we agreed not to make any inquiry about the time until we got home, just to see how far off we would be in our reckoning.

Coming through California, a country with which none of us were acquainted and where the seasons were so different from anything we had been used to, led us to believe it was a month or two later in the year than it really was when we reached Fort Benton, and nearly all of us made wild guesses as to the date of our arrival.[58]

Wyeth seemed to have relied solely on memory and previous journal entries, rather than referencing almanacs, a "stick" calendar, designation of a timekeeper, reckoning by the seasons, or checking in at a fort.

On August 24, once on Shoshone Creek, the men continued along that stream until they reached the vicinity of today's Jackpot, Nevada. From here, they traveled up Salmon Falls Creek to Cottonwood Creek, then worked their way northwest, around Grassy Mountain. Wyeth pointed out the presence of syenite, an igneous rock composed primarily of alkali feldspar and other minerals such as hornblende, which was common in the area.

Peter Ogden led an HBC brigade through this same area in May 1826. At that time local Shoshones told him "that about a month since a party of Americans about 30 in number had descended this Stream on their return from Salt Lake without Beaver." This was likely a reference to a troop led by Jedediah Smith.[59]

Wyeth also noted the presence of numerous Indian camps made by a tribe he referred to as "Diggers," calling this band of Shoshone "miserable."[60] Ethnologists write that

*Early non-Indian travelers in the Snake River Plain and Great Basin
did not generally differentiate between the Shoshone, Bannock,
and Northern Paiute peoples. Instead, they lumped them together
under the rubric "Snake Indians," a term apparently coined by other
Native groups in the region. Some observers did, however, distinguish
between "Snakes" and "Diggers" – the latter a somewhat derogatory
term. Although there was much confusion in terminology, "Snake"
commonly referred to horse Indians, while "Digger" often referred
to foot-going Indians who relied heavily on root foods for their
subsistence.[61]*

Osborne Russell, Warren Ferris, and Washington Irving all mention Diggers.[62] These were the Western Shoshone, also known as Sho-
shokos and sometimes as Walker Indians since few of them had horses.
Other sources call them White Knife Indians or Tosawi Shoshone.[63]

Most Shoshone bands were named according to their principle
food source: Sheep-eaters, Salmon-eaters, Buffalo-eaters, etc. Wyeth
later described "root digger" Indians using

*crooked sticks, the end used in the earth being curved and sharpened
by putting it in the fire and rubbing it against a rough stone, which
both points and hardens them; they are also made of elk and deer
horn, attached to a stick. They are used to obtain some small roots
which the country produces, such as kama, souk, yampas, onions,
tobacco-root, etc.[64]*

Wyeth made no comment in his later treatise on Indian tribes
regarding this band's inability to communicate in sign language, though
he did report:

*They differ from the other Snakes somewhat in language ... Our means
of communicating with them were very imperfect, and mistakes of the
meaning might occur. Their first answer to the question of "What is
the difference between the Bonacks and the Shoshonees?" if addressed
to one separate from the other, was, that they were good and the other
bad, meaning that they would trade beaver with the Whites, while the
other would steal from and murder them.[65]*

The August 24 journal entry provided the first hint that Wyeth might be collecting geologic specimens along the route. John Ball, in his articles for the *American Journal of Science and Arts,* made continual mention of his own geologic samples, ranging from puddingstone to sparry limestone to mica slate. Ball's indication of both "burnt and unburnt" rock formations confirmed Wyeth's description of "rock pretty well broke to pieces by heat."[66]

August 25-28, 1832   *Canyon Creek*

25th   We made in a W. direction along the same creek 20 miles.

26th   In a W by N. direction about 20 miles

27th   In a S W direction toward a snowy mountain and leaving the last creek 24 mils and struck one here running S.E.   Country desolate in the extreme   most of the creeks which have water in them on the mountains dry up in the plains of this region

28th   did not move more than 2 miles up.

For the next four days, the combined parties of the Rocky Mountain Fur Company and the Pacific Trading Company traveled predominantly westward through what is now northern Nevada before passing back into southern Idaho. The "snowy mountain" Wyeth mentioned on the August 27 was Elk Mountain. On the west side of Elk Mountain, the party found Canyon Creek running to the southeast and traveled up it a short distance.

August 29, 1832   *Slide Creek*

29th   About 5 miles in a S.W. Direction to cross a range of high hills until we struck a creek running in a N.W. direction which we followed 12 mils and encamped where the creek goes into the cut rocks   this day we parted from Mr. Subletts party with feeling of regrett for this party have treated us with great kindness which I shall long remember.

Skirting Biroth Ridge, the men crossed Wyeth's "range of high hills" and dropped onto Slide Creek, which runs northwest to its confluence with the Jarbidge River. The majority of the waterways in this region run through steep-walled canyons or "cut rocks."

August 29 brought Wyeth to a significant and sobering milestone: the experienced guidance of Milton Sublette and Henry Fraeb came to an end. These old hands separated from Wyeth to continue their quest for productive trapping grounds. Ball remembered the groups parting ways at the Owyhee River:

> *Sublette and Frapp kept on westward and we parted with them on the creek that ran north and which we followed. We were with these trappers more than a month, parting from them the 28th of August.*[67]

Joe Meek, a member of the Rocky Mountain Fur Company brigade, had been traveling with Wyeth since leaving Pierre's Hole but made little mention of this journey in his life story. When he did, he cited a different location for this event:

> *On the head-waters of the Humboldt River they separated, Wyeth proceeding north to the Columbia, and Sublette continuing on into a country hitherto untraversed by American trappers.*[68]

Meek said they took leave of Wyeth on the Humboldt, while John Ball thought they were on the Owyhee River.[69] None agreed with Wyeth, who placed them on the Jarbidge River, a tributary of the Snake. This can be inferred from Wyeth's later statement that the party was at the mouth of the Bruneau River on September 11.[70] Tracing Wyeth's route backwards from that location clearly identifies the Jarbidge, a tributary of the Snake River, as the site of the RMFC's departure rather than the Owyhee or Humboldt rivers. Though Wyeth never saw the Humboldt River, that did not stop Meek from recounting the following tale, with nearly forty years between himself and the events:

When Sublette's party first struck the Humboldt, Wyeth's being still with them, Joe Meek one day shot a Digger who was prowling about a stream where his traps were set.

"Why did you shoot him" asked Wyeth.

"To keep him from stealing traps."

"Had he stolen any?"

"No: but he looked as if he was going to!"

This recklessness of life very properly distressed the just minded New Englander.[71]

Unfortunately, historians have relied on Meek's version of autumn 1832, tracking Milton Sublette's RMFC brigade to the Humboldt, but that party likely never trapped so far south. As will be seen, Sublette's party reappeared in Wyeth's camp on September 18. To have made it to the Humboldt and returned to the Snake River in about three weeks would have been impossible. After separating from Wyeth, the crew probably trapped the Owyhee River or the headwaters of the Humboldt.

Interestingly, Wyeth included an anecdote nearly identical to Meek's (though without placing himself in the action) in his 1839 report to Congress, in which he inveighed against the lawlessness of American frontiersmen and their effect on Indian tribes:

[The] Indian country is becoming a receptacle for fugitives from justice. The preponderance of bad character is already so great amongst traders and their people, that crime carries with it little or no shame. I have heard it related among white American trappers, as a good joke, that a trapper who had said he would shoot any Indian whom he could catch stealing his traps, was seen one morning to kill one; and, on being asked if the Indian had stolen his traps, he answered, no, but he looked as if he was going to. An Indian was thus wantonly murdered, and white men were found to laugh at the joke. As long as there is no power in the Indian country sufficient to restrain or send home criminals, these things will occur.[72]

August 30, 1832   *Slide Creek*

*30th   We followed the creek in a N.W. direction about 12
mils through tremendous cut rocks   I went ahead to look the
route   I passed the smoking fires of Indians who had just left
4 of whom I saw running up the mountain   endeavoured by
signs to induce them to come to me but could not   Soon after
I came to another camp   I happened to find their plunder   this
induced them to come to me 3 men one boy 4 women   from
these Indians I procured fresh Salmon Spawn which was
very encouraging as we are nearly out of provisions and the
country would afford us a scanty subsistence   I gave these
Indians a few small presents to convince them of our friendly
disposition.   This day for the first time in this country saw
raspberrys   these Indians gave me a cake made of service
berrys quite good   they had about a Dozen of spotted fish of a
kind I had never seen resembling a Tom-cod.   These Indians
are small about 120 [lbs.] of a good countenance   they are
Snakes or Sosshonees.*

Wyeth's first solo day in the uncharted vastness west of the Snake
River Plains saw encounters with Indians and foodstuffs. It is unknown
what directions, if any, Milton Sublette had given Wyeth, although the
Bostonian must have known that reuniting with the Snake River was
the key to the Columbia. The Pacific Trading Company thus trekked up
the canyon of Slide Creek, Wyeth scouting the route before them.

John Ball's recollection of that day, years later, still betrayed his
apprehension:

*The first day after leaving the trappers, we traveled over a rough
country of all sorts of rock, burnt and unburnt, and encamped in
what is now called a canyon, between high basaltic rocks. We twelve
thus for the first time alone it seemed a little lonely. And though not
fearful, there was something like a deep curiosity as to the future,
what might happen to us in that unknown land. Our aim was to
get back on the Lewis river and follow that to its junction with the
Columbia. And I now presume we were on the headwaters of the
Owyhee, the east boundary of Oregon.*[73]

Wyeth had felt "regrett," but skirted the implications of being left to navigate on his own. The dozen greenhorns, of whom none "had been west of the Alleganies," must have shuddered at finding themselves in the midst of an immense wilderness.[74] Six months earlier these men had dined at the finest restaurants of Boston. Now they were struggling to subsist off the land. Realizing their route with Sublette had taken them out of their way, Ball pointed out that so far they had "gained nothing on our journey as to the distance to be traveled."[75]

Serviceberry, *Amelanchier alnifolia,* appeared frequently in primary accounts of the fur trade, sometimes as sarvisberry or juneberry. Besides an assortment of dietary applications, the berry had numerous medicinal functions as well. Lewis and Clark identified the berry and mentioned it throughout their journals. On August 13, 1805, for example, Lewis recorded that Shoshone chief Ca-me-âh-wait "had nothing but berries to eat and gave us cakes of serviceberries."[76] The western species of the fruit starts out red and turns a deep purple as it ripens, typically in late August. Serviceberry is a member of the rose family, thus is not technically a berry but a pome, akin to a miniature apple. John Ball described the various edible plants they harvested:

> *Occasionally we met with fruit, which, you may well think, was very acceptable to us – a berry growing on a shrub they called a service berry, resembling what is called in New England the robin pear, and red and orange colored currants.*[77]

Wyeth's "Tom-cod" was a saltwater fish found in the coastal waters off New England. The burbot, or ling cod, was the only freshwater cod in the Snake River region. The Idaho state record was a fourteen pound lunker caught in 1954.[78] The species is no longer legally harvested in the state.

7.
On the Columbia River

30th   We followed the same creek and made about 15 in a N.N.W. direction through a continued defile in many places admitting just room for the water through which in many places we were obliged to make our way   The mountains on each side are about 1000 feet above the creek which has a rapid decent   here are a small fish about 1/4 lb.[?] similar to a trout but with large dark spots.   We meet here plenty of cherrys currants and gooseberrys the latter sour.   The last of yesterdays and the first of todays route lay through Porphritic Granite rocks in their natural state   the latter part of to days was through a stratified blue sandstone untouched by fire for a short distance then assumed a volcanic appearance.   This day we assended the highest mountain in sight and found the exhibit an indescribable chaos   the tops of the hills exhibit the same strata as far as the eye can reach and appear to once form the level of the country and the vally to be formed by the sinking of the earth rather than the rising of the hills through the deep cracks and chasms thus formed   the rivers and creeks of this country creep which renders them of the most difficult character to follow   in the brooks we have fresh water clams on which we look with some feeling for the small quantity of Buffaloe meat now remaining admonishes us look for some other means of living   game there is little and being obliged to travel prevents our hunting much.   from this place the specimen in Bag No. 1 of vitrified quartz was taken.

This was the second day in a row Wyeth entered as August 30. The company kept on Slide Creek and continued downstream to its junction with the East Fork of Jarbidge River. The name "Jarbidge" is an anglicized version of the Shoshone word "Tsaw-haw-bitts," a mythical, cannibalistic giant whom the Shoshone believed lived in the Jarbidge Canyon. This giant was said to have preyed on native people, tossing them into a basket slung across his back, later cooking and eating the unfortunate victims. The Shoshone avoided the area until, so the story went, Shoshone braves chased the creature into a cave in the canyon and blocked its escape with rocks and boulders.[1]

The East Fork country continues to be so biologically and geologically unique that 64,000 acres of that area were set aside as the Jarbidge Wilderness Area with the passage of the National Wilderness Act of 1964. As Wyeth pointed out, the steep slopes of the canyon wall are 1,000 feet deep in some places. The average drop in the river is more than 250 feet per mile, creating quite a "rapid descent." Travel through the narrow, winding canyon must have been slow and arduous, yet at this time, Wyeth's troop did not elect to climb out to the plains and find a more direct route. As will become clear, finding water sources on the flats above would prove problematic; negotiating the river bottom might have been the lesser of two evils.

Given their reluctance to ascend, it is remarkable that Wyeth nevertheless did scale a high point in order to achieve a view of the Jarbidge region. The journal entry is not clear about which mountain Wyeth may have climbed, but any would have revealed to him the vast extent of the Snake River Plains, their great lava flow spreading before him.

This day of travel took the Bostonians from what is today northern Nevada back into southern Idaho. Several species of freshwater mollusks inhabit the waters of this region. The western pearlshell, *Margaritifera falcate,* once considered to be the most common mussel in the Pacific Northwest, was likely the clam Wyeth savored. Another candidate would have been the western ridged mussel, *Gonidea angulata,* also widely distributed throughout the waters of the Snake River drainage.[2] Wyeth noticed all potential food sources; the last time he dried buffalo meat had been a month back.

August 31, 1832   *Jarbidge River*

31st   We followed the same creek about 4 miles in a N. direction then took a dry ravine 2 miles in a S.E. then in a N. direction and then followed down another dry ravine about 1 mile when the rocks on each side closed over the top and formed a natural Bridge elevated about 50 feet while the sides approached to within 20 feet of each other and the bottom decended perpendicularly about 60 feet   we of course returned on our trail and then stered a N.E. direction about 4 miles and encamped on a little ravine in which there was only a little water standing in deep places and barely enough for us and our horses.   The first half mile of our route lay through the bed of the creek and among rocks from 1 foot to 3 or 4 in diameter   this was a very difficult task and several of our horses fell in the water   this day we lost two horses which gave out   the country still bears the same appearance as for several days past.

The description of this day's travel is one of the few entries allowing a positive identification of the party's location as it crossed the Snake River Plains. There is only one natural bridge in this region: the one in Arch Canyon in modern Owyhee County, Idaho, near where Cougar Creek enters the Jarbidge River. The "arch" is in fact a natural bridge, since the creek flows through the created gap, what geologists call a rincon. That Wyeth intentionally veered from his trail to see the formation suggests others had told him about it. The canyon creates a unique micro-climate – a cool, shady environment that encourages the growth of fern and moss, in sharp contrast to the hot, dry lands above the canyon rim. Homesteaders who pioneered the country at the turn of the nineteenth century carved their names into the rock.[3]

September 2, 1832   *Jarbidge River*

2nd Sept.   We left our camp in the ravine assended to the height of land which we found to be a high level plain over which we marched in a N.N.W. direction and found during a 10 hours march 2 springs which as the day was warm were acceptable   at the end of 30 miles we reached the creek which we left on the 31st   We found rabbits plenty on the plain   our camp was made surrounded by high and perpendicular clifts say 800 feet bearing every mark of fire   here we found little grass for our horses.

Since the previous day was recorded as August 31, the correct date here was likely September 1. On this witheringly hot day, the men climbed out of the ravine to travel along the rim of Jarbidge River Canyon. According to Ball, they had become "so shut in that [they] had to leave it by a side cut and get onto an extended plain above," only to return to the river's edge by day's end along an Indian trail.[4] Ball described the men's desperate search for water:

> we traveled 30 miles and found water but once, and in the dry atmosphere our thirst became extreme. On approaching the canyon we could see the stream meandering along the narrow gorge 1,000 feet down, and on and on we traveled not knowing that we should survive even to reach it to quench our thirst. Finally before night we observed horse tracks and that they seemed to thicken at a certain point and lead down the precipitous bluff where it was partially broken down. So by a most difficult descent we reached the creek, dismounted and down its banks to quench our thirst. And our horses did not wait for an invitation, but followed in quick time.[5]

The company marched along the lava plains, passing the confluence of the Jarbidge and Bruneau rivers, then descended to get water and make camp on the latter stream.

The name Bruneau was believed to have first been applied by French-Canadian trappers with Donald McKenzie's Northwest Company brigade in 1818. It derived from *brun*, "brown" or "dark," and *eau*, "water." Alternatively, the watercourse was named for Baptiste Bruneau of Three Rivers, Quebec, a trapper who supposedly discovered the river in 1815.[6] Robert Stuart referred to it as Rocky Bluff Creek when he found thirty lodges of Shoshone there on August 21, 1812.[7] Between 1825 and 1831, however, several sources, including William Kittson, Peter Skene Ogden, and John Work, had labeled this the "Bruneaus" or "Bruneau's" River, suggesting that it had been named after a person.[8]

However, a new twist was offered by Benjamin Bonneville's "Map of the Territory West of the Rocky Mountains," published in 1837 as a companion piece to Washington Irving's *The Rocky Mountains; or, Scenes, Incidents, and Adventures in the Far West*. This showed the Bruneau marked as Powder River.[9]

September 3, 1832   *Bruneau River*

3rd   We lay at the same camp and got fish from the brook enough for breakfast after which I took horse and followed the creek down about 1 mile and found another larger joining it a little below which there is a warm spring issuing from the bank about 40 feet above the stream   it gives out smoke when it meets the air and discharges a large quantity of water   about 2 miles farther down I found a small party of Indians from whom I obtained 8 fish weight about 4 lbs each and looking like a salmon   for these I gave 4 Hooks   they were friendly   they advise me to follow the right hand trail but I have determined to take the left and shall perhaps repent it.   The left heads N.W. which I think my direction   I returned to camp and three of the Indians with me.   One of these Indians had a bad wound on the side of his head and from his signs and appearance was made with a poisoned arrow.

Doubtless concerned that the canyon walls might again close in too tight for travel, Wyeth explored downstream, shortly arriving at the confluence of East Fork of the Bruneau River, known today as Clover Creek. This stream flowed into the main channel from the east, giving Wyeth a choice of two trails.

Wyeth's "warm spring" could have been one of many in this area. A geothermal aquifer underlies a major portion of the Bruneau watershed near present Bruneau and Murphy Hot Springs, Idaho, where water temperatures between 90 and 150 degrees F have been recorded. At least 204 geothermal seeps and springs have been identified in the area.[10] Ball described the river as "decidedly warm, made so by hot springs gushing in from porous bluffs. Quite a stream came in of the temperature of 100 degrees."[11]

The flow "issuing from the bank about 40 feet above the stream" was probably Austin Butte Falls, which dump into the Bruneau a short distance downstream from the East Fork's confluence. Wyeth later maintained that "about 70 miles from the mouth of the Bruneau a jet of hot water issuing from the basaltic rock, about 40 feet above the bed of the stream, is sufficient to carry the largest mills."[12] Wyeth's entrepreneurial spirit remained intact.

Ball also told of finding "Indians who had our future food, dried salmon." He explained that the New Englanders bought much-needed provisions in exchange for what the Indians "seemed most to need – awls of iron to prick their deer skins for sewing into garments, and knives, for they hardly possessed an article of our manufacture."[13]

The fish hooks of the day were not the snelled barbs of modern times. The tops of the shanks were typically not formed into an eye but were flattened to a thin, rounded, shovel-shape at the tip. Whatever line was to be used was then tied around this shank. All hooks of this period were handmade.[14]

Regarding Shoshone arrows, in his treatise on Indians Wyeth provided a detailed description of their construction, concluding, "It is said they poison these arrows, but I do not know the fact. They sometimes appear to have been dipped in some dark-colored fluid, which has dried on them."[15] In fact, this tribe was known to use animal-derived poison on arrow tips:

> *The Shoshoni and Bannack Indians state that the proper way to poison arrows, as formerly practiced by them, is to secure a deer and cause it to be bitten by a rattlesnake, immediately after which the victim is killed, the meat removed and placed in a hole in the ground. After the mass has become putrid the arrow-points are dipped into it. By this method the serpent venom is supposed to be the most essential in the operation; but it is extremely doubtful if the venom has time to fully enter the circulation in the short interval between the time that the victim is bitten and then killed.[16]*

If this method was actually practiced by these Indians the putrescent matter may have caused death by septicemia.[17] Discussing the arrows of Digger Indians, trapper Osborne Russell explained that

> *their arrows are pointed with quartz or obsideon which they dip in poison extracted from the fangs of the rattle snake and prepared with antelopes liver these they use in hunting and war and however slight the wound may be that is inflicted by one of them – death is almost inevitable but the flesh of animals killed by these arrows is not injured for eating.[18]*

September 3, 1832   *Bruneau River*

3rd   We moved camp in the proposed direction viz N.W. 16 miles   During which distance we found stagnant water once and encamped near about 15 Indians diggers   3 of our men we left at the last camp to set their traps at some signs there seen.   These Indians are very poor and timid   when I approached them alone on a gallop they all began to run but by moderating my pace and making signs the[y] suffered me to come to them   they gave me some sweet root to eat for which I gave them 3 Hooks   they had a young yellow legged eagle with them and most of the diggers we have met had a small kind of Hawk at their camps   these they feed and tame   this party also had a young bird tame resembling a King Bird   this days travel was on a high plain and good going on an old trail   these Indians had with them staves for fish spears so we presume they are going to the river for fish and so think ourselves on the right trail.   For three nights passed there has been no frost   a thing which has not befor happened for three nights in all since leaving rock Independence.   Snow spit we had the 28th Aug.   Today a slight sprinkle of Rain being the 2nd time since leaving the Rendezvous.

Wyeth recorded a second day as September 3. Leaving a few men behind to trap due to encouraging signs of beaver, the remaining nine men continued their northwest travel, essentially paralleling the Bruneau as it flowed toward the Snake River. Here the presence of stagnant water and no mention of following a creek indicates that the party moved out of the canyon to travel across the lava plain.

Again, they met a small band of Shoshone. Wyeth's "sweet root" is blue camas, *Camassia quamash*, a member of the lily family. The bulb was a primary food source of many indigenous people throughout the Rocky Mountains, where it grew in the meadows. In September 1805, after the Lewis and Clark Expedition had descended from the Bitterroot Mountains, the travelers encountered the Nez Perce who fed them camas. Lewis noted that what he called quawmash "are soft of sweetish tast, and much the consistency of a roasted onion."[19] Numerous trapper journals mentioned camas, and Washington Irving, describing edible tubers used by Native Americans, wrote, "Among these is the camash, a sweet root, about the form and size of an onion, and said to be really delicious."[20]

Wyeth found birds of prey in the Shoshone camp, yet there is little historical evidence that Native Americans practiced falconry. The area is a prime habitat for such birds, however. Today the Nelson Snake River Birds of Prey National Conservation Area is found less than eight miles from Wyeth's location on this date, and boasts one of the densest populations of nesting raptors in North America. Wyeth's "small kind of hawk" was undoubtedly a peregrine falcon. The large, yellow-legged eagle was more likely a Swainson's hawk. The western kingbird is "easily tamed" and "thoroughly enjoys the society and protection of humans."[21]

Weather conditions have seldom been cited in the journal thus far. Wyeth found the spit of snow that occurred a week earlier, however, noteworthy, perhaps because it occurred in August. On another rarity, Wyeth would later remark that the scanty rain this day amounted to less than one-eighth inch of precipitation.[22]

September 4, 1832   *Bruneau River*

4th   We left the camp early and proceeded over a high and pretty level plain gradually decending to the N.W. in a N.N.W. direction and after 20 mils travel without water came to ravines running E. and dry having gravelly and sandstone (untouched by fire) blufs and in 5 mils more came to the creek we had left on mng. of the 3rd.   the banks of which we found every 20 steps or thereabouts warm or hot springs and the creek tho large and discharging a great quantity water too warm to be palatable   Here we found an Indian and family of whom for 2 fish Hooks we bought 7 salmon of about 4 lbs weight each when green.   they were split and dried.   The two men left behind not having yet come up we intend halting here for them. The creek is here lined with volcanic rock   today saw the first fish Hawk in this country.

Another day of parched travel across the volcanic plains brought the Pacific Trading Company to the vicinity of modern Hot Springs, Idaho. Due to geothermal activity, many of today's agricultural wells pump water into cooling ponds before application to the fields.[23]

Wyeth's fish hawk was an osprey. This large bird of prey is the only North American raptor that feeds exclusively on fish. It is also the only raptor that plunges into the water feet-first to catch fish, which it then carries in a head-first position for better aerodynamics.[24]

September 4, 1832   *Bruneau River*

4th   La[y] at camp and repacked our goods and held a smoke with some Indians one of whom we engaged as a guide down the river and to Beaver   smoked too much and made myself sick

---

This was the second entry dated for September 4.

In a short list of Shoshone vocabulary compiled later, Wyeth wrote that "beaver" was translated as "Harnitze."[25] In that same treatise, he told a humorous story about the difficulty of communicating with this people:

> *In 1832, when I first went among the Shoshonees, we wished to know the name of the beaver, but could not succeed for several days. At last one of my trappers said he had learned it from an Indian, and that it was "bonaque." Subsequently we learned that this was a tribal name for a division of the Snakes.*[26]

From Wyeth's experience, the beaver and otter exceeded all other game in the homelands of the Shoshone he visited, though "they were by no means abundant; at that time the Indians had no traps, and therefore could obtain little food from the beaver."[27]

Wyeth had not mentioned his personal tobacco use until this point. Given that he made himself sick, it is a good guess he was not much of a smoker.

September 5, 1832 *Bruneau River*

5th   Moved on about 5 mils N.N.W. and again struck the creek and good grass   found Beaver sign very plenty and for the first time set all our traps at good sign   had a mess of fresh clams for dinner after which 2 Indians came to us with 4 salmon which we bought for 2 Hooks   This day heard what we all took for a cannon at about 10 mils distance time will determine whether we were mistaken.   In this creek there are a great number of snakes about 3 feet long with a large head and of a brownish grey color about the proportion of the striped snake of N[ew] E[ngland]   They Inhabit the water and I saw one catch a small fish within two feet of me while bathing at a warm spring which put into the main stream   The bathing at these warm springs is delicious   there are hundreds of them and some large enough to dive in   Some gush out of the rocks at an elevation of 40 feet above the stream and discharge enough water for a mill   I can perceive no unusual taste in the water.

Continuing down the Bruneau toward the Snake River, Wyeth's company swung away from the river early on, but returned to the mainstream as the day progressed. As the canyon walls grew farther behind them, the valley widened into a broad, fertile plain. The habitat was more favorable for humans and beaver as well. All of the party's traps were finally in the water.

The booming noise was rather mysterious. It may have been some volcanic or geothermal event, thunder, or even an earthquake. Meriwether Lewis described a similar curiosity on July 4, 1805 at the Great Falls of the Missouri River in what is Montana today. The Rocky Mountain artillery was heard again on July 11, 1805. Clark, too, was at a loss to explain the noise. But Lewis

now recollected the Minnetares making mention of the nois which they had frequently heard in the Rocky Mountains like thunder; and which they said the mountains made; but I paid no attention to the information supposing it either false or the fantom of a supersticious immagination. I have also been informed by the engages that the

*Panis and Ricaras give the same account of the Black mountains
which lye West of them. This phenomenon the philosophy of the
engages readily accounts for; they state it to be the bursting of the
rich mines of silver which these mountains contain.*[28]

The snakes Wyeth described may have been western terrestrial gar-
ter snakes, very common in Idaho. These brownish-grey serpents are
most often found near water and feed on fish, as well as slugs, worms,
small mammals, lizards, frogs and salamanders.[29]

Wyeth's warm spring and waterfall in this entry is another reference
to the Austin Butte Waterfall.

September 6-7, 1832   *Bruneau River*

*6th   Remained at same camp and were visited at 10 ock in
the morning by two Indians with whom we held a smoke   we
can learn nothing of any white post by these Indians   caught 7
Beaver*

*7th   Remained at same camp and exchanged two horses with
some Pawnack Indians three of whom visited us   also about
10 Sohonees with Salmon of which they have plenty   here
we caught a N. England Sucker also a fish a little resembling
pike of about 3 lbs weight but without teeth.   Caught 3
Beaver.   Ravens are here very plenty and tame   the[y] light
on the perpendicular sides of the creek waiting for fish on
which they live.   Gese and ducks are also plenty as well as
grouse.   Some of the Indians have guns but most of them go
unarmed   The creek here for about 10 miles runs W.N.W.*

For two days, the New England brigade stayed put in a camp along
the Bruneau River, due west of the eponymous modern town. In its
last few miles before flowing into Snake River, the Bruneau ran more
westerly than before. The valley's riparian and wetland habitat, with its
abundance of waterfowl and upland game, would have provided the
travelers quite a contrast to the previous weeks of hardship.

Wyeth's men were slowly learning the ways of the wilderness and
adding pelts to their packs. Ball wrote that "when two or three were away

for a night's trapping, we slept with our horse's long halters tied to a bush near us or sometimes in our hand." He explained that on these excursions for beaver, they "occasionally caught some, preserved and packed along their skins, knowing they would be acceptable to the Hudson Bay people in exchange for such things as we should need from them."[30]

September 8, 1832   *Bruneau River*

8th   Mooved camp down the creek about 12 miles and came to the village under the escort of about 20 Indians on Horseback one of whom by the direction of the chief shewed us the place for our camp where grass and water could be had   here the chief Harangued his people telling them not to come into our lines nor steal from the white people   he sent his squaws with wood for us and also sent salmon for us to eat   I gave him a present of tobacco awls Hooks Powder vermillion knives etc.   Here I traded a Beaver skin robe for two knives and six skins with many muskrat which are plenty here   I found these Indians great thieves in the small line knives etc.   Missing mine I went to one of the Sub Chiefs and told him of it   he made enquiry and pointed out the thief who refusing to open his Robe I gently did it for him but insted of finding the knife found a coat of one of the men which he held upon until I drew a pistol on which he gave it up and caught up what he supposed to [be] one of our guns but it happened to be my covered fishing rod   he was then held by the other Indians and sent to the village and I saw him no more

The mouth of the Bruneau was, according to Ball, "a favorable site for fishing."[31] In late summer of 1812, Robert Stuart had found a similar camp of Shoshones here. Thirty in number, these Indians had horses for which Stuart valiantly tried to trade. "Strong were the inducements we held out," Stuart wrote, "but they withstood our temptations."[32] The Astorian at last managed to exchange two of his worn out mounts for a couple of fresh animals.

Ethnologists have identified a specific tribal group as "Bruneau Shoshone," a band of Northern Shoshone who populated the region along the Bruneau River around the close of the eighteenth century.

MAP 4 *Bruneau River to Fort Walla Walla, 1832*

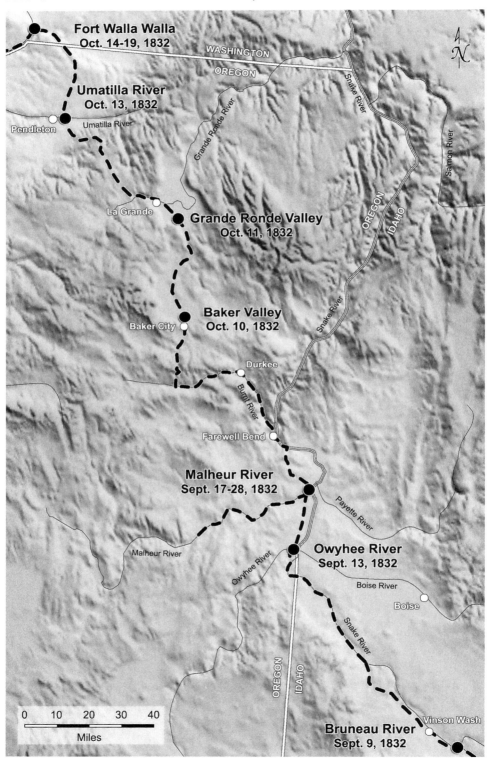

Pressured by the ascendency of mounted Northern Shoshone bands, primarily buffalo hunters, the Bruneau branch soon concluded it could get along just as well without horses. By the later years of the fur trade the Bruneau moved to the south bank of the Snake River where their seasonal migratory patterns cycled them into regions even further south. In 1868, their population would be recorded as 300 individuals.[33]

Although he seems to have taken the Shoshones' larceny in stride, Wyeth was particular and possessive about his fishing equipment. He had selected his gear "from the best materials of an angling ware-house," and he considered himself one "who professed to be a judge of such articles."[34] This angling rod was likely made of solid wood; the first split bamboo poles made in America would not be produced until 1845.[35]

September 9, 1832   *Bruneau River*

9th   In morning went to see the Indians catch Salmon which is done by entangling them in their passage up the creek among dams which they erect and spearing them   they catch an immense quantity   the operation commences in the morning at a signal given by their chief.   This chief is a good sized man and very intelligent and the President would do well if he could preserve the respect of his subjects as well or maintain as much dignity

---

Wyeth benefitted on numerous occasions from these salmon-eating people. This day he watched them catching fish using a type of weir. Ball gave further details:

Their manner of fishing was ingenious. The stream was shallow and they built a fence across it near its mouth and then some distance above, leaving weirs at one side, so that the fish coming down or going up would come in, but would not find their way out. They had spears with a bone point with a socket that fitted onto a shaft, and a hole through the point by which a string tied it to the handle.

At sunrise at a signal from the chief they rushed in from both sides,
struck the salmon through with the spear, the point came off, and
held by the string to the shaft, they towed them to shore and so soon
had hundreds on land.[36]

In his later treatise on Indians, Wyeth added that the weirs were
made from stone or brush, and that at night the people used torchlight
to watch for the salmon to enter their traps. When speared, "if the fish
is strong, the staff is relinquished, and operates as a buoy to obtain the
fish when he has tired." Wyeth also noted the strength of Shoshone fish
nets, made from "the outer bark of some weed."[37]

While Wyeth was in the mountains, Andrew Jackson, a Democrat,
served as President of the United States. Wyeth does not state his opinion of Jackson; his comment regarding the president can be taken a
number of ways, either positive or negative.

September 10, 1832   *Snake River*

10   Mooved down the main river in a S.W. direction which
here runs through moderate banks in a moderate current   We
are told that the next creek has beaver by the chief and that it
is 4 days march   The main river is here full of salmon which
continually jump above the surface like sturgeon.

The men of the PTC had reunited with the Snake River at last. Having left the Snake on August 14, it had taken them twenty-eight days to
traverse the rugged country. Wyeth's dates remained confused at this
time, but John Ball concurred that it was indeed September 10 when the
party reached what he called "Lewis River," an early name for the Snake.[38]

September 10, 1832   *Snake River*

10th   Mooved camp along the Bank of the river 3 miles   there
the river diverging to the Northward we left it and followed the
main trail   the river here goes[?] through cut rocks about 30
miles   We made this day 20 mils in all in a W.N.W. Direction

and encamped in poor grass on a small creek 1 mile from the
main river   during the march we crossed a small creek up
which about 2 mils is a fine camp.

Though he duplicated the September 10 date, Wyeth seemed to have recognized the errors in his chronology because from this entry on, his bearings appear to be on track. However, with the frequency of doubled and skipped entries since August 19, the actual date remains in question.

Wyeth now led the men confidently toward their Columbia River destination. Leaving its confluence with the Bruneau, the Snake trends to the southwest for a few short miles before making a decided bend northward. Wyeth kept to the south bank, moved away from the main channel, and then traveled overland. The looming canyon walls were higher on the opposite side.

Traveling down the Snake River, Wyeth passed modern Vinson Wash where in 1812 Stuart had made a miraculous discovery. Selecting a random spot to descend to the river for a drink of water, Stuart stumbled across four men who had separated from Wilson Price Hunt's overland expedition for a trapping excursion in 1811: John Hoback, Edward Robinson, Jacob Reznor and Robert Miller. The quartet had "suffered greatly by Hunger, thirst & fatigue, met us [almost in a state of nature]."[39]

At the end of this day, a dozen Bostonians were camped on today's Sinker Creek, once known as Burnt Creek due to the lack of grass along its banks.[40] About ten miles before stopping for the night, the party crossed Castle Creek. The "fine camp" that Wyeth marched past was likely near the junction of Catherine and Castle creeks, southwest of his route. The southern alternate to the Oregon Trail traversed this area, and it was along this meandering stream in 1862 that emigrant Henry M. Judson would report "grass higher than our heads."[41]

September 11, 1832   *Snake River*

11th   Moved at 3 A.M. and followed the trail 24 mils in a W.N.W.
Direction and encamped on the bank of the main river which is
here a fine stream about a 1/3 mile or over.   I swam across it

*and found it over my head all the way   here we found Indians
and bought Beaver 3 skins for 1 shoe knife and 4 charges
powder & lead   we also got salmon of them   the Basalt here
occurs resting on sand and gravel   in some places the rock is
not more than 4 feet thick and appears to have suffered from
intense heat   the country is barren in the extreme   there is
usualy a difference of 40 deg. between the day & night   the
heat at noonday about 75 to 85 deg.   The Indians here have
large nets made in the European manner of the hemp of the
country.   The trail on the river so far is fine and much used.*

Twenty-four miles downstream put the men near today's Sunrise Skypark, along the Snake River. They skirted Guffey Butte, following a path that roughly corresponded to modern Idaho State Highway 78.

Starting the day at three o'clock in the morning was not unusual for such travelers. Peter Ogden often got his brigade going well before daylight: "at three this morning all were in motion" and "at 3 A.M. I gave the call," appeared in his 1827 Snake Country journal.[42] Henry Spalding wrote a letter from the 1836 rendezvous describing his trip west from Fort William. He recorded, "the order of the camp was as follows: rise at half past three, A.M."[43]

Wyeth acquired a few pelts through trade. A shoe knife was essentially a skinning-type knife with a thin blade fixed by a tang in a wooden handle with a slanted tip. These were used by shoemakers for cutting and paring leather.[44]

Regarding fish nets, Wyeth's Indian treatise described how the Shoshone made cordage from a "weed which grows in the country, but I took no particular note of." He did note that

The nets are of two kinds: the scoop, which is precisely the same as used in the United States; and the seine, which is also in principle exactly the same; and the knot used in netting also appears to me exactly the same: but in this I may be mistaken, as I have never seen the operation performed. The leaded line is formed by attaching oblong rounded stones, with a sunken groove near the middle in which to wind the attaching ligature. Reeds are used for floats.[45]

Traveling upon such a clearly defined trail, for a change, must have been a relief for Wyeth. Now that he was heading downstream on the Snake, his course would simply follow the current north to its confluence with the Columbia River.

September 12, 1832   *Snake River*

12   Moved camp 15 miles on the trail in a W.N.W. direction and following the bank of the river which is here a gentle stream of about 4 miles and 1/2 mile wide.   Gnats here trouble us much and the days are extremely hot about 85 deg. and the nights warm enough for comfort   The river is full of salmon and a plenty of them are to be had of the indians whom we meet every few mils fishing on the banks of the stream   Some of the grass is here so salt that it can be washed in a pot of water and enough seasoning for boiling obtained   grass is generally poor. The banks are here generally sand   Many kinds of water fowl frequent the river here   today we bought a fish of the Indians dried excessively fat and when alive a large fish,   sturgeon probably

While traveling through almost the same place in 1812, Stuart had also complained of insects. Besides mosquitoes, Stuart griped that "another nearly allied in blood to the former, assails us vigorously in innumerable hordes for the greater part of the day – so that the Sand Flies these Champions of light may verily be paired with the Imps of Darkness."[46]

Salt grass, *Distichlis spicata*, has a tiny salt gland on its leaf surfaces that allowed for the extrusion of salt.[47] Many Indian groups used salt grass as a source for salt by cutting or pulling up the plants, then beating them to remove the saline crystals from leaves.[48] Grazing animals tend to avoid this grass if alternatives are available. Trapper Rufus Sage pointed this out: "The short buffalo-grass of the grand prairie had almost entirely disappeared, – in some places a blueish salt grass showed itself in plats uncropped by game."[49]

At the end of the day, Wyeth camped on the banks of the Snake, a short distance north of today's Marsing, Idaho.

September 13, 1832   *Snake River*

13th   moved camp along the bank of the river and following the trail 24 miles only deviating from the river about 3 mils of the last of the travel.   The first 6 miles the river is W. the next 3 N.W. then S.W. 3 then taking a circular sweep round to N. by E. which was 9 miles   then left the river and in 3 miles struck a creek about as large as Charles River at Watertown, where we found grass, salmon and Indians and the first timber we have seen since leaving the Mts. in sight on what appears to be a river coming in from the N. side   this I mean to ascertain tomorrow and the next day I shall start to explore the creek for Beaver.   This forenoon and yesterday forenoon were cloudy and the first cloudy weather for 2 months except as mentioned before.   Wether still as warm as 80 deg. in day time   buy salmon for a hook apiece.

Keeping to the Snake for another twenty-one miles, the course of the river in this area follows Wyeth's written itinerary almost to a tee. With the main river channel marking the roughly 200-mile border between today's Idaho and Oregon, Wyeth crossed into the latter near where he described a "circular sweep round to N. by E." At about present-day Adrian, Oregon, the river makes a northeast trend so that was likely the place where Wyeth left the river to go this day's final three miles.

The timbered creek that Wyeth compared to the Charles River near Watertown, Massachusetts, was the Owyhee River, which appeared in many early diaries as Sandwich Island River. This stream derived its name from Hawaiian Islanders, who by 1800 were coming to this country as fur trade employees. "Owyhee" was a phonetic spelling for Hawaii, also then known as the Sandwich Islands. Donald McKenzie had sent three Kanakas, natives of those islands, along with other Northwest Company trappers to trap these waters in 1819. This trio left the main brigade to explore unknown terrain and never returned. The men were believed to have been killed by Indians, and the river was subsequently named in their memory.[50]

September 14, 1832   *Snake River*

*14th   Mooved camp in a N.N.W. Direction 5 miles and
encamped on the main river   being out of provisions I sent
a man on a mule to buy some salmon   he went up the river
about 3 miles and called to some Indians on one of the Islands
to bring some   these he bought   afterward another Indian
came over with some   the man thinking he had got nearly
enough offered him a less price   this displeased the Indian
who slapped him in the face and at the same time hit the mule
a kick which set him out on the run and the Indian ran quick
enough to avoid vengeance   the man came to camp much
displeased having had to walk most of the way and carry his
fish   this day also visited by Indians from below with salmon*

Riding horseback along the bank of the Owyhee to its union with the Snake, Wyeth set up camp on the main river about five miles south of today's Nyssa, Oregon. One of Wyeth's men got a hard lesson in fair trade.

September 15-16, 1832   *Snake River*

*15th   Sent 3 men and 4 animals to examine the small river for
beaver   this day a N.W. wind much like the N.E. of the Atlantic
with some little rain (at the same camp)   this day took a ride
down the river to examine for a camp*

*16th   N.W. wind still   took a ride up the river to find a camp
where timber, fit for a raft which we propose to build to carry
some of the loose baggage and some men who are on foot
can be found, found none   saw some beaver sign   in trading
for some salmon an Indian attempted to snach a paper of fish
hook from me but he did not make out   returned to camp and
sent two men to trap for the beaver   they left their horses and
went into the willows to look [for] the sign during which time
the Indians none of whom were in sight stole a cloak from Mr.
Ball.   They found the beaver had lately been trapped out say
within 3 weeks   next morning they returned to camp*

Fish hooks of the period, especially those made in England, were often wrapped in paper, in varying quantities, for ease of transport. American-made hooks were more commonly sewn onto a rectangle of cheap pasteboard or pushed though punched holes in a card. These papers might contain as many as one hundred hooks.[51] A Lewis and Clark Expedition memorandum mentioned "4 papers of fish hooks" to supply their angling needs.[52] Fish hooks were also a valuable trade good; losing them to thievery would not do.

John Ball described how the trappers picketed the horses and posted a couple of men on guard duty. "One night when thus encamped I had my old camlet cloak stolen from my saddle and our horses' halters cut, but they, the horses, did not leave us, and we did not see by whom done."[53] Camlet was a fine fabric made from wool (originally from camel hair, but later goat) combined with silk. Ball used this cloak and its large cape for "bed purposes," along with half a buffalo robe and a blanket, the cloak pulled over his head "to shut off the wind or the moon."[54] He slept profoundly with this arrangement, so it was an unfortunate loss for Ball.

Interestingly, these greenhorns were able to determine that the beaver had been trapped out, though it may not have occurred within the previous few weeks. John Work had been on the Owyhee the year before, in the spring of 1831. That May, his journal reported that, fulfilling the HBC "fur desert" mission, he had

> *separated a party this morning and sent 8 men ... to hunt to the Westward on the heads of small rivers which run into Snake river and on the Eastern fork of Sandwich Island River, while I with the remainder of the party proceed to the southward to Ogden's river, and then to the head of Sandwich Island river.*[55]

September 17, 1832   *Malheur River*

17th   Mooved camp N. by W. 16 miles and encamped on a creek about as large as the last near a few lodges of Indians   the main river about two miles to N.E.   This creek appears to run S.W.   The Inds. say there is beaver on

*it   the main river here makes a considerable detour to the
N.   Yesterday had hail and rain & snow and today the Mts. to
the Northward are white with it.*

After a few days spent surveying the area, Wyeth moved north to
the Malheur River, camping about a mile and a half due north of today's
site of the Ontario Municipal Airport. Wyeth had his bearings reversed
– the Malheur runs to the northeast.

Malheur is a French word meaning misfortune, bad luck or disaster;
the literal translation being "evil hour." Ogden explained the source of
the river's name in his journal entry of February 14, 1826: "We encamped on the River au Malheure (unfortunate River) so called on account
of property and Furs having been hid here formerly discovered and Stolen by the Natives."[56]

Historians have identified Donald McKenzie as the unlucky NWC
brigade leader whose furs were stolen.[57] Bonneville's 1837 map showed
the Malheur as the Little Wyer River; the map drawn by Warren Ferris
in the same year has the correct name in the correct place.[58]

September 18-28, 1832   *Malheur River*

*18th   with 2 men I went up the creek   this I followed about
50 miles and found its general course about W by N.   the first
15 miles S.W. then W. 20 then N.N.W. 15 where the cut rocks
begin   This is a large stream when the waters are high in the
spring but now is sluggish   here we got a few beaver   It had
been trapped by the H.B. 2 years before   we saw no Indians
on it during the 9 days I was up.   On the 10th day [Sept. 28]
I returned to where I left the party and feeling in the mood of
banter I told the Indians at the mouth of the creek (the party
having left) that I had eaten nothing for two days   this to see
if they would give me anything for charity sake.   One of them
went and looked at my saddle and pointed to me the fresh
blood of a beaver I had that morning caught and left with the
two men   I then bought 2 salmon for one awl   afterward I
told him I had three children at home   he brought forward*

three tawny brats and his squaw who was big　I backed out of story telling with Indians.　I then proceeded on until the moon went down when seeing a light I made for it　after traveling 5 miles I found it to be an Indian camp on the other side of the river　I then unsaddled my horse and slept until 4 ock when I mounted and at 9 ock found where my party had camped the same night and a notice in the trail of their motions　at 11 ock I overtook them with my horse lame and jaded.　I found an Indian with the party who seems to know the route to Wallah Wallah and he intends going with us　During my absence the three men sent up the creek above the one I went up returned without accident, and during the same time Mr. Sublette with Mr. Frapp & party joined our camp and crossed by fording to the other side of the river intending to divide into 3 parties and trap up three streams coming in opposite　the upper one of which we thought to be salmon river　it proves to be called Big Woody on account of the timber on it.　They attempted to come down on the creek above the one I asscended but after toiling long and wearing down their horses in a cruel manner they crossed to the one that we decended and arrived at the Indian village the day after we left it　he left before I returned　I regretted much not seeing this party.　from Information gained here we suppose that we shall meet no Indians between this and the fort　have therefore provided as much salmon as we could get and put ourselves on allowance.　Subblette who went to 2 creeks further than I did saw a large stream running S.W.　this must either turn and be some large river coming into Lewis below here or be the head water of some river going to the Gulph of California.　After joining camp we proceed on to a creek coming from the N.W. which is our route　the river here being impracticable and taking a great bend to the N. and shall wait here until the two men who went up with me come to camp　The river from where I lef[t] camp runs about N. 20 miles then west 10 miles then N. again into cut rocks　found the party all well and the horses much recruited

Wyeth left off writing in his journal for ten days while he explored the Malheur River. Upon his return, this catch-up entry filled in recent events. Taking two unidentified men, Wyeth had followed the Malheur nearly fifty miles upstream, trapping as he went. At about the point that Squaw Creek enters the Malheur, near the extreme southern end of present-day Harper Valley, Oregon, Wyeth turned and headed back, alone, to rejoin the nine men still in the main camp. He managed to catch some beaver, but again realized the stream had been trapped out. Once back at the former basecamp, Wyeth discovered the main company had moved on. He chose not to wait for the two trappers he had left on the Malheur, and went in search of his other men. A rare glimpse of Wyeth's sense of humor shows him attempting to trick Indians into thinking he was someone he was not. Not surprisingly, he was outwitted at his own game.

Wyeth had also sent three men to reconnoiter up the Payette River while he was gone, and they had returned after a short, uneventful excursion. This watercourse was named for Francois Payette, a Canadian fur trapper who first arrived at the mouth of the Columbia in John Jacob Astor's second Pacific Fur Company ship, the *Beaver*, in May 1812. Payette hired on with NWC, and was believed to be the first Euro-American to have entered the Payette River region, having accompanied Donald McKenzie in 1818.[59]

John Ball had held a significant parley with some Shoshone in the Captain's absence. Using sign language made up as they went along, the Bostonian managed to get good directions for the course ahead. The Shoshone man used a paddling motion to mean river, pointed to a horse to indicate a trail, and laid his head on his hands and shut his eyes to represent how many days on each.

We made the Indians understand that we were going to Walla Walla, the name of that place being the only word we had in common. All else was by signs, talk with the fingers. Inquiring the way, one of the Indians said that he had been to Walla Walla and made in the sand a map of the country. He said that such a mark meant the river and another the trail, that the road kept down the river three sleeps, always reckoning distances by day's journeys, or in two if we whipped up; that then the river went into mountains, it does pass through a canyon and for a hundred or two miles, and the road left the river and up a creek, and then we should go so many days and come to a mountain, go over that and encamp, then over another and encamp, then a plain and in two days Walla Walla.

I felt confident I understood him, though this all by signs, and it proved just as he had said, and of great help to us.[60]

It must have been disappointing for Wyeth to learn that during his absence, Milton Sublette and Henry Fraeb's contingent had stopped by. The parties had been separated for the past month and Wyeth missed them by one day. While apart from the Bostonians, the Rocky Mountain Fur Company brigade had come close to perishing in the desolate country between the Owyhee and Humboldt rivers. Meek told Frances Fuller Victor that Sublette

finally resolved to turn north, in the hope of coming upon some better and more hospitable country. The sufferings of the men now became terrible, both from hunger and thirst. In the effort to appease the former, everything was eaten that could be eaten, and many things at which the well-fed man would sicken with disgust ... In this condition, and exposed to the burning suns and the dry air of the desert, the men now so nearly exhausted began to prey upon their almost equally exhausted animals. At night when they made their camp, by mutual consent a mule was bled, and a soup made from its blood. About a pint was usually taken, when two or three would mess together upon this reviving, but scanty and not very palatable dish ... hungry as they were, the men were cautious in this matter; and it generally caused a quarrel when a man's mule was selected for bleeding by the others.

A few times a mule had been sacrificed to obtain meat; and in this case the poorest one was always selected, so as to economise the chances for life for the whole band. In this extremity, after four days of almost total abstinence and several weeks of famine, the company

reached the Snake River, about fifty miles above the fishing falls,
where it boils and dashes over the rocks, forming very strong rapids.
Here the company camped, rejoiced at the sight of the pure mountain
water, but still in want of food. During the march a horse's back had
become sore from some cause; probably, his rider thought, because
the saddle did not set well; and, although that particular animal
was selected to be sacrificed on the morrow, as one that could best
be spared, he set about taking the stuffing out of his saddle and
re-arranging the padding. While engaged in this considerate labor, he
uttered a cry of delight and held up to view a large brass pin, which
had accidentally got into the stuffing, when the saddle was made,
and had been the cause of all the mischief to his horse.

The same thought struck all who saw the pin: it was soon converted
into a fish-hook, a line was spun from horsehair, and in a short
time there were trout enough caught to furnish them a hearty and a
most delicious repast. "In the morning," says Meek, "we went on our
way rejoicing;" each man with the "five fishes" tied to his saddle, if
without any "loaves." This was the end of their severest suffering, as
they had now reached a country where absolute starvation was not
the normal condition of the inhabitant.[61]

Wyeth learned from his men that Milton Sublette had forded the
Snake to give his trappers access to three streams that entered on the
east bank. One of these waterways was the Boise River, which Wyeth
called "the Big Woody on account of the timber on it." Earlier French-
Canadian trappers, having traveled over many miles of the volcanic,
arid Snake River Plains, were reported to have exclaimed, "Les bois!
Les bois! Voyez les bois!" ("The woods! The woods! Look at the
woods!") The river was known by other forms of that name: Riviére
Boisée, Boisias River and Boise. It was also called Wihinast (boiling
rapidly) by the Shoshone, and the Reed River, for John Reed (a Pacific
Fur Company man murdered by Indians while trapping this stream
in 1814). In 1819 Donald McKenzie called it the Skamnaugh, after a
band of local natives.[62]

The other two tributaries Milton Sublette intended to exploit were
the Payette and the Weiser rivers. Meek related:

After the incident of the pin and the fishes, Sublette's party kept on to the north, coursing along up Payette's River to Payette Lake, where he camped, and the men went out trapping. A party of four, consisting of Meek, Antoine Godin, Louis Leaugar, and Small, proceeded to the north as far as the Salmon river and beyond, to the head of one of its tributaries, where the present city of Florence is located.[63]

Wyeth learned that Sublette had tried to ascend the Owyhee River, the next major tributary of the Snake west of the Bruneau. But due to the strenuous nature of the country, which wore down already-weakened men and horses, they abandoned that stream and forged their way over to the Bruneau. Milton Sublette and Fraeb had arrived at the Shoshone village at the Bruneau's junction with the Snake the day after Wyeth had led his men onward. Sublette had clearly traveled farther west than Wyeth after parting ways the previous month, so the reported "large stream running S. W." could have been the Humboldt River in what is today northern Nevada. If Sublette only "saw" the Humboldt, reports of him trapping it that summer were incorrect.

On September 28, Wyeth followed his Indian guide north about twenty-five miles overland to the mouth of Benson Creek. His trail closely approximated what would become a portion of the Oregon Trail through this area in a few short decades. Wyeth dropped back down onto the Snake River for the final few miles to the creek upon which he would camp before heading into the Blue Mountains.

Earlier wayfarers had also stayed at this Benson Creek location. On December 23, 1811, Wilson Price Hunt had overnighted at the site. The next morning, as he bid farewell to the Snake, Hunt recorded that thoughts of that current "will always cause us some moments of unhappiness."[64] The following year, Robert Stuart camped there on August 12.[65] John C. Fremont stopped there in 1843 and wrote in his journal, "we hear the roar, and see below us the commencement of rapids where it enters among the hills."[66] The site at Benson Creek came to be known as Farewell Bend to overland emigrant trains. Here, after following the Snake River for upwards of 350 miles, covered wagons would veer away as the Snake entered the upper reaches of Hell's Canyon, with its rushing current headed for the Seven Devils Mountains.

Wyeth followed his Indian guide from Farewell Bend to a new campsite on Burnt River without saying how many miles he traveled with the reunited group. Twenty-two miles, a likely distance, places them in the vicinity of present Durkee, Oregon.

Tradition has it that Burnt River derived its name from either charred timber on the banks of its upper reaches or from the cauterized appearance of rocks at the river's mouth.[67] The stream was known to the Astorians in 1812 as Wood Pile River. Ogden wrote both Brulé and Burnt in the journal he kept while trapping there in the winter of 1825-26.[68] Work's journal also described his travels along Burnt River in 1830-31.[69]

September 29 - October 3, 1832   *Burnt River*

29th   We lay at same camp.

30th   Mooved about 5 miles   the creek running about W.

1 Oct   Mooved camp along same creek about 5 miles still W.

2nd   At same camp   at this place the bears dung was plenty but we saw but one.

3rd   Moved camp about 15 miles   creek still west and trail good.

A day of rest helped men and animals build up strength for the rough road they would travel through the Blue Mountains. Wyeth knew few landmarks, and so he never named this range in his 1832 journal. He would be able to describe many more by the time of his second expedition, in 1834. David Thompson referred to the range first as the Shawpatin Mountains, in July 1811, but a month later called them the Blue Mountains – likely the earliest mention of this name.[70] Ross Cox pointed out "the chain of craggy mountains" visible in the distance, and reported that "from their colour the Canadians call this chain *Les Montagnes Bleues*" (the Blue Mountains).[71]

The trail from Burnt Creek to Fort Walla Walla was used frequently by Hudson's Bay and Native Americans. John Work described this section of trail in his journal, though he traveled the reverse direction Wyeth was about to undertake.[72]

For several days, the party marched upstream through the Burnt River Canyon. The trail, for the most part, kept to the north bank.

October 4, 1832   *Burnt River*

4th   With an Indian and 4 men I left camp in order to explore this creek the N.W. trail here leaving it   after leaving camp I proceed over bad hills about 18 miles and encamped among cut rocks on the same creek it here being W. by S.   during the march we observed a range of high snowy mountains to the N. of us but wether on our side of the river or not could not determine.

Taking time for a brief exploration, Wyeth entered the north fork of Burnt River. From a high point, Wyeth spotted the Wallowa Mountains whose highest point is Sacagawea Peak (9,838 ft.).

October 5-7, 1832   *Blue Mountains*

5th   Made about 5 miles through intolerable cut rocks   some beaver

6th   At same camp.

7th   5 mils on same creek which bears W. by S   here left it.   having sent a messenger to camp with orders to proceed on the route to Wallah Wallah and stering north passed some snow clad mounts. which we walked up with bare feet and after 25 mils struck a small run going into the next creek   during this day we passed through an immense forest of pine of different kinds and unknown to us altho very similar to some of ours   on these mountains we found unripe service berrys, cherrys and thorn apple all of which are gone on the rivers   it snowed and rained most of the day   many of the pines were 4 feet through

---

October 5 saw Wyeth's company work its way five miles north, leaving the branch of Burnt River and ending the day somewhere along Rock Creek, trapping as it went. Wyeth sent an express back to the main camp with orders to head north though Ball indicated this instruction was given on the same day Wyeth split from the group.

Wyeth noted "an immense forest of pine of different kinds"; the Blue Mountains were home to some of the largest stands of old growth forest, particularly ponderosa pine, in North America.[73]

October 8-9, 1832   *Blue Mountains*

8th   Moved 4 miles to the main creek and laid down cold and hungry and supperless hoping that our traps would give us beaver in the morning

9th   Got 7 beaver and went to eating like good fellows mooved this day 6 miles down   creek here running about N.

Wyeth had taken care earlier to stock up on salmon and place the men on rations, knowing that no Indians would be encountered on this route. Nevertheless, by the time the group camped on Rock Creek, nothing to eat remained. Ball's party, following a few days behind Wyeth, were similarly short on food. He wrote "not knowing just where we were, and not taking the precaution to buy a supply of dried fish, and meeting no more Indians, we soon got short of food."[74]

As luck would have it, the morning found seven beaver upon which Wyeth's men dined greedily.

October 10, 1832   *Baker Valley*

10th   Moved N. and down creek about 15 miles and found the rest of the party who had come on the main trail in an average N.W. direction about 45 miles   This day rain   this creek from where we struck it to this place runs in an extensive plain of fertile soile equal to the best I ever saw of about 5 mils average width   here we raised a great smoke and am told by our Indian that the Nez Perces will see it and come to smoke with us

Working downstream, Wyeth found the Powder River in today's Baker Valley, Oregon. He had traveled fifty-eight extra miles to reach the same destination as his men who had followed the main trail. With the Wallowa Mountains to the east and the Elkhorn Range to the west, Wyeth noted the suitability of the basin for settlement.

The Astorian parties traveled both directions through this Powder River region in 1811-12.[75] It was near here that Marie Dorion, wife of Hunt's guide/interpreter Pierre Dorion, gave birth while on the trail to Astoria.[76] Ogden trapped on the Powder River in the fall of 1827 and experienced similar weather.[77] The river got its name from a Chinook term, "polallie illahe" (powdered or sandy soil).[78]

The New Englanders had ventured into Nez Perce territory and attempted to contact them by building a smoky fire. Though Wyeth did not give a reason, no doubt he hoped to trade for food. It is surprising they never attempted to catch their own salmon.

October 11, 1832   *Grande Ronde Valley*

11th   To the S.W. of us is a range of snow clad Mts.   the Indian says it is 7 days to Wallah Wallah.   This creek runs about N.E. by E.

11th   started at 8 ock and moved about N.N.W. 30 miles over high ground of good soil

---

Unlike previous duplications, these two entries may have been made on the same day, rather than an error in timekeeping. The reunited brigade traveled north thirty miles, entering the Grande Ronde Valley through which flowed a river of the same name. *Grande Ronde*, French for "great circle," was visited by many early trappers, particularly those from the Northwest and Hudson's Bay companies. Stuart called this river the Glaise, the French word for clay.[79] In 1827, Ogden noted in his official journal that the brigade "reached Clay River or commonly called Riviére de Grande Ronde."[80] Bonneville showed it on his 1837 map as the Way-lee-way, a phonetic transcription of the Nez Perce name for the river, referring to its yellowish color.[81]

October 12, 1832   *Blue Mountains*

12th   Left the party after killing a horse of the poorest kind for food in order to go ahead to find indians or whites or food   The party here remained one day in a valley of about 20 miles long and 15 wide of a very fertile soil   in this valley saw extensive camps of Indians about one month old   here they find salmon in a creek running through it and dig the Kamas root but not an Indian was here at this time   we put out in a N.W. direction and assended the hills which soon became wooded with good timber   our course this day was about N.N.W. and 40 miles   I had with me an Indian and three men and a little horse meat   we camped this night in the woods without water.

Ball remarked on the meat of the exhausted horse, "as hungry as we were, we did not relish it. We vowed if we killed another we would take a young one. The meat of a good horse tastes like venison." Wyeth and four companions pressed ahead toward Fort Walla Walla hoping to find succor for his men along the way.[82]

Ball wrote that Wyeth took the best horses but promised to "get food and send back for us." Ball also recalled that he was instructed to take command of the remaining crew and follow on the next day.[83]

To the Nez Perce, the Grande Ronde Valley was a key locale for gathering camas. Summer was prime for digging camas, but another harvest was typically made in the early fall. William Clark first encountered this tribe on September 20, 1805, in the Weippe Prairie, about two hundred miles to the northeast, where the women were laying in their winter supply of the root.[84]

Forty miles was a remarkable distance for a day's travel, particularly for near-starving travelers. The trail, mainly following a route that would become the Old Oregon Trail Highway through the mountains, took Wyeth past the modern town sites of Meacham and Kamela, Oregon. From there it led over Deadman Pass and to the edge of the Columbia Plateau.

Like Wyeth, John C. Fremont would find the timber impressive when he explored the area in 1843:

*October 20 After travelling occasionally through open places in the
forest, we were obliged to cut a way through a dense body of timber,
from which we emerged on the open mountainside, where we found a
number of small springs, and encamped after a journey of ten miles.*[85]

October 13, 1832   *Umatilla River*

*13th   Arose early and continued our route until 9 ock and
stopped for breakfast of bad Horse meat on a creek of
some size where we found the red thorn apple and a few
cherries   after 3 hours stop we moved across the creek which
runs West and is called Ottillah   on ascending the opposite
bluff we saw a smoke about 20 mils down on it to which we
went and found some poor horses in charge of a squaw and
some children   the men were all out hunting   they had no food
but rose berrys of which we made our supper   they were much
frighted at our approach there having been some Indians of this
tribe viz Walla Walla killed by the snakes above, and this family
was murdered the night after we left them*

The river Wyeth encountered that morning was the Umatilla. This
river's name was Anglicized from a Nez Perce term meaning "water rip-
pling over sand."[86] Primary documents of the early 1800s contain many
variant spellings of the name. Lewis and Clark, returning east, passed its
mouth on April 27, 1806, and recorded the name as "Youmalolam."[87] In
1811, Alexander Ross called it the "Umatallow" and Hunt wrote "Euo-
talla." Stuart noted the stream as "Umatalla" a year later.[88] Bonneville
labeled the watercourse "Ottolais" on his 1837 map.

This entry may have been written or completed after Wyeth reached
Fort Walla Walla, which could explain how he knew the Indian family
had been killed the night after he left them.

Under Ball's leadership, the rest of the brigade was making its way
north at the same time. The ground was frozen; travel was tough, but
the men found an Indian trail into the Grande Ronde Valley. Several of
them had opted not to pack any of the dried horse meat and now, being
hungry, stole from those who did. Ball, "having schooled myself to one
meal a day," had been able to save a few rations of dried salmon.[89]

October 14-18, 1832   *Fort Walla Walla*
Written October 20

In the morning of the 14th we put out about N. and arrived at fort Walla Walla about 5 ock in the evening   distance 30 miles   near the fort the river Walla Walla was crossed which is about 75 feet wide and about 2 feet deep   current moderate   the size of the last creek passed   I was received in the most hospitable and gentlemanly manner by Peanbron the agent for this post   the fort is of no strength merely sufficient to frighten Indians   mounting 2 small cannon having two bastions at the opposite corners of a square enclosure   there were 6 whites here.   My party arrived on the 18th having fared for food in the same manner as myself but for a longer time.   They met a Nez Perce village on the 16th and got a supply of food   they passed my trail and went N. of it and struck the main river above the fort   they brough[t] in all the horses   At the post we saw a bull and cow & calf, hen & cock, punkins, potatoes, corn, all of which looked strange and unnatural and like a dream.   They gave me a decent change of cloths which was very acceptable   I took a ride up the river 9 miles to the junction of Lewis River which comes in from the S.E. and soon takes a S. course   the Columbia comes here from the N.W.

This entry, written several days after Wyeth's arrival at HBC's Fort Walla Walla, catches up on events through October 18, when Ball and the other seven men arrived to rejoin him. After seven long months of travel, the Pacific Fur Company had finally reached the Columbia River.

The Walla Walla River, as well as the fort built upon its bank, shared their name with a local Indian term meaning "small, rapid stream."[90] This waterway, which empties through the south bank of the Columbia River, was noted by Lewis and Clark in 1805-06 as the "Wal-ler wal ler," spelled variously throughout their journals. A Native American tribe, denoted by the Corps of Discovery Captains as the Walula, lived on this river.[91] Stuart pointed out in 1812 that the river "possesses a good many beaver."[92]

Wyeth arrived at Fort Walla Walla in the late afternoon of October 14. This fort had been built in the summer of 1818 by the Northwest Company under Donald McKenzie. It was originally christened as Fort

MAP 5   *Fort Walla Walla to Fort Vancouver and back, via Columbia River, 1832-33*

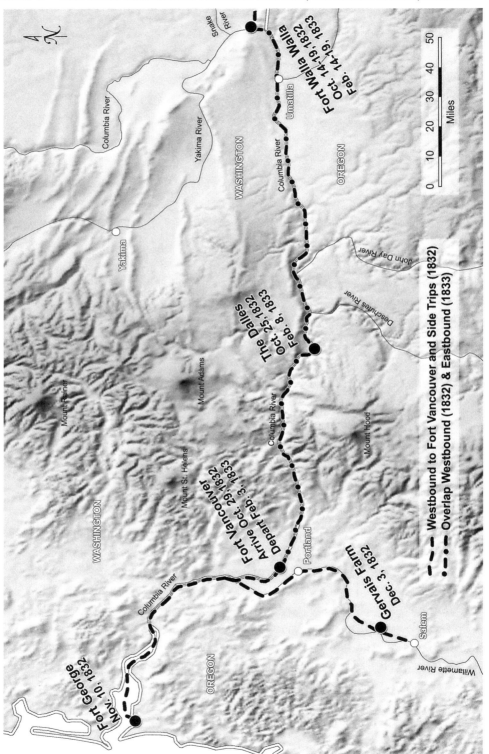

Nez Perce but passed to the Hudson's Bay Company when the two firms merged in 1821 and, shortly after, was renamed Fort Walla Walla.

The site was on the Columbia, a few miles downstream from the mouth of Snake River, which Wyeth inspected during a brief tour. Fort Walla Walla held a commanding view from the south shore of the Walla Walla. Alexander Ross noted that the surrounding landscape had been depleted:

> By far the greater part of the timber had to be collected in the bush and conducted by water the distance of a hundred miles, for not a tree or shrub was on the spot itself! ... [The natives] insisted on our paying for the timber we were collecting. They prohibited our hunting or fishing. They affixed an exorbitant price of their own to every article of trade, and they insulted any of the hands whom they met alone.[93]

This passage helps explain the need for fortification. Although Wyeth deemed the fort "of no strength," Ball described it as "built of upright timbers set in the ground. The timbers were some fifteen or eighteen feet high. A small stockade, with stations or bastions at the corners for lookouts."[94] Apparently, the fort was strong enough to deter the natives from outright attack.

In 1837, Narcissa Whitman would visit the post for the first time, and wrote about its abundant foodstuffs and hospitality:

> The dooryard was filled with hens turkeys pigeons & in another place we saw cows hogs & goats in abundance, & I think the largest & fattest cattle & swine I ever saw ... Having arranged our things, we were soon called to a feast of mellons, the finest I think I ever saw or tasted. The mushmelon was the largest measuring eighteen inches in length, fifteen arround the small end and nineteen around the largest end. You may be assured we were not any of us satisfied or willing to leave the table untill we had filled our plates with chips.[95]

Pierre Pambrun, whom Wyeth called "Peanbron," had been appointed by HBC Chief Factor John McLoughlin as the fort's chief clerk in March 1832. HBC Governor George Simpson kept notes on many of his key personnel in what he referred to as a "Character Book," each man identified by number rather than name. After Simpson's death, a single sheet was discovered among his papers that proved to be the code to solving identities of those described. Pambrun was number 70. Simpson described Pambrun as

> *A Canadian about 45 years of age – 17 years in the Service. – An active, steady dapper little fellow, is anxious to be useful but is wanting in judgment and deficient in Education: – full of "pluck," has a very good opinion of himself ... Does not manage the business of his Post well, owing more to a want of discretion & foresight than to indifference or inattention.*[96]

Simpson had visited the fort just a few years earlier and reduced the complement of men assigned to Pambrun from eleven to the six Wyeth found upon his arrival. While mediocre in terms of fur harvest, Fort Walla Walla's proximity to the Cayuse and Nez Perce tribes, famous for immense herds of prime horses, was integral to keeping the HBC supplied with mounts and pack animals. Several Snake Country Expeditions, from both Northwest Company and HBC, were outfitted from Fort Walla Walla.[97]

Though destroyed by an accidental fire in 1841, the fort was reconstructed out of brick, and stayed in operation until 1855.[98]

The fort was an important jumping-off point for the interior, particularly the Snake River country. Consequently, many travelers became acquainted with Pambrun, including fur trade notables Benjamin Bonneville, John Townsend, Joe Meek, Robert Newell, Marcus Whitman, William Craig and numerous Americans traveling the Oregon Trail.[99]

Although Simpson's evaluation of his chief clerk's management skills and HBC loyalty may have been lukewarm, Bonneville ran up against another side of Pambrun altogether:

> *As he stood in need of some supplies for his journey, he applied to purchase them of Mr. Pambrune; but soon found the difference between being treated as a guest, or as a rival trader. The worthy superintendent, who had extended to him all the genial rites of*

hospitality, now suddenly assumed a withered-up aspect and demeanor, and observed that, however he might feel disposed to serve him, personally, he felt bound by his duty to the Hudson's Bay Company, to do nothing which should facilitate or encourage the visits of other traders among the Indians in that part of the country.[100]

Pambrun was promoted to chief trader in 1839 and retained that position until his death in 1841. In May of that year, he was thrown from a horse; the injuries sustained in the mishap proved fatal.[101]

While Wyeth enjoyed getting to know Pambrun and Fort Walla Walla, Ball continued moving the men north on the trail from Grand Ronde Valley, as Wyeth had ordered. October 14 for these travelers brought a clear day except for large cumulous clouds gathered on the western horizon. Ball noticed one that seemed stationary and after watching it for an hour realized the "cloud" was "the grand and snowy Mount Hood," which the entire party "hailed as a discovery."[102]

By the end of the day, Ball's troop had descended from the mountains and found itself on the Columbia Plateau, "a prairie extending without apparent limit before us."[103] The men were weary but the horses more so. Ball declared that "an old pack mule turned around to me the moment I dismounted to be unpacked."[104]

On October 15, Ball urged the men onward, selecting the deepest worn trail among several choices. The next day, he proposed to kill another horse for food – this time "the best conditioned one" – but the men agreed they could endure one more day. On October 17, the Walla Walla River brought them to an Indian encampment where they were able to obtain some dried bear meat and elderberries. Benefitting from his extra bits of horded salmon, Ball "did not feel as ravenous as the other men, who ate until I urged them to stop, for fear of the result."[105]

The next day, a fifteen-mile ride brought the famished and exhausted men to the fort, four days behind their Captain, who had apparently forgotten to send relief to the trailing party. According to Ball, once at Fort Walla Walla, the Bostonians tasted bread for the first time since June 1 and the forks of the Platte.[106]

Mount Hood viewed from The Dalles. The highest mountain in Oregon, this inactive volcano was a major landmark for travelers on the Columbia River. When John Ball spotted it on October 14, 1832, the party "hailed [it] as a discovery." JOHN MIX STANLEY; UNIVERSITY OF MICHIGAN MUSEUM OF ART. GIFT OF MRS. EDITH STANLEY BAYLES AND THE LATE MRS. JANE C. STANLEY 1940.426

> **October 19, 1832**   *Columbia River*
> *Written October 20*
>
> *On the 19th I took leave of my hospitable entertainer in one of the Cos. barges with my party leaving my horses in his charge at the fort and proceeded down the river about 4 mils and s[t]opped to tighten our boat   the river forms fine eddies to work up with and about 3 mile current down   the 2nd run of fish failed this year in the river and the Indians are picking up the most nauseous dead fish for food   the course of the river about S.W.*

After five days, Wyeth left his livestock in the care of Pambrun at Fort Walla Walla, and set off in a company boat with the eleven remaining men of the PTC. They were at last headed down the Columbia River on their way to the Pacific Ocean. Fort Vancouver, where Wyeth would have anticipated meeting the supply-laden *Sultana*, was just ten days downriver. Presumably, Wyeth's long-range plans would have included research on the best locations to establish PTC settlements and trading posts on the Columbia.

The boat Wyeth called a "barge" was commonly known as a *bateau* – a flat-bottomed, shallow-drafted boat similar in length to the York boat in use at HBC posts in Canada. Bateaux were narrower in the beam and smaller in capacity, but the lighter weight was better suited to the long, steep portages of the Columbia River.[107]

Four miles downriver, the two HBC employees manning the boat stopped to "tighten" it. Bateaux were nailed and gummed with a mixture of sawpit resin and tallow. En route, the vessels had to be re-gummed frequently because sunlight melted the pitch above the water line, opening the seam. Tightening involved beaching the craft, turning it bottom up, and letting the boat dry. Then a burning torch was moved slowly along the gum line to soften it, while a small spatula was used to smooth it back into the seam. More pitch could be added if necessary.[108]

Wyeth noted that the autumn salmon run had not occurred as the Indians had anticipated. Understanding the salmon cycle was integral for survival along the Columbia, and for survival in any business involving salmon, as Wyeth knew. The midsummer run was huge, the river choked with fish swimming upstream to their breeding beds. The fall run brought the leaner and drier dog, or chum, salmon. Their flat taste caused the Astorians, twenty years earlier, to derisively call them "fish with seven barks" since after cleaning and cooking, the fish were found to have "almost no nutritive substance."[109] The quality of the fall salmon run was of no consequence to Wyeth's fish-pickling scheme, because he had his eye on the premium summer catch.

That night, the men climbed onto the bluffs above the river's current to camp. Ball remembered seeing the Cascade Range and snow-clad Mount Hood to the west.[110]

October 20, 1832	*Columbia River*

20th   Left the beach at sunrise the River still S.W. and kept on until about noon when a furious wind arose from the S.W. and stopped our further progress   the sand flew so as to obscure the air   Here we traded a few fish from the natives for Hooks awls powder &c   made 10 miles during which we passed some rapids of a bad character at which in times of high water portage is necessary   the gese are numerous seated on the banks of the river.   River W. by S.   a large snowy mountain S.W. by W. ahead which the river leaves to the left called by the French "Montagne de Neige"   made 10 miles

Ball found the Indians in this section of the river "not so respectable in appearance as those we had seen," noting they subsisted mostly on "bad fish and a few roots."[111]

Mount Hood was often called *Montagne de Neige* ("snowy mountain") by HBC men. In 1818, two Canadian explorers were said to have made their way into the region of modern Dog River, east of the peak, and climbed a glacier upon it.[112] Mount Hood (elevation 11,240 feet) was named in 1792 by Lieutenant William Broughton, a member of Captain George Vancouver's expedition, in honor of British admiral Lord Samuel Hood.[113]

October 21, 1832   *Columbia River*

*21st   Wind same but more moderate   Put down the river still
W by S.   passed a large Island at the lower end of which we
stopped for the night.   Ther. 22 deg.   Made 16 miles during
the day   our boatman bought a colt which we found fine
eating   shagg and gese plenty*

Wyeth's party was in the vicinity of the present-day Umatilla National Wildlife Refuge, just downstream from modern Irrigon, Oregon. Many of the islands and rapids in this area are now under the waters of Lake Wallula, the reservoir behind the McNary Dam. The thermometer dipped below freezing as autumn deepened.

The Indians who supplied the colt were acquainted with the HBC boatmen, according to Ball, who wrote that "Although we had brought plenty of food from the fort for the voyage, the horse did not taste like the poor one killed by us in the Blue Mountains." Indeed, Ball said, it was "as good meat as I had ever eaten."[114]

The "shagg" Wyeth noted was a cormorant; the bird's short, upright crest was known as a "shag." As various species of this sea fowl were discovered by English-speaking sailors and explorers throughout the world, some of the birds were called cormorants and some shags, depending on whether they had crests or not.[115]

October 22, 1832   *Columbia River*

*22nd   Made 30 miles   wind moderate and no rapids of much
dificulty   stopped at night at a village where was a chief sick
to whom our conductor administered some medicine and bled
him   his eyes were exceeding yellow and his blood after
standing a short time was covered with a scum of yellowish
green   he gave us a horse to eat of which he had 260 in fine
order and of good breed   we found the meat equal to any
beaf and quite different from the poor and sick old ones we
had eaten.   They here sell Horses for 100 loads amunition 1
Blankett and 1/4 lb tobacco.*

Thirty miles down the Columbia took the bateau past Crow and Golgotha buttes, landing in the vicinity of today's Arlington, Oregon. The ailing chieftain they met here may have suffered from jaundice – an effect of conditions such as liver failure. Due to the liver's inability to release bilirubin into bile, the yellowish-green-colored substance builds up in the bloodstream, causing a yellow discoloration of the skin, the whites of the eyes and other tissues. This discoloration in the whites of the eye had led to the expression "to look at something with jaundiced eyes" by about 1800.[116]

It is doubtful that bleeding the chief would have affected his condition. Bloodletting was described by Hippocrates in 400 B.C. Eighteenth- and nineteenth-century medical practice included the technique as a mainstay. Today, known as therapeutic phlebotomy, it is reserved for a few specific disorders but has largely been abandoned.[117]

October 23, 1832   *Columbia River*

23rd   The chief much better and we left him Yesterday   our people in search of wood of which there is none but drift   here found a pile which they brought to our fire but were soon told by the natives that they had robbed the dead   we will avoid the like mistake in the future   we made this day 28 miles during which distance we passed one bad rapid and the river John Day from a trader of that name.   This river is large but obstructed by rapids and enters from the S.   is 79 miles below Walla Walla   no rain as yet but we are informed that the rain is now constant below the falls   we see Indians every few miles who come off to trade what little articles they have   sometimes with nothing to beg a chew of tobacco sometimes with a little wood for fuel   sometimes with two 3, one or 1/2 a fish a few berrys   our conductor appears to have a wife at each stopping place   4 already and how many more sable beauties god only knows   these Indians are tolerably honest but will steal a little.

On the rocky barrens of the Columbia Plateau, finding firewood was a problem. Discovering a pile of wood, Wyeth's men freely helped themselves only to find out it was a burial site for local natives. Indians in the Northwest sometimes interred the dead in vaults made from slabs of boards, broken canoes and stacked wood. William Clark described such a crypt in his journal entry for October 20, 1805:

> On the upper part of this Island we discovered an Indian vault our curiosity induced us to examine the methot those nativs practicd in disposeing the dead, the Vaut was made by broad poads [boards] and pieces of Canoes leaning on a ridge pole which was Suported by 2 forks Set in the ground Six feet in hight in an easterly and westerly direction and about 60 feet in length, and 12 feet wide, in it I observed great numbers of humane bones of every description perticularly in a pile near the Center of the vault [118]

John Ball, perhaps realizing what he had seen after the fact, provided a similar description:

> Their way of burial here was to wrap their bodies in their clothing and mats, and place them in canoes, which they place on some conspicuous place on shore or on an island, one is called Coffin Island, then cover the boat with boards, split slabs, and load them down with stone so that the wolves or other animals could not get at the body and put the deceased's property in and about the canoe. To steal from a grave they view a great crime.[119]

Today, there are two John Day Rivers in Oregon: one in the northwest, and the one Wyeth was passing in the northeast portion of the state. Both are tributaries of the Columbia and both are named for the same member of the Wilson Price Hunt Astorian overland party. Virginia backwoodsman Day and Ramsay Crooks had fallen behind Hunt and the others while in the Snake River region in the winter of 1811-12. In the vicinity of Wyeth's northeastern river, they were robbed by Indians, leaving them naked and destitute, without so much as flint and steel. A party from Fort Astoria led by Robert Stuart later rescued them. From Astoria, Day started east with Robert Stuart the following year but was escorted back to the post when he exhibited symptoms of derangement. He recovered and went to work for the Northwest Company when Astoria passed into its hands. Day died in the Salmon River Mountains of Idaho in 1820.[120]

Lewis and Clark tried to name the northeastern stream Le Page River in honor of Expedition member Jean Baptiste Le Page, but by late 1825, Ogden would write of reaching "Dey's River." That name stuck.[121]

Wyeth's HBC boatman had apparently acquired a number of spouses along the river. This was not an uncommon practice of the day. Michel Laframboise, for example, boasted to Charles Wilkes that "He ... travelled in all parts of the country, and says that he has a wife of high rank in every tribe, by which means he has insured his safety."[122]

October 24, 1832   *Columbia River*

24th   Started about 9 and after about 6 miles [written here but crossed out] passed the grand falls of the Columbia just above which a small river puts into the Columbia about the size of the small rivers above the Wallah for instance   these falls now the water is low are about 25 feet   when the water is high these falls are covered   the water not having a sufficient vent below the water here rises about 40 feet   just before arriving at the falls are considerable rapids   the falls are easily passed in boats at high water   we hired the Indians about 50 for a quid of tobacco each to carry our boat about 1 mile round the falls   the goods we carried ourselves   shortly after passing the falls we passed what are called the dalles (small) or where the river is damed up between the banks steep and high of not more than 100 feet apart through which the whole waters of the mighty Columbia are forced with much noise and uproar   I passed through with some Indians while my men went round they not being good boatmen enough to trust and frighted withall.   We are now camped at the Great Dalles which are still narrower and more formidable than the small having stoped after making 20 miles the wind being high and unfavorable for passing at the gorge of this pass   the water rises[?] by the mark on the rock at least 50 feet forming a complete lock to the falls above the back water covering them entirely.   The Indians are thieves but not dangerous   before us and apparently in the river rises the most formidable mountain we have seen   the country ahead is clothed with forest to the river side which has not been the case before and the western horizon is covered by a dense cloud denoting the region of constant rain during the winter.

Wyeth and his men had been coursing through the Columbia Gorge, a series of waterfalls, rapids and canyons, and on October 24 contended with a cascade known variously as the Celilo, Columbia or Great falls, and sometimes simply as the Chutes. The river that put in above these falls was the Deschutes, so called not for having a waterfall but for being close to the Chutes.[123] This was a busy fishing and trading location for Native Americans.

The name Celilo was Indian jargon for "floating sand cloud" suggestive of the dense swirls of sand that often wafted through the air on the area's windy days. For Lewis and Clark, these were the "Great Falls" of the Columbia.[124] In low water such as Wyeth found, the drop could be as much as forty-seven feet. During spring, increased water volume submerged the falls enough to enable boats to shoot the rapids safely, if the crew was brave enough.[125] Fortunately, Wyeth found Indians there whom he hired to assist in portaging the boat across a rocky point on the north bank. A "quid" has been defined as the amount of tobacco typically put into the mouth at one time.[126]

The site had been noted frequently by earlier explorers. For Lewis and Clark on the Columbia, this cataract was the first major barrier the Corps of Discovery encountered. The portage, with the help of local Indians, took all of October 23, 1805. Hunt recorded passing Celilo Falls on January 31, 1812, and Stuart camped there to repair a leaky boat in July of the same year. Naturalist David Douglas joined Work's Hudson's Bay brigade at "the Chute" in July, 1826.[127]

Three miles below Celilo Falls, the PTC came upon the Dalles, which meant "sluice" or "flagstone," a reference to the columnar basaltic rocks carved by the current. This stretch of rapids consisted of a lower and an upper cascade.

This first or upper obstacle, the "short narrows," was also called Les Petites Dalles, Ten Mile Rapid, and the Little or Upper Dalles. In modern times, Lake Celilo reservoir inundates both falls and narrows.[128]

Gabriel Franchére's 1814 mention of the Dalles may be the earliest written description of these narrows:

> On [April] 12th, we arrived at a rapid called the Dalles: this is
> a channel cut by nature through the rocks, which are here almost
> perpendicular: the channel is from 150 to 300 feet wide, and about

Wyeth ran into several obstacles on his trip down the Columbia River, including a portage around Celilo Falls, photographed here by Benjamin Gifford circa 1900. The falls are now under the waters of Lake Celilo Reservoir. OREGON HISTORICAL SOCIETY, # BB000093

*two miles long. The whole body of the river rushes through it, with
great violence, and renders navigation impracticable. The portage
occupied us till dusk.*[129]

Ball described walking past the "wonderous chute of flume through
which all the water rushes at its low stage, but the boat passed through
it," confirming Wyeth's claim that the men had been too frightened to
shoot these rapids. No doubt the HBC boatmen piloted the craft safely
through with Wyeth hanging on for dear life.[130]

That night, they camped at the second or lower obstacle, the Big
Dalles, sometimes called the Long Narrows, Five Mile Rapid and Les
Grand or Great Dalles, ten miles downriver from the smaller rapid.[131]

Wyeth pointed out that the landscape ahead was changing to forested slopes on the river banks – the party would soon experience the
lush rain forests of the Pacific Northwest. But, for a few days more, they
floated through what Scottish naturalist David Douglas depicted as
"nothing but extensive plains and barren hills, with the greater part of
the herbage scorched and dead by the intense heat."[132]

October 25, 1832   *Columbia River*

*25th   Made this day 6 miles and passed the great dalles
similar to the small ones which we passed yesterday but still
narrower being 75 feet about in width   through this pass we
went with an unloaded boat at an immense speed   the goods
and Baggage were carried past on the backs of my men and
some Indians hired for that purpose   my men not being good
boatmen and timorous I hired Indians to work ours through
going with them myself to learn the way   during part of this
day we had a fair wind   the river still W. by S.   here we saw
plenty of grey headed seals   we bought some bear meat from
the Indians which we found very fine.   We encamped for the
first time on the river among timber among which I saw a kind
of oak and ash.   Indians Plenty   one chief at whose lodge
we stopped a short time gave me some molasses obtained
from fort below to eat   He had a large stock of dried fish for
the winter   4 tons I should think roots &c   he was dressed
in the English stile Blue frock coat pants. & vest   comported*

In late October 1832, Wyeth and his men traveled through the turbulent Dalles (photographed here in 1915) using boats crewed by Hudson's Bay Company boatmen. This stretch of the Columbia was a mecca for Native salmon fishing. WASHINGTON STATE HISTORICAL SOCIETY

himself with much dignity   enquired my name particularly and repeated it over many times to impress it on his memory   his sister was the squaw of an American of the name of Bache who established a post on the river below the great dalles three years ago last fall and who was drowned in them with 11 others the following spring   the remains of the fort I saw as also the grave of the woman who died this fall and was buried in great state with sundry articles such as capeau vest pantaloons shirts &c.   A pole with a knob at the top is erected over her remains   at the foot of the Dalles is an island called the Isle of the Dead on which there are many sepulchers   these Indians usually inter their dead on the Islands in the most romantic scituations where the souls of the dead can feast themselves with the roar of the mighty an eternal waters which in life time aforded them sustenance and will to all eternity to their posterity.

After Lewis and Clark, the Astorians were among the first Euro-Americans to describe the Big Dalles. Ross Cox portrayed them as "a succession of boiling whirlpools."[133]

Alexander Ross explained that through this bend of the Columbia River

the whole body of water must pass. Through this gap it rushes with great impetuosity; the foaming surges dash through the rocks with terrific violence; no craft, either large or small, can venture there in safety. During floods, this obstruction, or ledge of rocks, is covered with water, yet the passage of the narrows is not thereby improved.[134]

The portage around the Big Dalles was nine miles long. Again, Wyeth reported his men were too "timorous" to chance riding the bateau through the swift current though the Captain gamely tried to "learn the way." Though Wyeth harped on his men being fearful, while showing himself to be daring and brave, in fact, the men were doing their job (accompanying the portage), and Wyeth was doing his job (accompanying the boat). Once men and gear were safely past the narrows, they camped among trees for the first time since reaching the Columbia.

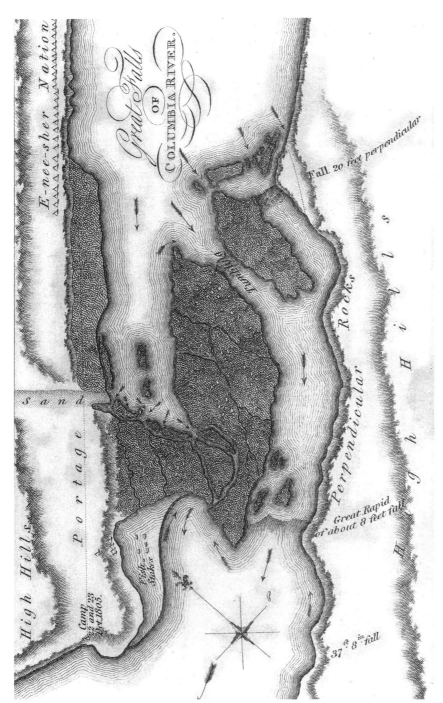

Wyeth arrived at the Great Falls of the Columbia River in October 1832. This map, drawn by William Clark at the same time of year but twenty-seven years earlier, shows the constriction of the river at the site. The portage trail is on the north bank. MANUSCRIPTS, ARCHIVES AND SPECIAL COLLECTIONS, WASHINGTON STATE UNIVERSITY LIBRARIES, PULLMAN, WA

Here, Wyeth encountered Nez Perce chief Tilki who traded extensively with the HBC posts along the river. He first appeared in the historical record in the journals of Fort Nez Perce on January 25, 1832, as "Watilka, chief of The Dalles."[135] Wyeth seemed delighted with the chief's European clothing, polite demeanor, and attempts to learn his name. Samuel Parker had several contacts with Tilki in 1835-36, describing him as "a man of more than ordinary talents."[136] Referring to the chief, John Townsend also spoke highly of the man:

> *I had often heard of this man, but I now saw him for the first time. His person is rather below the middle size, but his features are good, with a Roman cast, and his eye is deep black, and unusually fine. He appears to be remarkably intelligent, and half a century before the generality of his people in civilization.*[137]

Around 1829, an American and former employee of the HBC named Bache established an independent trading post at the Dalles. No known connection exists between this Bache and the former member of the Pacific Trading Company, Theophilus Bache, who turned back at Pierre's Hole. Captain Dominis, of the brig *Owyhee*, and Captain Thompson, of the schooner *Convoy*, had contracted with Bache to set up a business to compete with HBC by trading at the Big Eddy of the Great Dalles, where eastbound travelers began their portage around the narrows. Coincidentally, Dixie Wildes, the mariner with whom Wyeth had first contracted to ship goods to the mouth of the Columbia, was part owner of both of these vessels. Bache was married to chief Tilki's sister and thereby gained a strong liaison with the tribe.

Using his prior trade experience, Bache initially drew a significant amount of business away from the British, impacting forts Okanogan, Colvile and Walla Walla. HBC Chief Factor John McLoughlin soon responded by sending James Birnie and three men to compete with Bache, setting up their station across the river, on the south bank of the Columbia. The site, at the west end of the Lower (Big) Dalles, was near the eventual location of the Wascopam Mission. Birnie, backed by HBC's massive resources, consistently outbid the American for furs and drove prices for goods down. Bache's post went bust by mid-March 1830, and he once again became an HBC employee.[138]

The burial chamber Wyeth mentioned in this entry would have been similar to those discussed earlier. These crypts were frequently constructed on islands in the Columbia River, hence names like "Mount Coffin" appear in accounts by Irving, Ross, Franchére and others.[139] What Meriwether Lewis referred to as "Sepulchar Island" is known today as Memaloose Island, derived from a Chinook term meaning "land of the dead."[140] Wyeth's list of the woman's grave goods reveals that Euro-American clothing had infiltrated the culture of this tribe. Luxury goods such as a *capeau* (often spelled *capote*) or blanket coat, vest, pantaloons and shirts marked the grave as that of an elite person.[141]

October 26, 1832   *Columbia River*

26   After 30 miles of beautiful navigation with little current and fair strong wind and no rapids we arrived at the Cascade or lower obstruction of the river   here it is necessary to carry the boat and the Indians are all dead   only two women are left a sad remnant of a large number   their houses stripped to their frames are in view and their half buried dead   this portage will be a hard job   during this day I went ashore to a small lake near the river   I killed at one discharge of my double barrelled gun 5 of them which gave 5 of us a hearty supper   no rain as yet but constant appearance of it ahead   at these rapids are a great many seal   it is a mystery to me how they assend them.   The direction of the river is here about W by S. and a little snow on some of the highest of the hills   this day we passed the high mountain covered with snow hertofore mentioned   it is on the left of the river and is a more stupendous pile than any of the Rocky Mts.   Always covered with snow and is called the Snowy mountain.

The lower-most obstacle on the Columbia before Fort Vancouver was the Cascades Rapids. As the landscape became hillier and greener, the river became "broad, deep, and rapid, with several sunken rocks, scattered here and there, which often injure the canoes."[142] Here the rushing waters of the Columbia cut through the Cascade Mountains, dropping forty-five feet at high water in four and half unnavigable miles. The portage along the north bank varied in length from season to season:

Here we came to the cascade where the mighty river rushes for some miles through the break in the Cascade range of mountains, a continuation of the Nevada range of California. The mountain on the north side somewhat subsides giving a land pass way, but abrupt and thousands of feet high on the south side, down which leap from the immense height beautiful cascades.[143]

Wyeth's report of massive numbers of Native American deaths along this lower portion of the Columbia refers to an epidemic the Chinook people called "the cold sick" that began about 1830 and reached its peak in 1832, about the time the Bostonians drifted through. One witness reported that the high fevers, chills, muscle cramps, intestinal upsets and coughs resulted in vast devastation and that "scarcely one of the original race is now to be seen."[144]

Realizing that without local assistance the portage was going to be difficult, Wyeth temporarily avoided the work by going hunting. Most likely, the unnamed prey was some type of waterfowl, because the hunt took place at a small, nearby lake. Although the Bonneville Dam submerged the Cascades Rapids in 1938, there are still a number of small lakes in the vicinity, Wauna Lake being one of the largest.

Just below the Cascades, Lewis and Clark had, like Wyeth, remarked on the number of harbor seals found in the Columbia. So many, that on March 31, 1806, they named a river after "the great abundance of those animals" seen about its confluence. The stream they called Seal River is today known as the Washougal River, from the Chinookan term for "rushing water."[145]

Mount Hood, a "stupendous pile" to the south of the river, was again within view during this day of downstream travel.

October 27, 1832   *Columbia River*

27th   in the morning commenced carrying the boat and goods which we finished at 1 ock. and making 9 miles in all stopped to repair the boat which was leaky from damage sustained in carrying   rained all this day and saw but two[?] Indians

The Hudson's Bay Company sawmill provided lumber for Fort Vancouver and boards for export to Hawaii. Built in 1828, it was the first sawmill in the Pacific Northwest. JOHN MIX STANLEY; WASHINGTON STATE HISTORICAL SOCIETY

Without Native labor, it fell to Wyeth and his men to muscle the bateau and goods over the portage to navigable water. In 1811, Ross Cox complained that "the path was narrow and dangerous, one part greatly obstructed by slippery rocks and another ran through a thick wood."[146] Cox bitterly described this portage of "up hills, down hills, and side hills most of the way ... to say that there is not a worse path under the sun would perhaps be going a step too far, but to say that, for difficulty and danger, few could equal it would be saying but the truth."[147] With their boat and gear around the Cascades Rapids, the party finally reached tidewater on this date.[148]

October 28, 1832   *Columbia River*

28th   With a fair wind and a little rain we decended the river at a great rate   on the route we killed a goose which dropped in the water   a white headed Eagle from a distance seeing this took occasion to come   he seized it and lifted it into the air a few feet but our near approach frighted him away   made this day 26 miles and stopped at a saw mill belonging to the H.B. Co. under charge of a Mr. Cawning[?] a gentleman who came here 22 years since with a Mr Hunt   he is in the service of the Co.   We were treated by him with the greatest kindness   he gave us mocasins and food in plenty

---

Fall rains were becoming more frequent as the Pacific Trading Company drifted downriver. The HBC sawmill at Fort Vancouver was located on Mill Plain, about six miles upriver from the post. In a lengthy dispatch to Governor Simpson in 1831, Chief Factor John McLoughlin informed his superior that the mill had been rebuilt and "It commenced regular work, on the improved plan, in the middle of April ... during which time it cut 90,000 feet of inch boards ... The Saw Mill works from 6 to 10 saws and when in full operation employs 25 men." Vast quantities of lumber not needed at the fort were shipped to Hawaii.[149] Ball was surprised and intrigued by several of the mill's employees:

*Stopped over night at a sawmill of the company on a creek, and saw
there, two strange looking men, saw at once they could be neither
Caucasian, Indian or African. And so it proved, they were Kanakas,
Sandwich Islanders, in the employ of the traders. And the mill was
under the superintendence of one of Astor's men who had remained
in the country.*[150]

People of Hawaiian descent had been involved in the maritime
and fur trades since the late 1700s. "Kanaka" was a Hawaiian term for a
native Hawaiian commoner. These laborers were also called Sandwich
Islanders, from an early Euro-American name for the island chain. In
1776, when Captain James Cook first arrived in Hawaii, he christened
these islands in the Pacific after the sponsor of his voyage, the Earl of
Sandwich.[151]

Wyeth called the millwright "Cawning," but Ball correctly named
him as Cannon. William Cannon came west with Wilson Price Hunt's
overland expedition in 1811, arriving with the first group that straggled
into Fort Astoria in January 1812. His name occasionally arose in the
record as Canning, and thus was he listed on at least one Pacific Fur Company roster. Cannon, a Virginian, had been hired by Hunt as a hunter
at Mackinac, where he appeared in the expedition's account for the first
time on August 6, 1811. He joined the Northwest Company when Astoria was sold, then the HBC upon the 1821 merger of the two firms.[152]

Wyeth spoke of "a Mr. Hunt" as though he was unfamiliar with the
role Hunt had played in the earlier history of the Pacific Northwest. By
contrast, Ball had visited former Astorians Seton and Crooks in New
York City before setting off with the PTC, and either made the connection regarding Hunt while visiting the mill, or while compiling his
account years later.

8.
Fort Vancouver

At last the New Englanders had arrived at the Hudson's Bay Company's Fort Vancouver. Until now, the post may have signified to Wyeth only his planned reunion with the *Sultana*, but it would also turn out to be an excellent vantage point from which to scope out PTC's future.

Located on the north bank of the Columbia, nearly one hundred miles above its mouth and about six miles above its junction with the Willamette, Fort Vancouver was the headquarters of HBC activity in the Pacific Northwest. Supply-laden ships from London arrived at the post's docks annually, as did canoe and overland brigades from Hudson's Bay.[1]

Wyeth and his remaining men had traveled more than 3,000 miles in the eight months since leaving Boston. More than half the overland party had been lost due to sickness, desertion and Indian attack, but the Pacific Trading Company had finally reached a long-sought destination.

October 29, 1832   *Fort Vancouver*

29th   Started at 10 ock and arrived at the fort of Vancouver at 12, 4 miles   Here I was received with the utmost kindness and Hospitality by Doct. McLauchland the acting Gov. of the place   Mr McDonald Mr Allen and McMckay gentlemen resident here   Our people were supplied with food and shelter from the rain which is constant   they raise at this fort 6000 bush. of wheat 3 of Barley 1500 potatoes 3000 peas a large quantity of punkins   they have coming on apple trees, peach Do. and grapes.   Sheep, Hogs, Horses, Cows, 600 goats, grist 2, saw mill 2.   24 lb guns   powder magazine of stone   the fort is of wood and square   they are building a Sch. of 70 tons   there are about 8 settlers on the Multnomah   they are the old engages of the Co. who have done trapping.   I find Doct. McLauchland a fine old gentleman truly philanthropic in his Ideas   he is doing much good by introducing fruits

*into this country which will much facilitate the progress of its
settlement (Indian corn 3000 bush)   The gentlemen of this Co.
do much credit to their country and concern by their education
deportment and talents.   I find myself involved in much
difficulty on acc. of my men some of whom wish to leave me
and whom the Co. do not wish to engage no[r] to have them in
the country without being attached to some Co. able to protect
them alledging that if any of them are killed they will be obliged
to aveng it at an expense of money and amicable relations
with the Indians.   And it is disagreeable for me to have men
who wish to leave me.   The Co. seem disposed to render me
all the assistance they can   they live well at these posts they
have 200 acres of land under cultivation   the land is of the
finest quality.*

Named in honor of British explorer George Vancouver, the fort had
originally been erected in 1825 on Belle Vue Point, three quarters of a
mile from the river's bank. Four years later, Fort Vancouver was rebuilt
closer to the Columbia's edge, with a 90,000-square-foot stockade.
Upon completion, it was the grandest post operated by the Company
below the Forty-Ninth Parallel.[2]

John Ball provided a succinct description of the HBC's main post in
the Columbia District:

> *We arrived at Fort Vancouver, it having taken us nine days to
> come down the river, some two hundred miles. Fort Vancouver is
> an extensive stockade, enclosed on a prairie back from the river. It
> includes the storehouses and the houses for governor and partners,
> as the clerks were called. For the servants and Frenchmen there
> were little houses outside of the fort. This was the main station of
> the Hudson Bay Company west of the mountains, and to this place
> shipping came ... There had been some farming done about the fort
> for some seven years previous.*[3]

In charge of the trading post since its inception was forty-eight-year-
old Chief Factor John McLoughlin. His six-foot, six-inch height and bull-
like build manifested a commanding but dignified authority. His wrath

was as well known as his generosity and fair dealing. "The White-Headed Eagle," as he was sometimes called, supervised HBC trading as far south as San Francisco, California, as far west as the Hawaiian Islands, and throughout the interior bounded by the Rocky Mountains.[4]

On October 29, 1832, the very day of Wyeth's arrival, McLoughlin informed his superiors what he had gleaned concerning the American interlopers. Though the manuscript says "Dwight," McLoughlin was obviously writing about Wyeth:

> *This morning a party of eleven Americans under the direction of a Mr. Dwight, from Boston, arrived here; they left that place in March, & St. Louis in July. He says he came to ascertain if possible to make a business of curing Salmon in this River, & at the same time to supply the American Trappers in the Rocky Mountains, but that from what he has seen on the way here, he thinks the latter would not answer, & that if possible, he will endeavor to go to St. Francisco, & return next Summer from thence across land to Salmon River, where American Trappers are to assemble, & go home with the party that brings their supplies. He says Salmon would sell for 14 cents p. lb. in the States. It is impossible for us to say, in the short interview we have had with him, if these are his views or not; & though it may be as he states, still I would not be surprised to find that his views are in connexion with a plan which I see in a Boston paper of March 1831, to colonise the Willamette. It seems he started with a party of 35 men. Several of them left him in the Snake Country to join the American Trappers, & that he had a battle en route, with the Black feet tribe of Indians.[5]*

McLoughlin's business acumen would not allow him to take Wyeth's explanation at face value. News of Hall J. Kelley's plan had reached the Pacific Northwest some time ago. The HBC man would not be fooled by Wyeth's smooth insistence that he had found the fur trade of little interest.

John Ball recognized that his cohort's very presence bore the stamp of American infringement in a region solidly monopolized by the Hudson's Bay Company: "We were a hard looking set, owing to our hard life, but we were most hospitably received in spite of the awkward and suspicious circumstances in which we appeared."[6]

Established in the winter of 1824-25, Fort Vancouver served as headquarters for the Columbia District of the Hudson's Bay Company. In this 1854 image, a U.S. Army post, with prominent American flag, sits on the hill at left, while the trading post is visible on the right, near the river. SUBLETTE COUNTY FUR TRADE PAPERS #2010.551.0100, MUSEUM OF THE MOUNTAIN MAN, PINEDALE, WY

Wyeth's initial conference with Fort Vancouver VIPs had included McLoughlin, Archibald McDonald, George Allan, and Thomas McKay. McDonald was chief trader in charge of nearby Fort Langley and made occasional visits to McLoughlin. The *Eagle* had landed at Fort Vancouver on October 14 with that post's returns and McDonald had likely been on board.[7] George Allan was a young clerk who, after serving a year in the trade house, had been promoted to overseeing the company farms at Fort Vancouver. Allan had been at the fort for only a year. Thomas McKay was McLoughlin's stepson. Alexander McKay, Thomas's father, had been blown up in the 1811 *Tonquin* fiasco. As an HBC clerk, the younger McKay had accompanied the expeditions of Peter Ogden and Alexander McLeod, but by the time of Wyeth's arrival, he had expressed a wish to retire.[8]

During this discussion, Wyeth learned of the crop yields, presumably from Allan, the man in charge of those operations. Interestingly, just the day before, McLoughlin had mentioned expected harvests in a letter to directors in London, and his numbers differ significantly from Wyeth's. The Chief Factor reported 3,000 bushels of wheat, 2,000 bushels of barley, 6,000 bushels of potatoes and 2,000 to 3,000 bushels of peas.[9] Later in the fall, McLoughlin wrote Chief Trader Alexander McLeod that the harvest (in bushels) was 3,500 wheat, 3,000 barley, 3,000 peas, 1,500 potatoes, and 2,000 oats – enough to satisfy the needs of the post for two years.[10] John Ball said McLoughlin had raised "1,200 bushels of wheat, barley, peas, Indian corn, potatoes and garden vegetables." Ball's figures were so out of line with other reports of the harvest that year that it seems he was either misinformed or had misunderstood.[11] Wyeth thought only two hundred acres of land were under cultivation; Allan put the figure at "about seven hundred acres."[12] Production figures like these surely encouraged Wyeth's plan for farming in the Pacific Northwest.

As for livestock, McLoughlin was determined to increase the cattle herd at Fort Vancouver until it was large enough to sustain slaughter – the goal was six hundred head – and so did not consistently butcher beef until 1836. By the spring of 1833 McLoughlin could report that the farm's cattle numbered between 400 and 450 "exclusive of what we supplied to other places." In late 1836, Henry Spalding wrote that the cattle at Fort Vancouver totaled seven hundred head.[13]

John McLoughlin (1784-1857), sometimes hailed as the "Father of Oregon," was Chief Factor at Fort Vancouver during Wyeth's time in the West. Though they competed head-on, the two men developed a life-long friendship. OREGON HISTORICAL SOCIETY, #BA018865

Wyeth's understanding of HBC shipbuilding plans was distorted as well. He thought the Company was building a schooner when in reality it was repairing the *Vancouver,* which had run aground at the entrance to Portland Canal on the coast of British Columbia. In June 1832, McLoughlin informed the Company that the post shipbuilder, James Anderson, had died of fever, so work on another boat had not begun.[14] The sixty-ton *Vancouver,* built at the post in 1827, was pulled from the water in 1832 for repairs and a complete overhaul.[15] "Every timber in the least decayed is taken out of her; she will be planked (which is almost done), have new ceiling, Beams, & Decks," the bosses were told.[16]

The river today known as the Willamette was first called the Multnomah by Lewis and Clark in November 1805. Initially spelled "Mulknomah," the word may have been a corruption of a Chinookan term meaning "downriver." The section of the stream between the waterfalls and the mouth of the Columbia was known to Natives as the Multnomah and the segment upriver from the falls was apparently the Willamette. In

October 1792, Lieutenant Broughton of Vancouver's expedition named the watercourse the River Mannings, but that name obviously did not stick. The map created by William Clark showed the headwaters of the Multnomah near the Great Salt Lake, and this "fact" may have helped establish the Forty-Second Parallel as the U.S. boundary with Spain.[17]

Wyeth was well aware that there were already settlers on the Multnomah, or Willamette River. Former Astorian Etienne Lucier was likely the first to set up house on what became known as French Prairie, north of present Salem, Oregon. Lucier was a freeman, which meant that he was carried on the HBC rolls, but could trap where he chose. He could join a Company expedition so long as he sold his furs to the HBC, typically on a fifty-fifty basis. In 1828, Lucier had asked McLoughlin for seed and tools with which to establish a farm on the Willamette. McLoughlin turned him down.

Lucier renewed his appeal, and received McLoughlin's approval, in 1830; perhaps the HBC headman hoped to prevent the trapper from joining "the first opposition that came here."[18] Conditions had changed. About the same time, several employees retired from Company service and requested similar accommodation to which McLoughlin also agreed. The Chief Factor realized the precedent he was about to set; HBC policy had been to discourage independent settlement in the district, preferring that retirees return to Canada.[19]

McLoughlin's conscience mandated that he support the retirees, but he did not want deadbeats populating the valley. He required each man to maintain a fifty-pound credit on the HBC books, have a family, and live on his own farm rather than with a wife's native people. None of these policies actually fell within HBC's purview, so McLoughlin kept the men's names on the employee roster as if still employed, but without pay or duties. Thus, the Chief Factor managed to circumvent the letter of the law in order to accomplish what he deemed humanitarian.

The strategy worked. Several French-Canadians settled in the Willamette Valley, among them William Cannon and Joseph Gervais, two other former Astorians.[20] Hall J. Kelley accused McLoughlin of implementing this plan in order to

secure himself and the servants of the company, the first choice of farming lands, mill privileges, and positions for cities, and commercial towns, sent five or six Canadians to take up lands near the falls of the Wallamet; the very place which he had good reason to suppose the American pioneer would first occupy ... Those Canadians were the first settlers in Oregon; and its clearly inferable ... by whom Mr. Mc'Laughlin was moved to make them such.[21]

Before he retired, McLoughlin bought out the HBC's interest in the land claim on the Willamette, putting the claim in his own name.[22]

Wyeth's journal entry suggests that the remaining PTC members renewed their grumbling talk about disbanding at about the same time they witnessed the region's bounty.

October 30 - November 5, 1832   *Fort Vancouver*

30th to 5th. Nov   remained at Vancouver and except the last day rain.

Wyeth neglected his journal entries for about a week while resting at the fort and getting to know the HBC personnel working there. He may also have accompanied several of the men on a short adventure downriver. Some of the New Englanders felt they had not reached the end of their journey until they had seen the Pacific. Therefore, a few days after arriving at Fort Vancouver, they paddled down the Columbia, past the mouth of the Willamette and as far downstream as Tongue Point. Ball's account makes clear that the journey made a deep impression on him.

November 3 Five of us started down the river in an Indian canoe. We could not go before, as it had rained. The country continued low on both sides of the river. Mount Hood on the south, Saint Helens on the north, in the rear of which appeared an hexagonal cone, white and beautiful (not then named; afterwards known as Mount Rainier).

November 4 We passed many of the company's sloops, and Indians singing as they paddled their canoes. We saw also many white geese and ducks. We encamped on the shore opposite an island, used by the Indians as a burial ground ... As we went on shore to camp here, we went to a house, and got some wappato a root much eaten by the Indians.

November 5 We continued down the river. The banks became broken and heavily timbered as far down as Tongue Point, where we encamped in sight of Fort George, and overlooking the sea. The next day we went to Fort George, or "Astoria," and were well received. A tree near the fort had recently fallen. Some said it was forty-seven feet in circumference, and others said seven fathoms. I do not think either exaggerated.

November 8 We went over the hills to Young's Bay, where Lewis and Clark wintered, calling their camp "Clatsop Camp." We saw many enormous trees, two hundred feet high and from forty to fifty feet in girth. In fact, everything, even to the brakes, were of gigantic size. Still the potatoes on the clearing near the fort were small, and the soil looked poor.

November 9 We got a yawl and a man to sail it, and crossed over to Chinook Point on the east, encamped, and at low tide went three miles around the point to the seashore. I urged the men to go with me, but all declined. So I went alone to look on the broad Pacific, with nothing between me and Japan. Standing on the brink of the great Pacific, with the waves washing my feet, was the happiest hour of my long journey. There I watched until the sun sank beneath the water. Then by the light of the moon, I returned to camp, feeling I had not crossed the continent in vain.[23]

The canoes made by tribes along the Columbia were remarkable vessels. Lewis and Clark created extensive descriptions and drawings of five distinctly different canoes in use on the waters of the Pacific Northwest:

The Canoes of the nativs inhabitting the lower part of the Columbia River from the Long narrows down make their canoes remarkably neat light and well addapted for rideing high waves. I have Seen the nativs near the Coast rideing waves in these Canoes in Safty and appearantly without Concern ... they are built of Arborvitia or white Cedar generally, but Sometimes of fir. they are cut out of a solid Stick of timber, the gunnals at the upper edge fold over outwards and are about ⅝ of an inch thick and 4 or 5 broad, and Stand out nearly Horizontially forming a kind of rim to the Canoe to prevent the water beating into it. they are all furnished with more or less Cross bars agreeably to thier sizes ... Some of the large Canoes are upwards of 50 feet long and will Carry from 8 to 12 thousand lbs. or from 20 to 30 persons, and Some of them particularly on the Sea Coast are waxed painted and ornimented with curious images on bow and Stern; ... when the nativs are engaged in navigateing their Canoes, one Sets in the Stern and Stears with a paddle the others Set by pars and paddle over their gunnals next them, they all kneel in the bottom of the Canoe and Set on their feet ... those paddles are made verry thin and the middle of the blade is thick and hollowed out.[24]

The "wappato" Ball and the men shared for dinner on November 4 was a favorite vegetable for many of the people living in the Columbia region. Commonly known as broad-leaved arrowhead, *Sagittaria latifolia* is a member of the water-plantain family. The bulb of the plant is about the size of a hen's egg and, when cooked or roasted, tastes a lot like a potato. Wapato was a staple in the diet of Lewis and Clark during the 1805-06 winter at Fort Clatsop.[25]

Tongue Point may be the first geographic feature in Oregon country to have been named by Euro-Americans. In 1792, Captain George Vancouver failed to bring his ship into the mouth of the Columbia and abandoned the attempt. His lieutenant, William Broughton, had safely crossed the Columbia Bar in the ship's tender and was left to continue explorations. Broughton noted "a remarkable projecting point, that obtained the name of Tongue Point." Lewis and Clark tried to bestow "Point William" on the location, after William Clark, but the name did not stick.[26] Young's Bay was named in 1792, also by Lieutenant Broughton, for Sir George Young of the Royal Navy. Lewis and Clark had tried to rename the inlet Meriwether Bay, but like their attempt to rechristen Tongue Point, the name did not take.[27]

Ball, thinking of his childhood neighbor, wrote his parents, "I have seen the country the description of which John Ordway gave you so interestingly when he returned from his tour with Lewis and Clark in 1806."[28]

If Ball's long ordeal across the continent possessed a peak moment, standing on the Pacific shore was surely it. Ball later reminisced, "Here I stood alone ... entranced ... I had gone as far as feet could carry me west."[29]

November 6-14, 1832   *Mouth of the Columbia River*
Written November 19

6th   started down the river to look with a view to the Salmon business   we decended the river at about 4 mils per hour and accomplished the journey in parts of 4 days   the river is full of islands but they are all too low for cultivation being occasionally overflowed as also the praries (what few there are) on the main land   with the exception of these small levells the country is so rough that a great part of the earth must be inhabited before this but the soil is good and the timber is heavy and thick and almost impenetrable from underbrush and fallen trees   the description of Mess. Lewis & Clark and others is fully borne out as to size and more also   the river is so well known at this part of it that I will not insert any observations of my own   there are a great number of fowl on this river at this time and there will be more as they say soon   there are large swan white gese a goose with a motled breast and yellow bill a trifle smaller than the goose of N[ew] E[ngland]   A white goose almost exactly like the domestic goose of N.E. yellow feet and legs as also the former   there is another goose like that of N.E. but I think smaller   there is the tame duck of N.E. with 19 tail feathers and a fine duck to eat   there is the grey duck of N.E.   green winged teel   Buffle heads   Cape Races   Dippers of the Sea   loons   seal   deer   I killed one swimming the river   I saw no elk but only tracks   fort George now occupied as a trading post by the H.B. Co. is well scituated on a sloping bank of the river about 2 miles outside of Tongue point and 6 miles inside of Clatsop point   Chinnook point is opposite the latter and inside   Chinnook is a river of small size   is also inside Tongue point   above Tongue point about 6 miles are

> *the Cathlametts they are an archipelago of reedy Islands overflown at high water Here are ducks innumerable. the Indians in this part of the river are of late much reduced they appear good and hospitable as far as an Indian ever is that is they are willing to sell provisions for all they can get for them they appear to live well and I believe any one may with plenty of powder and lead on this river either as a purchase or to shoot there are no beaver here*

Though the dates were different, Wyeth's canoe trek to the Pacific was probably the same excursion as Ball's. The pragmatic Wyeth wrote about the salmon trade, flora and fauna, and made observations about people and commerce, rather than pondering the significance of having reached the Pacific Coast.

The impressive list of waterfowl Wyeth recorded in this entry speaks to the rich habitat along the river. William Clark was similarly amazed when he paddled through in 1805, reporting "Great numbers of Swan Geese Brant Ducks & Gulls in this great bend which is Crouded with low islands."[30]

Throughout their journey, Wyeth and Ball both made so many references to Lewis and Clark that it begs the question of whether they carried with them a copy of the Corps of Discovery journals.

The reedy islands that Wyeth referred to as the "Cathlametts" are known today as the Hunting Islands, and are part of the Julia Butler Hansen Refuge. A tribe known as the Kathlamets occupied settlements along the south shore of the Columbia from about Tongue Point, upstream to the area around Puget Island in modern Clatsop County, Oregon.[31]

On November 10, about one hundred miles downstream from Fort Vancouver, Wyeth visited another HBC post – Fort George, originally John Jacob Astor's Fort Astoria. Built in 1812, it had been sold to the Northwest Company in 1813 and renamed. Wyeth found James Birnie in charge at the post. A Scot from Aberdeen, Birnie entered the service of the Northwest Company in 1817 then transferred to HBC at the time of its merger with NWC. As mentioned earlier, McLoughlin had sent him to drive Bache out of business at the Dalles in 1829.[32] Now at Fort George, Birnie proved the perfect host.

After this short visit to Fort George, Ball, like Wyeth, recorded observations about the local Indians:

November 11 We began returning slowly up the river. The Indians we found always peaceable, these traders having had the good sense and tact to keep them so, by always keeping faith and a good understanding with them. That day we went but five miles, keeping along the south shore. In the evening we were visited by Indians in a friendly way.[33]

November 15-19, 1832   **Fort Vancouver**
Written November 19

We arrived at the Fort of V. on the 15th Nov having had no rain during this time.   I must here mention the very kind gentlemanly conduct of Mr. Jas. Bernie superintendent of Ft. G. who assisted me to a boat and pilot for the outer harbor and acted the part of host to perfection   I had much pleasure with a little liquor and a pipe in his company   he has seen much of this country and is of the old N.W. concern   I derived much information from him   on my return to the fort my men came forward and unanimously desired to be released from their engagement with a view of returning home as soon as possible and for that end to remain here and work for a maintance until an opportunity should occur.   I could not refuse   they had already suffered much and our number was so small that the prospect of remuneration to them was very small   I have therefore now no men   these last were Mr. Ball Woodman Sinclair, Breck, Abbot, Tibbits   they were good men and persevered as long as perseverance would do good   I am now afloat on the great sea of life without stay or support but in good hands i.e. myself and providence and a few of the H.B. Co. who are perfect gentlemen   During my absence Guy Trumbul died on the 7th of Nov. of the Cholic an attack of which he had on the Platte of which he nearly died   in this case he was taken in the evening and died early in the mng.   His funeral was attended by all the Gentlemen at the place and prayers were said accord to the form of the Church of England   for this attention to my affairs in my absense was considerate to

*my feelings and I hope will be duly appreciated   service is
here performed on sunday and on the days prescribed by the
church of Eng.   our excursion down the river was performed in
an Indian canoe which we hired for a 3 1/2 point Blankett   We
found it very kittish but withall a good craft for sailing and easy
to paddle but the men were exceedingly awkward.*

Soon after returning from the canoe trip to the Pacific Coast, Wyeth and Ball were invited to dine at Chief Factor McLoughlin's table. Ball and the Captain were lodging within the Factor's house; the remaining men quartered with McLoughlin's men, outside the fort proper. Ball recalled the honor of having been invited to dine with the Chief Factor:

The gentlemen of the fort were pleasant and intelligent. A circle of a dozen or more sat at a well-provided table, which consisted of partners, the clerks, Captain Wyeth, and myself. There was much formality at the table. Men waited on the table, and we saw little of the women.[34]

John Dunn, a British naval apprentice who had reached Fort Vancouver on the bark *Gannymede* the year before, remembered his own evening at McLoughlin's table:

The dinner is of the most substantial kind, consisting of several courses. Wine is frequently allowed; but no spirituous liquors. After grace has been said, the company break up. Then most of the party retire to the public sitting room, called "Bachelor's Hall," or the smoking room: to amuse themselves as they please, either in smoking, reading, or telling and listening to stories of their own, and others' curious adventures. Sometimes there is a great influx of company, consisting of the chief traders from the outposts who arrive at the fort on business; and the commanders of vessels. These are gala times after dinner; and there is a great deal of amusement, but always kept under strict discipline, and regulated by the strictest propriety.[35]

In 1837, Mrs. Jason Lee vividly detailed the meal she enjoyed at the fort:

We were all seated around a long table 18 of us, the table set with blue. Our first course was Soup, the next boiled salmon, then roasted ducks, then such a roast turkey as I never saw or eat it was a monster, it was like cutting off slices of pork, then wheat pan cakes, after that bread and butter and cheese all of their own make, and excellent too.[36]

On November 17, Ball delivered news that must have surprised both McLoughlin and Wyeth:

I soon gave Doctor McLoughlin and Captain Wyeth to understand that I was on my own hook, and had no further connection with the party. But not liking to live gratis, I asked the doctor (he was a physician by profession) for some employment. He repeatedly answered me that I was a guest and not expected to work. But after much urging, he said if I was willing he would like me to teach his own son and the other boys in the fort, of whom there were a dozen. Of course I gladly accepted the offer.[37]

At about this same time, the remaining members of the Pacific Trading Company also asked to be released from their contracts. Yet in his journal entry Wyeth named only six men who quit; left unmentioned were Smith, Whittier, Sargent, and Burdett. These four must have previously advised the Captain of their withdrawal from the company, because Wyeth was now alone.

The factors that triggered the mass exodus are unknown but not difficult to conjure. The men were no doubt exhausted from the demanding, dangerous journey west. The apparent luxury of life at Fort Vancouver may have caused some of them to wonder how the PTC could truly compete with the well-oiled machinery of the Hudson's Bay megacorporation. And the supply ship *Sultana's* delay somewhere on the far side of the Columbia Bar must have been dispiriting, to say the least. In a letter Wyeth would write to his brother Jacob in March 1834, he would look back and summarize the misfortunes that had accumulated in late 1832:

We arrived at the Coast where we found the vessel that I had
expected had been lost. This was a signal for the rest to desert and
truly I was glad to be rid of them although thereby all the proceeds of
the expedition were sacrificed or buried in the Mountains.[38]

Wyeth's letter implied that word of the *Sultana's* fate, minus any details, had reached the PTC on the Columbia and may have played a role in the desertions. And in a letter McLoughlin wrote to John McLeod on March 1, 1833, the Chief Factor said of the Bostonians, "their plan has failed for the present in consequence of the vessel being wrecked, with their supplies being wrecked on their way there."[39]

Many historians, relying on these letters, have asserted that the men quit the company only after they knew the supplies would never arrive. But in his journal, during the entire return journey from Fort Vancouver to Boston, Wyeth never mentioned the ship or its fate. There is in fact no way to ascertain exactly what Wyeth knew about the ship's progress, or when he knew it.

Frances Victor uncovered the likely fate of the *Sultana* while researching trapper Joe Meek's life story. Victor conducted interviews with Francis Lemont, a *Sultana* crew member in 1832, who described his experience.[40] In a dramatic sequence of events, the unlucky *Sultana* hit an uncharted reef off Bow Island (today's Hao Island in French Polynesia) on February 29, 1832, at two o'clock in the morning. The ship rapidly filled with water. By noon, the crew and as much equipment and supplies as could be salvaged were marooned on the island. Tents were set up, and a huge kite made from the ship's sails was hoisted as a signal to passing vessels. There was no fresh water on the island and the flora provided limited food sources of any kind. The primary sustenance of the castaways was a green-colored fish and "geography," hard biscuits that were charred and soaked in a pot of water to make them palatable. The sailors had recovered some tea, but it had gotten wet in the salty waters and had lost its flavor.[41]

The men collected rainwater and dug a well that afforded them potable water. Two weeks later, Captain Lambert set out for Tahiti in the ship's launch. In his absence, natives arrived in a state of nakedness that compelled the crew to offer them the cotton cloth that had been destined for Wyeth's inventory. A case of looking glasses, brought from

the wreck, also came in handy for trade. After four months, the schooner *Pomare* arrived, and brought the men and remaining cargo to Tahiti,
to be reunited with Lambert near the end of June.

Lambert auctioned off all the goods in his charge, including those
Wyeth might have wanted, to buy passage on board the *Meridian*, bound
for New Bedford, Massachusetts, for himself, chief mate George Sweet-
land, and supercargo Curtis Clapp. The rest of the crew, in a make-shift
native boat, sailed for sixty-eight days from Tahiti to Valparaiso, Chile,
where each man was left to find his own way home. Lemont, for example, traveled to Cadiz, Spain, before arriving back in Boston in June 1833.

The *Sultana*'s demise had been reported in the *Niles Weekly Register* by September 1832, so Wyeth's backers likely heard the news well
before he did.[42]

Wyeth apparently knew the ship's fate before returning from the
West. He may have received word from Captain William McNeill of the
American brig *Llama*. In July 1833, Wyeth would write of receiving letters from McNeill, who had sailed all over the Pacific in the previous
months. Mentioned only in passing, the content of McNeill's correspondence is unknown. Another letter Wyeth wrote the same day, however, mentioned "the loss of Capt. Lambert's Bg." and that, while at Fort
Vancouver the year before, he had given letters to McNeill to deliver to
the *Sultana*'s owner, Joseph Baker and Sons, "if he fell in with [their]
vessells."[43] This suggests that during their concurrent time at Fort Vancouver in late 1832, Wyeth and McNeill both assumed the *Sultana* was
still at sail.

In any case, Wyeth would have been fully apprised of the vessel's
destruction after his return to Boston in November 1833. Apparently
undaunted, Wyeth would once again hire James Lambert to command
a supply ship, this time for his second expedition. Historian Hubert H.
Bancroft, pulling together the available information, sketched a credible
storyboard for Wyeth's hopes, apprehensions, and ultimate dismay:

> *Unfortunately for Wyeth and his Boston associates, the* Sultana
> *failed to put in an appearance at the time and place appointed. All
> this winter of 1832-3 Wyeth watched her coming, looking eagerly
> every day westward into the opaque mists of the Columbia for tidings
> of her approach, and it was not until after he had given up and*

returned to Boston that he learned her fate ... One of the first persons
to greet Wyeth on his return was Captain Lambert, who informed
him of the wreck of the Sultana.[44]

In the middle of November 1832, meanwhile, without supplies
or personnel, Wyeth's dream of commencing a fur trading operation
became the victim of harsh realities. The scanty supplies he had packed
from Boston had been for the most part either submerged in the Sweetwater River or cached back in Snake Country. His plan to purchase
salmon from the Indians had been scratched due to bad timing. Everything the Captain had visualized for the Pacific Trading Company had
failed to materialize. But Wyeth had not abandoned his dream – he had
merely postponed it.

It is noteworthy that, as Wyeth developed a new approach, he never seemed to view – or express in writing, at least – the Hudson's Bay
Company as a serious competitor against his business plan. In fact, the
area where Wyeth proposed to operate had been aggressively harvested
by HBC brigades since the early 1820s precisely to dissuade interlopers
like him. The Boston ice man seemed oblivious to the possibility that
the great conglomerate might not welcome him.

November 19-29, 1832   ***Fort Vancouver***
Written November 29

> *19th   From this to the 29th I remained at Fort Vancouver*
> *eating and drinking the good things to be had there and*
> *enjoying much the gentlemanly society of the place.*

This brief entry, while it said so little, communicated so much.
Wyeth lingered at the fort, sorting out all he had learned. Without
doubt, Wyeth was also building relationships with these Englishmen
that would not only serve him well from a business standpoint, but that
would be lifetime associations. Of particular note was his long-term
connection with John McLoughlin.

November 29 - December 8, 1832   *Willamette River*

*On the 29th. with Abbot and Woodman in an Indian canoe
I started for a journey up the Wallamet or Multonomah
River   this river which is highest in the winter was so at this
time but is not rapid until near the falls   the subjoined scetch
will shew its course as I made it   distance by the river by my
estimate 27 1/2 miles to the falls which are perpendicular about
20 feet   past these we carried our canoe about 1/4 mile and
launched above the falls   the water though generally more
rapid above would admit of the running of a steam boat.   In
this river at this time there is more water than in the Missouri
and not of a more difficult character to navigate   the tide flows
to within 8 miles of the falls   below the fall the banks of the
river are not suitable for cultivation being overflowed as far
as the bottom extends which is not far and beyond these the
country rises into rocky hills unfit for tillage but producing very
large timber mostly if not all of the pines   On the bottoms
there is considrable oak of a kind not found in the States but
of excellent quality for ship building and is the only kind of oak
found in the country of the Columbia   I noticed but two streams
coming into the river below the falls   the river to within 6 mils
of its junction with the Columbia runs along the N.E. side of
a range of hills or as they would be called in N[ew] E[ngland]
mountains   at the falls it passes through this range   this river
has two mouths   the East one is the one I assended the west
one follows the range of hills above described to their falling
on the Columbia about 3 miles below   the eastern entrance
[of] the mouth of this river is in Latt 45 deg. 36 min. 51 sec.
Long. 122 deg. 48 min.   Above the falls for 22 mils by estimate
the banks of the river are high enough to prevent flowing but
timbered and not fertile and rough and the country apparently
not valuable except for timber which is here mostly of the pines
except a small quantity of cotton wood and alder   the latter is
here a tree of sometimes a foot and a half through   at the falls
the H.B. Co. are erecting a saw mill to which they contemplate
adding a grist mill   the scituation for mill priviledges is beyond
any thing I have ever seen   22 mils from the falls are 3 or 4
Canadians settled as farmers   they have now been there one
year have Hogs, Horses, Cows, have built barns, Houses,
and raised wheat, barely, potatoes, turnips, cabages, corn,*

punkins, melons   The country here becomes open, but still wood enough and a much greater proportion of oak   prairies of from 1 to 30 miles in extent bound by a skirting of timber   this country seems a valley between the mountains to the East and West of about 50 miles wide including both sides of the river and is very level   of nearly uniform soil   extremely rich   equal to the best of the Missouri lands.   Accounts vary much as to its southerly extent   I have seen it at least 75 mils in southwardly direction and from all I can learn I think it extends with but little interuption as far south as the vally of the Buneventura which is also of the same description of the country.   and I have never seen country of equal beauty except the Kansas country and I doubt not will one day sustain a large population   10 mils by land above the first settlement and 30 by the river is another by a Mr Jervie which was a very fine beginning of one years standing of the same character and product as the one below   in all about 9 settlers are on this river   if this country is ever colonised this is the point to commence   the river is navigable for canoes to its very sources but as I understand very circuitous   deer abounds in this district and wolves one of which a large devil I shot   these settlers I found exceeding attentive to my comforts especially Mr Jervai at whose house I slept 2 nights   I was absent from the fort this time 10 days.

Having quit Wyeth's employment two weeks earlier, Abbott and Woodman had apparently maintained an equitable enough relationship with Wyeth to accompany him on an exploration of the fertile Multnomah River Valley upstream from the fort. Indeed, by mid-January, 1833, these two men would be back on Wyeth's payroll for the journey east.[45]

As mentioned earlier, the Indians who lived along the "Wallamet or Multonomah" River likely referred to the section of the stream between the waterfalls and the mouth of the Columbia as the Multnomah; the segment upriver from the falls was apparently called the Willamette, a name that may have meant "to spill or pour water."

Wyeth was impressed with the resources he witnessed as he paddled upstream, sketched a map, and entered observations in his journal. It was no wonder McLoughlin sought to tie up this region for the Company, and for his own personal gain.

On the Multnomah, too, Wyeth recorded the first and only location by latitude and longitude in his 1832 journal. John Ball had purchased a sextant to bring on the expedition but never recorded its use in his diary. Nor was there evidence that any of the three men on this canoe trip possessed the knowledge to use such a tool. Perhaps McLoughlin provided Wyeth with the geographic specifications of the site.

Speculating that the Willamette might take its rise as far south as California, Wyeth named the "Buneventura" (Buenaventura) as a possible source. This name was often applied to the Sacramento River in the northern part of the state. Buenaventura was also the name of a mythical river thought to flow from the Rocky Mountains in the vicinity of the Great Salt Lake, westward across the Great Basin, to the Pacific Ocean.[46] The north-flowing Willamette is the longest river entirely within the boundaries of the modern state of Oregon; its source is not in California.

Joseph Gervais, former Astorian, was one of the first farmers in the region. As an employee of the Northwest Company, he had made several beaver hunts to the Willamette River Valley, often with his friend Etienne Lucier. In 1821, Donald McKenzie reported that "Lucier and Gervais are trapping the Walamet as usual." When Gervais built his farm, McLoughlin provided him with tools, seeds and lumber, as well as loaning cattle with the understanding that any calves produced were to be returned to the Company.[47]

The wolves Wyeth described played a role in the establishment of a provisional government in 1843. Residents of the Willamette Valley met in February and March of that year to discuss the issue of predators attacking livestock, and to create a system of bounties on those wild animals. The second of these so-called "Wolf Meetings" was held in the home of Joseph Gervais.[48]

As 1832 drew to a close, John Ball made good on his commitment to teach the young men at the fort:

The boys were sent to my room to be instructed. All were half-breeds, as there was not a white woman in Oregon. The doctor's wife was a "Chippewa," from Lake Superior, and the lightest woman was Mrs. Douglas, a half-breed, from Hudson Bay. I found the boys docile and attentive, and they made good progress. The doctor often came into the school, and was well satisfied and pleased. One day he said: "Ball, anyway you will have the reputation of teaching the first school in Oregon."[49]

Among the two dozen students taught by Ball were McLoughlin's eleven-year-old son, David, and grandson Willie McKay, oldest son of stepson Thomas McKay with his first wife, the daughter of Chinook Chief Concomly.[50] The pupils conversed in a variety of languages including Klickitat, Nez Perce, Chinook, Cree and French. Initially, only the Factor's son spoke English.[51]

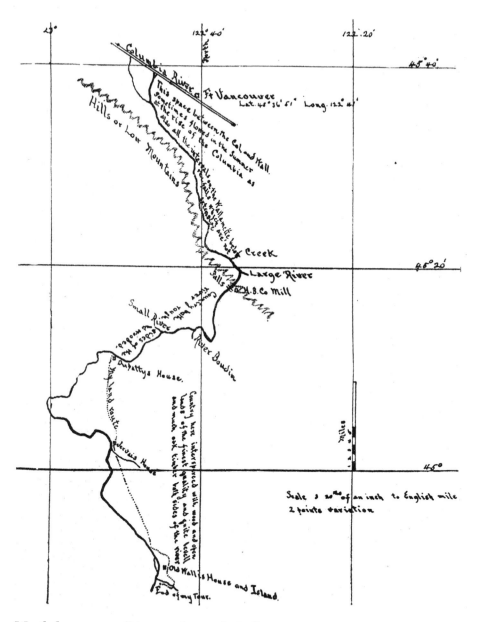

Wyeth drew a map of his excursion up the Willamette River, noting the HBC sawmill, Gervais's farm, and other landmarks. Given that the map is scaled to the English mile, the latitude and longitude information Wyeth included probably also came from his HBC hosts. This is one of the few extant maps Wyeth drew based on his Western expeditions. OREGON HISTORICAL SOCIETY, #BB010166

9.

A New Year and the Return East

After his October 29, 1832, arrival at the Hudson's Bay outpost, Wyeth kept a patchy account of daily activities. Frequently, he put the chore off for days at a time, then logged multiple days' events, creating gaps and inconsistencies in his timeline. Undoubtedly, the missing *Sultana* and the demise of the Pacific Trading Company weighed heavily on him. Incessant rain, by Wyeth's reckoning nine and a half inches in December alone, could only have oppressed him further.[1]

Wyeth neglected to comment on the Christmas and New Year holidays that would have been celebrated exuberantly at Fort Vancouver. Samuel Parker participated in the celebration in 1835; his recollections were probably quite similar to events Wyeth witnessed just a few years earlier:

The holidays are not forgotten in these far distant regions. From Christmas until after New Years, all labour is suspended, and a general time of indulgence and festivity commences. Only this once in the whole year are ardent spirits given to the laborers, when they have a free allowance, giving them the opportunity to exhibit fully what they would do, if spirits were easily and always accessible. On Christmas morning they dress themselves in their best attire, accelerated movements are seen in every direction, and preparation is made for dinners, which are sure to be furnished in their first style, and greatest profusion; and the day passes in mirth and hilarity. But it does not end with the day; for the passions and appetites pampered through the day, prepare the way for the night to be spent with dancing, and the loud and boisterous laugh, shouts, and revelry, consume the hours designed for rest. They continue these high-strung convivialities until they pass the portals of the new year, when labor and toil take their place.[2]

December 9, 1832 - January 10, 1833   *Fort Vancouver*
Written January 10

To the 4th Jany. the weather was little better than a continual rain not however a hard rain often but a drizzling uncomfortable air   during December there fell 9 1/2 inches rain by a pluviometer   on the 4th the wind came strong to N.N.E. with fair and cool weather   Ther. averaging about 19 Deg.   this continued to the 8th when there is much floating ice in the river and those here think that with two days more of this weather the river will close.   The readiness w[it]h which the river frezes must arise from the water getting intensely cold in the upper country.   During this month Mr. McKay gave our room a treat of Buffaloe meat salted and smoked and this being the first opportunity of comparing good Buffalo meat with other good meat was highly acceptable.   I think it equal to the best meat ever eaten.   Up to the 4th there was no frost in the ground and ploughing is commonly done all the winter   during the latter part of January the River rose about 4 feet which must have arisen from the rains as there could be no melting of snow on the Mountains at this season   these rains must have I think extended farther back than is described to be their range viz the falls at which the timbered country terminates.   Carrots are here finer and larger than I have ever before seen   one I think was 3 inches through and of fine flavor.   There appears much sickness amon[g] the people here especially among the common people which I think arises from low diet and moist weather for as far as I can observe the gentlemen who live well are not much subject to disorders.   the main disorder is an intearmittent fever which has carried off all or nearly all the Indians who live even worse than the engages.   The Lima which sailed a month since had not to the 1st Jany. got out of the river.   I have been Informed by Mr Douglas and Mr. Finlesson that vessells have laid off the bar 7 weeks before they could enter.

The opening days of January saw the start of the seasonal wet weather for which the Pacific Northwest became well-known. A pluviometer, sometimes called a udometer, was a nineteenth-century term for a rain gauge. Wyeth apparently had access to one at the fort and recorded the December precipitation. Rain had also been the constant companion of the Corps of Discovery's winter of 1805-06, spent in close proximity to Wyeth's 1833 location. Patrick Gass had lamented that "from the 4th of November 1805 to the 25th of March 1806, there were not more than twelve days in which it did not rain, and of these but six were clear."[3]

The man who brought Wyeth buffalo meat was surely Thomas McKay, whom the Yankee had met the day the Pacific Trading Company had first arrived at Fort Vancouver. Since McLoughlin would not butcher cattle until the herd was self-sustaining, buffalo would have been a welcome alternative to yet another plate full of salmon.

Regarding the 1835 New Year celebrations at the HBC post, the Reverend Samuel Parker commented,

> *The expiring year vanishes, amidst the noise and revels of many ... and too many give as they profess, but a decent honor and respect to those festival days, when from house to house of their best or more indifferent friends, the wine is circulated until they become genteelly inebriated.*[4]

No doubt Wyeth applied his best efforts to such gentility.

The growing season in the Pacific Northwest was lengthy. Vegetables grew well in the relatively mild oceanic climate. The Astorians reported in 1811-12 digging up "a Turnip in the Garden weighing 8 lbs; Circumference 28 Inches," and as for potatoes, "among them were two weighing 3-3/4 lbs."[5]

Wyeth presumed that fevers at Fort Vancouver were connected to bad food and too much rain. The New Englander would have known about malaria, the "intearmittent fever," because it could be contracted even in Boston at this time, but apparently the mosquito's role in the spread of the disease was as yet unknown. The ailment's frequency among Indians and "common people" makes the case for higher incidences among those who spent most of their time outdoors, and in prime mosquito habitat. Fort Vancouver agriculturist George Allan's memories of administering quinine to the ill hints at the presence of malaria:

> *In the fall of the year 1832, the fever and ague was very prevalent at Vancouver, and at one time we had over 40 men laid up with it; and great numbers of Indian applicants for La Medicine, as*

they called it ... [McLoughlin] was himself attacked with the fever, when he appointed me his deputy, and I well remember my tramps through the men's houses with my pockets lined with vials of quinine.[6]

Wyeth records the name of the ship *Llama* or *Lama* as the "*Lima.*" This 145-ton brig, captained by William McNeill, was purchased by the HBC in 1832 to replace the damaged *Vancouver*. The Chief Factor's superiors in London were not pleased that McNeill, an American citizen, had been hired to work for the British company. In fact, prior to being employed by McLoughlin, McNeill had competed against the HBC fur enterprise in northern British Columbia. The *Llama* had arrived at the Fort from Oahu on October 28, 1832 – the day before Wyeth and his men – and set sail again shortly after.[7]

The journal entry does not say whether Wyeth actively sought information about the Columbia Bar, but Wyeth was surely interested in conditions that might have affected the *Sultana's* arrival. A succinct description of the Columbia Bar's shifting hazards for getting in and out of the bay was penned by Samuel Parker in 1835:

A difficulty, of such a nature as is not easily overcome, exists in regard to the navigation of this river, which is the sand bar at its entrance. It is about five miles across the bar from cape Disappointment out to sea. In no part of that distance is the water upon the bar over eight fathoms, and in one place only five, and the channel only about half a mile wide. And so wide and open is the ocean, that there is always a heavy swell, and when the wind is above a gentle breeze, there are breakers quite across the bar, and there is no passing it except when the wind and tide are both very favorable. Without the bar there is no anchorage, and there have been instances, in the winter season, of ships laying off and on thirty days, waiting for an opportunity to pass; and always a good pilot is needed. Perhaps there have been more lives lost here, in proportion to the number of those who have entered this river, than in entering almost any other harbor in the world.[8]

Parker summarized several ships' encounters with that shoal:

*In 1811, the Tonquin, sent out from New York by Mr. Astor, to form a
fur trading establishment at or near the mouth of this river, lost eight
men in crossing the bar. The calamity resulted from the ignorance of
Captain Thorn of the dangers, and his great want of prudence.*

*In the year 1828, the ship William and Anne was cast away a
little within the bar. All on board, twenty-six in number, were lost,
and it could not be ascertained what were the circumstances of the
lamentable catastrophe, as no one was left to tell the story.*

*On the 23d of May, 1830, the ship Isabella was cast away upon a
sand-bar projecting from Sand island, which is a little within the
capes. As soon as she struck, the men all deserted her, and without
stopping at Fort George, made their way to Fort Vancouver. It is
thought, that if they had remained on board and waited the tide, she
might have been saved.*[9]

One of Wyeth's informants about the Columbia's treacherous navigation was James Douglas, who had apprenticed with the Northwest Company at age 16. Two years later when the NWC merged with HBC, he was brought on as a clerk. Douglas had become an accountant under McLoughlin in 1830. The other informant, Duncan Finlayson, began his career with HBC as a writer, the apprentice rank below clerk, in 1815. Working under Donald McKenzie at the Red River post, Finlayson was promoted to chief trader in 1828, then transferred to the Columbia River District three years later. He supervised trade between Fort Vancouver and Hawaii.[10]

January 11, 1833   *Fort Vancouver*

*11th Jany.   The River closed with ice and I am detained
here until it opens.   Last winter the river remained frozen 5
weeks   there is yet no snow.   Today heard by Mr Hermatinger
of the death of Mr Vandeburg killed by the Blackfeet   up to this
time the weather continued clear and cold for this country the
Ther. varying from 12 deg. to 20 deg.*

The Columbia was usually closed by ice in the wintertime for a period lasting from a few days to as long as two months, suspending all navigation.[11] Wyeth learned that "the Columbia as near as I can find freezes up about half the years. Last winter and this it has frozen."[12]

Francis Ermatinger enlisted in the Hudson's Bay Company in 1818 and was assigned to the Columbia District in 1825. He accompanied the Snake Country Expedition of 1831 and was often in the field for most of the next seven years, trapping as far away as French Camp, California.[13]

This well-traveled Company man brought Wyeth news of William Henry Vanderburgh, an American Fur Company trapper whom Wyeth had likely met at the Pierre's Hole rendezvous. Vanderburgh's co-leader with the American Fur Company, Andrew Drips, is mentioned several times in Wyeth's journal so it is likely Vanderburgh and Wyeth were introduced. That Ermatinger carried such relatively fresh news may have indicated that his brigade encountered American trappers while working east of the Continental Divide – in U.S. territory.[14]

Vanderburgh's death became a well-known story in the annals of fur trade history. Although Vanderburgh's fur trade experience was extensive, having worked under Manuel Lisa in the Missouri Fur Company and Kenneth McKenzie at Fort Union, he and Drips were unfamiliar with the Rocky Mountains. To make up for this deficiency, Drips and Vanderburgh had left the Pierre's Hole rendezvous soon after the Rocky Mountain Fur Company brigade led by Jim Bridger and Thomas Fitzpatrick, shadowing the better-schooled men. At this point, a desperate game of hide and seek began; Bridger was determined not to teach the newcomers where prime beaver was to be found. Leading them north, directly into hostile Blackfoot territory, they trapped tributaries of the Jefferson River around Alder Gulch. There, Vanderburgh and another mountaineer were killed by Indians in an ambush.[15]

Wyeth wrote letters to family members and business partners on January 16. He would have been reluctant to elaborate upon the dismal commercial aspects of his venture thus far for various reasons, but alluded to difficulty preserving the privacy of his mail when he wrote, "no business letters can go out of this country by this conveyance." He did inform his brother that several caches of goods remained at various locations in the Rockies, and if he could find an American company to provide escort, he would attempt to recover that merchandise. Despite the hospitality and comforts the HBC afforded Wyeth, the prying eyes of the competition were of great concern to him.[16]

For twenty-five cents postage, the HBC express transported correspondence eastward by an elaborately laborious route, as described by John Ball:

> I wrote to my friends in New Hampshire and New York and by the Hudson express that leaves Fort Vancouver on the 20th of March, goes up the North, the main branch of the Columbia, to about the latitude of 52 degrees and by men on snow shoes over the mountains in about two weeks to where they take bark canoes on the La Bashe, that flows into the Arctic Ocean. Descend that a distance then make a short portage at Fort Edmonton to the Saskatchawan and down that to Lake Winnipeg, and by its outlet, the Nelson, to Hudson Bay and also up the said Lake to Lake Superior, etc., to Montreal, from which place my friends got my letters by September.[17]

Wyeth wrote his parents that he expected to be home by October, 1833; he told his brother Leonard a letter would "reach you near the same time as myself."[18] When corresponding with brother Charles, Wyeth allowed himself to reflect on how his western adventure had affected his priorities:

> When I am in a country where I can get horses to ride, Buffaloe to eat, and Deer skin to wear I am as well off as I can be anywhere and if I make no money, I shall loose none and so much of life will be gone, all the trouble of life will be all the same a hundred years hence.[19]

Wyeth wrote with open affection to his uncle, Leonard Jarvis. "I write you, because it would be unpardonably in me not to do so whenever I have an opportunity." Wyeth tended to copy only business correspondence into his letter book; few personal letters were duplicated there. This may explain why no letter to his wife was found there for this period. Though he asked both Leonard and Charles to pay respects to their wives on his behalf, neither letter requests a similar salutation to his own mate.[20]

January 18, 1833   *Fort Vancouver*

*On the 18th at 2 oclock it commenced hailing and at day
light the hail was about 2 inches on the ground   the River
closed on the 10th and so remains at present   on the 14th I
walked across the Columbia and found the ice about 6 inches
thick where it lay smooth but it was much turned up edge
wise   afternoon of the 18th commenced Raining and on the
19th rains still   the hail was at one time from 1 1/2 to 2 inches
deep on the 18th.*

Due to his not making daily journal entries, Wyeth's dates often con-
flicted. This entry disagreed with his earlier date for when the Columbia
froze solid. He must have recalled, as he walked across the ice and examined its characteristics, images of Cambridge, Fresh Pond, Tudor and
his wife. Wyeth resignedly wrote "Since this [ice] trade will not soon
thrive in this quarter it ceases to be a subject of interest."[21]

January 19-27, 1833   *Fort Vancouver*

*19th   after raining hard all night there is no snow left   it is
warm and showery to day   Ther. 54 deg.*

*20th   Raining stil and Ther. 52 deg.   River not yet cleared
ice stationary.*

21st   22nd   warm and Rainy.

*23rd   The river Broke up   still warm   Ther. 51 deg.   I am
informed by Mr Dav. Douglas that a Mr Woodard whom he
saw in Calafornia was intending to come to the Columbia
for Salmon   he is a Brother-in-law to Capt. Ebbets and is
from New York   Mr. Douglass saw him in Calafornia in July
1832.   I am informed by Doct. J. McGlaucland that he has
seen strawberrys ripe here in Dec. and blossom in Jany.   the
weather warm up to the 28th with occasional rains   there is
now little ice on the river   on the banks the wreck and rubbish
of the breaking up of the river.   The H.B. Co. are now making a
fort at Nass. to counteract the Am. vessells on the coast.*

The day Wyeth reported the Columbia breaking up, January 23, he was visited by botanist David Douglas. The Scot had first visited Fort Vancouver in 1824, on an excursion to collect specimens on the Pacific Coast. After a voyage to England and back, Douglas had returned to the Columbia District in 1830. He had made another tour of California at that time, aboard the HBC brig *Dryad* at which time he met Woodward.[22]

Scant information is available regarding the man "Woodard" and his salmon plan, though a John Woodard acted as a "witness at Mont[erey]" in 1832. Since the *Dryad* landed at that port in 1830, this might be a relative or even the same man Douglas named.[23] Though Wyeth only briefly mentioned Woodard, surely the idea of someone else eyeing the salmon industry perturbed him.

Captain John Ebbets first sailed the Pacific Coast in 1810 under orders from John Jacob Astor to "prepare the Indians for a friendly reception to some white men who would come to stay with them." In other words, Ebbets was to exhibit trade goods and proffer gifts to prepare the local inhabitants for the arrival of the Astorians. Ebbets's first visit to California came in 1830 when he served as supercargo of the *Volunteer*.[24]

The post Wyeth heard about at Nass River in today's northern British Columbia was the already-established Fort Simpson, and the rumors concerned its relocation. In 1829, American ships (including the aforementioned William McNeill's *Llama*) were enjoying successful trade with the natives in the Nass River area. This spurred the HBC to build a fort there, with Peter Ogden, John Work and Aemilius Simpson, cousin of Governor George Simpson, in charge of the effort. Delayed by an epidemic, the post began operating the summer of 1831. Aemilius Simpson died the following September and the post was named after him. The Tsimpsean peninsula was later determined to be a better location, placing the post equidistant from the mouths of the Nass and Skeena rivers. Fort Simpson was relocated in 1834. Nass (a Tlingit word meaning "food depot") referred to the enormous candlefish run in the early spring.[25]

January 28, 1833   *Fort Vancouver*

28th   Warm still and fair   the Co. are about sending a party under Mr. Manson to make a fort at Milbank Sound.

Donald Manson had been an HBC employee since 1817 and became a clerk in the Columbia District in 1825. He had been sent to build Fort Langley on the Fraser River in 1827 and was stationed at Fort George two years later. Before relocating, Manson married the daughter of Etienne Lucier. He was put in charge at Fort Simpson in 1831, and in the spring of 1833, he built Fort McLoughlin on Milbank Sound – the post Wyeth mentioned in this entry. Fort McLoughlin was built two hundred miles south of Fort Simpson on a protected bay of Campbell Island, at Lama Passage in Fitzhugh Sound. It was said to be in the midst of "a Native world."[26]

Wyeth made no entry for January 29, 1833, which would have been his thirty-first birthday.

January 30, 1833   *Fort Vancouver*

30th   Today a party sent to enquire after another reported to be cut off beyond the Umquoi or near the Clammat River under a man by the name of Michelle returned having ascertained that one white and two Inds. only of said party had been killed   this party I [am informed] was under a man by the name of Duportt   I requested to accompany him but the Gov. would not consent alledging the[y] would conceive that I came to avenge the death of Mr. Smiths party who was cut off by the Umquoi Indians, all which I interpreted into a jealousy of my motives   this party brought back 200 skins which they had traded   they did not go beyond the Umquoi,   they were gone 2 months   lost no men and but 2 horses which Died of Fatigue.

The tributaries of the Snake River had been trapped hard due to HBC Governor Simpson's decree to denude the region of beaver.[27] As a result, HBC trappers had been moving farther west and south of the

Snake in search of beaver, and were working streams in California at the time of Wyeth's visit. Brigades had developed what came to be known as the Siskiyou Trail through Oregon, leading over the mountains and into Mexican territory.

Since the mid-1820s, brigades had been trapping the waters of the Umpqua River, which empties into the Pacific near the modern town of Reedsport, Oregon. "Umpqua" was the local Indians' name for the region, and over time the term attached itself to the river and the tribe itself. By 1832, Hudson's Bay had an establishment there, alluded to in early documents as Old Fort Umpqua, the Old Establishment, or McKay's Fort.[28]

Wyeth's "Clammat" River was the Klamath, a stream also named for the people who lived along its banks. It flows 263 miles, predominantly to the southwest, through what is now southeastern Oregon and northern California. The Klamath cuts through the Cascade Range to meet the Pacific Ocean near today's Klamath, California. The name was the Euro-American mispronunciation of "Tlamatl," an Upper Chinookan word meaning "they of the river."[29]

Rumors of Indians having attacked and killed a group of trappers had recently flooded into Fort Vancouver. McLoughlin dispatched a search party to find out what happened to the brigade led the previous spring by Michel Laframboise. An experienced HBC field leader, Laframboise had originally come to the Oregon coast on board Astor's *Tonquin* in 1810. He became known as "Captain of the California Trail" due to frequent expeditions into California.[30]

Wyeth stated that this returning search party had been led by Jean Baptiste Desportes. Appearing in fur trade journals as Dupate, Depaty, Jean Baptiste McKay, and other monikers, Desportes was yet another overland Astorian who had stayed in the territory. He had traveled regularly to the Umpqua country since 1825. Complicating matters further, Desportes was also known by his *dit* name, McKay. It was a custom of many Frenchmen to give "dit" names, nicknames by which a man might be better known than by a surname. Unlike English nicknames, these might be passed on from father to son and were considered significant enough to be used in official records. Commonly they derived either from a personal characteristic, a birthplace, or place of residence.[31] A freeman rather than an HBC employee, Desportes was, like Joseph Gervais and Etienne Lucier, an early settler on French Prairie.[32]

The search party set out shortly after the New Englanders arrived at Fort Vancouver at the end of the previous October. Although Wyeth did not mention this in his journal at the time, by the January entry he seemed to have resented not being allowed to join the outgoing group. McLoughlin had cited the bloody encounter between Jedediah Smith's men and the Kelawatset Indians in July 1828 along the Umpqua River. Only Smith and three of his eighteen men had survived.[33] The Chief Factor may – or may not – have concocted the danger of reprisal in order to control Wyeth's movements within the territory HBC had monopolized.

January 31 - February 3, 1833   *Columbia River*

31st to the 3rd. Feb.   we had warm and wet weather   on the 3rd at 10 ock. we started for Wallah Walla   I had with me two men and am in company with Mr Emmatinger of the H.B. Co. who has in charge 3 boats with 120 pieces of goods and 21 men.   I parted with feelings of sorrow from the gentlemen of Fort Vancouver   their unremitted kindness to me while there much endeared them to me more so than it would seem possible during so short a time   Doct McGlaucland the Gov. of the place is a man distinguished as much for his kindness and humanity as his good sense and information and to whom I am so much indebted as that he will never be forgotten by me   this day we came to the Prarie Du Li[s]   15 miles   raining most of the day.

From the day Wyeth departed Fort Vancouver (February 3 by his calculation), no alternate primary accounts corresponded with his travels, unlike his journey from Cambridge to the Columbia. For the remainder of this volume, Wyeth's journal can be supplemented, contrasted, or confirmed only through fragmentary reports and known events during the same time period.

Wyeth had experienced enough major setbacks on his initial foray into the West that for now, he could accomplish nothing more on the Columbia. When the frozen river opened, Wyeth would head for New England. Informing McLoughlin of his impending exit but assuring the Chief Factor of an eventual return, Wyeth arranged to accompany an HBC brigade led by Francis Ermatinger – partly for company but more so for protection.[34]

Though never stated directly, one of Wyeth's planned destinations was probably the 1833 Rendezvous in the Green River Valley, where other travelers, if not business opportunities, would present themselves. At rendezvous, Wyeth could readily attach himself to other groups aiming for St. Louis, an essential stop on his route home.

Departing Fort Vancouver on his return to Boston with the re-hired Abbott and Woodman, Wyeth joined the brigade of four or five men led by Francis Ermatinger, now headed for the Flathead country in today's northwestern Montana. The usual inland-bound supply outfit generally left Fort Vancouver in June of each year, taking needed merchandise and equipment to the company's upriver trading posts.[35] Ermatinger's winter excursion, however, was an experiment, possibly instigated by Wyeth's discussions with HBC managers. Rather than leading a party devoted to trapping, Ermatinger also carried a supply of trade goods and planned to follow the Flatheads as they roamed the mountains. The emphasis would shift to trading for furs while living with this tribe or, for that matter, anyone else who had pelts to swap.

McLoughlin later indicated the brigade left on January 31 rather than Wyeth's February 3 date. Possibly Wyeth delayed Ermatinger's expected departure by three days.[36] A "piece" was a bundle of goods weighing from eighty-five to ninety pounds, so Ermatinger's outfit of 120 pieces weighed in excess of five tons. They would travel up the Columbia River to Fort Walla Walla by boat, then proceed east via pack train. Based on the freight load, sixty horses would be needed to carry the HBC merchandise to customers once the party left the Columbia.[37] In addition, Wyeth had his own gear and horses to contend with. In April, he would write of having started from Fort Walla Walla with forty-seven mounts.

Wyeth probably hoped to salvage some of his own expedition's capital by recovering the pelts and supplies he had cached in the mountains on his way west. If he succeeded, he would be able to sell these at the upcoming 1833 summer rendezvous. As he left Fort Vancouver, Wyeth must have realized that when he returned to Boston financial backing for a renewed Oregon country enterprise might prove elusive. Wyeth sorely needed evidence to bolster his investors' confidence in him.

Wyeth never lost his gratitude toward McLoughlin or the other HBC men. They had made his life easier throughout his tenure in the Pacific Northwest, and had provided a wealth of information that he would attempt to profit from in the coming years. Whatever his business condition, Wyeth could not blame the HBC.

Paddling fifteen miles up the Columbia River on this day brought the Ermatinger-Wyeth party to what the Bostonian understood to be "Prairie du Li" but was probably Prairie du Thé, or Tea Prairie, at the junction of the Washougal River with the main current of the Columbia. Wyeth's editor, F. G. Young, inserted an "s" believing Wyeth meant "Prairie du Lis." It may have been a misinterpretation of Wyeth's penmanship, likely "Té." According to Ross Cox, the lowland was so named "by the Canadians from a species of mint which grows on it, and which they are fond of using as a substitute for tea."[38] John C. Fremont referred to Tea Prairie River when he passed through the area in November, 1843.[39]

At Fort Vancouver, meanwhile, John Ball reported that some of the other New Englanders who had abandoned Wyeth entered the employ of the HBC. These men were Breck, Burdett, Sargent and Whittier. For the moment, Ball stayed at the fort and continued operating his school.[40]

February 4, 1833   *Columbia River*

4th   Left the prairie Du Li on the lower end of it   this prairie is about 3 miles long and through it the River Du Li a small creek enters the Columbia   we made but 2 miles when one of our boats ran foul of a rock and was stove   it landed its cargo without wetting much   this accident detained us till 1/4 before 12 ock when we started and kept on till 2 ock and stopped 20 minutes to dine then kept on till 1/2 past 5 ock making 17 mils this day   this River is at medium water   the rivers banks high precipitous and rocky   from the Lea prairie in one place the bank on the N. side rises to 200 feet perpendicular   I saw a hawk light on a projecting crag about half way up which gave me a good idea of the height of the rock   from this rock a small stream casts itself into the Com.   wether a permanent one or not cannot say but should think not   there are here many white headed Eagles   one skunk we saw today   the timber appears much smaller than below   no rain but cloudy this day   wind west and Ther. about 40 deg.   now at 8 ock at night the full moon is looking down calmly upon us aparently thinking that the cares of us humble individuals concern her little.

Wyeth's "River Du Li" was likely today's Washougal River; that stream traverses Tea Prairie.

February was still a wintery month in Oregon country so the water levels of the river were not as high as they would be in spring. With rocks exposed or barely submerged, lower water made a more hazardous passage than in later months and forced portages in several places that could be safely canoed at high water.

The high cliff Wyeth noticed on the north bank was Cape Horn. This massive basalt outcrop, located on today's Washington side of the Columbia River, was noted in William Clark's November 2, 1805, journal entry as a "point of rocks of a high clift of black rocks."[41] In modern times, the Columbia River still provides open water and an excellent source of fish for migrating bald eagles. Cape Horn's secluded roosting habitat shelters the birds from mid December through early March.[42]

Camp was made that evening on the south side of the river near present Dodson, Oregon.

February 5-6, 1833   *Columbia River*

5th   We left camp at 7 ock and made 4 miles to breakfast and in 7 mils more the foot of the Cascades   our breakfast was made on a small island abreast of a rock rising perpendicular from the bed of the river as I should think 400 feet high   Lewis & Clark call it I think 700 feet   this rock is nearly surrounded by the waters of the river

*The Cascades occasion a portage of 100 rods   our goods
were carried across this day   the river is here compressed into
a very small place and the bed is full of rocks   I should think
the fall to be about 8 feet in the space of the 60 rods   There
are here two fishing villages both now deserted as the people
here say from the inmates being all dead of the fever but I
suspect some are dead and the rest and much larger part
frighted away   we made the portage by the North side on
which is one of the above villages   it is near the river on a
little clear spot with a little lake in the rear   here the Inds were
once hostile and great caution was once used   in passing
now but little is requisite   it rained all the latter part of the day
and night and morning of the 6th finished the portage but our
boats were so bruised that the rest of the day was taken to gum
them   took a look about me the rest of the day   found that the
tripe de roche grew on the rocks here but small   here there are
many petrifactions of wood in a bank of gravell some of which
are perfectly petrified and will not burn in the fire but others
appear only half so and burn and cut freely   they are found
bedded in stone composed of rubble of some former world   the
gravel is cemented together by finer gravell   the whole being
volcanic and water worn.*

The morning meal on February 5 was probably eaten on today's
Pierce Island, across from Beacon Rock. Lewis and Clark saw this olivine basaltic plug on October 31, 1805, and initially named it Beaten
Rock but referred to it in April 1806 as Beacon Rock. They estimated
the size of the rock at "about 800 feet high & 400 paces around."[43] This
landmark was called Inshoach Castle by Alexander Ross in 1811 and
Pillar Rock by Samuel Parker in 1835.[44]

The "Cascades" Wyeth noted in this entry were the rapids now
under the reservoir formed by the Bonneville Dam. In describing the
length of the route around this obstruction, Wyeth used the "rod" as
a measurement for the first time in his journal. Defined as a length of
16.5 feet, a rod was a basic distance unit used by Anglo-Saxon residents
of England before the Norman conquest of 1066.[45] Wyeth probably
acquired this usage from his recent familiarity with so many Britishers.

Though Wyeth reported two Indian villages at this location, Alexander Ross wrote in 1811 that there were three "small camps" of natives at the site, numbering "250 or 300 at most."[46] Though Ross identified the people as Cathleyacheyachs, they were in fact the Watlalas, with whom the Corps of Discovery had a confrontation in April, 1805. These natives resented outsiders who threatened to interfere with their control of river trade at this place. Lewis and Clark, as well as Ross and his party, were continuously harassed while making their portages. The explorers' efforts to get canoes and equipment around the Cascades was made more miserable and strenuous by the Indians' stone throwing, petty thievery, and other threatening behaviors. Although making a portage in the rain was surely unpleasant, Wyeth was fortunate to have avoided such aggravation.[47]

Wyeth noted *tripe de roche* growing on the rocks in the area. This was edible lichen known to the people of the Pacific Northwest. John Macdonell's 1793 journal reported that the voyageurs on his expedition considered this moss

> *a last resource men have to subsist upon in the inhospitable regions of the dreary North, and has been Know[n] to keep men alive for months, boiled in water, after having the sand well washed off.*[48]

The following year, Duncan McGillivray, of the Northwest Company, penned "our Stock of Provisions ran short. We had to make use of some wild vegetables & *tripe de roche* which when boiled with a little Pemican made a kind of soup."[49]

February 7, 1833   *Columbia River*

7th   At 1 1/2 mile above the Cascade is a small river from the N. and 4 1/2 above this a creek from the N.   rained all the 6th and rains a little today   came in all 27 miles   passed many Indian habitations on the river and canoes   15 mils above the Cascades is a Torrent that precipitates itself into the river from about 60 feet   17 mils from same on same side viz south is a creek   both small   one between them   on the N. side timber growing gradually thinner.

The two streams Wyeth observed after moving upriver from the Cascades were Rock Creek and Wind River, respectively, both on the Washington shore of the Columbia. The "torrent" he described was in a section of the river with no less than half a dozen sizeable waterfalls between the mouths of Summit and Starvation creeks. Based on Wyeth's estimate of its height, the most likely candidate for his "torrent" was Lindsey Creek Falls. While paddling through this same portion of the river on October 30, 1805, William Clark reported that he "Saw 4 Cascades caused by Small Streams falling from the mountains on the Lard. Side."[50]

On this date, the Bostonian passed the site where the small hamlet of Wyeth would develop in the years ahead. Present-day Hood County, Oregon, chose to honor the Boston entrepreneur by attaching his name to a railroad station that was the site of a "tie pickling plant."[51] The site, on the south bank of the Columbia between Gorton and Harphan creeks, included a post office between 1901 and 1936 but today features only the Wyeth State Recreation Area.

February 8, 1833   *Columbia River*

8th   We found that a Capeau and 2 blanketts had been stolen by some Inds. from one of our men and went to the village just below our camp to recover them   they acknowledged the theft but the thieves had run off   we took two canoes to our camp and breakfasted   immediately after breakfast the man who had lost the articles took an ax and broke the worst canoe for which he was reprimanded by Mr Ermatinger   the other he left and a little after we left I saw the Ind. come and take it   we made 29 mils to the Dalles which are one mile or thereabouts long and encamped having passed two of the boats   the other owing to some mistake had she[e]red out and forced the line from those who were towing and forced one Indian into the stream and was drowned   he was in a bank about 15 feet high   he swam until he got into a whirl pool and went down.   Just below the Dalles the timber ceases   there are here many Indians   Tilky & Casineau are here the chiefs and very clever ones   all this day we saw Indians on the banks   the water passes even now at a furious rate and at high water it is impassible and boats are

> *carried as much as two mils and all the goods   for assisting
> through this place a little tobacco is given the Inds.   we gave
> the usual quantity and saw a personal struggle for the division
> of it.*

Theft by Indians along the Columbia River was frequently docu-mented in the early journals of fur traders traveling this route. Com-merce here was jealously controlled and nearly everyone who passed through paid some form of toll, voluntarily or not. Confrontations with local Indians at the Dalles were common. For example, in spring 1811, Astorian David Stuart came by on his way to Fort Okanogan. Natives stole two bales of goods and "maliciously threw large stones" at the canoes, damaging at least one. The Indians became "so audacious as to pillage the poor fellows, even of their knives and pocket handkerchiefs."[52]

The treacherous nature of the rapid itself dealt a tragic blow on this date. As the boats were being towed upstream through the roil-ing current, the line slackened enough to allow one craft to career out of control. The rope was yanked from the hands of the men on shore and knocked an Indian into the water. Projecting boulders and recesses in the steep rock walls had formed staggering waves and whirlpools. Though the man made a valiant effort to swim to safety, he drowned.

East of this point, the Columbia River cuts through the virtu-ally treeless basalt plateau region between the Cascade Range and the Rocky Mountains.

With the assistance of the local Wishram tribe, Ermatinger suc-cessfully got the boats and equipment to the upper end of the narrows, paying the customary price for labor. Here, they also met the Chinook chieftain Casineau, who held sway over much of the river from Astoria to the Cascades. Fur trade journals spelled Casineau's name variously, from "Kyeassino" to "Cassanov" or "Cassino." He was said to be the sec-ond most powerful American Indian on the lower Columbia River. Only the legendary Concomly, who had met Lewis and Clark at the mouth of the Columbia on November 20, 1805, was considered greater.[53] Casineau married one of Concomly's daughters, Illchee, in about 1820. Six years earlier, Illchee had wedded Duncan McDougall, an Astorian who later joined the Northwest Company, but upon his departure from the Indian country, she had become the wife of Casineau.[54] Paul Kane painted the chief's portrait at Fort Vancouver in the late 1840s and reported

> *Casanov is a man of advanced age, and resides principally at Fort Vancouver. I made a sketch of him while staying at the fort. Previously to 1829 Casanov was considered a powerful chief, and could lead into the field 1,000 men ... Casanov is a man of more than ordinary talent for an Indian, and he has maintained his great influence over his tribe chiefly by means of the superstitious dread in which they held him. For many years, in the early period of his life, he kept a hired assassin to remove any obnoxious individual against whom he entertained personal enmity.[55]*

Also at the Dalles to greet the white traders was the leader Tilki, whom Wyeth had met in late October on his westward journey. Tilki oversaw the region from the Dalles upriver to the mouth of the Walla Walla.

February 9, 1833   *Columbia River*

9th   Left the Great Dalls and in three miles came to the little dalles which we passed by towing in which we were delayed by reason of having only two lines one having been lost at the time the Indian was drowned   in three miles more I arrived at the Shutes or falls of the Columbia which are not in this stage of the water more than ten feet perpendicular but much more than that including the rapids above and below in the immediate vicinity   these falls once during the times the whites have been here have been sailed up owing as I suppose to the Dalles at such times affording a slow outlet to the accumulated waters and their being raised by this circumstance to above the level of the falls   this day got our baggage and goods over at the G. Dalles   I traded one horse which I sent on by Abbot   at the Shutes we found about 150 to 200 Indians who were very troublesome to pay for very trifling services   however they stole nothing.

Company bateaux were equipped with square sails and, when the prevailing winds were favorable, the boats went *á la voile* – under sail.[56] The idea of sailing up the Columbia as far as Celilo Falls was not unheard of, especially at high water. John Work's 1826 brigade, though already above the falls, had found mid-July breezes to be a great help. Work reported they "had a nice sail wind all day" and that "a fair aft Breeze throughout the day assisted our progress very considerably" the next day.[57] Governor George Simpson commented that

> *The Chutes vary very much in appearance according to the height of the waters. At one season may be seen cascades of twenty or thirty feet in height, while, at another, the current swells itself up into little more than a rapid, so as even to be navigable for boats.*[58]

In the fall of 1839, Father Modeste Demers recorded that

> *One may be astonished to learn that these chutes, so terrible at low water, are smooth and still at very high water, which does not happen every year. Then it is that, instead of fearing them, the voyageurs hasten to approach them, to light their pipes and rest.*[59]

Wyeth traded for a horse although he would soon be back at Fort Walla Walla, where he had left all of his pack animals in the care of Pambrun the previous October.

This day's camp was made on the north bank of the Columbia, in the vicinity of today's Maryhill State Park in Klickitat County, Washington.

February 10, 1833   *Columbia River*

10th   Passed over and gummed the boats and at 1/2 past 12 started up the river having traded another horse and sent it on by Woodman   one mile above the river Aux Rapide comes from the south   the size of the stream I cannot tell as I only saw the mouth of it   here on the N. side of the river Abbot came to me having lost the horse entrusted to him   I took Mr. Woodmans and gave Abbot with orders to wait until 10 ock tomorrow and then to come on whether he got the horse or

*not   we came today 9 miles and 6 yesterday   here we have
to give a piece of tobacco for every stick of wood we get   last
night was the first frost I have seen since the river broke   the
grass is somewhat green   this part of the river affords trout in
small quantity.*

Based on the mileage Wyeth reported, his "river Aux Rapide" must
be the Deschutes River. In earlier days, this waterway was often called
Riviere des Chutes or *Riviere aux Chutes*, meaning River of the Falls.[60]

The Captain traded for yet another horse and put this one in Woodman's charge only to learn a little while later that Abbott had not been
able to keep track of his own animal. Though a minor point, it is not
clear exactly what Wyeth has written here. F. G. Young edited the original entry to suggest that "gave" should be replaced with "left." In a 1984
reprint of Wyeth's journals, editor Don Johnson of the University of
Idaho modified the same line to read "I took Woodmans and gave [it to]
Abbot with orders to wait..." though Johnson was probably not working
from the original Wyeth manuscript. Since Wyeth said two days later
that he was glad to see "Abbot come up but without having found the
lost horse," it is more conceivable that Abbott was left afoot to hunt for
the missing animal and Woodman remained mounted. Abbott apparently spent the night by himself on the north shore.

Firewood was at a premium on the Columbian Plateau. In 1839, F.
A. Wislizenus described the plateau region thusly:

*This enormous stretch of country is really only one huge prairie,
rolling on in wave-like hills and broad plateaus, plentifully traversed,
it is true, by brooks and rivers, but so scantily provided with wood,
that even the mere traveler cannot always find the necessary
firewood.*[61]

William Clark had noted a similar shortage as he paddled downriver in October 1805, writing "fire wood is verry Scerce."[62]

February 11, 1833   *Columbia River*

11th   Started at an early hour and made the mouth of a considerable stream coming from the S. called John Days River from a hunter of that name formerly in this country   distant from our 1st camp 7 1/2 miles   we camped 22 1/2 miles from this on the North side of the river having had a strong and fair wind all day   one thing I observed in this part of the River is that the savages are civil and as much as one in ten has lost an eye as I suppose from the effects of the fine sand of the river being blown about or the violent wind for which this part of the river is noted   we found some few roots and little game with the natives   the night was windy and uncomfortabl but no frost but a little rain

This was the same John Day River Wyeth passed in late October 1832 on his way to Fort Vancouver.

Meriwether Lewis had noticed that blowing sand irritated the eyes of the Indians along this section of the river. On April 28, 1806, Lewis penned,

> *We gave them some eye-water which I beleive will render them more essential service than any other article in the medical way which we had it in our power to bestoe on them. soar eyes seem to be a universal complaint amonge these people; I have no doubt but the fine sand of these plains and river contribute much to this disorder.*[63]

John Work commented in the summer of 1828 that "the people were nearly blinded with driving sand" above Celilo Falls.[64]

David Douglas experienced "soar eyes" along the river first hand. Near the junction of the Walla Walla and Columbia rivers, the naturalist wrote, "My eyes began to trouble me much, the wind blowing the sand, and the sun's reflection from it is of great detriment to me ... My eyes so inflamed and painful that I can scarcely see distinctly an object ten yards distant."[65]

Paul Kane reported that in this region "furious gales of wind ... rush through the opening hills with inconceivable violence, and raise the sand in clouds so dense and continuous as frequently to render travelling impossible." Kane added that the windblown sand permeated everything to the point that the dried salmon eaten by the Walla Walla people was full of enough grit "as to wear away the teeth of the Indians, and an Indian is seldom met with over forty years of age whose teeth are not worn quite to the gums."[66]

Having traveled twenty-two-and-a-half miles beyond the mouth of John Day River, the party made its evening camp in the vicinity of modern Roosevelt, Washington.

February 12, 1833   *Columbia River*

12th   At 1/2 past 6 we started and made 2 miles to breakfast on the N. side   fair wind and clear   one boat stove and must stop to repair and gum   found two small logs of drift wood   at 10 ock. recommenced our journey with a fair light wind and made in all this day 17 miles   during the day had the satisfaction of seeing Abbot come up but without finding the lost horse.

This was the third time on this trip that the boats needed to be gummed, attesting to the constant maintenance required by these vessels. Firewood was in such short supply that Wyeth deemed finding driftwood noteworthy. Abbott rejoined Wyeth and Ermatinger without the missing horse.

February 13, 1833   *Columbia River*

13th   Calm in mng. but after breakfast had a fair and midling strong wind   at 1 ock passed the upper end of Grand Island   an Indian to day brought me a pouch and horn stolen from one of my men going down but the balls and powder used up which I redeemed for a little tobacco   last night a frost not

*severe   made this day 25 miles   found wood enough for use
on the banks but it is a custom of the Indians to run along the
beach and take possession of the wood there may be and
sell it [to] you for tobacco which appears to be their greatest
luxury   a quid is pay for almost anything.*

Wyeth's "Grand Island" was Francis Ermatinger's brother Edward's
"Gros Isle" in the journal of his trip from Fort Vancouver to York Factory in 1827.[67] John Work called it "Big Island" when he camped there
in 1826 and 1831; other fur traders called it "Long Island."[68] In Wyeth's
time, the island was about six miles long. The entire island was purchased in 1899 by Dr. Nelson G. Blalock, a Civil War surgeon and pioneer railroad developer. Renamed Blalock Island, it was later flooded by
Lake Umatilla, the reservoir behind the John Day Dam. Only the high
ground remains as a group of seven smaller islands known cumulatively
as the Blalock Islands.[69]

Tobacco was a common gift/currency along the river for most of
the early nineteenth century. Lieutenant Charles Wilkes, traveling from
Fort Vancouver to Fort Okanogan in 1841, related that Indians always
followed the expedition boats and provided assistance at the cost of two
leaves of tobacco for half an hour of help. The Indians also sold firewood
in exchange for tobacco.[70]

February 14-19, 1833   *Fort Walla Walla*

*14th   We started at 6 ock and in one mile passed the River
Ottillah   one mile above which rapids commence   the[se]
we passed one mile long making 3 to breakfast and started
at 1/2 past 10 with a fair and strong wind and reached Walla
Walla at 5 p.m.   just befor reaching this place the cut rocks
close into the river in such a manner that there appears but
a small perpendicular sided gap to look through   past these
and at W.W. both bank[s] fall down to a nearly levell plain   we
were again hospitably received by Mr. P.C. Pambrun   we
remained at this post until the 19th of Feb.   the weather mild
and clear but high S.W. winds   W.W. is a place noted for high*

winds   a little frost during the nights only   gras just getting green   My horses in tolerable good order and all found   eat horse meat all the time at this post   On Sunday took a ride up the river W.W.   found its bottoms good but not extensive and no wood   the corn for this post 150 bushells last year was raised at least 3 miles from the fort   none was stolen by the Indians   a good test of their honesty as they are all most always starving.   This place is kept by about 5 men   Inds. are freely admitted inside of it   about 1200 skins traded here   it is kept up mostly for trading horses and the safty of the communication   the course of the Wallah river is E. by N. near the fort when I saw it.

This entry was apparently written just prior to leaving Fort Walla Walla, because it contained a summary of Wyeth's stay at Pambrun's post. The combined group would travel north and east, toward the headwaters of the Walla Walla River, which Wyeth called the "Wallah" or sometimes simply "W. W."

This final leg of the journey up the Columbia River took Ermatinger and the party past the Umatilla River and the Grand Rapids. Ross Cox, traveling in the opposite direction in 1812, reported similar geography:

> *A few miles below the Walla Walla the land on the south side rises into rocky cliffs, near two hundred feet high, which extend some distance inland. There is a long and very dangerous rapid at their base, which, by way of pre-eminence, the Canadians call the Grande Rapide.*[71]

Cox added that he saw "immense numbers of rattlesnakes here, basking in the sun, and under rocks." Half a dozen men with Cox fired simultaneously at a batch of snakes lying under one rock and killed or wounded thirty-seven of the reptiles.[72]

At the post, Wyeth found all of the horses he had left with Pambrun the previous fall in tolerably good condition, and added the newly purchased mount to the cavallard. As mentioned before, Fort Walla Walla's

MAP 6 *Fort Walla Walla to Bitterroot Valley, 1833*

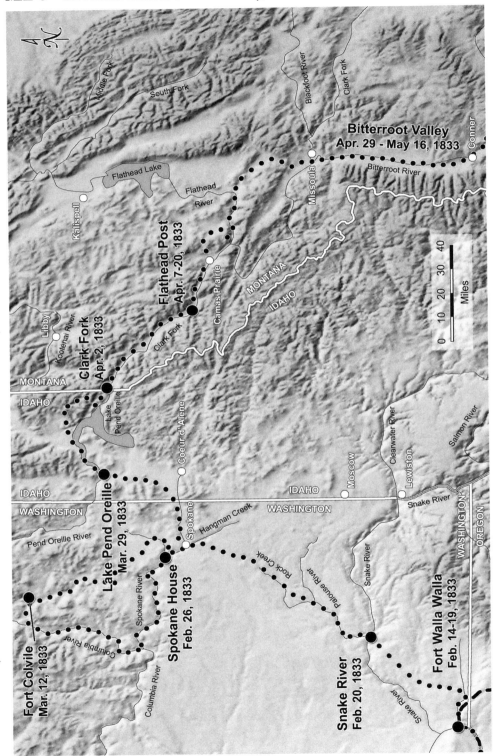

easy access to Indian horseflesh allowed the HBC to maintain a breeding program that kept the Company supplied with mounts.

When he visited the fort in 1825, HBC Governor Simpson was dismayed by the copious amount of horse meat consumed by the post's eleven men:

> *Some time ago no less than Seven Hundred Horses were slaughtered for the use of this Establishment in three Years besides Imported Provisions and it has been left for me to discover that neither Horse Flesh nor Imported Provisions are at all required as the River with a Potatoe Garden will abundantly maintain the Post.*[73]

Wyeth's report of 1200 pelts, presumably beaver, was typical of Fort Walla Walla's unimpressive fur trade revenues. Simpson had estimated 2000 beaver hides would be collected in 1824, but most years showed far fewer. When Simon McGillivray had been in charge here, his post journal indicated that between March 26, 1830 and November 29, 1831, eleven hundred beaver skins were drying in the storehouse – 340 more than the prior year. The successful horse trade, however, made maintaining this remote post worthwhile.[74]

Since the weather held mild and clear, Wyeth took a side trip to reconnoiter the area around the fort, and found the river bottoms disappointing. More surprising to Wyeth, Indians were allowed into the fort commons, probably due to there being only five men on staff. John Dease, trader at the post from 1823 to 1825, had relaxed restrictions on the natives, giving them much freer access. Attempts to reassert control over the Indians had met with little success.[75]

February 19, 1833   *Fort Walla Walla*

19th   Just as we were leaving the fort an Indian brought in the horse which Abbot lost at the Dalles and a short time after leaving the fort an Indian sent by Mr. P. brought one other which had strayed from Abbot at this place   we made this day 17 miles to a branch of the Wallah river here coming from the N.   the space nearly a plain and barren and sandy but good grass   this branch appears to be about half the Wallah

On the Columbia River a few miles downstream from its confluence with the Snake, Fort Walla Walla was an important trade center for the Hudson's Bay Company. It was built in 1818 and was originally known as Fort Nez Perce. WASHINGTON STATE HISTORICAL SOCIETY

> *river   encamped a little after sundown and for 12 yards blue clths. 1 Blkt. 2 1/2 pt 50 balls & powder 2 knives 1 lb. Tobacco bunch beads, 10 fish Hooks traded a good horse   this appears a fair price here.*

Transferring the freight to horses and leaving the Columbia River behind, Wyeth and Ermatinger began an overland segment of the journey to the interior.

The return of Abbott's two horses proved again the goodwill of the HBC employees and their influence on the Indians. It also reiterated Abbott's inability to supervise horses after almost a year on the trail.

In March 1832, about a year prior, Simon McGillivray documented several horse trades that provide comparison to Wyeth's "fair price here." McGillivray bartered for a "Stout Young Horse" from a Nez Perce chief. The goods exchanged were:

1 Int. Blanket 3 Points	1 doz. Rings
8 yd. Fine transpt. Beads	1 Japanned Tobacco Box
6 yd. Aquamarine ditto	with Glass
1 yd. Tobacco	1 Large Knife
1/2 yd. Common Strouds	1/2" Copper Kettle 2/2"[76]
1 doz. Thimbles	

In addition, McGillivray threw in "1 Flint, 1 Awl, 1 G Worm, & verm" as a gift. A "G Worm," or gun worm, was a coiled wire that attached to the end of a ramrod to aid in cleaning the gun's barrel. "Verm" was vermillion, a red grease paint much sought after by many Native Americans.[77]

Wyeth's evening bivouac on this date was at the confluence of the Touchet and Walla Walla rivers. Lewis and Clark had camped there in late April or early May 1806, as they took a shortcut to the Snake River.[78] The name Touchet derives from "Tú-se," the Nez Perce name for this waterway. The word means "roasting"; according to legend, Coyote roasted salmon here after breaking the fish dam guarded by the five Swallow sisters at Celilo Falls.[79]

February 20, 1833   *Snake River*

20th   We made a late start and after travelling 9 hours without water arrived at the Snake river   here running W.   our course was this day N. by E. 22 1/2 miles over a country which would be considered light sandy land with little sage   grass good and in tufts   very level except some trifling roundly swelling hills   these make one think of gently swelling breasts of the ladies.   Day warm and clear   We in the first of the day followed the branch of the W.W. mentioned yesterday say four miles on which I saw blackbirds which Mr. Pambrun says stay at W.W. all winter.

At day's end, the party camped on the Snake River across from the mouth of the Palouse River, named for a Sahaptin group known as Palus, though variously spelled.[80] Earlier, Lewis and Clark had called it Drewyer's River, after Expedition member George Drouillard. Astorians had named it Pavion in 1812; Alexander Ross later noted it as Pavilion and John Work dubbed it Flag River in 1825. In 1845, Paul Kane referred to the stream variously as the Pavilion, Paluce and Pelouse river.[81] More likely, the name of the river and the Indian tribe derived from the French *pelouse*, meaning grassy plain. During the spring, the fertile hills north of the Snake were covered in green bunch grass. Voyageurs traveling in the region often referred to the area as the palouse country.[82]

The topography, characterized by picturesque rolling hills, random humps and hollows, reminded Wyeth of the "gently swelling breasts of the ladies." Although fur trade era place names abound with references to human and animal body parts, such as French trappers naming the mountains Wyeth saw while in Pierre's Hole the *Tetons* (French for "breasts"), the remark seems rather out of character for the staid New Englander.[83]

February 21, 1833   *Palouse River*

21st   No frost in morning.   Crossed the river to the mouth of a creek coming into the river from the N. for 10 miles which was the length of our march this day   this creek is through cut rocks of moderate height for this country.   We followed the stream on the east bank.   These banks were about 300 feet high to the levell of the plain if that can be called a plain where the hills rise to an almost equal height and the gullies are abrupt and narrow.   The soil was what would be called in N[ew] E[ngland] a poor sandy soil producing good grass but still no wood   Traded two horses this day at the usual rates   The people who are most used to this country are so little afraid of the indians that they either travel without guns or with them unloaded.

The site of their Snake River crossing was where the Palouse Ferry would be constructed in 1860. Later known as Lyons Ferry, this current-powered transport operated well into the 1960s.[84] Passing along roughly the same route as Wyeth in this vicinity, the Mullan Military Road, completed in 1862, also ferried across the Snake at this location.[85]

Once on the north side of the river, Wyeth, Ermatinger and the string of supply-laden packhorses tramped along the east bank of the Palouse on a northerly bearing, following the rim of the canyon carved by the river through finely-grained basalt. The silty soils that Wyeth noted are "erosional remnants of what was once up to a 75 meter layer of windblown loess in this region."[86]

Wyeth referred briefly to the continual lack of firewood in this locale. When the Corps of Discovery was on the Palouse in mid-October 1805, Sergeant John Ordway reported that "we can Scarsely git wood enofe to cook a little victules." Most of the fuel the Corpsmen found had been gathered and stored by Indians who "raft all their wood down the River a long distance and they put it up on Scaffels and take great care of it." Expedition members ultimately raided these high stands, stealing wood from the Indians' storage.[87]

As for traveling essentially unarmed through this region, historian Alvin M. Josephy wrote:

Under [McLoughlin's] policy, benign and fair to its subjects, the roaming Nez Perces had gradually acclimated themselves to conforming to the standards of relations that the British traders demanded. At the heart of the Indians' change were such things

as continued desire for access to the white man and his trade and
alliance with him against common enemies, as well as a wish to
avoid trouble – all of which were guaranteed only by the stoppage of
horse thefts, pilfering, threats with arms, and other acts that angered
the traders. As the Indians abandoned those traits, their relations
with the British had grown more harmonious.[88]

After being tutored in weaponry and battle preparedness by the
Sublette brothers, Wyeth was no doubt surprised to find men in the
mountains without loaded guns.

February 22, 1833   *Palouse River*

*22nd   A pretty hard frost in the morning   followed the river one
mile on the North side then crossed it and made North 3 miles
and crossed a branch of it coming from the N.W.   Our course
this day N. by E. and encamped at a little run of water running
S.E.   This is inconsiderable   Saw about 20 antelope this day
in one herd   at our camp this nigh[t] observed about 2 inches
of frost in the ground   this days ride over very rocky country
the valleys of which are very good but small otherwise more
sandy than common   grass good   Made 22 1/2 miles*

To go from a morning with no frost at all to the next dawn covered
in hard frost must have intrigued the New Englander. Once in camp,
Wyeth apparently dug into the earth to find out just how deep the frost
line extended.

Following the Palouse River, the party passed Cow Creek early in the
day. Wyeth's "inconsiderable" southeast-running stream would have been
unusual because most of the currents flow westward in that area. Rock
Creek, running predominantly south, entered the Palouse near the end of
the day's trek. This was likely the stream to which Wyeth referred.

Wyeth's antelope sighting may be the only historic record of the presence of pronghorn in what is now the state of Washington. Prehistoric
remains are relatively common in the region's archaeological sites, but
these creatures were thought to have been extirpated from the state. A

1997 synopsis of Washington State mammals does not include any reference to pre-1900 pronghorn. Pronghorn were re-introduced in 1938.[89]

February 23, 1833   *Rock Creek*

23rd   N. 17 miles over a rough and Rocky country with a few small bottoms which are good land   at 9 miles from last camp passed some of the best specimens of Basaltic colums which I have seen   They were 5 sided and about 50 feet high some standing independent others tumbled down to the foot of the wall like demolished Towers   This days march [passed] many small lakes whether formed by the snow or not I can not say but I think some of them are permanent   none larger than a few acres   Camped at a stream coming from the N. and were visited by three Indians who report the road to Colville impassable for snow   a hard frost last night and frost in the ground beside the lakes mostly frozen over but not thick   these made me think of the old business of my life.

Wyeth and his party had reached an area south of Rock Lake packed with lakes of all sizes; Hergert, Stevens, Duck, Johnson, and Texas lakes, to name a few. Camp was made near the site of present Ewan, Washington. Unsurprisingly, the sight of so many iced-over lakes brought images of Wyeth's former profession to his mind.

Fort Colvile, their next planned destination, was the new HBC headquarters for the region, having replaced Spokane House in 1826. Named for Andrew Colvile, a high-ranking London HBC official, the post was constructed on the Columbia River near Kettle Falls – closer to HBC trade routes. The original spelling of the fort's name would be changed to "Colville" after the U.S. Army took over the post in the early 1860s.[90] Even though Spokane House had well established trade connections, Governor Simpson thought Fort Colvile better located, reasoning that:

> *a very heavy expense and serious inconvenience in transporting the Outfits and returns between the Main River [Columbia] and the present Establishment by Land a distance of about 60 Miles will be avoided.*[91]

A snow-blocked trail to Fort Colvile held little concern for Ermatinger and he maintained his plan to transport his equipment down the Clark Fork via boat, and into his projected sales district to serve the Flathead tribe.

February 24, 1833   *Rock Creek*

24th   20 miles N. through timber in the first of which we encamped last night   the stream which we camped on here forks   no game except two small prairie hens   passed many little lakes one of which is as large Fresh Pond and one nearly so   the rest smaller   Patches of snow and one third of the trees prostrated last year by southerly gale   their trunks much obstructed the path before us   on the right are snow covered and moderately high Mts.   found good wood at our camp by the light of which I now write   the scene reminds me of my Ice men at work by torch light   not frost enough in the ground to prevent driving tent stakes   the little [rain] and snow made streams run Southerly

---

Following Rock Creek, the brigade passed its confluence with Buckeye Creek before stopping for the night. Of the nearby lakes comparable to Fresh Pond back home, Rock Lake and Bonnie Lake, both long and narrow, were two of the largest on the route. The topography began to include sparse stands of ponderosa pine and other conifers. Recent gale-force winds had apparently knocked over many of these, blocking the trail but providing ample firewood – a pleasant change from the last few weeks.

The snow-covered range on the eastern horizon was likely the Tekoa Mountains, a low, outlying ridge of the Bitterroot system that reached to nearly 4,000 feet in elevation.[92] The name was taken from Old Testament references to a fortress city on the eastern slopes of the Judean hills about twelve miles south of Jerusalem. Tekoa was believed to have been the home of the prophet Amos and is mentioned in the Old Testament books of 2 Samuel, 2 Chronicles, Jeremiah and Amos.[93]

Here Wyeth described his routine of sitting in the orange glow of a roaring campfire, writing in his journal at the end of the day. The scene reminded him of the warm winter temperatures in Massachusetts that had forced him to harvest ice at night by torchlight.

February 25, 1833 *Spokane River*

25th   in a N. direction 15 miles to Spokan River a stream now about half as large as the Snake River   it is now high from the melting of the snow   its sources are not distant and in a range of Mts. in sight   this Range runs about N.W. which is here the general course of the stream but how far I cannot say as it is visible but a short distance   at this place are the remains of the old Spokan House   one Bastion of which only is now standing which is left by the Indians from respect to the dead   one clerk of the Co. being buried in it   the banks of this river are here rocky and precipitous   I observed among the rocks of its bed Granite Green Stone Quartz sandstone Lava or Basalt   the country on approaching this river from the South resembles the pine plains of N. Hampshire near Concord   we passed the divide between the waters of this and the last river about 5 mils from our last nights Camp   striking then after passing the isolated wood in which we had camped and a large plain devoid of wood   a deep valley running N.   Crossed the most of our baggage today

Leaving the Rock Creek camp, Wyeth described a route that took the pack train away from the creek on a bee line for the Spokane River. He spoke of a "divide" between the waters flowing predominantly south toward Rock Creek and those streams now headed more northward toward the Spokane. However, there was not a drastic shift in landscape but a subtle change as the Columbia Plateau, Wyeth's "large plain devoid of wood," gradually gave way to the hills and mountains on the east. The deep valley mentioned was probably the gorge through which flows Hangman Creek as it winds its way north to drain into the Spokane River.

The name Spokane derived from the Spokan Indians, a Salish-speaking tribe that Lewis and Clark called the "Sket-so-mish." David Thompson called them the "Sleetshoo," yet in 1810 dubbed his newly-built post Spokane House. In 1812, Ross Cox referred to the nation as the Spokans. The people called themselves "Spukanee," which was translated as "Sun People" or "Children of the Sun."[94]

The mountains Wyeth pointed out were the southernmost peaks of the Selkirk Mountains and the northernmost portion of the Bitterroots, sometimes called the Coeur d'Alene Mountains. The Spokane River took its rise from the outlet of Lake Coeur d'Alene, about twenty miles east of the modern town of Spokane, Washington. Coeur d'Alene, meaning "awl hearted," was the name applied to the local Indians by French traders who found them shrewd businessmen. Cox referred to them as "Pointed Hearts."[95]

The Northwest Company's David Thompson built Spokane House at the confluence of the Spokane and Little Spokane rivers – a location that had, for centuries, been a gathering place for Indians to catch and dry fish. From 1810 through the next eleven years, Spokane House was the principal distribution point for the NWC on the upper Columbia. Operations continued after Hudson's Bay merged with the NWC in 1821, until the disadvantages of its location became too evident. The Spokane was unnavigable during certain seasons, thus horses had to be kept on hand for transportation from the post to the Columbia and back. During the spring, however, when the river was full from runoff as Wyeth described it here, boats could float to the Columbia.[96]

In March of 1826, the post was dismantled and Fort Colvile was built along the Columbia near Kettle Falls. Jacques Finlay, a former NWC clerk long associated with Spokane House, chose to stay behind with his family. He died in 1828 and was buried under the southeast bastion of the post. All of the other buildings and the stockade had been used by the local tribes for firewood. Finlay's grave marker, the southeast bastion, was still standing in1836 when Reverend Samuel Parker passed by. However, when German naturalist Charles A. Geyer visited the site in 1843, nothing was left.[97]

February 26, 1833   *Spokane House*
  26th   Arrived [at Spokan House]   After perusing the enclosed loose papers I proceed

The "loose papers" included in Wyeth's journal had been lost by the time Young edited the original diary. Young believed that these sheets contained Wyeth's notes about an unexplained journey from the site of Spokane House to Fort Colvile and back. A March 12, 1833, letter Wyeth wrote from Fort Colvile, addressed to HBC Governor George Simpson, makes the case for such a trip. Wyeth's upcoming journal entry for March 28, 1833, will also refer to this excursion. Unfortunately, whatever Wyeth may have noted on these unattached pages between February 26 and March 26 has been lost.

On or about February 26, Ermatinger left the freight in care of a small crew and proceeded to Fort Colvile with Wyeth and a handful of men, probably by horseback. Ermatinger wrote his brother Edward on March 11, "I arrived [at Fort Colvile] a few days ago and must be off tomorrow." While at the district headquarters, Ermatinger made final arrangements with trader Francis Heron for conducting the eastbound goods down the Clark Fork, and cleared his accounts with the post.[98]

Francis Heron, chief trader at Fort Colvile from 1829 until 1835, had worked for HBC since 1812. Simpson noted privately that Heron "was getting into habits of Drunkenness but found they were likely to injure his prospects of advancement and therefore Changed from Grog to a rigid Water Drinker." Heron had more than one violent quarrel with his supervisor, John McLoughlin.[99] Based on the tone of Ermatinger's letters, he and Heron were not on the best terms either. He had written the previous year that Heron was "altogether a mean fellow, and if he does not go out as expected by the express, I shall refuse to serve under him."[100]

Wyeth, however, seemed to tolerate Heron. In a letter to McLoughlin, Wyeth, thanked "Mr. Pambrun Mr. Herron and Mr. Hermatinger" for their attention to his needs while in the Northwest.[101] Heron and Pambrun must have been intrigued by Ermatinger's unique Company venture. Discussions between the men while at Fort Colvile surely covered the prospects of such an undertaking. Wyeth suggests that the three HBC men encouraged Wyeth to propose a business relationship with the British firm.

Despite the loss of the *Sultana*'s valuable goods, and the disappearance of PTC members, the intrepid Wyeth showed firm resolve. Ever the entrepreneur, Wyeth wrote a letter to Governor George Simpson with an ambitious offer to partner with the Hudson's Bay Company.

Fort Colville March 12th 1833

Sir

I am induced by gentlemen in this country to suppose that you would enter into some arrangement for a supply of goods and therefore send the enclosed proposal. I left Boston in March last with 32 men with the intention of forming on the Columbia or south of it [a post] for collecting furs and salmon to be sent to the States by vessells ordered therefrom such vessells to bring out the goods required for the trade. My plan was based on the following grounds viz. that Salmon (worth in the States 16$ per Bbl. of 30 gallons) would pay all the expenses that goods introduced by this route would be entitled to the drawback and this would be a consideration as they are nearly all foreign to the States and being coarse pay a heavy duty, that the saving made in the purchase of horses here instead of at St. Louis is at least 25$ per head, that the danger of transporting this side of the mountains is infinitely less than on the other and the distance to the Fur country much less. In the first part of said undertaking I have completely failed. All my men have left me and what goods and valuables I had with me have been expended or deposited where they will probably be lost to me. I am now on my return to the States for the purpose of forming new arrangements to carry my original plan into execution. In case I make no arrangement with the Co. I shall if I arrive in Boston by the 1st Nov. next come to the Columbia the following summer, if I arrive later I shall be delayed until the next.

It appears to me that as an American I posses some advantage that an Englishman would not inasmuch as I can visit parts of the country from which he is excluded and still not so remote in point of distance difficulty or expense as from St. Louis.

I have already lost largely from a capital at first small and am therefore desirous to proceed on a more secure plan even if it should offer less prospect of profit. I have to observe that in case of agreement being made I will give surety satisfactory to the Co. for fulfilling any part of the same or if required will deposit in their hands a sufficient sum for the same purpose. The only objection to the latter would be the difference in the rate of interest in the states and with you.

In case of an agreement for supply of goods the supply of men would still be a consideration. If men could come to this side of the Ry. Mts. as early as July a fall hunt might be made which is all that can be done from St. Louis. Canadians are to be had cheaper than Americans and are for some purposes better men. Their conveyance would not be so expensive as horses would be saved which cost 30$ at St. Louis and the same set of animals are fit for a full hunt. I would not wish more than 15 Canadians. These might be procured by myself or agent or furnished me by the Co. as they might elect and the residue of the men required might be procured in the Mts. without the expense of bringing them into the country or learning them the ways of it. If no political dificulty exists there must be some advantage in using a few Canadians. Should you deem it for the interest of the Co. to close with me an agreement not essentially different from the enclosed proposal you would much oblige me by forwarding to my address care of Mess. Jarvis & Brown Merchants Baltimore Maryland a contract to the purpose which I will execute and immediately proceed to fulfill. I request this mode of proceedure because I will have but one month after my arrival at Boston to prepare for a voyage to the Columbia, in case of failure of this negotiation with the Co.

To Geo Simpson Esq. Gov. H.B.C. York Factory

Yrs &c N J W

Copy of the proposal enclosed in the two foregoing letters[102]

1st The Hon H.B.C. to furnish at their store at Vancouver to N.J.W. such goods as he may select at the same rate that the clerks of the said Co pay for the goods supplied them viz 50 pr ct on their original cost

2d The said Co to lay no obstruction in the way of the said Wyeths trading at any post or place for provisions or animals to be used in his business or to his trading furs anywhere south of the Columbia and not within a 100 miles of their posts and generally in matters indifferent to their interest to forward his views and operations

*and to give him such information as may be in their power and not
inconsistent with their immediate interest*

*3d The said Co to Cr the acc. of said Wyeth at the rate of $5 for full
Beavers and in proportion for kittens and yearlings and for all other
furs and skins usually secured by the said Co. as merchandise at the
same prop. to their markett value in London or wherever that Co.
dispose of their furs as 5$ is to the markett value of the Beaver skin.*

*4th The said Wyeth to deliver all Furs and skins of every description
of which he may get possession to the Co.*

*5th Said Wyeth to continue the arrangement for five years and in
case of his not doing so to be bound not to do a Fur business in any
country to which the H.B. Co. have access.*

*6th In case said Wyeth faithfully performs this said agreement, then
the H.B. Co. at the end of the time agreed on is to pay over to him
any balance that may be due him in cash or goods as the said W. may
elect and at all times he is entitled to claim from them in case any
balance which may be due him over and above $1000.*[103]

This was not the first of such schemes Simpson had seen from an American. In late December 1828, American trader Joshua Pilcher had written to the Governor, offering his services to his competitor. Short of men, trade goods, and equipment, Pilcher's fur company had gone out of business at that summer's rendezvous. His partners had scattered and future prospects looked bleak. Pilcher thus proposed that the British supply him with goods that he would take to the eastern side of the Continental Divide to compete with other American traders in the upper Missouri country. He suggested the expedition be in his name to get around the regulations restricting foreigners from trapping on American soil.[104]

Simpson wasted no time in rejecting Pilcher, even as he admitted that the idea had merit:

*If a difficulty of a formidable character did not present itself, which is
Territorial rights of the United States Government to that Country.*

*These rights, we as British subjects cannot infringe openly, and
although the protecting Laws of your Government might be successfully
evaded by the plan you suggest still I do not think it would be reputable
in the Hon[orable] Hudson's Bay Coy to make use of indirect means to
acquire possession of a Trade to which it has no just claim.*[105]

Wyeth's offer of paying fifty percent advance on original cost appears lucrative for the HBC at first glance. But an understanding of HBC business practice adds perspective. Original or prime cost was the actual invoice value of goods sent from England to the Columbia via Company supply ships. An "advance" or markup, including costs for such things as freight and insurance, was then added to the original invoice value to arrive at the total cost the post was charged on goods. Wyeth no doubt had determined the existing price structure at Fort Vancouver during the months he was there. The advance had initially been set by the Governor and Committee at seventy percent back in 1821. McLoughlin had pled to have this reduced but it was not until 1827 that the HBC controllers lowered it to fifty percent and then, two years later, authorized a further reduction to thirty-three and one third percent. A lower cost to McLoughlin allowed better advantage in trade, providing more room to manipulate retail prices on merchandise.[106]

Yet that thirty-three and one third advance was only a paper exchange. It would certainly make the accounts of a trading post look more profitable, but the Governor knew that a lower cost of goods would "not probably cover the charges" for acquiring inventory. To Simpson, such a loss was "a matter of little importance as the expenses actually incurred, be they more or less," would be charged off to the fur trade.[107] Therefore, Wyeth's proposal of fifty percent advance on prime cost was not as advantageous to the Company as might be presumed.[108]

Simpson never replied to Wyeth's proposal, and Wyeth would withdraw it eight months later. By 1834, however, HBC would warm to the idea of using Americans to compete in U.S. Territory. That year, Warren Ferris managed just such an agreement. Partnering with HBC employee Nicholas Montour, Ferris bought trade goods and headed for the Green River Valley. Though the merchandise was charged against Montour's Company account as surety, Ferris was specifically named as leader of the enterprise.[109]

In early March 1833, McLoughlin had written to fellow HBC bureaucrat John McLeod. McLoughlin acerbically remarked,

> *A party of Americans made their way to this place they intended to Establish a Salmon fishery, but their plan has failed for the present in consequence of the vessel being wrecked, with their supplies being wrecked on their way there – and though he is off to Boston his people are here and he says he will be Back.*[110]

Though McLoughlin did not name anyone, he was obviously referring to Wyeth.

About this time, John Ball was ready to abandon teaching at Fort Vancouver. His role in schooling the children there was taken up by Solomon Smith, another former member of Wyeth's company. Seeing no opportunity to return east in the near future, Ball had traveled up the Willamette River, looking over the country where a handful of retired HBC men were already settled. On March 1, Ball began farming on French Prairie with a rough start:

> *I came to this place and commenced farming under many disadvantages. I boarded the first three months at J. B. Desportes, a half-breed, whose family consisted of two wives, besides one absent, by all seven children, four or five slaves and two or three hired Indians, besides cats and dogs without number. All inhabited one room in common.*[111]

McLoughlin loaned him seed and tools, which Ball took up the Columbia by boat. His journal continued,

> *I caught from the prairie a span of horses with a lasso, made a harness, and set them to work. For harness I stuffed some deerskins, sewed in proper form, for collars, fitted to them for the harness, crooked oak limbs tied top and bottom with elk skin strings. Then to these strips of hide was fastened for tugs, which I tied to the drag made from a crotch of a tree. On this I drew out logs for my cabin, which, when I had laid up and put up rafters to make the roof, I covered with bark pealed from the cedar trees.*[112]

Solomon Smith took over teaching duties at the Fort Vancouver school when John Ball chose to start farming in 1833. Smith married Celiast Kobaway, daughter of the Clatsop chief, in 1837. OREGON HISTORICAL SOCIETY ORHI #14130 BB006419

With the aid of his neighbors, Ball managed to plow a sizeable field, fenced it and planted crops. John Sinclair, who had joined Wyeth's company at the same time as Ball, was a frequent companion at Ball's farmhouse. Ball also sporadically housed a "young wild native" to help him catch the horses.[113]

Having returned to Spokane House from Fort Colvile, Wyeth and Ermatinger promptly headed their brigade eastward, toward the Flathead villages.

March 27, 1833   *Spokane River*

27th   March   due N.E. by N   24 miles we made this day   This line cuts the Spokan river   This point we turned but I call the course direct for convenience   this course is through a tolerable fertile prairie   the grass good and flowers plenty   on the W. side are low range of rocky hills which are granite and a better development of the broken rock named

yesterday   I find it to be volcanic by its being [a word omitted]
blending with porous rock   on our left and about half way
of the days march passed a mile distant a little lake 1/2 mile
across   to the E. by N. of this is a lake 3 miles across from
which the Spokan flows   neither of these I have seen but
take this from hearsay   arrived at our camp and all well and
in better order   I have forgot to mention that the stream that
comes into the Spokane near the House brings down pebles
of volcanic rock   also that the streams near our present camp
come from the hills enter the prairie of the Spokan River and
disappear in the ground.

Wyeth started out following the Little Spokane River along the base of Lookout Mountain, then veered southeasterly around Little Baldy Mountain, where the "line cuts the Spokan river." At this point the party turned almost due east, passing through the "fertile prairie" of Spokane Valley. Toward the end of the day, near the modern border of Idaho, the route finally began a sweep to the northeast across the Rathdrum Prairie.

The first lake mentioned in this entry was likely Liberty Lake, named for Louis Laliberte, a well-connected Northwest Company man who joined Wilson Price Hunt's overland Astorian party at Lachine, Quebec, and came to the Columbia River region.[114] The larger body of water Wyeth heard about but never saw was undoubtedly Lake Coeur d'Alene, the source of the Spokane River. Ross Cox depicted the prairie through which the Spokane River flowed as "a perfect plain, with a light gravelly bottom." It was the scene of many horse races in which "some of the rearward jockeys were often severely peppered in the face from small pebbles thrown up by the hoofs of the racers in front."[115]

March 28, 1833   *Spokane River*

28   Made 18 miles N. through a level and wooded country and
camped with only snow water and poor grass   the rocks seen
to day are bolders of granite and observed that the compass
in one place would not Traverse   this happened while going

to Colville from Spokan and coming from there back   also observed Today and yesterday the effects of some former gale in prostrated trees   direction here S.W.

Continuing northward, the brigade crossed into the panhandle of what is now Idaho. They traveled in the shadow of Rathdrum Mountain, flanking Round Mountain by the end of the day to make camp near modern North Pole, Idaho.

Numerous lateral basalt flows in the area lay exposed near the surface as talus, heavily veined with iron. These can become highly magnetic, especially when struck by lightning. These mineral deposits interfered with the swing of the needle in Wyeth's compass.[116]

March 29, 1833   *Pend Oreille River*

29   horses missing in mng. and not found till noon   went N. 9 miles and struck Flat Head River   compass again refused to traverse   through deep snow today and yesterday and thick young trees and fallen timber   observed here the white pine and Hemlock   snow and rain all yesterday   found our people at the river with the boats.

With a full morning spent catching horses, Wyeth and Ermatinger covered few miles on this date. But they were able to rendezvous with HBC crewmen, who had brought empty boats either from Fort Colvile or Flathead Post to the planned meeting place on what Wyeth called the Flat Head River, today's Pend Oreille. Here, Ermatinger's brigade would load the horse-packed Flathead supplies onto the boats for transport by water to Flathead Post.

Lewis and Clark had originally called this river the "Flat Head," but on May 6, 1806, they changed the name to "Clark's river." The explorers believed that the Pend Oreille, Clark and Bitteroot all comprised the same river.[117] Ross Cox explained that the Flat Head "falls into the Columbia over a foaming cascade, caused by a large collection of immense rocks, which choked up the entrance."[118] Today, this waterway is the Pend Oreille River, which rises from the western outlet of the lake of the same name. It drains into the Columbia River near Montrose, British Columbia.

Pend Oreille meant "hangs from ears," a name given by early French trappers to the Indian tribe that wore shell ornaments dangling from their earlobes. The Indians called themselves Kalispels. Alexander Henry, writing in 1808, reported "The Kullyspell or Earbob Indians are also a tribe of the Flat Heads and speak the same language."[119]

March 30, 1833   *Pend Oreille River*

30th   Remained at the same place   crossed the river   I here saw an Indian who was entirely blind   he seemed to be taken good care of by his relatives   made him a small present for which he thanked me   parted company with Mr Ermatinger he to go on with the goods by water myself with horses by land   last night the coldest for some time   today warm and pleasant

On the north bank of the river, near today's Laclede, Idaho, Ermatinger's packs were transferred from horses to the flat-bottomed barges that would be poled across Lake Pend Oreille and up the Clark Fork to the Flathead Post near Thompson Falls. Ermatinger and his boats set off as soon as the loading was finished, leaving Wyeth to make his way eastward to the post, leading more than 100 horses belonging to both men. The pack animals would be loaded up again in a few weeks.

10.
The Road to the Buffalo

Once he parted with Ermatinger, the trail Wyeth followed around the northeast side of Lake Pend Oreille, up the Clark Fork, and eventually to the steppes of the Great Plains was also known as the "Road to the Buffalo." Several mountain tribes used it for semi-annual forays to hunt bison east of the Continental Divide. Meriwether Lewis reported that the Nez Perce called it "Cokahlarishkit"; David Thompson labeled it the "Great Road of the Flathead." Today it is often referred to as the Kootenai Trail.[1]

Nicolas Point described an 1842 Flathead party setting out on this worn path, clearly marked from many years of use:

> *Since these hunts were long affairs, the hunters took with them everything they possessed. Each wigwam counted usually seven or eight persons, and these, together with their provisions, required the use of about twenty horses. Some fifteen parallel trails, formed by dragging wigwam poles, wound between two chains of mountains.*[2]

This ancient highway to the plains served mountain tribes until the late nineteenth century.

March 31, 1833   *Lake Pend Oreille*

31st   Moved early N. 7 miles passing a point and two little streams   Excessively bad going in crossing the point from snow and brush   E. two mils along the river   N.N.E. 5 miles to the Lake then a line to our camp cutting the lake   5 mils more N.N.E.   This lake is about three miles broad and indeed the river so far resembles a long lake little or no current and 3/4 miles wide   plenty of patridges, gese, and Duck and some deer meat of the Indians   all clay country   mountainous   one Horse gave out and left him   a good lo[d]ge made of Branches

of Pine had almost made me forget that it had snowed and
rained all day   ourselves and goods were wet through   we
had no human comfort except meat enough to eat and good.

Crossing the point of land immediately north of modern Laclede, Idaho, Wyeth essentially followed the river to the shores of Lake Pend Oreille. Wet spring weather brought heavy snow and rain that made travel difficult. The streams he noted in the initial few miles were most likely Johnson and Smith creeks. Passing the site of today's Sandpoint, Idaho, Wyeth and his party had no trouble shooting game birds, which supplemented the venison provided by local native people.

Wyeth spent the night in a brush shelter, protected from the weather. It was not clear whether Wyeth's men constructed the hut themselves, whether the Indians who supplied them with meat had also offered him room, or if the party found an abandoned dwelling. Use of makeshift brush shelters was common among tribes on the move. Warren Ferris, for example, availed himself of such lodgings while traveling to Flathead Post. On the Clark Fork in January 17, 1834, he "passed down the river about twelve miles, where [he] found a comfortable bush cabin, and halted for the night." Two days later, he "traced along the path about half a mile, and came to a large bush cabin."[3]

In September 1809, David Thompson built a Northwest Company trading post on Lake Pend Oreille's Memaloose Point near present Hope, Idaho, which he dubbed Kullyspel House. Wyeth indicated he saw "all clay country" but Thompson said "the soil was light, and had no blue clay, which is so very necessary for plaistering between the logs of the house and especially the roof."[4]

April 1, 1833   *Lake Pend Oreille*

1st April   E. 2, N 3, E by S. 3, and found that from this spot
the place where I entered on the lake bore S.W. N. by E. 2, E.
by S. 5 N. 3 and made the traverse of a large peninsular   at
one mil E. by N. struck the head of a creek which after 3
miles more led us back to the Lake at the entrance into it of

the River Tete Plate.   This Lake is a large and fine sheet of water   it appears of a good depth   There looks as if a large river entered on the S. side   at the east end it is widest and there are two Islands   it is surrounded by lofty and now snowy Mts. but their summits are timbered   yesterday saw nothing but Granite   today saw Slate and Sandstone   not the least volcanic appearance in this part of the Country.

Working his way east, then north around Kirby Mountain, Wyeth led the pack string across the Sunnyside Peninsula and into the Cabinet Mountains. Lightning Creek brought the team back onto the river running into Lake Pend Oreille. Wyeth again called this the Flat Head River, though he used the French *Tête Platte*. Today, this tributary is known as the Clark Fork, named for William Clark of the Corps of Discovery.[5] Ross Cox, too, knew this section of the Clark Fork as the Flathead River.[6] Today's Flathead River, which rises in the lake of the same name, is a tributary of this Clark Fork of the Columbia which should not be confused with Clark's Fork of the Yellowstone.

The origin of the name Flathead, or Tête Platte, for the tribe and numerous geographic namesakes, has long been obscure. Tribal members have suggested that the term was adopted by early traders from sign language gestures indicating these people. The gesture was to press the hands against the sides of the head, hence "flat head." Another version of its origin was that long ago, two tribal groups lived in the Flathead country, the "Leg People" and the "Wide-Head People." The ones whose heads looked broad were imagined to have pressed them to increase the spread though Warren Ferris was convinced that "not one living proof of the existence at any time of that practice can now be found among them." Their tribal name was Salish.[7]

Wyeth was correct regarding the apparent depth of Lake Pend Oreille. Over 1200 feet deep in places, this glacially carved body of water hosts the United States Navy's Farragut Naval Training Center at its southern tip, near Bayview, Idaho. The base was the second largest submarine training center in the world during World War II, but today is used for underwater acoustic research.[8]

Wyeth was mistaken, however, in believing that a large river entered the lake on its south side. While Cape Horn Creek enters Scenic Bay on that end, it is not of substantial size. Wyeth probably saw simply an arm of the lake extending several miles southward.

Although Wyeth reported two islands in the lake, there are at least four in the area around the mouth of the Clark Fork. These include present-day Warren, Cottage, Pearl and Memaloose islands. Warren Island, named for Civil War veteran Charles S. Warren, was once known as "Wasunka" (Mother of Twins). The twins were Cottage Island, named for a building on the island, and Pearl Island, named after the daughter of settler Joe Childs. Memaloose, which translates as "dead," had earlier been used by local Native Americans as a burial ground.[9]

The number of islands Wyeth could see may have been reduced by higher water levels caused by early spring snow melt. The construction of the Albeni Falls dam in the 1950s would end these dramatic seasonal fluctuations. The dam, located just beyond where Priest River enters the Pend Oreille River, allowed the Army Corps of Engineers to regulate water levels in the lake. Today, there is a six to ten foot difference between spring and winter levels, depending on the needs of resident fish species, particularly Kokanee salmon and bull trout.[10]

April 2, 1833   ***Clark Fork of the Columbia***

2nd   Made E.S.E. 6 mils through a difficult swamp over a hill and to the main river again during which time we passed two small streams   this swamp had the largest cedars apparently the same as those of the N.E. that I have ever seen   I measured one at my height from the ground of 31 feet circumferance and I presume some were larger   no rocks to day but sandstone and slate   camped on acc. of my horses having had no feed lately   the slate is tortuitous and I think mica slate   here my Indian brought me in some onions and two kinds of trout   some of the trout I have bought of the Indians as large as 10 lbs.   they are plenty and taken with the hook   there are plenty of ducks and gese   the Ducks are the [same] as the tame ducks of N[ew] E[ngland]

Lightning, Cascade, Spring and Mosquito creeks all flow into the Clark Fork from the north side and create the beginning of the river's mouth – a lush marshy, wetland and home today to the Panhandle Wildlife Management Area. In more recent times, this delta has been affected by logging, forest fires and development of the town of Clark Fork, Idaho; thus the open swamp seen by Wyeth is now predominantly wetland scrub, shrubs and forested area. Wyeth moved up Mosquito Creek to traverse Antelope Mountain, circling around back to the Clark Fork.

Western red cedar (*Thuja plicata*) is still common in these riparian wetlands. Sometimes called Pacific red cedar, this coniferous tree is actually related to the cypress. Red cedars often top two hundred feet in height, and as in Wyeth's example, can be ten to twelve feet in diameter. They are long-lived, sometimes surviving more than a thousand years.[11]

This was Wyeth's first mention of an Indian traveling companion. Ermatinger may have supplied the Bostonian with someone who knew the terrain to insure the pack horses would reach Flathead Post. Alternatively, Wyeth's journal will later reveal that a twenty-year-old Salish man was returning back east with him. This man may be the person mentioned in the current entry, but his origin is unknown and is never satisfactorily explained by Wyeth.

Lake Pend Oreille was home to many species of trout, most notably bull, cutthroat, rainbow and lake trout. The lunkers Wyeth purchased could have been any of these. The Idaho state record rainbow, a thirty-seven-pounder, and the record bull trout, weighing in at thirty-two pounds, were both caught in the lake in the 1940s; bull trout can no longer be legally harvested.[12]

April 3, 1833   *Clark Fork of the Columbia*

3d   10 mils almost due E. cutting a mountain and through almost impenetrable wo[o]d and deep snow   much trouble and delay to keep the trail   from the mountain 4 mils from last nights camp saw our last camp on this Lake which bore W. by N.   to night we camped without grass but could not go further   some of the horses strayed in the trail behind

Passing below the base of Sugarloaf Mountain, Wyeth drove his herd across the modern Idaho border and into the present state of Montana. From a high point of his traverse, he was able to look back and see the spot where the party had camped a few nights before. Snow covered whatever grass might have been available. Still, the party was too tired to go on, and camped without feed for the stock. The more worn-out horses were left behind on the trail.

April 4, 1833   *Clark Fork of the Columbia*

4th   Started our Indian early to find the strayed horses and started camp ahead 9 mils E. following the river the whole way altho the trail cuts off the point and encamped where the trail again strikes the river   at this place there is a considerable [creek] coming from the E. by N. into the river   here for the first time since reaching Walla Walla I saw fresh Beaver sign   the Indian has not yet come up with the horses and little feed for those we have with us   to day saw a small sized Bear but he was off to soon for a shot

---

This day's trek took Wyeth's small party upstream along the Clark Fork's north bank as the steep slopes of Pillick Ridge rose on the left. The group stopped for the night at Bull River.

April 5-6, 1833   *Clark Fork of the Columbia*

5th   12 mils E.S.E. through deep snow and thick wood most of the way sometimes miry sometimes slippery with ice and always obstructed by the great quantity of fallen wood   Last night late the Indian brought up all the lost horses

6th   9 mils E.S.E. trail better   slate rock only   Camped on the river last night in the mountains.   Yesterday two horses gave out   left a man to keep them and bring them up if possible   to day one gave out which I will leave at this camp for same man

---

From the mouth of Bull River, Wyeth pushed the horse herd along the riverbank, the precipitous walls of Government Mountain looming above them. They passed the site of modern Noxon, Montana, across the river. Snow continued, making the going slick with mud and ice as the party splashed through Rock and McKay creeks and ended the day near Swamp Creek on April 5. Nine miles farther upstream on the Clark Fork the next day found Wyeth's small band camped at the confluence of the Vermillion River. Lack of feed, rigorous work getting over downed trees, and slippery footing took its toll on the horses.

April 7-17, 1833   **Flathead Post**

7th   Arrived at the Flathead post kept by Mr. Rivi and one man after a ride of 17 mils E.S.E. through thick wood   not very good trail and a snow storm which loaded the pines in such a manner as to bend them down to the ground frequently loading me with the snow as passing I disturbed the branches   trees loaded down in this way and frozen so as to be firm constitute much of the difficulty of the route from Flathead or Ponderay Lake to this place   want of grass at this time of the year the residue with some mire   rock mica slate   this place is scituated on a fine prairie 2 mils long 1 wide and seems pleasant after coming through thick woods and mountains   counting my horses found 32 of 47 with which I started but think I shall recover all but one left on the Lake having sent men and Indians in search of them   Mr. E. came in the boats in 5 days   I have now news by four Indians who came in on the 6th on foot   the Nez Perces have lost all but 4 horses of their band of about 500 stolen by the Blackfeet   The Flatheads expected in about 15 days   on the 11th started out to see if there were many beaver in the country with intention of staying 12 days but was recalled by the arrival of the buffaloe Indians   found few beaver and the country can only be trapped on foot   plenty of patridges to be found in this country   arrived again at the post on th[e] 17th of April   my route was back on the Flathead River.

After a gap of more than ten days, Wyeth again picked up his quill and ink on April 17 to catch up on events. Then operated by the Hudson's Bay Company, Flathead Post was originally constructed in 1809

by the Northwest Company's David Thompson. After building Kullyspell House on Lake Pend Oreille's Memaloose Point, Thompson had
ascended the Clark Fork to establish Flathead Post. Originally dubbed
Saleesh House by the NWC, for the traditional name of the local tribe,
it was located a few miles upstream from present-day Thompson Falls,
Montana. When the two fur conglomerates merged in 1821, HBC took
over operations.

Flathead Post would occupy a succession of locations along the
Clark Fork. Sometime in the 1820s, the post burned and was rebuilt
farther upstream, possibly near the now-defunct railway town of Eddy,
Montana. The Archives of Manitoba name 1828 as the year that Flathead
Post was relocated; however, historian Dale Morgan suggests that when
Jedediah Smith visited the site in 1824, it had already been moved.[13]
At the time of Wyeth's visit, Flathead Post was on the grassy plain of
Thompson Prairie, evidently in the first open area he encountered as he
ascended the Clark Fork. In 1836, William Gray would report the loca-
tion of "the house" as being five miles above Thompson Falls.[14]

At Flathead Post, Wyeth was welcomed by Francois Rivet, known
to his friends as "Old Rivay" due to his advanced age. Born in 1757, he
was still spry enough in 1804-05 that he "danced on his head," meaning he danced on his hands, during the winter spent at Fort Mandan
with the Corps of Discovery. By 1813, he was a freeman engaged by
the NWC as an interpreter at Flathead Post, having lived among the
Salish people and married a woman of the tribe. He remained at that
station through the HBC merger in 1821, and in 1829 was transferred
to Fort Colvile. By 1832, Rivet had been reassigned to Flathead trade.
He would retire to French Prairie in 1838.[15]

Rivet and Nicholas Montour had worked together at Fort Colvile
but, for undisclosed reasons, Chief Factor John McLoughlin had dis-
approved of the liaison and had ordered the two to separate, without
much success. Finally, in 1832 McLoughlin authorized Fort Colvile
Trader Francis Heron to engage Rivet for three years "if Montour goes
to the Flat Heads."[16] Wyeth's description of Flathead Post being "kept
by Mr. Rivi and one man" suggests that Montour and Rivet were still
together and that Wyeth perceived Rivet to be the man in charge.

Montour was the son of an NWC partner of the same name. The
junior Montour worked as a Nor'wester clerk and was trading among

the Kootenay Indians in 1812. Transferred to the HBC, he was reported as indolent and fond of alcohol, but was allowed to join the Snake
Country Expedition led by Alexander Ross in 1824 as a freeman.
Montour was one of the men who deserted Ogden the next year, but
returned to Company service several years later and was put in charge
of the Kootenay Post. He was associated with Warren Ferris in 1834-35
in establishing a semi-private trade venture underwritten by HBC. By
1840, Montour was listed as a "Columbia freeman."[17]

    The rumor Wyeth heard concerning the theft of Nez Perce horses
by Blackfoot raiders is unsubstantiated. The Nez Perce were known for
the quality of their stock in horseflesh. In February 1806, Meriwether
Lewis wrote of the Nez Perce,

> *Their horses appear to be of an excellent race; they are lofty eligantly
> formed active and durable; in short many of them look like the fine
> English coarsers and would make a figure in any country ... marked
> much like our best blooded horses in virginia, which they resemble as
> well in fleetness and bottom as in form and colours.*[18]

    At first glance, so many stolen horses would seem a remarkable loss.
However, Father Pierre-Jean De Smet noted in 1840 that "the [Nez
Perce] own a great number of horses; some have as many as 500 or
600."[19] Nevertheless, no report of such devastating horse stealing has
been found in either Euro-American or Indian accounts for the years
Wyeth was in the mountains.

    Spring and summer were the preferred seasons for Blackfoot horse
raids. The favorite passes used by the Salish and Nez Perce as they
headed east on buffalo hunts also became the chosen passes for Piegan and Blackfoot parties who came to steal horses.[20] But rarely was an
attempt made to raid tribes west of the Rocky Mountains when deep
snows clogged the high passes.[21] Benjamin Bonneville, while camped
with a mixed group of Nez Perces, Flatheads and Pend Oreilles, claimed
these people took the greatest of care of their stock when in a dangerous neighborhood. But in an encampment of "fancied security" many
of their normal precautions were omitted. "They merely drive them, at
nightfall, to some sequestered little dell, and leave them there, at perfect
liberty, until morning."[22]

On April 11, Wyeth had taken off on another of his explorations; this time his intent was to assess the beaver population in the area. When he got back to camp on April 17, he discovered that Ermatinger and the boats loaded with supplies had arrived the day after he left in search of beaver. Now the American entrepreneur and the HBC trader would repack the goods for horseback travel and finalize preparations to continue east to join the Flathead tribe.

April 18-20, 1833   *Flathead Post*

18th to 20th   remained at the post having now found all my horses   started camp 2 miles East up the river and to the upper end of the prairie on which the house is built   at this place is a large creek coming from the N.

Abbott, Woodman and a few Indians had successfully rounded up the fifteen missing horses. With the stock having grazed for nearly two weeks in the vicinity of Flathead Post, good grass was probably scarce. Therefore, Wyeth relocated camp two miles away, near the mouth of Munson Creek.

April 21, 1833   *Clark Fork of the Columbia*

21th   rained hard last night and from the 17th to this day have had one or more slight showers each day   the plain is now good grass   we are much anoyed by the dogs of the Indian village which are numerous   they eat all our cords and fur flesh they can get at in the night   this is always a great trouble while travelling with Indians until you get to Buffaloe where they find better food   for three nights no frost   This valley is the most romantic place imaginable   a level plain of two miles long by 1 wide   on the N a range of rocky and snow clad Mts.   on the S. the Flathead river a rapid current and plenty of good fishing running at the immediate base of another lofty Snowy and Rocky range of Mts.   Above and below the vally the mountains of each range close upon the river so as apparently to afford no outlet either way   about 200 horses feeding on the green plain and perhaps 15 Indian Lodges and numerous barking dogs with now and then a half breed on horseback galloping gracefully with plenty of gingling bells attached to all parts of himself and horse   it is really a scene for a poet nought but man is wanting to complete it

This Indian camp probably comprised the Flatheads whom Wyeth had heard would arrive "in about 15 days." Ferris told of similar problems with hungry Indian dogs:

We were annoyed almost beyond endurance by the hundreds of famishing dogs belonging to the Indians. They devoured every leathern article that lay within reach, even to the bullhide thongs, with which we fastened our horses. We were compelled to keep guard by turns or risk the entire loss of our baggage, their depredations were so bold and incessant. I performed my watch at the salient angle of our tent, armed with an axe, which I hurled among them without respect to "mongrel, puppy, whelp or hound," and not infrequently sent some of them back yelping a serenade of pain to their sleeping masters. Once, however, on returning with the axe which I had thrown unusually far, I discovered a scury cur, coolly trotting off with my saddle bags, which the rascal had stolen from within the protection of the tent. It is needless to say that I pursued and recovered them, but ere I could return to my post, I perceived three large fellows marching leisurely homeward, with a bale of dried meat, weighing not less than forty pounds. Grounding an inference hereupon that in spite of the axe and my utmost efforts they would prove victorious, I thought it advisable to let my manhood take care of itself, and call up my dreaming companions. No sooner said than done, when we called a council of war, and deeming discretion with such an enemy the better part of valour, we suspended all our baggage in a tree that overhung the tent, and went to rest without apprehension of the consequences. In the morning we found every thing safe as we had left it, while our less careful neighbours were seen busily collecting the scattered relics of the night's devastation.

*One of them lost above forty dollars' worth of furs, and another, a
jolly old Frenchman, drew his pipe from his teeth to swear with more
emphasis that the scoundrelly dogs had devoured his axe.*[23]

Despite incessant downpours, Wyeth found time to ply his fishing
rod and had some success in catching a few of the trout for which the
Clark Fork is still known today. The river was hemmed by Koo Koo Sint
Ridge and Big Hole Peak looming to the north, and Eddy and Cherry
peaks, in the Coeur d'Alene Mountains, rising over the valley to the
south. Koo Koo Sint ("Star-Looker") was also the Salish nickname for
David Thompson, known for gazing at the heavens with his telescope.[24]

In one of Wyeth's rare descriptive passages, he pondered how the
"romantic" scene before him might be more complete if it were immor-
talized by a (presumably Euro-American) poet.

April 22, 1833   ***Clark Fork of the Columbia***

*22nd   Moved 8 mils E.N.E. along the river   at 6 miles passed
a very bad rock called le Roche Mauvais   the mountains as
yet closely follow the river on both sides but seem declining
in height   as we stopped early we spent the rest of the
day in preparing to prevent the blak Foot from stealing our
horses   they have have never but once passed the bad rock
and then the Flatheads gave them such a beating as keeps
[them] since in better order   the[y] infest much the country we
are now about entering*

At the Bad Rock (known as "Es-em-mowela" in the local tongue
and *Roche Mauvais* in French), an extremely steep, rocky ridge fell off to
the very edge of the river. Surrounded on three sides by nearly vertical
shale slides and with its base submerged in the swift waters of the Clark
Fork, Bad Rock was one of the most hazardous sites on the Road to the
Buffalo. Many travelers along this route during and after the fur trade
period would recount their experiences at Bad Rock.[25]

While constructing his army road in 1860, Lieutenant John Mullan
described the site:

*a rock point running out to the very water's edge, terminating there in
a perpendicular bluff. The Indian trail ... winds high up on the bluff
side, and regains in the same serpentine manner the bottom, about
three hundred yards above the place where it left it.*[26]

One of the most graphic accounts of the crossing at Roche Mauvais
was penned by Father De Smet:

*Our path during a great part of the day was on the declivity of a
lofty, rocky mountain; we were obliged to climb a steep rough pass
from 400 to 600 feet high. I had before seen landscapes of awful
grandeur, but this one certainly surpassed all others in horror. My
courage failed at the first sight; it was impossible to remain on
horseback, and on foot my weight of 211 pounds was no trifle. This,
therefore, was the expedient to which I resorted; my mule Lizette was
sufficiently docile and kind to allow me to grasp her tail, to which
I held on firmly: crying at one moment aloud, and at other times
making use of the whip to excite her courage, until the good beast
conducted me safely to the very top of the mountain ... On descending
from this elevation I had to make new precautions. I preceded the
mule, holding her by the bridle, while she moved cautiously down to
the foot of the "Bad Rock" (as it is called by the savages), as though
she feared stumbling and rolling with her master into the river which
flowed beneath us.*[27]

While "Blackfoot" raiding parties often clashed with the Salish, it was
not clear whether the Flatheads in Wyeth's tale defeated Piegans, Bloods
or Blackfoot proper. Of the three nations comprising the Blackfoot
Confederacy, the Piegans most often clashed with mountain people.[28]
Although available Blackfoot histories do not validate Wyeth's report,
ethnologist John C. Ewers has noted that "the causes of intertribal wars
in which the Blackfoot engaged, and which were initiated prior to 1810,
cannot be specifically documented from historical records."[29]

Given that Wyeth was receiving stories of the tribe's history, it
appeared as though he and Ermatinger were now accompanying the
band of Flatheads from Flathead Post. Their camp on the night of April
22 was on the lowland across from the mouth of Swamp Creek.

April 23, 1833   *Camas Prairie*

*23d   Moved 8 mils E.N.E. to Horse plain thence N.E. 5 mils
cutting a hill and leaving the River which we had hertofore
followed   decending the Mts E.N.E. 6 mils to a large open
vally in the hills with little timber and much grass   opposite
to our Camp is a mountain where 200 Flatheads Conterays
Ponderays and other Inds. were killed by the Blackfoot
Inds.   During the first part of the last division of the days
march passed a small lake with many waterfowl and one
sand hill crane.   We are now fairly in the dangerous
Country   through Horse plain and into the R Flathead is a
small brook   to day 2 Indians arr[i]ved from the main Flathead
Camp at Porte D'enfer with news that the Blackfoot have made
2 h[a]uls of horses from them   the Flathead Camp consists of
men of various tribes*

After a few miles, the trail left Clark Fork in order to pursue a short-cut to Camas Prairie. The route made its way northward over Locust Hill, through the open valley of Dog Lake (sometimes called Rainbow Lake today), and down onto Camas Prairie via Camas Creek.

David Thompson visited Horse Plains, known today simply as Plains, Montana, during his traverse of the Kootenai Trail. Stopping at a "fine Brook," probably Lynch Creek, he depicted "a very fine Plains beyond it, & a great extent of Meadow Knowles &c." Thompson also rode past Dog Lake and, like Wyeth, shot a partridge.[30] Warren Ferris said his journey took him "over a low pine covered mountain, from the summit of which we descended into a large valley, called Horse Plains."[31] Also known as Horse Prairie, De Smet wrote of how following "a mountainous defile ten miles long led us thence to the lovely Horse Prairie."[32]

Wyeth recorded a fragment of tribal lore in this entry, concerning a massacre by Blackfoot in the mountains adjacent to Camas Prairie. In the last half of the eighteenth century, once the Blackfoot tribes acquired horses and firearms, they pushed Salishan peoples, who lacked guns, from ancestral grounds on the Plains immediately east of the Rockies. The Salish fled to the wooded valleys west of the mountains. Around 1810, the Salishan nations began to obtain the new weaponry and united in buffalo hunting expeditions onto the Plains, often via Camas Prairie and Hell's Gate. Still, they found strong opposition there from the Blackfoot, who remained their enemies through the end of the buffalo days.[33] While the death of so many people in one battle was not confirmed, it was conceivable.

What Wyeth called "Porte D'enfer" was also known as Hell's Gate, Hell Gate Ronde, Hellgate, or simply "the Gates," located near the west end of the Missoula Valley in what is now Montana. One early Montana historian wrote

> *when the war-like Blackfeet overran the whole of Montana, the romantic and picturesque pass or canyon where the Hell's Gate river cuts through the mountain above the town of Missoula, was a regular rendezvous for their war parties, and so constantly did they infest this place, that it was almost certain death for an individual or even small parties to enter this pass, and so great was the dread and fear entertained by the Indians of the Western tribes and the Canadian voyageurs, that it became a saying with them, that it was as safe to enter within the gates of hell, as to enter into that pass, and it was called by the voyageurs, in their language Porte d'enfer, Gates of Hell, or Hell's Gate.[34]*

Ogden's 1824 Snake Country Expedition "passed opposite to the well known place Called the Gates of Hell ... why So Called I cannot Say but it appears there is Something awful attached to it as even the Buffalo will not dare to pass through." William Kittson, clerk on the trip, learned that "Hellsgate" was "a defile much dreaded by the natives from the different attacks they have met in it from their enemies ... Its name is well appropriated for it looks very dismal and dark."[35]

In 1832 Warren Ferris passed through Horse Plains and on to Hell's Gate, which he portrayed as

> *a high rocky conical elevation attached to a plain jutting into the bottom on one side of the river precisely opposite to the bluff rocky termination of a plain of considerable height, on the other side, which gives them the appearance of formidable gates.[36]*

According to the messengers who arrived at Wyeth's camp, Blackfoot raiders had twice hit the main Flathead encampment at Hell's
Gate, and stolen ponies from the tribal herd. Wyeth recognized the vital
nature of the horse in Native American culture and would later write

> *It is a well-established fact that men on foot cannot live, even in the*
> *best game countries, in the same camp with those who have horses.*
> *The latter reach the game, secure what they want, and drive it beyond*
> *the reach of the former.*[37]

April 24, 1833   **Flathead River**

24   mooved E. by S. down the valley to Flathead river then 4
miles E. following the river then Forded it and made 3 mils E.
by N. and encamped on it at a place where last year a man by
the name of La Couse was [killed] by the Blackfoot Inds.   the
river is not now high   when so it is not fordable and is here a
good sized stream   the salts here whiten in the ground and
the animals are almost crazy after it which makes them bad to
drive   the morning was sult[r]y and I travelled without my coat
but in the afternoon we had a fine [s]hower with some thunder
of good quality   the vally we left today abounds with the finest
Kamas I have yet seen   as provisions are scarce in camp the
women dug much of it

Keeping to Camas Creek, the travelers soon came to the Flathead
River, a major tributary of the Clark Fork. When the band reached the
divide between the valley and the river, it could have followed Camas
Creek on through the gorge to the river. However, based on the mileage
Wyeth recorded after reaching the Flathead, they must have climbed
up the ridge, perhaps via Cottonwood or Clear creek, then picked their
way down, hitting the main channel near Knowles Creek.

Once on the Flathead River, the eastbound troop followed it
upstream, crossing to the south bank after four miles, stopping for the
night near the intersection of modern Highway 200 and County Road
382. Of the Frenchman La Couse, or more probably La Course, no
record has been found. He was apparently an HBC trapper known to

Ermatinger. This is another instance in which the opportunity to view Wyeth's original journal would provide a cross check of the spelling of the man's name. Le Course or La Course were both relatively common names in the fur trade. For example, there was an M. La Course with Ross Cox in 1812, a Claude La Course in the Columbia District in the late 1820s, and a Pierre La Course was mentioned by Ermatinger as a boat builder in 1829.[38]

Warren Ferris negotiated the Flathead River about seven months after Wyeth, in December 1833, and as the Bostonian had visualized, Ferris succeeded only "after considerable difficulty, in fording it, still deep and rapid, even at its lowest stage."[39]

April 25, 1833   *Flathead River*

25th   Mooved Camp up the main river 12 mils E 1/2 N. then up a large but fordable branch 3 mils E. by S.   trail fine   grass good   weather beautiful   no frost for three nights   the Climate appears much as at Baltimore at this season

---

Continuing up the Flathead River's south bank, near today's Old Agency, Montana, Wyeth's party struck the Jocko River, turned up that, and rode a final three miles. The Jocko River was named for one of David Thompson's men, the clerk and interpreter Jacques Finlay, often called Jocco. When Finlay died in 1828, he and his sons were reputedly the best woodsmen, trappers and hunters in the Northwest. Ferris may have referred to the Jocko River as Wild Horse Creek.[40]

April 26, 1833   *Jocko River*

26th   made E. along the creek last named 5 miles then crossed and followed it 4 mils S.E. then recrossed it and followed it E.S.E. 3 mils crossing a small branch   then 2 mils recrossing the main creek again then followed 1 mile E S.E. and recrossed it and followed a small branch of it S.E. 1 mile   crossed the branch and followed it 2 mils S.E. to Camp   clear except 1 shower but only comfortably warm   Count[r]y hilly but open   E. lay a heavy pile of snowy Mts. 5 mils distant aparently running N. & S.   the rocks for a few days have been Sandstone mica slate   this day saw a white bear which we surrounded to kill but he broke through and escaped   earth in some places whitened with salt which makes the horses bad to drive   horses getting fat   grass good as also the bottom lands which are tolerably extensive

Nine miles of crossing and recrossing the Jocko River and its tributary, Finley Creek, took the outfit past today's Ravalli, Montana, up the river valley several miles beyond modern Arlee, Montana, to camp near the junction of Schley Creek. The Rattlesnake Mountains, source of the Jocko River, were the snow-covered range to the east. The spring weather was noticeably warming, with grass beginning to green and grizzly bears coming out of hibernation.

April 27-28, 1833   *Finley Creek*

27th   Remained at same camp   snowed a little this day   the Inds went hunting and got one Deer

28th   Abbot brought in one Beaver   started Camp 2 mils S.E. 2 S.S.E. 2 S. 4 S. by W. thus far through woods and a defile crossing the divide between the creek which we were on and another going to that branch of the Flathead river to [which] we came this day.   then into open plains   snowy mts on each side   3 mils S.S.E. then 5 mils S E by E crossing two slews of the Flathead river and Camped on a third and larger one which we shall be obliged to raft over   I judge it twice as large as the one we crossed some days since   the river here runs S.W.   a little snow today   quarrelled and parted with my man Woodman   he appeared to think that as I had but two he might take libertys   under such circumstances I will never yield an inch   I paid him half as I conceive he had gone half the route with me   here we met some Inds from the great Camp which they say is a moderate Camp distant

An extra day in camp allowed everyone a bit of rest and an opportunity to hunt. Not only did one of the Salish bring in a deer, but Wiggin Abbott managed to trap a beaver. This was the first indication that any of the Boston trio was trapping along the way, and likely this had been the first opportunity to get traps in the water.

The day's route took Wyeth in a southerly direction, on up Finley Creek. Entering O'Keefe Canyon, the travelers crossed over the low divide that separates Finley and O'Keefe creeks, about four miles beyond present Evaro, Montana. The Salish knew this area as Place Where You Come Out to a Clear Area.[41] When the sun went down, camp was made on the Clark Fork, which Wyeth described as a fork of the Flathead. Though it ran southwest at the place where Wyeth struck it, the Flathead River essentially flowed toward the northwest, merging with the Clark Fork and, ultimately, the Columbia. This camp was across the river from where Orchard Homes, Montana, a suburb of Missoula, is today.

O'Keefe Canyon was once called the Coriacan Defile, named for an HBC Kanaka trapper named Koriaka. HBC archives include a record of employee Corriacca, who came from Hawaii sometime in 1830 and was killed by Blackfeet, probably in the Flathead area, in 1835. However, oral history indicates he was a member of Neil McArthur's brigade, sent in 1846 to trade with the Flathead near where Frenchtown, Montana, is today. After a successful season, the crew headed back to headquarters, Koriaka riding the bell mare at the head of the line. Blackfoot raiders waylaid the returning caravan in the gulch where the Marent railroad trestle is today. The ambush was not a total success, because the Blackfoot fired before the main body was in range. The traders fell back, rallied, and drove the attackers from the field. The only fatality was the Hawaiian, hence the canyon was named for him. Koriaka's Canyon soon became the Coriacan Defile, and was renamed after rancher David O'Keefe in the mid 1800s.[42]

The substance of the quarrel between John Woodman and Wyeth is unknown. Given Wyeth's autocratic and suspicious nature, the disagreement might have been about something real, or as easily about something imagined. In any case, Woodman was paid and sent on his way – alone and in Blackfoot country. Wyeth was now down to one employee: Wiggin Abbott.

April 29, 1833 *Clark Fork of the Columbia*

29th   Forgot to mention in proper place that I saw Plumb trees at the place we left W. branch of the Flathead river   these are said to be good   about inch through   ripe in Sept. and found nowhere else but at this place   I tried hard to get some stones but could not   Moved this day S.S.W.   we crossed by fording contrary to expectation by loading high and taking high horses   at 8 miles struck another branch of same river as large as those already passed   at 4 miles further a creek from opposite side   ford tolerably good   at 20 miles came to main Camp of 110 Lodges Containing upward of 1000 souls with all of which I had to shake hands   the Custom in meeting these indians is for the Coming party to fire their arms   then the other does the same   then dismount and form single file both sides and passing each other shake hands with men women and children   a tedious job   buffaloe have come here and even further but they are killed at once and do not get wonted   her[e] the racine amani or Spetulum is found   this Camp is on the river   good grass   river direct S.S.W.   six nights since the Blackfoot stole horses from this Camp   here I found thre[e] Canadians one of whom was one who came to us the night before we were fired on on the heads of the Spanish River   this days march between two parralled ranges of Mts   now Snowy but I think not always so   there is much kamas in this region   we find little meat in the Indian Camp and are therefore much shortned for food

Wild plums still grow in thickets along stream bottoms and coulees in what is now central and eastern Montana. The Flathead told a story about Coyote riding on his gray horse along the Jocko Valley. At present Dixon, Montana, Coyote threw the branch he was using as a quirt to the ground and it grew into a plum tree. "In the generations to come, there will be plum trees growing right here," he prophesied, which was why the Indians called Jocko River the Creek of the Wild Plum Trees.[43] Though Wyeth hoped to gather some plum stones, no doubt with future propagation in mind, he was not able to do so. Nor is there mention of the *Prunus Americana* in the collection of plant samples Wyeth brought back to Boston.

Instead of having to build a raft to get across the Clark Fork, the troop managed to ford by rearranging loads, centering the packs on the backs of the tallest horses rather than their sides. Packers use this method when water depth is about belly high on the animal. Though it makes the load a bit top heavy, it prevents the animals from getting swept under by side-loaded packs.

Heading southwest, Wyeth paralleled the Bitterroot River until its main channel cut across the width of the valley and necessitated another ford. Throughout the day, the Bitterroot Mountain Range bounded them on the west, and the Sapphire Mountain Range loomed in the east. Farther south down the valley, Lolo Creek soon crossed their path. The Bitterroot River was known to the Salish as the Waters of the Red Osier Dogwood.[44]

The spot was a stone's throw from Traveler's Rest, where Lewis and Clark stopped September 9-11, 1805, before taking the arduous Lolo Trail across the Bitterroot Mountains. The Expedition visited the site again on its return trip, this time recuperating for several days, June 30 - July 3, 1806. From this point, the Corps of Discovery split into several smaller groups to explore more territory as it returned east.[45]

Another eight miles southward, Wyeth's party found the main Flathead camp, which had relocated from Hell's Gate (see Wyeth's April 23 entry) to the Bitterroot Valley, near present-day Florence, Montana. The area had been a campground and crossroads for Native Americans, most notably the Salish, for generations. The major tribal gathering Wyeth encountered had converged on the plains to hunt buffalo, and consisted of 110 lodges, or more than 1000 Salish.

This was likely the primary Flathead encampment for which Ermatinger had been aiming from the time he left Fort Vancouver, and he had probably been apprised of this location before leaving Flathead Post. Ermatinger had come to trade with these people; guns were fired in salute by all parties, then introductions were made. Wyeth may indeed have had to shake hands with every person in the valley. Ferris endured a comparable meeting with the Flathead in 1831:

> When they had approached within fifty paces, they discharged their guns in the air, reloaded, and fired them off again in like manner. The salute of course, was returned by our party. The Indians now

dismounted, left their arms and horses, and silently advanced ....
When the Chief had come up, he grasped the hand of our Partizan,
(leader,) raised it as high as his head, and held it in that position
while he muttered a prayer of two minutes duration ... His example
was followed by the rest, in the order of rank. The whole ceremony
occupied about two hours, at the end of which time each of us had
shaken hands with them all.[46]

Meriwether Lewis told of a similar episode when he met the Shoshone for the first time, greeting and embracing everyone in the village
until the Americans were "all carressed and besmeared with their grease
and paint." Lewis admitted he was "heartily tired of the national hug." In
1836, missionary and early Oregon pioneer William Gray also met the
Flatheads and provided a description of the assembly nearly identical
to Wyeth's.[47]

Wyeth's "racine amani or Spetulum" was the bitterroot plant – Montana's state flower since 1895. In the *Journal of the Academy of Natural
Science*, naturalist Thomas Nuttall cataloged the collection of plants that
Wyeth brought back from this expedition. Item #41 was described as
"Lewisia *rediviva*, plate 2. Spoet'lum of the Sailish or Flat-Head Indians. Racine d'Amare of the Canadians." Alexander Ross spelled the
term "Racine aux Mere," literally "mother root."[48] The Flathead dug the
bitter-tasting root for food, usually prepared by boiling and serving with
meat or berries.

Flathead tradition told of an elderly woman crying for her starving
sons on the banks of what would become the Bitterroot River. The Sun
heard her mournful pleas and sent a red spirit-bird to comfort her. The
creature promised that from her falling tears a new flower would grow
that would be rose-colored, like his feathers, and white like her hair. It
would grow from a root as bitter as her sorrow but as nourishing as her
love. The prophecy came true and her people called the plant "spetlem"
("bitter").[49]

The plant's scientific name, *Lewisia rediviva*, was bestowed in hon-
or of Meriwether Lewis by botanist Frederick Pursh, who examined
Corps of Discovery specimens that had been collected on the Corps'
return trip. Lewis first reported on the root in August 1805. The sample

was much mutilated but appeared to be fibrous; the parts were brittle, hard of the size of a small quill, cilindric and as white as snow throughout, except some small parts of the hard black rind which they had not seperated in the preperation. this the Indians with me informed were always boiled for use. I made the exprement, found that they became perfectly soft by boiling, but had a very bitter taste, which was naucious to my pallate, and I transfered them to the Indians who had eat them heartily.[50]

Despite "much kamas" and bitterroot available, Wyeth complained that little meat could be found in the Indian camp, thus his men were "shortened for food." Although it sounds at first like a greenhorn's distaste, Wyeth's hesitancy to feast on roots after a diet of meat may have been the right strategy. William Clark wrote in October 1805, "Capt Lewis & my Self eate a Supper of roots boiled, which filled us So full of wind, that we were Scercely able to Breathe all night [from] the effects of it."[51]

In the busy Salish village, Wyeth found three American Fur Company men (he noted them as "Canadians"). Their names were not recorded but Wyeth recognized one of them from his 1832 trip west with William Sublette's rendezvous-bound supply caravan. On July 2, 1832, after crossing South Pass and spending an eventful night near the Green River, six trappers had come over for a visit; this man had been one of the six.

The American Fur Company presence meant that there was already competition for Flathead furs. Trapper Robert Newell recorded that in the spring of 1833, "I was Sent [by] fontinell & Drips to the flat heads to trade with 7 men after 31 Days travel I found them on Bitter Root River (near a place called hellsgates) on a large fork of the Columbia."[52]

The men Wyeth remarked upon could well have been members of Newell's small AFC brigade. Ermatinger would not have been terribly happy to see a rival delegation among his customers.

April 30, 1833   *Bitterroot Valley*

30th   went out to collect some flowers for friend Nuttall afterwards to see the Camp   find 120 lodges of us today some having arrived   they are collecting to go to the Buffaloe in force to meet the Blackfeet   looked at their games   one is played by two men at a time   a level place is made on the ground about 15 feet long by 3 feet wide with a small log of wood at each end to stop a small iron ring which one of them rools from one end of the ally to the other   both following it   each having an arrow which they endeavor to throw after and under it so that when stopped it will rest on one of them   the one on whose arrow it is wins   at least this is all I understand of the game   the game is kept by a third by means of placing sticks on one side or the other   another feat much in practice from the smallest to the largest in Camp is two with some arrows throw them so as to go as near the first thrown as possible advancing continually untill all are expended then throwing them back again in same manner   another game is two or more opposite the one side having some small article in their hand keep changing it from one hand to the other as swift as possible accompanied by a tune and motion of body and limbs except feet (for they sit all the time)   the get is for the other party to designate the hand in which it rema[i]ns at the last   this is the most practised game and requires much dexterity on both sides   it is kept with sticks as the first   every morning some important indian addresses either heaven or his countrymen or both I believe exhorting the one to good conduct to each other and to the strangers among them and the other to bestow its blessings   he finishes with "I am done["]   the whole set up an exclamation in concord during the whole time   Sunday there is more parade of prayer as above   nothing is done Sunday in the way of trade with these Indians nor in playing games and they seldom fish or kill game or raise camp   while prayers are being said on week days everyone ceases whatever vocation he is about   if on horseback he dismounts and holds his horse on the spot until all is done   Theft is a thing almost unknown among them and is punished by flogging as I am told but have never known an instance of theft among them   the least thing even to a bead or pin is brought you if found and things that we throw away   this is sometimes troublesome   I have never seen an Indian get in anger with each other or strangers.   I think you would find among 20 whites as many scoundrels as among 1000 of these Indians   they have a mild playful laughing disposition and their qualities are strongly portrayed in their countenances. They are polite and unobtrusive and however poor never beg except as pay for services and in this way they are moderate and faithful but not industrious. they are very brave and fight the blackfeet who continually steal their horses and kill their straglers with great success beating hollow equal numbers They wear as little clothing as the weather will permit sometimes nothing on excep a little thing to cover the privates and sometimes but rare this is ommitted at play but not when there are women and allways at a race the women are closely covered and chaste never cohabiting promiscuously with the men the pox is not much and perhaps never known among them it dies here of itself when brought from the coast where it is rife the young women are good looking and with dress and cleanliness would be lovely today about 100 of them with their root diggers in their hands in single file went out to get roots they staid about two hours and returned in the same order each time passing the chief's lodge it was evidently a ceremony but the import I could not learn in a lodge or other place when one speaks the rest pay strict attention When he is done another assents by "yes" or dissents by "no" and then states his reasons which are heard as attentively it is a practice when a woman has her courses to make a little lodge outside her husbands lodge and there remain until they are finished. The more peaceable dispositions of the Indians than the whites is plainly seen in the children I have never heard an angry word among them nor any quarrelling altho there are here at least 500 of them together and at play the whole time at foot ball bandy and the like sports which give occasion to so many quarrells among white children

Wyeth started his day with the intentions of collecting specimens ("samples") for his friend Thomas Nuttall, back in Cambridge. Wyeth's efforts to bring back a variety of plants, rocks and other natural oddities to further scientific knowledge of the West was well received by academics and would result in two scientists accompanying his next expedition.

As another ten lodges of Indians arrived in the valley, however, Wyeth's entry ultimately focused instead on the lifestyle and practices of the people around him. Throughout his journey, Wyeth made ethnological notes regarding the nations he encountered. Many of these entries were later expanded into a series of question and answer letters between Wyeth and noted American ethnologist Henry R. Schoolcraft, who reproduced them in his six-volume catalog of Native Americans of the United States. Wyeth's series of letters focused heavily on his impressions of the Shoshone, thus little of the information in this entry relating to the Flathead saw ink.[53]

Warren Ferris, while spending time with the Flatheads in 1831, also recorded several of their games. The first sport Wyeth described, the ring-and-dart game, Ferris said the French called "roulette." Ferris noted that the gambling contest of "hand" or *lehal*, was universally played by men and women. Ferris provided additional details about both of these games.[54] "Bandy," which Wyeth mentioned late in the journal entry, is a game much like field hockey.

As to the collective Flathead character, Ferris seemed as smitten as Wyeth. He testified that they

> *are noted for humanity, courage, prudence, candour, forbearance, integrity, trustfulness, piety, and honesty. They are the only tribe in the Rocky Mountains that can with truth boast of the fact that they have never killed or robbed a white man, nor stolen a single horse ... I have, since the time mentioned here, been often employed in trading and travelling with them, and have never known one to steal so much as an awlblade ... The Flatheads have received some notions of religion either from pious traders or from transient ministers who have visited the Columbia. Their ancient superstitions have given place to the more enlightened views of the christian faith, and they seem to have become deeply and profitably impressed with the great truths of the gospel. They appear to be very devout and orderly, and never eat, drink, or sleep, without giving thanks to God. The doctrines they have received are no doubt essential to their happiness and safety in a future state of existence, but they oppose, and almost fatally, their security and increase in this world. They have been taught never to fight except in self defence, or as they express it, "never to go out to hunt their own graves," but to remain at home and defend manfully their wives and children when attacked.*[55]

Ross Cox had noted earlier that

> The Flat-heads have fewer failings than any of the tribes I ever met
> with. They are honest in their dealings, brave in the field, quiet and
> amenable to their chiefs, fond of cleanliness, and decided enemies to
> falsehood of every description.[56]

Wyeth witnessed – and recorded what may be the first Euro-American written account of – the Flathead First Roots Ceremony. Held in early spring prior to the wild harvest, the rite ensured abundant and robust camas and bitterroot. Anyone gathering roots before the ceremony had been completed might cause the roots to be shriveled and scarce. Two elder women appointed by the chief would count off a specific number of female assistants. They would proceed to a traditionally fruitful area where the senior matron would pray to the sun and to the earth for success, security and blessing. The women then dug up a supply of tubers to be prepared in a cooking pit by the wives of the village chief. Once the meal was ready, the chief gathered the tribe and made similar entreaties to the sun and earth. Finally, the food, symbolic of all they would gather that season, was distributed to the people.[57]

Wyeth carefully described the "root digger" the women used to harvest edible bulbs:

> Root-diggers are crooked sticks, the end used in the earth being
> curved and sharpened by putting it in the fire and rubbing against
> a rough stone, which both points and hardens them; they are also
> made of elk and deer horn, attached to a stick.[58]

Ross Cox's portrayal of Flathead women echoed Wyeth:

> The women are excellent wives and mothers, and their character for
> fidelity is so well established, that we never heard an instance of one
> of them proving unfaithful to her husband. They are also free of the
> vice of backbiting ... and laziness is a stranger among them ... [They]
> are comparatively very fair, and their complexions are a shade
> lighter that the palest new copper after being freshly rubbed. They are
> remarkably well made, rather slender, and never corpulent.[59]

Father De Smet, by contrast, was not impressed with females of the tribe:

The women are very filthy. Their hands, faces, and feet are black and stiff with dirt. They rub them every morning with a composition of red and brown earth mixed up with fish oil. Their hair, always long and disheveled, serves them for a towel to wipe their hands on.[60]

As Wyeth noted, Salish tradition dictated that women were considered unclean during menses and required them to live in a separate lodging where they were subject to frequent ablutions. After they were "purified," the women resumed their usual place within the family.[61] Regarding menses, numerous Native American societies had cultural taboos involving women's monthly cycles. For example, trapper Osborne Russell remarked that Crow women were required to remain apart for seven days.[62] While in a Nez Perce encampment, Meriwether Lewis noticed that

at all these lodges of the Chopunnish [Nez Perce] I observe an appendage of a small lodg with one fire which seems to be the retreat of their women in a certain situation. the men are not permitted to approach this lodge within a certain distance and if they have any thing to convey to the occupants of this little hospital they stand at the distance of 50 or 60 paces and throw it towards them as far as they can and retire.[63]

May 1, 1833   *Bitterroot Valley*

May 1st.   Same camp   the day reminds me of home and its customs   it is a fine and almost summer day altho the nights have been frosty of late but the days are warm   This morning the squaws left camp with their root diggers singing in good accord the tunes of their country   Yesterd[ay] Mr. Ermatinger traded 29 beavers   I find an Indian Camp a place of much novelty   the Indians appear to enjoy their amusements with more zest than the whites altho they are simple   they are great gamblers in proportion to their means bolder than the whites

In a rare interval, Wyeth allowed himself a nearly utopian reverie concerning the life of a white man among the Flathead. The presence of American Fur Company men did no disservice to Ermatinger, because the HBC partisan's British goods were cheaper than those presented by his competition.[64]

May 2-4, 1833   *Bitterroot Valley*

2nd   Moved Camp 2 miles S.E. by E. 4 miles S by E. over a hilly but open country and diverging a little from the main river to the Eastward and Camped on a small river going to the same river   the two parallel ranges of Mts still continue on either side of the river   It rained a little of the last night and some this morning   the day is cloudy and moderately warm   The absence of quarrells in an Indian Camp more and more surprises me when I come and see the various occasions which would give rise to them among the whites   the crowding together of from 12 to 1800 horses which have to be driven into Camp at night to stake in mng. to load the starting of horses and turning of loads the seizing of fuel when scarce, often the case, the plays of men and Boys &c.   At the Camp yesterday saw the bones of a buffalo bull not old being the first sign of buffaloe yet seen.

3d.   Same Camp.

4th   Same Camp   To day heard a sound like a heavy piece of ordonance and I suppose arising from the fall of some mighty fragment of rock from the mountains   The sound seemed to come from the N.   I suppose the sound heard in the Snake country arose from the same cause altho then no heavy mountains were in sight but there were cut rocks enough   weather somewhat smokey but warm and clear   A party of hunters who proposed to go out for beaver deferred the thing on acc. of the water being too high to set a trap.   A Thunder storm in the afternoon with high wind from the S.W. and Rain.

To have packed up an entire village and moved six miles up the Bitterroot was probably due to diminishing forage for the immense horse herd. The Flathead likely reset their lodges close to North Burnt Fork

Creek, about a mile north of today's Stevensville, Montana. Father Pierre Jean De Smet would establish St. Mary's Mission for the Jesuits in 1841 just south of this encampment site in an area the Salish referred to as Red-Topped Peaks.[65]

Spring rains and melting snow in the surrounding mountains had raised water levels in nearby streams, signaling a temporary suspension of the spring beaver trapping season.

May 5, 1833   *Bitterroot Valley*

5th. Sunday according to our reconing   there is a new great man no[w] getting up in the Camp and like the rest of the wrld covers his designs under the great cloak religion   his followers are now dancing to their own vocal music in the plain   perhaps 1-5 of the Camp follow him   when he gets enough followers he will branch off and be an independent chief   he is getting up some new form of religion among the Indians more simple than himself   like others of his class he works with the fools women and children first   while he is doing this the men of sense thinking it too foolish to do harm stand by and laugh but they will soon find that women fools and children form so large a majority that with a bad grace they will have to yield.   These things make me think of the new lights and revivals of New England   rains a little today

In this entry it is unclear whether Wyeth's own cynicism about religion, informed by his experiences growing up in New England, gave him special insight into the spiritual life of the Flathead encampment, or instead obscured his understanding. Anthropologist Leslie Spier was convinced Wyeth was describing the appearance of a prophet or a prophet's apostle, gathering to himself a set of followers to set up an independent band through what Spier defined as a "Prophet Dance," which centered on a revitalization of ancestral culture. Regarding this particular Wyeth quote, Spier commented on the difficulty of connecting it to other native religious activity in the region.[66] However, chieftainship among the Flathead was not necessarily hereditary, thus everyone was eligible for election. If all of the candidates for leadership were about equal in popularity, then the person with the largest following in camp was elected. Wyeth's "new great man," whatever his motivation, seemed well on his way to a leadership position within the tribe.[67]

In America, the nineteenth century saw several powerful waves of religious revival, and Wyeth had witnessed their effects. The terms "New Lights" and "Old Lights" referred to pro- and anti-revivalists in most denominations. Originally coined during the First Great Awakening (1730-60), which spread through the colonies, the terms found new usage in the early years of the nineteenth century as a new movement gained momentum. Wyeth grew up during the Second Great Awakening (approximately 1800-1840) when reactions to the growing revival pushed many normally orthodox believers into strongly anti-Calvinist positions, particularly in New England. Several missionary societies that would soon set out to evangelize the western territories were founded during this period.[68]

Yet, despite his exposure to extremes, Wyeth managed to maintain a tolerance for many views: "I do not ridicule nor would I persecute although I do not believe but am willing that all should enjoy their own opinions and am convinced that all honest opinions will be tolerated."[69] Wyeth managed to escape the fervor of the Second Great Awakening, despite having met Presbyterian minister Lyman Beecher, considered by many as the leader of the movement.

In a letter to his brother-in-law, Reverend Clark Perry of Newbury, Vermont, Wyeth railed against the lack of religious tolerance he found in the States:

> *There can be no greater hazard than death (in my crede) and that all must meet at some time and if there were I should not much regret leaving the land of religious freedom as you call it but it is not so to me finding in it none of that freedom of religious opinion of which you speak, by freedom of opinion I mean the exercise and avowal of ones ideas without harm accruing therefrom ... And yet you call this a land of civil and religious freedom. I repeat I have not found it such.*[70]

May 6, 1833   *Bitterroot Valley*

6th.   Bright and clear   found all of my horses three of which had been missing   Moved 4 mils S. and encamped on a creek of the main river about 1 1/2 mils from the latter

Once again, the village moved south, partly to find better feed for the livestock, but undoubtedly to continue closing in on the buffalo range of the Great Plains. The new camp was four miles south, on today's Willoughby Creek at the eastern edge of the Bitterroot Valley, over a mile from the main river.

May 7-9, 1833   *Bitterroot Valley*

7th.   Same Camp   cloudy all night and today but warm

8th.   Same Camp   last night had a false alarm   Some Inds. of the camp who were gambling for a gun discharged it before laying [it] on the stakes   This though a common occurrence gave the horses a fright and one frightens another in those cases until all are alarmed   the running of those that have got loose the snorting stamping and rearing of those who cannot when there are at least 1500 the Howling of dogs men running with guns   the contrast of firelights with the darkness of the night make altogether a scene of confusion to be recollected   This day hunters went out 2 only   one returned sun two hours high with one antelope   the other at night with 4   To day a small boy broke his arm but as I understood that the Indians reduce fractures well and as I am quite ignorant I did not meddle with it

9th.   Moved S. by E 6 mils and camped on the main river   on the march saw two blakfeet who ran with all the speed of their horses to the mountains   a little rain but warm   high wind and somewhat dusty   The rain does not seem to lay the dust in the least   The country covered for the first time with sage and so far the same kind of minerals as near the Ponderay Lake   This afternoon came to us a Snake a Nez Perce and a Flat head on foot   they came from Salmon River and bring no news except that the Nez Perce Camp is at Salmon river and that they are mostly without horses

As the camp moved southeast, Blackfoot scouts were seen high-tailing it into the mountains. Wyeth and the Flatheads relocated about two miles south of modern Victor, Montana. Before the dusty day was over, a three-man multi-tribe delegation arrived with information about the location of the main Nez Perce camp, roughly 160 miles to the south. The Flathead contingent planned to join the Nez Perce for the seasonal buffalo hunt which also worked out well for Ermatinger. In reaching Wyeth and the Flatheads, the three men had followed the same track from the Salmon drainage over Lost Trail Pass used in September 1805 by the Corps of Discovery as it headed north.[71]

May 10, 1833   *Bitterroot Valley*

10th   Mooved 7 mils E. by E.[?]   rained a little shower but clear in the afternoon.   This moment Chief Guineo is saying the usual afternoon prayers   I observe that he first makes a long one which is responded to by the usual note in accord then a short one followed by the same note   on horse back the whole time walking about the Camp   hat on   in an audible voice and directed as though addressing the men below rather than "him" above   To day 11 Flatheads started on foot to steal horses from the Blackfeet

---

Wyeth likely wrote or intended "S. by E.," which Young apparently transcribed as the confusing "E. by E." Seven miles south by east would have pushed the Flathead village down the Bitterroot Valley to just north of modern Hamilton, Montana, a credible destination. Today, Salish elders have offered two translations for the traditional name of this area: Sacred Trees Growing on Open Ground or Trees Standing in Water.[72]

The Flathead chief Wyeth called "Guineo" may have been the same leader who provided the blessing of the First Roots Ceremony a week and a half earlier. Ferris also mentioned this same "Flathead or rather Pen-d'oreille chief" on numerous occasions. Ferris translated this man's name as "French for bad-luck," spelling it variously Guigneo, Guigueo, Guignon, Old Gurgeo and Ginquro. According to Ferris, after a disastrous battle with the Blackfoot, the Flathead chief had led his band, along with some forty wounded men, to the 1832 rendezvous in Pierre's

Hole, where they stayed for six weeks. This chief and some of his warriors had participated in the Battle of Pierre's Hole. On William Gray's return trip east in 1836-37, the missionary also mentioned meeting "old Gineo, the Chief of the Flat Heads."[73]

May 11, 1833   *Bitterroot Valley*

11th   Started out early hunting for the first time this trip   We are now short of provisions.   The Camp moved 10 mils S. by E. and camped on the river   the wide botom of which is done   it is now jammed in between the hills   during this distance passed two small creeks big enough for beaver   only saw four antelope   killed nothing   saw two olived green snakes about 2 1/2 feet long   blunt tail but slender   afternoon clear and warm

At day's end, the Flathead had reached a narrow point in the Bitterroot Valley where the hills closed in around them. During their travels they would have passed several creeks that could easily have maintained suitable habitat for beaver. Wyeth must surely have seen Skalkaho Creek, which meant "place of beaver" in Salish.[74] A likely candidate for the second beaver stream was either Cow or Camas creek. With over one thousand people pursuing the region's wildlife, a scarcity of game comes as no surprise. It is remarkable that Wyeth claims this was the first time he had hunted since heading east from Fort Vancouver.

May 12, 1833   *Bitterroot Valley*

12th   Being Sunday remained at same Camp   the hills here are of Granite with large bed of quartz.   Mica slate is common   Gneiss also in some places   the same rock as at Kittle falls   observed in one place a black mineral like that found at Franconis[?], covering iron ore   it looks like horse hair in a mass combed straight   the hills are now well covered with grass   the river is now at its highest but is fordable   this morning long prayers in form as usual   at some lodges the Inds. are singing as an act of devotion

Wyeth apparently had traveled to New Hampshire quite a bit, because earlier in his Rocky Mountain adventure, he noted trees on the Spokane River that reminded him of the pine-covered hills of that region. Now, he observed a black mineral and thought of the iron factories of Franconia, a town in the Granite State, and the hornblende that often coated the ore deposits of that area.[75]

Like Wyeth, Warren Ferris noted the religious aspects of the Flathead people:

> *Their religious exercises consist of singing and dancing, in which they all assemble and engage on every Sabbath in the open air. Their customs are almost identical with those of the ancient Jews, with the single exception of burnt offerings or sacrifices, in which blood is displayed ... To one who has been familiar with their manners and customs, it would seem that in ancient times, they had had a Jewish Jesuit among them, who had instructed them in all the ancient doctrines of the Pentateuch.* [76]

Washington Irving wrote about the topic in *The Adventures of Captain Bonneville,* but his remarks were so nearly identical to Wyeth's May 10, 1833, journal entry that it is likely he obtained his information from interviews with Wyeth rather than from Benjamin Bonneville:

> *The Flatheads, have a strong devotional feeling, which has been successfully cultivated by some of the resident personages of the Hudson's Bay Company. Sunday is invariably kept sacred among these tribes. They will not raise their camp on that day, unless in extreme cases of danger or hunger: neither will they hunt, nor fish, nor trade, nor perform any kind of labor on that day. A part of it is passed in prayer and religious ceremonies. Some chief, who is generally at the same time what is called a "medicine man," assembles the community. After invoking blessings from the Deity, he addresses the assemblage, exhorting them to good conduct; to be diligent in providing for their families; to abstain from lying and stealing; to avoid quarrelling or cheating in their play, and to be just and hospitable to all strangers who may be among them. Prayers and exhortations are also made, early in the morning, on*

*week days. Sometimes, all this is done by the chief from horseback;
moving slowly about the camp, with his hat on, and uttering his
exhortations with a loud voice. On all occasions, the bystanders listen
with profound attention; and at the end of every sentence respond
one word in unison, apparently equivalent to an amen. While these
prayers and exhortations are going on, every employment in the
camp is suspended. If an Indian is riding by the place, he dismounts,
holds his horse, and attends with reverence until all is done. When
the chief has finished his prayer or exhortation, he says, "I have
done," upon which there is a general exclamation in unison.*[77]

In point of fact, some Iroquois trappers led by Old Ignace La
Mousse have been credited with settling in the Bitterroot Valley sometime before 1828. They may have taught the first notions of Christianity
to the Flathead. Old Ignace was Catholic and trained the Flathead in
saying the Lord's Prayer, making the sign of the Cross, and to observe
Sunday as a day of rest.[78]

May 13, 1833   *Bitterroot Valley*

*13th   Went out hunting   killed one N.E. patridge only   saw 4
cubs 4 deer   Camp moved 6 mils S.S.E. and camped on the
W. side   we approach the head of this river fast*

Six miles closer to the end of the valley, Wyeth saw that they would
soon be entering the mountains. Now camped on the left bank of the
Bitterroot River, he spotted more game than on previous hunts, but
managed to kill only one grouse, which he erroneously identified as a
New England partridge, better known as a ruffed grouse. More likely, the
bird was a blue grouse (*Dendragapus obscurus*) since the Bitterroot Valley
has historically been home to vast numbers of this species. Meriwether
Lewis wrote the first description of this bird on August 1, 1805, while
in the Tobacco Root Mountains of Montana. Among the details Lewis
recorded was that "the feathers of the tail are reather longer than that of
our phesant or pattridge as they are Called in the Eastern States."[79]

> **May 14-15, 1833**   *Bitterroot Valley*
>
> *14th. remained at same Camp   snow and sleet all day   An Indian died in camp to day but I do not think the Camp was delayed on this account   it was a bad day which I think the reason   his friends now singing over him according to their custom*
>
> *15th   made 6 miles S.S.E. and crossed the river and camped on a little creek   crossing two on the W. side all too small at low water for beaver.   snowed last night and until 8 this mng.   altho as much as 4 inches of snow has fallen it is at 11 oclock all gone except the hills which are white   grass good   Granite country and fertile in the bottoms and on the hills and mountain sides*

Passing the present town of Darby, Montana, the throng forded Fern and McCoy creeks, then crossed the Bitterroot to camp near the mouth of Rye Creek. The area was known to the Salish traditionally as Place Where They Would Lift Something. At this major campsite, people would often bet on who could move a boulder that sat along the trail.[80]

> **May 16, 1833**   *Bitterroot River*
>
> *16th   made 9 mils S.E. following a creek of the main river about 1/3 the size of the same   this we crossed 6 times during the day   this morning 4 inches snow which fell during the night but all gone at 9 ock   fair at 4 in afternoon   this day finishes all our provisions   in above distance river crooked.*

Near today's Conner, Montana, the village picked up the East Fork of the Bitterroot River. With six stream crossings during the day, the camp was definitely out of the valley, following a twisting, winding flow upstream to halt in the vicinity of Laird Creek. Though Wyeth reported that his hunters killed five antelope a week earlier, he had not recorded much of a game harvest since; the party had consumed all of the meat on hand.

MAP 7 *Bitterroot Valley to Pierre's Hole, 1833*

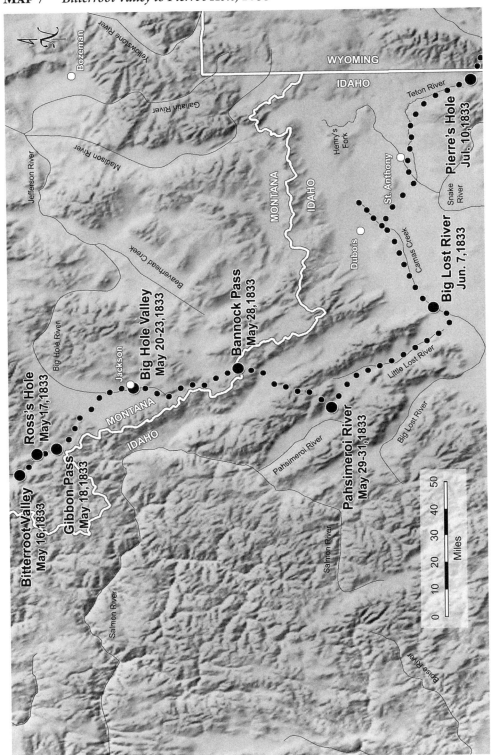

Interestingly, Wyeth did not mention passing the Ram's Horn Tree about five miles southeast of Conner. The site held great significance for the Flathead. Perhaps, since the trail was on the west side of the river and the tree was on the east bank, Wyeth did not notice it. The Ram's Horn Tree was first described by Alexander Ross in 1824; Warren Ferris also wrote of it in the 1830s.[81] According to Ross,

> *About five feet from the ground is growing up with the tree, a ram's head with the horns still attached to it! and so fixed and embedded is it in the tree that it must have grown up with it. One of the horns and more than half of the head is buried in the tree; but most of the other horn, and part of the head, protrudes out at least a foot.*[82]

Sometime around 1890, a pioneer cut off all of the exposed horn. Bark has grown over the scar, though scientific tests indicate the horn and portions of the skull are still embedded in the tree.[83]

May 17, 1833   *Ross's Hole*

17th.   2 miles S.E. 3 E and cutting a high mountain 1 mile S by E. and struck the river again in a large and fertile plain   here crossed the main branch of it and followed 2 miles a creek running S by E   at the place where we left the river it receives a small creek from the S and where we struck it again another quite small from the N.   The main branch appears to run about E. from the plain   when arrived at Camp finding no meat I took my traps out to catch beaver   when returning saw the squaw bringing in moss and roots   when I came in found the hunters had come in with one bear one Elk and several deer and 5 beaver   this makes a timely supply   Indians are gone ahead to see the mountain is passiable   This mountain divides us from the heads of the Missouri.

At or near the junction of Warm Springs Creek, which entered the East Fork from the south, Wyeth turned from the waterway and led his pack string up Sula Gulch and over Sula Peak. This route avoided the remaining canyon and cut about a mile off the trip. Alexander Ross reported in 1824 that he "left the river and crossed what we named Little Mountain."[84] William Clark had met the Salish for the first time in September 1805 on the east side of this same ridge. When the Corps of Discovery left the valley two days later, it passed to the west over Sula Peak because, as Clark explained, "the Mountains Close on each Side of the river."[85]

Descending from the mountain onto Cameron Creek, Wyeth's party was now in Ross's Hole, the basin named for Alexander Ross, who with his HBC brigade spent thirty-three days in the spring of 1824 confined on this flat by deep snow. Their escape from what he called "the Valley of Troubles" required the remarkable exertions of forty-five men, eighty horses, and twenty-six days to break a trail. A man on snowshoes led the first horse forward while a second man applied the whip, urging the animal ahead. After several plunges, that horse stalled, completely tired out, its head and shoulders barely above the snow's surface. Another horse was maneuvered into place and the whole scene repeated. The second horse would make it six or seven yards in front of the first before it played out. Then a third did the same, and so on.

Getting the horses dug out of the snow was more difficult than goading them forward, but Ross reported, "We were partly recompensed by the novelty of the scene and the mirth and glee the operation diffused among the people ... but the men and horses soon got tired of it." In nine hours, they had managed less than 600 yards of road. On the second day of such effort, only twenty-eight men and fifty horses showed up for road duty, making less than a quarter of a mile of progress in their labors. Nevertheless, having begun the trail work on March 20, they made it over the pass on April 14. Today, the hamlet of Sula, Montana, is situated in Ross's Hole.[86]

Now entering Ross's Hole, known to the Salish as Coming Out into a Big Open Place, Wyeth crossed the East Fork of the Bitterroot and went up Camp Creek a couple of miles.[87] This location turned out to be a good place to replenish food stores. The edible "moss" brought in by the women would have been the black tree lichen sometimes called "Bear Hair."[88] The moss was boiled into a gruel, sometimes flavored with a bit of meat or berries, then formed into a cake.

May 18, 1833   *Big Hole Valley*

*18th   2 miles up the creek S. by E.   then assending the
mountain S.E. 2 more then S by E down the mountain and
struck a little thread of water which during 28 mils increased
gradually to a little river and S.E. to another coming from the
S. and both go off together N.   this is one of the heads of the
Missouri   we crossed it and camped   here we found both
Bulls and cows which makes all merry   this pass is good
going when there is no snow   now there was about one foot in
places drifted more   we took 8 hours to pass   there is a visible
change in the appearance   vegetation is not so forward   the
trees appear stinted and small   the land poorer and covered
with Sedge   the other side there is little   on the W. side all
is granite   as soon as I passed the divide I saw Pudding
Stone   we had showers of snow and rain this day but this I
believe is constant in this region at this time of the year   the
Mt. is much higher the W. than the E. side   This I observed
also at the Trois Tetons   The grass is poor and has started
but little   the prairie in some places has snow   The vally runs
N. and S. and is bounded E. and W. by a range of Mts.   this
day my horse keeper left me taking an offence at some
misinterpretation about a horse.   The 16th. Woodman came to
camp from his hunt for beaver tired and famished having eated
nothing for three days*

On up Camp Creek, they came to the base of what would become known as Gibbon's Pass, after General John Gibbon's 1877 battle with the Nez Perce at the southeast foot of this divide in the Big Hole Valley.[89] Regarding the capricious climate of the Rocky Mountains, Ross in 1824 had found seven feet of snow at the same time of year; nine years later, Wyeth contended with just one foot and some drifts.

The "little thread of water" on the east side of the pass was Trail Creek. Wyeth, and Alexander Ross before him, identified Trail Creek as a source of the Missouri River. The HBC brigade leader told of finding the spring that issued into the creek, and standing astride the outflow for some time while smoking his pipe.[90] As Trail Creek runs east, numerous feeder streams join it and increase its size until it merges with the North

Fork of the Big Hole River, a tributary of the Jefferson River that is in turn one of three rivers forming the headwaters of the Missouri.

Having crossed to the east side of the Continental Divide, Ermatinger and his HBC team were technically in violation of United States law, but no one seemed concerned. Joint occupancy provisions allowed British commercial interests to operate west of the Divide, but the east side was undisputed United States territory, acquired in the 1803 Louisiana Purchase. By law, Ermatinger required a trade license.

After more than twenty-eight miles in the saddle that day, the band continued across the Big Hole River and camped a few miles south of today's Wisdom, Montana. The Big Hole River was known to the Salish as Waters of the Pocket Gopher but had been dubbed the Wisdom River by Lewis and Clark. Settlers later changed the name of the river, but kept the old name for their town.[91] Wyeth pointed out the landscape's transition from densely forested hills to sage-covered prairie, bracketed by the Pioneer Mountains on the east and the Anaconda Range to the west. The presence of buffalo and the availability of fresh meat raised the spirits of the crew.

Wyeth's troubles with employees continued with the departure of his "horse keeper" and the unwelcome reappearance of John Woodman. The horse keeper may have been the man Wyeth referred to as "my Indian" at the beginning of April. Woodman, having been dismissed by Wyeth on April 28, had been on his own for nearly three weeks.

May 19, 1833   *Big Hole Valley*

19th   Same Camp   snowed by fits most of the day   being Sunday the medicine chief had devotional exercises with his followers   he formed them into a ring men women and children and after an address they danced to a tune   in dancing the[y] keep the feet in the same position the whole time merly jumping up to the tune keeping the hands in front of them   at intervals he addressed them   at night Blackfeet were seen prowling about the camp at least so the Indians say   erected myself a lodge for the first time in the country and paid a treat of rum &c to the whites in Camp and some of the principal Indians to wet the same as it is called.

On this Sunday, Wyeth may have described the Flathead Jumpin'
Dance, as his account "appears to tally with what little is known" of
the ritual. The dance got its name from the short hop performed while
dancing in place. However, May was not characteristic timing for this
typically winter celebration.[92]

The lodge Wyeth set up for himself was probably one of the canvas
tents he had brought from the East for the trip, last noted being set up
in late February. However, it was also possible that he had bartered for
a Flathead buffalo-skin lodge, the primary dwelling used by the Salish
when traveling.[93]

Wyeth had not previously mentioned having any kind of alcohol in camp, and his reticence is surprising considering the long and
presumably dry miles traveled from Fort Vancouver. John McLoughlin was a temperate man, and since taking over as Chief Factor of the
Columbia District, he had worked hard to decrease, if not halt, the sale
of alcohol to Native Americans. Wyeth may not have been aware of
McLoughlin's position at this time, but he would certainly learn of it
when he returned to the Pacific Northwest the next year. In 1834, he
would initially compete against HBC by employing liquor in his dealings with the local clientele. McLoughlin would request the Bostonian
desist in the sale of liquor not only to Indians, but to all area residents,
and Wyeth would comply. But the presence of alcohol in Wyeth's party
now is not much of a mystery.[94]

In spite of his stance on alcohol, McLoughlin had purchased two
puncheons (168 gallons) of rum from Captain McNeill of the *Llama*
back in July 1832, just a few months before Wyeth arrived at Fort Vancouver. With that much quality rum on hand, it was probably not difficult to supply Wyeth's outfit when he left for the East.[95]

Wyeth's closing phrase, "to wet the same as it is called," brings to
mind "wetting one's whistle," or having a drink. Grose's 1796 *Classical Dictionary of the Vulgar Tongue* defined "whistle" as the throat.
"Whet," seen in some forms of this phrase, was an early term for a
morning's draught, commonly of white wine, supposed to sharpen
the appetite. Grose also defined a "wet Quaker" as a member of that
sect who has no objection to wine, giving the word "wet" a clear connection with alcohol.[96]

> **May 20, 1833**   *Big Hole Valley*
>
> *20th.   Snowing hard in the morning   one horse so lame that if we move Camp to day he will remain for the Blackfoot or wolves.   Much the same.   Started at half past 12 found the horse could be drove a little   got him along about four miles   shall return for him to morrow   this day 9 miles E.S.E. over a level plain of rich deep soil   wet and miry in the extreme   saw our Indians running buffaloe ahead   At 5 mils crossed a little brook running N by E and camped on a considerable creek running N. by E. and all falling in to the same as the creek we left   At about the junction it doubles round a point of mountains and apparently takes a north[?] eastwardly course   rain snow and sunshine as usual today. 4 hunters left us to day to hunt beaver in the Blackfoot country, Pellew, Charloi, Narbesse, Rivey.*

After a late start due to foul weather, the group crossed Cow Cabin Creek, then camped on Warm Spring Creek, which doubles around Jackson Hill and enters the Big Hole River near today's Jackson, Montana. During the spring thaw, a myriad of springs and creeks combine with snow melt, runoff and standing water to create a virtual swamp along the route.

Four trappers, probably HBC freemen rather than employees, broke off on their own, heading north to trap in Blackfoot territory. "Rivey" may have been Antoine Rivet, son of Francois, whom Wyeth had seen at Flathead Post. The senior Rivet would have been in his mid-seventies, a mite old for trapping excursions.

> **May 21-23, 1833**   *Big Hole Valley*
>
> *21st.   Same Camp   sent back and brought the lame horse into Camp   Went out to the mountain to cut log poles   found a Blackfoot lodge recently occupied   snow as usual   saw the Indians cooking a root resembling the yellow dock, but not so yellow   tasted like parsnip raw, informed by them that it is bad before being cooked   suppose it is more or less poisonous*

> *22d   Same camp   Blue Devils all Day   Turned in*
>
> *23d   6 miles S.S.E. and up the valley 3 S E by S. 3 S.E.   This valley is all good land about four miles wide and perhaps 50 long and how much further it goes N. I cannot say.   Went out to hunt buffaloe   killed one Elk out of a large band   mountains with snow each side of valley   snowed a little as usual*

On an errand into the Pioneer Mountains, Wyeth found a temporary brush lodge of the style many tribes used when hunting or raiding and on the move. Prince Maximilian described such a war lodge he had seen on the Milk River in 1833:

> *We reached, on the south bank, an Indian fort ... it is a kind of breastwork, which Indian war parties construct in haste of dry trunks of trees. When such parties intend to stop for the night, they erect a breastwork, sufficiently large, according to their number, composed of trunks of trees, or thick branches, laid one on the other, generally either square or triangular. In thus bulwark they lie down to sleep, after having placed sentinels, and are there able to repel an attack.*[97]

The alarm raised a few days earlier about prowling Blackfoot may have been more valid than Wyeth believed at the time. With evidence of recent use, this shelter had probably housed those raiders for the night.

Salish diets included well over a dozen different roots. The tubers Wyeth noted, gathered in a seasonal, wetland habitat, may have been swamp parsnip (*Sium suave*). It is easily confused with the poisonous western water hemlock.[98] Among Wyeth's plant specimens, Nuttall described another yellow-flowered member of the same plant family, *Umbelliferae*, with "round and small tubers, having the taste of parsnips and is employed for food by the natives."[99]

In the early 1800s, "Blue Devils" alluded to low spirits, suggesting that Wyeth was depressed and had gone to bed early. However, by the mid-1830s the term had come to mean the forms and figures seen by a hallucinating drunkard experiencing delirium tremens.[100] Given that rum had flowed a few nights previous, and in light of later accusations of overdrinking, perhaps Wyeth suffered from a form of alcohol withdrawal.

May 24, 1833   *Beaverhead Mountains*

24th   A double portion of the usual weather viz. rain Hail snow wind rain and Thunder into the bargain   we are so near where they make weather that they send it as if cost nothing   Course S.E. 6 miles up the creek then by N.E. 3 cutting a height of land but low and perfectly good going to the head of another river running S.E.   down this two miles and camped   hunted today   killed one cow   saw some hundreds

Wyeth's sense of humor rebounded in comments about the weather. The camp worked its way out of the Big Hole Valley and over the Beaverhead Mountains, but the information provided does not allow identification of which streams the group followed. A likely course would have been up the Big Hole River to its sources in the area of Skinner Meadows, across the Divide and onto Bloody Dick Creek.

May 25, 1833   *Horse Prairie Creek*

25th   Followed the creek 5 miles S.S.E. then it turned round a point more eastwardly   We continued same course 4 mils and struck a creek going into the same about 2 mils below the point spoken of   rain snow & Hail today with sunshine   grass better   to day had a long ride before sunrise after the lame horse which I brought to Camp.

Keeping to Bloody Dick Creek until its course heads more easterly, the party would have struck Horse Prairie Creek and worked its way south, up that stream.

May 26, 1833   *Horse Prairie Creek*

*26th   Same Camp   A blackfoot Trail discovered in our
vicinity   a numerous camp of them   better weather than usual
to day   Sunday according to our reconing.   At night one of two
Indians who started on an express to the Nez Perces Camp
returned with three blankets one white shirt and tobacco and
powder which articles they found buried with a Blackfoot Indian
who was unscalped   two bullets through his head and one
through his body   We apprehend that there has been a battle
between the Blackfoot Indians and perhaps the whites.*

Wyeth's assumption on this predictably quiet Sabbath that a battle had occurred between the Blackfoot and "whites" was likely due to the body not having been scalped.

May 27, 1833   *Horse Prairie Creek*

*27th   17 mils S. crossing two small forks of the Missouri and
camping on the third of small size   near Camp found a red
blankett Hat and some small articles but no body.   soon after
Camp arrived one Indian with news and soon after 2 more
and three squaws comprising the only survivor of the battle
which happened thus   21 Nez Perces 18 Flathead and two
Iroquois and 1 Ponderai started with intent to steal horses
from the Blackfeet near the head of Salmon River   they saw
4 and some horses   these they attacked   just at this moment
a horse threw one of the Flatheads   he seized on one of the
horses of the Blackfeet and ran after him up a mountain   he
looked back and saw a large number of Blackfeet killing his
companions   not one survived but himself   he made the
best of his way to the Nez Perce Camp to tell the sad tale to
the wives and children of the dead   in this Camp [where] the
relatives of the deceased Flathead are there is weeping and
wailing.   Fair all day and comfortably warm.   there were 46
lodges of the Blackft.   do not know if women were with it or*

> not   if not it is a much larger Camp than ours,   the blanketts
> &c found are accounted for in the practice that the Blkft. have
> of cutting a piece of flesh from near the shoulder tying it to
> an article and throwing it away to propitiate the Deity   the
> circumstances of the flesh being tied with them I did not at first
> know.

In 1834, Warren Ferris heard of this battle between the Flathead and the Blackfoot bands. Little Chief, a Salish headman also known as Insula, told the trapper

> *that thirty of his people were massacred last spring [1833], at*
> *one time, by a large party of Black-feet, on the east fork of Salmon*
> *river. The little devoted band had started expressly to retake horses*
> *from, or fight the Black-feet, who were, it appears, approaching in*
> *considerable numbers, at the same time, determined to fulfil a threat*
> *they had made last fall, that they would exterminate the Flat-*
> *heads, root and branch. The two parties met on the summit of the*
> *[Lemhi] pass from that fork to Horse prairie, and a most desperate*
> *conflict ensued, which resulted in the total defeat of the Flatheads,*
> *who fought to the last, and perished to a man. The only individual*
> *of the party who escaped was separated from the rest in the early*
> *part of the action, and fled to tell the disastrous tale. There were*
> *among the slain several of the bravest warriors of the nation, who*
> *were well known to the hunters as hardy, bold, and heroic in war;*
> *sage and experienced in council, and hospitably courteous, even to*
> *inconvenience and self-privation, in their humble dwellings ... It is*
> *believed that the Black-feet sustained great loss in this engagement;*
> *at least they abandoned the design of attacking the village, and*
> *returned to their own country.*[101]

A few of the details vary from Wyeth's report but the skirmish described by Insula was undoubtedly the same. William Marshall Anderson met Insula in 1834. Anderson explained that this Salish chief's name "signifies in English the War Eagle's Plume," in reference to the cap he wore.[102]

May 28, 1833   *Bannock Pass*

28th   Moved S. 8 miles following the left branch of the creek which forks at our last nights camp then S.S.W. 4 miles and camped on the same creek   a little rain just after we came to camp   a band of Buffaloe passed the camp which gave a fine chance to the Indians to run them   one of them they chased into camp and then killed her a fine cow.

Crossing Bannock Pass, and descending Canyon Creek to the Lemhi River, the party returned to the Columbia drainage, reentering the modern state of Idaho. Killing a bison cow in the middle of camp would certainly be convenient in terms of butchering the meat, and apparently such a chase was not unheard of. A similar event occurred at the 1834 rendezvous when a Nez Perce named Bull's Head drove an old buffalo bull through the middle of camp.

Whilst dining in our tent to-day, I heard the simultaneous cry from English, French and Indian mouths, of a bull, un caiac, tsodlum and oh, Spirit of Nimrod, what a spectacle! A huge buffalo bull, booming through camp like a steamboat, followed by an Indian yelling and shaking his robe ... and whiz, whiz, went a dozen arrows, bang, bang, as many guns, and poor John Baptist leaped from the bank and floated, broad side up, down the rapid current of Green River.[103]

Bull's Head was known to most trappers as Kentuck in consequence of his ongoing attempts to learn the song, "Hunters of Kentucky." William Gray described him as "good natured, sensible, and yet apparently crazy," which might explain why this daring feat was performed merely to please William Sublette.[104]

May 29, 1833   *Lemhi Mountain Range*

29th   Moved S. by E. 6 miles cutting the divide of waters and struck a small creek going into Salmon river then 7 miles S by E. following the creek through high hills of lime rock on which

> *we found plenty of sheep some of which were killed   then*
> *3 miles S.W. and struck Salmon River   here a small creek*
> *running through a fine open plain valley about 6 miles wide and*
> *extending each way as far as the eye could reach   the river*
> *runs here about W. by N.   On the S. side is a high range of*
> *snowy mountains perhaps not covered the whole year   this*
> *range is parrallel with the river.   the country I should call for*
> *two days back volcanic   flints are found in abundance   some*
> *of the stones have a white crust on the outside of them whether*
> *of lime or Epson salts can not say   both abound   the lime*
> *rock is mostly slate blue but is found in layers of all shades*
> *from white to deep blue and very much contorted and forming*
> *frequent caves and holes.   It is the intention of the chiefs to*
> *remain at this camp until the Nez Perces come to us and then*
> *to move together.   This morning left my wounded horse.*

While crossing the Lemhi Mountain Range between the Lemhi and the Pahsimeroi rivers, the camp managed to shoot a few bighorn sheep. In 1831, John Work had added "plenty of sheep" to the larder when his HBC brigade traversed this area.[105]

Wyeth could not have been on the Salmon River, as he claimed. First, the mileage logged since leaving the Big Hole was not far enough to get him there. Second, the Salmon does not run west by north, but rather to the southeast, eventually emptying into the Snake River. Wyeth was likely on the Pahsimeroi River, which does flow to the northwest and was often called the Little Salmon by other fur traders.[106] Certainly Ermatinger would have known the difference. Historians have taken at face value that Wyeth was on the actual Salmon rather than the Little Salmon River. Subsequent diary entries and study of accurate maps will offer additional proof that Wyeth and his cohort were not on the Salmon.

May 30, 1833   *Pahsimeroi River*

30th.   Same Camp   rained all last night and all day   Went up
into the mountains to hunt sheep   wounded one but a snow
storm coming on his trail was covered and I lost him   Saw

> *plenty   it is surprising to view the places where they go   no one would imagine it possible for an animal to climb the rocks they do   Got nothing and hearing a firing hasted to the top of a hill to see if the Camp was attacked but found that the Nez Perces had arrived with 9 whites   a Mr. Hodgskins at their head.   This party is 16 lodges and only escaped the Blkft. by the latter falling in with 31 Indians 30 of whom they killed   It is supposed the 30 killed about 50 of the Blkft.   They mustered about 700   all men and were sufficient to cut off all our Camps if they would trade man for man.*

Using Wyeth's April 29, 1833, estimate of 1000 people in 110 lodges, the sixteen lodges of Nez Perce joining the Flathead camp on this date would have totaled approximately 145 Indians. The Nez Perce band had been larger by thirty-one souls, but those had perished in a skirmish with Blackfoot raiders.

William D. Hodgkiss was a clerk for Benjamin Bonneville. In March, the Captain had sent him out in charge of a trapping brigade with a small stock of trade goods. Hodgkiss and his nine men had met up with the Nez Perce and stayed with them for protection against marauding Blackfoot bands seen in the area.[107]

Bonneville had learned the details of that deadly encounter from Hodgkiss, who heard the story from the Nez Perce. Three hundred enemy warriors had been spotted in the hills around the Nez Perce village. The Nez Perce were not numerous enough to cope with so large an enemy in an open fight. A Pierced-nose chief, whom the whites had named Blue John, volunteered to lead a small hand-picked band through a defile opening onto the Blackfoot encampment, aiming to drive off the rival horse herd. Blue John had consulted his medicine. His stealthy raid would succeed, provided no rain should fall before he had passed through the defile; but if it rained, his band would be wiped out.

The weather was clear until the warriors reached the gorge. Just as they were entering it, however, a black cloud rose over the mountain crest, releasing a sudden shower. The warriors turned to their leader but Blue John was resolute, and they pressed forward. A short way into the defile, an enemy scouting party appeared. The Nez Perce attacked and drove the Blackfeet among the hills. While in hot pursuit, shouts and yells rose behind them as the main body of the Blackfeet advanced. As Irving tells the tale, the Nez Perce second-in-command wavered at the sight and proposed retreat.

> *"We came to fight!" replied Blue John, sternly. Then giving his war-whoop, he sprang forward to the conflict. His braves followed him. They made a headlong charge upon the enemy; not with the hope of victory, but the determination to sell their lives dearly. A frightful carnage, rather than a regular battle, succeeded. The forlorn band laid heaps of their enemies dead at their feet, but were overwhelmed with numbers and pressed into a gorge of the mountain; where they continued to fight until they were cut to pieces. One only, of the thirty, survived. He sprang on the horse of a Blackfoot warrior whom he had slain, and escaping at full speed, brought home the baleful tidings to his village … To their surprise the Blackfeet refrained from pursuing their advantage; perhaps satisfied with the blood already shed, or disheartened by the loss they had themselves sustained. At any rate, they disappeared from the hills, and it was soon ascertained that they had returned to the Horse Prairie.*[108]

May 31, 1833   *Pahsimeroi River*

31st   Got news that 20 lodges of Blkft. are now camped at our camp of 21st Inst. and I think likely that these are the same who killed the 30 Indians and as usual 10 times over rated.   This day moved 7 miles S.E. up the river and following a small creek   near our camp of last night a creek comes in from the S.   one which we followed coming from N.W.   this one fro[m] the S.S.E.   the main river S.E   went into the mts.   saw antelope   killed nothing in the mountains   heavy thunder with snow and hail storm and high wind.

With Blackfoot lodges set in the Big Hole Valley, the enemy was not too many days behind the main Flathead camp. The Blackfoot camp, located at the Wyeth party's May 21 site, could have accounted for as many as 240 warriors if these were all war lodges.[109] However, if this was a traveling band of Blackfoot rather than a raiding party, twenty lodges represented about 200 men, women and children. Wyeth pointed out the exaggeration of warrior numbers, but his skepticism was no doubt edged with relief; the Flathead camp now swelled to over 1,200 people.

Wyeth's report that the camp moved "S. E. up" the river was further evidence that they were not on the Salmon River as he stated. If the travelers had been on the Salmon, they would have moved "down" the river. Along the day's route, Wyeth passed the point where the Pahsimeroi emerged from its mountain sources. The small creek the party followed was Goldburg Creek.

June 1-2, 1833   *Little Lost River*

June 1st   Same Camp   some snow on Mts.   got wet.

2nd   17 miles S. E. 1 E. by N.   through an open plain nearly level   finished the streams of Salmon river and struck one called little Goddin   it terminates near the three butes in a little lake   here goes S.E. through the valley   the mts. appear terminating on both sides   a fair day   the S. range comprises much more of a stone which I will call quartz   the same as is found at Kettle falls   there is also lime stone   Blue and without organic remains.

Working its way upriver on the Pahsimeroi, the camp eventually struck today's Little Lost River, then known as the Little Goddin River. It was named after Iroquois trapper Antoine Godin who found the stream in 1824.[110] He and his father Thyery worked initially for the Northwest Company and its successor, the Hudson's Bay Company. The son was a key instigator of the Battle of Pierre's Hole at the 1832 rendezvous.[111] The river disappeared completely underground in several places and at various times of the year, hence its modern name.[112] Once again, details show that the party's location on the map is not the Salmon River drainage.

In this instance it is most likely that Wyeth's reference to getting "wet" is about the weather.

June 3, 1833   *Little Lost River*

*3d   15 miles S.E. through the same vally   gradually
decending   the stream became a rapid and pretty large
one   as large as some that pass 300 miles   We camped
at a narrow pass formed of low hills   here is between the
hills a slough of clay saturated with Epsom salts   the hills
are of Basaltic rock in columns   the first I have seen in this
region   lime rock is found here in pudding rock   Killed plenty
of Buffaloe here*

The only thing resembling a "narrow pass" along this stretch of the
Little Lost River is where Deer Creek joins it from the west and Badger
Creek joins it from the east. It must have been near these "low hills" that
the party set camp on the night of June 3.

The location seems to have been a good place to encounter bison.
In 1832, while in the Pahsimeroi River Valley, Ferris claimed to have
killed "upwards of an hundred head of buffalo, which were numerous
for sometime."[113]

June 4-5, 1833   *Little Lost River*

*4th.   Moved through the valley following the river called as I
am informed little Goddin in a S.E. by E. 6 miles during which
space I found the lower hills of Basalt   the mts. are of lime
rock   the same as passed hertofor   Wind high   N.W.   which
brings warm weather here and clear   grass very bad.*

*5th.   Clear warm day   moved S.E. by E. 8 miles   went in
search of Buffaloe   found none   Saw an old Blkft. Camp of
65 fires   half as large as our present camp   Saw several
whirlwinds which raised the dust at a distance and appears
much like smoke.   Saw the three Butes come in sight one by
one and then the Trois Tetons   the Butes S.E. by S.   20 mils
distant about   so far this river rapid and little brush and no
beaver   grass worse and worse.*

As they moved down the Little Lost River, they inched their way closer to the Snake River Plains. Wyeth had traversed the southern portion of these plains on his way west the previous fall. Now, he was working his way toward the familiar territory of the north bank of the Snake which he could backtrack eastward. The three buttes are volcanic cones on the plains between modern Idaho Falls and Arco, Idaho. These mounds, known today as East Butte, Middle Butte and Big Southern Butte, often appeared in early fur trade journals as the Three Tetons, which has confused scholars and historians over the years.[114] The sinks of Big Lost River are near the base of these hills.

The Trois Tetons, one of the most important landmarks in the Far West, loom over Pierre's Hole, where Wyeth had attended the rendezvous of 1832. Astorian Wilson Price Hunt named them the Pilot Knobs for their ability to orient the traveler.[115]

June 6, 1833   *Little Lost River*

6th. Same Camp   last night arrived 3 Kootenays with 25 beaver who left us on Flathead river being on foot the whole time   last night sent out Indians to see in what direction were the most Buffaloe   one came back this mng.   reports cows to the S.

No mention was made in April when these three Kootenai men separated from the main camp. Wyeth does not identify whether these were Ermatinger's HBC men or independent Natives on their own quest for fur. Either way, a harvest of only twenty-five beaver pelts was a meager result from nearly two months' labor.

June 7, 1833   *Big Lost River*

7th   Moved E.N.E.15 miles and without water the whole route   the Trois Tetons bearing E. perhaps 90 miles distant over a level and dry plain without grass or extemely little   in the afternoon had a gale from the S.W. which blew down the lodges accompanied with a little rain and enough dust to suffocate one   on our left there is a range of high hills from which come numerous streams but they sink in the plain and are warm and muddy   went out this evening to bring in the meat of a cow killed in the forenoon and found a horse extremely fat   it is surprising how fat a horse gets by being left to himself   no grooming that I have ever seen will make a horse appear as beautiful as to be left to his own resources   the Butes bear due S.

From a campsite near present Howe, Idaho, Wyeth moved out onto the Snake River Plains, traveling northward presumably picking up the intermittent bed of the Big Lost River and working his way along it until it diminished. Early maps show this stream extending various distances onto the plains before reaching its sink. An early twentieth century map shows the Big Lost River reaching to nearly the border of Idaho's Butte and Jefferson counties, close to Circular Butte, before draining into the basin floor.[116] The amount of rain in a given year likely affected the length of the river.

The open prairie presented no protection from the afternoon winds. Once past the sinks, most of the day's route was without water. The mountains on Wyeth's left were the Lemhi Range and the Beaverheads, from which several streams originate – primarily Birch, Warm Springs and Medicine Lodge creeks and their tributaries. All of these waterways flow onto the Snake River Plain then disappear into the porous, lava-based floor of the basin to feed the Snake River Aquifer below.

June 8, 1833   *Camas Creek*

8th   5 miles N. following the same creek up which grows larger as we assend   had a fine rain & Hail and Thunder today which is Sunday.   Water very muddy   grass little and but a little.

As the travelers crossed the plains of what is now northeastern Idaho, there were no large rivers to follow. The next likely watercourse of any size or consistency would have been Camas Creek.

June 9, 1833   *Camas Creek*

9th.   10 miles N. and following the creek   has some tolerable wild[?] cotton wood and willow on it   wind N.   clear and windy   country same   Three Nez Perces arrived at camp   Bring news that Payette is with four Nez Perce Chiefs.   Capt Serrey with 7 is detained by snow   that the Blackfeet village is camped at the spot where we met the Nez Perces.   We find that Payette will meet us at the forks   Capt Serrey has got 31 horses   this day a bull was run into camp which I shot at my lodge door   To day an Indian was running bulls   he turned   the horse stopped and threw him   the bull gored him into his chest so that his breath was made through the apparture   by the help of the women he reached camp.   When Mr. Ermatinger dressed his wound he very composedly made his will by word of mouth   the Indians responding in concord at the end of each sentence.   He appeared not in the least intimidated by the approach of death.   I think the Indians die better than the whites   perhaps they have less superstition in regard to the future and argue that as the deity makes them happy here he will also hereafter if there is existence for them.

Francois Payette was an Astor man who arrived in the Pacific Northwest on board the *Beaver* in 1812. He became a Nor'wester, then an HBC employee. He was John Work's second-in-command in several brigades. The modern Idaho town of Payette, Payette River and Payette Lake were named after him.[117] Wyeth's suggestion that Payette would meet them "at the Forks" surely referred to the junction of Henry's Fork and the Snake River.

Michel Sylvestre Cerré was one of Benjamin Bonneville's lieutenants. Cerré had been previously involved in the Santa Fe Trade and was a partner in P. D. Papin and Company, better known in St. Louis as the French Fur Company. During the 1832-33 winter camp, Bonneville had assigned Cerré to accompany the Nez Perce on their spring hunt.[118]

Wyeth's comment that the Blackfoot village was camped where the Flatheads met the Nez Perce apparently referred to their previous camp on the Pahsimeroi River where Hodgkiss and his party joined the New Englander. The enemy was still about ten days behind them.

Wyeth's ruminations on spiritual matters, after witnessing the Indian's death, again reveal his skepticism regarding New England religious conventions, but provide little concrete information about Native American beliefs. Perhaps influenced by Christianity, Flathead informants explained to early ethnologists that the good spirit Amotkin was thought of as dwelling in the sky, while Amtep, the dark spirit, dwelt underground. The soul of a good person lived with Amotkin after death, while the bad person's soul was sent to Amtep.[119]

The danger of hunting bison also made it exciting. Rufus Sage recalled a similar instance in which a trapper was gored by a bull. A party had killed two buffalo:

> Both animals were extended upon the ground, one entirely and the other apparently dead the hunters, having butchered one of them, proceeded to the other, and were in the act of raising him to the right position for the commencement of operation. The old fellow, not relishing the like familiarity from new acquaintances, sprang to his feet, and made a plunge at the afrighted hunters, who only escaped the fatal charge by one of those admirable feats of quick dodging so often in requisition among mountaineers.
>
> The bull, passing between them, fell head foremost against the ground, two or three feet beyond the spot they had occupied scarcely a second previous; then rising, with glaring eyes and distended nostrils, and mouth foaming with blood and rage, he pursued one of them in hot chase, for a distance of several hundred yards. So close was the bull in a few leaps, that with a sweep of his horns he gored the hunter's back, tearing away his pantaloons and coat, and prostrating him upon all-fours at the edge of a deep ravine, down which he tumbled; the enraged beast followed, but the force of an unbroken headway landed him, with a tremendous shock, against the opposite bank, far beyond the hunter. Improving the advantage thus gained, the latter escaped through the windings of the ravine, and ascended the bank, without the reach of his pursuer.

Having procured his rifle, after nine more shots had riddled the lights of the bull's carcase, the business of butchering was again commenced and terminated without further mishap.[120]

It is easy to imagine why this mountaineer would have fired, reloaded, and fired again – nine times – in retaliation for such a heart-thumping escapade.

June 10-13, 1833   *Camas Creek*

10th. Same camp   another Indian came to camp who had been looking out for the Blkft.   He was ambuscaded by two of them and narrowly escaped by the goodness of his horse being wounded slightly in the nose.

11th   Same camp   fresh news of the Blkft.   Made horse pen that my horses might be safe.   I do not apprehend any serious attack but only that they will come suddenly with a great noise of voices and guns and fright the horses   on such occasions horses become wild   one frights another   they run over the lodges   this increases the confusion and the yelling firing and running & snorting of 1200 Indians and 1800 horses is frightfull indeed.   Sometimes a camp with as many horses as the above loose every one   it is commonly whole or none.   Day warm, clear fresh   wind W.

12th.   Same camp   warm day   The Blackft camp about 15 mils from this   they are very numerous.

13th.   Same camp   cloudy and cool with high wind from S. E.   Blakft. still near but have attempted nothing yet.   Child died in camp yesterday   remains to bury today.   Find I have missed one day in my journal which has been done while laying at some camp and accordingly date tomorrow the 15th.

It is not clear why the camp stayed put for so many days with the Blackfoot raiders nearby and closing in. Perhaps it was to provide a period of recovery for the wounded hunter.

A horse stampede was not an unexpected occurrence when in unfriendly territory. This excerpt from Irving's tale of Bonneville's adventures sounds remarkably like Wyeth's description:

*Captain Bonneville was also especially careful to secure the horses,
and set a vigilant guard upon them; for there lies the great object
and principal danger of a night attack. The grand move of the
lurking savage is to cause a panic among the horses. In such cases
one horse frightens another, until all are alarmed, and struggle to
break loose. In camps where there are great numbers of Indians, with
their horses, a night alarm of the kind is tremendous. The running
of the horses that have broken loose; the snorting, stamping, and
rearing of those which remain fast; the howling of dogs; the yelling
of Indians; the scampering of white men, and red men, with their
guns; the overturning of lodges, and trampling of fires by the horses;
the flashes of the fires, lighting up forms of men and steeds dashing
through the gloom, altogether make up one of the wildest scenes of
confusion imaginable. In this way, sometimes, all the horses of a camp
amounting to several hundred will be frightened off in a single night.*[121]

June 15-16, 1833   *Camas Creek*

*15th   Last night some Blackfoot fired into our camp   a ball
passed through a lodge   some straggler disappointed of
stealing horses I suppose.   Moved N.N.E. 5 miles and camped
on a creek now almost dry and soon will be wholly.   There is
little but cotton wood on this creek.*

*16th.   8 miles N.E. by N. to a small creek which about a
mile below this joins another larger one.   Country nearly
level   day windy   S.W. wind cool and cloudy   Trois Tetons
bear E.S.E.   Today saw the Indians carrying the man who was
wounded by a Buffaloe   no one could receive more attention,
one person to carry water   he was on a good bed made on
poles the front of which like shafts were carried by a horse
led by his wife   the hinder part by 6 men and women on their
shoulders   the camp moved slower than usual for him   these
things give a favorable impression of the Indians.*

The man who had been gored by a buffalo the week before was carefully transported along the trail on a travois. Wyeth seemed somewhat
surprised that in this case, the trailing ends of the poles were supported

by people, rather than being dragged on the ground, in order to keep the wounded man more comfortable.

Ethnological reports indicate that while the Flathead used horses to drag lodge poles in flat, open country, they seldom used a horse travois for general transportation, even when hunting buffalo.[122] Nevertheless, Warren Ferris documented their use for transporting wounded a year earlier:

> *The wounded Indians were carried on a kind of litter simply constructed, by fastening the ends of two long poles to opposite sides of a pack horse, and tying cross bars six feet assunder, to prevent the long poles from approaching to, or receding from each other. A buffalo robe is then fastened loosely to the four poles, and the wounded person placed upon it. These litters, of which there were eight or ten, were followed by numbers of young men, ever ready to administer to the wants of the sufferers.*[123]

June 17-18, 1833 *Camas Creek*

17th. Same camp   rained very hard all last night and until noon of today   an alarm of Blkft last night but I believe little of these things in so large a camp when it is known that there are Blkft. near   a man straying out of camp is enough to give rise to a report and a report once raised it gathers like a snow ball.

18th. Same camp   Severe hail & snow yesterday afternoon and rain most of last night and until noon today.   Camp about out of provisions so we are in hopes of moving soon.   Nothing but necessity and that immediate will induce an Indian to do the least thing, any excuse serves to stop business with them and a small party of whites who are not strong enough to move alone will find in traveling with them occasion for all the patience they may have.

After spending so many weeks on the trail in their company, Wyeth had come to admire many aspects of Native American culture. Yet it is difficult to imagine a profit-driven, nineteenth-century business tycoon embracing all facets of a hunter-gatherer's approach to life. The self-centered Boston entrepreneur probably puzzled the nomads of the Plains in equal measure.

June 19, 1833   *Camas Creek*

*19th.   1 1/2 miles to the main river here going S.W.   this
we found quite deep enough to ford for horses the mules   I
was obliged to unload and put the loads on the horses   3[?]
miles more passed   three slews of our stream joining the last
river mentioned.   3 miles more camped on another branch
of it   making 10 1/2 miles N.E. by E.   day clear   snow in
patches in shaded places but the country green with herbage
and mostly in blossom.   All rocks for some days past
volcanic.   This stream looses itself in the plain.*

There is no major stream in the vicinity, but in all likelihood Wyeth
was still on Camas Creek, one of the largest drainages in this part of
modern Idaho. The creek got its name from the abundance of camas
that thrived in the valley. Today the region is drained by numerous man-
made canals and ditches (similar to Wyeth's "slews"). Some late-nine-
teenth-century maps showed Camas and Beaver creeks ending at a sink.

June 20, 1833   *Camas Creek*

*20th.   Moved 11 miles E. by N. and camped on Kamas River
so called from the abundance of that root   in some spots it is
so abundant as to exclude other vegetation.   This Prairie is
very extensive perhaps 15 miles each way and is intersected
by numerous little streams which form one going to the S.
and ends in a small lake on the plain between this and Lewis
river   day clear & cool   frost last night   snow on all the high
hills   Trois Tetons bear E.S.E.   I should think about 80 miles
distant   found Buffaloe here   the first for 10 days   when we
found the last I think at least 100 were killed in one day   42
tongues were given to Mr. E. H. and myself.*

Camas Creek originates in the Beaverhead Mountains, northeast
of present Dubois, Idaho. As mentioned, early maps often showed
Camas Creek disappearing into the plains; however, it was almost

as frequently shown flowing into Market Lake, known today as Mud Lake, and likely Wyeth's "small lake." This shallow body of water with no outlet harbored thousands of migratory water fowl including geese, swans and a variety of ducks.

Having not seen buffalo for more than a week, now that a herd was found, the Indians made a full day's work of killing and butchering. Wyeth, Ermatinger and Hodgkiss were rewarded with over a dozen tongues each. The bison tongue, considered one of the prime cuts, was relished by many mountaineers. As Warren Ferris put it, trappers often feasted "luxuriously upon the delicate tongues, rich humps, fat roasts, and savoury steaks of this noble and excellent species of game."[124]

June 21, 1833   *Camas Creek*

21st.   Late last night arrived 5 hunters   Pillew, Nasben, and Churboye and two Indians who left us on the head of the Missouri having seen plenty of recent sign of the Blkfeet but happily saw none   they killed 94 Beaver.   Today went out to hunt   killed one Bull.   forenoon showers and lowery   Kamas in bloom   the Indians are taking large quantities of it   this plain is extensive but about 7 miles across of it only is rich and that is as good as any land I ever saw   the main plain is much of it bare rock   the surface of which looks like a pan of milk when you push together the cream   evidently it was once a fiery and fluid plain or lake of lava, probably the whole plain between these mountains and the Trois Tetons   the rock is porous like honey comb   the surface shows plainly the heads of Basaltic colums and in some places the colums stand not perpendicular but at an angle of 50 degrees about,   same camp.

The hunters who had gone off from the main party on May 20, while they were still in the Big Hole Valley, rejoined the group. Their ninety-four beaver hides no doubt pleased their boss, Ermatinger.

June 22, 1833   *Camas Creek*

22nd.   Same camp   arrived this mng. an express from
Bonneville   this express came from the forks in three
days   they saw Blkft. by the way   this afternoon Mr. Hodge left
to go to Bonneville   day clear and warm   Buffaloe were run
into camp.

Benjamin Bonneville was camped to the southeast of Wyeth's group, at the junction of the Henry's Fork with the Snake River. Bonneville was about 22 miles away but unsure of Wyeth's whereabouts, thus it took three days for Bonneville's messenger to track him down. The man came to recall Hodgkiss from his trapping excursion in Nez Perce country and rejoin the Company. Hodgkiss started out the same afternoon.

When Bonneville's express arrived, Wyeth saw an opportunity. He hurriedly wrote to Bonneville with a business proposition. Wyeth had as yet received no response from Governor Simpson regarding his earlier overtures to the Hudson's Bay Company; perhaps the Bostonian felt he should hedge his bets by offering a similar deal to the U.S. Army officer-cum-trader. Hodgkiss carried this proposal to his superior:

To Captain Bonneville of Salmon River June 22d 1833.
Sir
I send you the following proposition for a mutual hunt in the country
south of the Columbia river which I visited last autumn and winter.
As to the prospect of Beaver there I will only say that I have no doubt
of taking 300 skins fall and spring. As much sign as would give me
this I have seen. I have little doubt much more might be found, but
in that country a hunt cannot be made with horses alone, boats
must be used. I have obtained some maps of the country beside my
own observations in it, and I have little doubt but I can make my
way through it without guides, who cannot be procured. As this
country is distant an immediate answer is required. As it regards
the mules Horses would do but are by no means so good for grass
in some places is very bad. If the number required is a very great
objection 9 would do but goods enough to buy 3 more must be given

in their stead. The men that are wanted must be good, peaceable and industrious, but need not be trappers. I would prefer good men who have not been more than one year in the country. In case of agreement being made you are to engage to deliver what letters I wish to send home, a boy about 13 years old and about 25 lbs. sundrys. The expenses of the boy in the States my brother in N. York will pay to whom he is delivered. The boy will have a mule to carry him. With so many animals as I have and so few men I cannot come to the forks and I think these Indians will go no further than where in your route to Green River you strike the plain of the Three Butes. There I hope to see you and in case you acceed to the proposal, with all the things required in it, this hunt to be for one year to meet you at your rendezvous of next year the furs to be equally divided between us and I to have the right to take mine at any time during the year yourself to have the right to send a man to see to your interests –

PROPOSITION.

To be furnished by Mr B.	To be furnished by Mr. Wyeth
9 men, armed, clothed for the year with saddles &c	19 horses
12 mules	3 mules
9 skins dressed for making boats	20 traps
40 good traps	3 men with myself
1 doz files	2 doz knives
4 doz knives	1 Lodge
20 lbs tobacco	Cooking apparatus
200 lbs grease, if possible	vermillion.
3 bales Indian meat	fish Hooks a few sundrys
a few small tools	10 lbs. powder and lead.
3 axes	14 pr. Horse shoes
12 pair Horse shoes (if you have them.)	4 pack saddles and Harness.
4 pack saddles and Harness.	
6 pair of lashes	
25$ for cost of sundrys	
25 lbs. powder and lead with it.	

*– said man to do duty the same as the other men and to have no
other control than to secure your interest in the division of the skins.
In case you are ready to make this arrangement you need make no
doubt of my being ready to enter at once on it except that in the mean
time I loose my animals.*

*You to have the liberty of sending a load of goods to pay off the
men you furnish. All property at the risk of its owner, neither to be
responsible for the debts of the other.*

Yrs &c.[125]

Wyeth's offer appeared to be heavily in his own favor; it required
Bonneville to put up nearly double what Wyeth would provide. Perhaps
Wyeth viewed his recently gained knowledge and first-hand experience
in the Columbia region (though he had done little trapping himself) as
ample collateral to balance the risks. He sounded confident that a pool-
ing of resources would net both men a substantial return on their invest-
ments. Wyeth's proposal to hunt in the coming fall meant he would have
to postpone his plans to return to Cambridge.

Still, it is hard to believe Wyeth was convinced that abundant beaver could be harvested from the fur desert of the Northwest, which he
had just traversed. Perhaps that is why he told his backers he intended
"to reach the vicinity of St. Francisco" on this trapping excursion.[126]
Historian Bernard DeVoto confirmed that

> *no part of California west of the Sierra divide and south of the San
> Joaquin Valley was good fur country. Even in such fur country as
> there was, the resources and the elaborate system of the Hudson's Bay
> Company were required to turn a profit – if indeed the Hudson's Bay
> Company which had been working the field for eight years, did show
> an overall profit.*[127]

Wyeth's motive for attempting such an alliance with Bonneville may
have been based in part on a stubborn refusal to return home as a failure, or again, on the possibility of retrieving his cached furs and goods.
If he could recover these and sell them at Eastern prices, Wyeth felt he

could pay all the expenses he had incurred thus far.[128] Even as he detailed his proposal to Bonneville, Wyeth was optimistic about collecting these items on the return trip from California. He wrote to financiers back East, "I shall make a hunt, and probably reach the Spanish settlement of St. Francisco, and on my return obtain my last years deposites of furs &c."[129]

June 23-25, 1833   *Camas Creek*

23rd. Sunday   Indians singing and dancing as usual   day warm and clear.   These Inds. do nothing on Sunday.

24th.   Moved across the plain 3 miles N.E.   Day warm and clear.

25th   Yesterday at night some Inds. came in from hunting Buffaloe reported that they saw two Blkft. and fired on them   at night we saw their fire in the Mts.   Same camp   fine clear warm day   employed in making a saddle.

Keeping to Camas Creek, the party moved slowly upstream toward the headwaters. This camp was northeast of modern Dubois, Idaho. A person can see for many miles in all directions from the volcanic flats surrounding the creek. In one letter, Wyeth referred to the area as "Plain of the Three Buttes" which remained visible to Wyeth from this location.[130]

Wyeth did not disclose why he was constructing a saddle or whether it was for riding or packing. Nez Perce were known to have a talent for saddle-making so perhaps Wyeth was learning from one of their craftsman. Sergeant Patrick Gass, a Lewis and Clark Expedition carpenter, described the Nez Perce technique:

The frames of their saddles are made of wood nicely jointed, and then covered with raw skins, which when they become dry, bind every part tight, and keep the joints in their places. The saddles rise very high before and behind, in the manner of the saddles of the Spaniards, from whom they no doubt received the form; and also obtained their breed of horses. When the Indians are going to mount they throw their buffaloe robes over the saddles and ride on them, as the saddles would otherwise be too hard.[131]

June 26, 1833　　　　　　　　　　*Camas Creek*

26th. Same camp went out hunting saw a few Buffaloe but killed nothing but a grouse as I had some dispute with Mr. David Douglass about the grouse of this country I subjoin a discription; the bird had 10 pointed drab colored, mottled with white, tail feathers the outer edge of the feathers are only mottled until you approach their end when both sides are mottled under the tail are 10 or 12 dark brown feathers 2/3 as long as the tail feathers white at the termination. The tail feathers are about 8 inches long. The wing feathers are nearly white underneath and dark drab outside. From the head of the breast bone to the tail are many black feathers. On the body under the wings are redish grey feathers above the breast and nearly on the neck is a place devoid of feathers of a dirty olive color each side and a little below this is a tuff of short sharp pointed dirty white feathers they look as if they had been clipped with a shears. The tail feathers look as though they had been burnt off leaving the stalk of the quill projecting. The bill is short and curved downwards above the bare spot on the neck are short mottled feathers cream, white and black. It is feathered to the toes which are three and a small one behind. The hinder part of the leg is not feathered from the knee downwards Toe nails short and obscure. its back pretty uniformly mottled with deep brown dirty white approaching dirty yellow and dun colored weight 4 1/2 lbs. Length from point of tail feathers to tip of bill 25 inches from tips of wings 3 1/2 ft. We were regaled by thunder shower on our return to camp saw Blkft. trail and a cow recently killed by them.

Such an in-depth description of this sage grouse (*Centrocercus urophasianus*) makes one wonder about the intensity of the argument between Wyeth and botanist David Douglas, whom Wyeth had not seen since Fort Vancouver. Wyeth seemed to believe that he knew as much as the naturalist did about regional varieties of upland game.

June 27-30, 1833   *Camas Creek*

27th.   Same camp   nothing remarkable.

28th.   Same camp   nothing but lice and dirt.   Cool today.

29th.   Same camp as yesterday   went out to hunt   killed one Buffaloe which fell into the river and had to butcher him up to my middle in cold water.   Some hunters who went out today came in with news that they had seen the Blkft. camp on Tobacco river   one of the heads of the Missouri   they say it is larger than ours.

30th   Same camp   Sunday   Indians praying, dancing & singing.

Wyeth described the Tobacco River as "one of the heads of the Missouri." However, the identity of this particular Tobacco River is unknown. The Madison River was sometimes referred to as the Tobacco Root River but this name was not in use until the 1860s. There was a Tobacco River in northern Montana, near the Canadian border, though clearly this was not the stream mentioned by Wyeth.[132]

July 1, 1833   *Camas Creek*

1st July.   Moved 2 miles S. and down the creek   clear moderately warm day the first for three days   nights have been frosty   ice made in our pots & pails.   Men came from Bonneville in the evening.

Reversing track, the camp moved back down Camas Creek, and received more visitors from Bonneville's party. The army captain was still somewhere to the east of Wyeth's position. Wyeth will mention in a later entry that on this day, about forty lodges of the Flathead village separated from the main camp. As Wyeth noted, even mid-summer temperatures at elevations above 5,000 feet can be cold.

> **July 2, 1833**   *Camas Creek*
>
> *2nd.   Moved S. 12 miles and camped on same creek   on the
> way observed some fine luxuriant clover   grass good   about
> 9 miles down the creek wich rapidly increases in size from
> numerous springs wich are of fine cold water   we camped in
> a cluster of large cotton wood   large for this place   about 10
> inches through.*

Twelve miles downstream placed the night's camp at today's Camas, Idaho, near the former Union Pacific Railroad station.

> **July 3, 1833**   *Camas Creek*
>
> *3rd.   Last night a Bear made his way into camp among the
> horses and gave a considerable alarm but was off before
> guns could be got out.   Today moved 16 miles S.S.W. and
> camped on same creek with Mr. Bonneville with about 40 men
> bound for Green river.   I have heretofore forgot to mention
> that at our camp of 1st July we left about 40 lodges of the
> Flatheads   country this days route dry and barren   day warm.*

Keeping to Camas Creek, Wyeth moved downstream, back toward Mud Lake, where he was joined by Benjamin Bonneville and his contingent. They were getting ready to head for the summer rendezvous, to be held that year in the Green River Valley – the first of six such annual events to occur in the fertile bottomlands of the stream the Shoshone called the "Sisk-a-dee Agie" (Sage Hen River), and the Spanish called the *Rio Verde*.[133] The journey to Wyeth's camp was a bit out of the way for Bonneville, but perhaps discussions concerning the business proposal then on the table caused the slight detour.

July 4-6, 1833   *Camas Creek*

4th.   Same camp   at night saw a band of Blackfeet a little above camp   clear warm day.

5th.   Same camp.

6th.   Same camp   very warm weather.

Though Wyeth wrote virtually nothing in his journal, several letters he wrote while at this campsite indicate that a lot was going on. On Independence Day, Wyeth penned letters to his brothers, Leonard and Charles, his Uncle Leonard Jarvis, his friend Thomas Nuttall, former employer Frederic Tudor and several of his financial backers. All of these letters were infused with an overriding feeling of drama, describing the risks and dangers that awaited Wyeth in the months ahead. But more significantly, each letter conveyed Wyeth's excitement about the future, about the potential for his own fortunes, and by proxy, about the stake each addressee held alongside him. Wyeth wrote as if he wanted to keenly attune each of them to the gamble he would take on their behalf. He was also particularly sensitive about the mortgage on his Cambridge house, which would be due before he could return home.

In these letters, Wyeth exulted in the "power to make up jointly" with Bonneville, writing that his plan would keep him away from home for another year. He described recruiting a dozen men, although he seems to have added just nine new hands, because in the dozen, he counted two previous employees and himself. The faithful Wiggin Abbott was one; the second may have been John Woodman, whom Wyeth had discharged at the end of April, but who may have been rehired when he reappeared in mid-May.[134]

As it turned out, most of those letters were never mailed. Wyeth's letter book has "Not Sent" written across the face of six of them. The following day, July 5, he wrote to John McLoughlin, Chief Factor at HBC's Fort Vancouver, in a distinctly different tone. Wyeth told his British friend that he was then on a "direct train for the States," and expected to reach Cambridge, Massachusetts, by October.[135] Bonneville must have experienced a change of heart, perhaps wary of Wyeth's situation.[136] Whatever the cause, the abandoned pact did not keep Wyeth and Bonneville from traveling together toward rendezvous for the next few days.

From this camp, Wyeth wrote his friend, naturalist John Nuttall, that he was sending a package of plant specimens via brother Leonard, hoping the samples would hold together during shipping. Wyeth even invited Nuttall to consider accompanying him on a "pursuit of science" in the coming year, suggesting that the cost would be less than living at home.

In his tale of Bonneville's adventures, Washington Irving made no mention of Wyeth's and Bonneville's mutual encampment or Wyeth's business proposal, although Irving had access to the journals of both men.[137] One event that Irving did include in his account of Bonneville's expedition, but which Wyeth tellingly omitted, could only have happened during this time together:

> *During his sojourn on the Snake River plain, Captain Bonneville made one of his first essays at the strategy of the fur trade. There was at this time an assemblage of Nez Perces, Flatheads, and Cottonois Indians encamped together upon the plain; well provided with beaver, which they had collected during the spring. These they were waiting to traffic with a resident trader of the Hudson's Bay Company, who was stationed among them, and with whom they were accustomed to deal. As it happened, the trader was almost entirely destitute of Indian goods; his spring supply not having yet reached him. Captain Bonneville had secret intelligence that the supplies were on their way, and would soon arrive; he hoped, however, by a prompt move, to anticipate their arrival, and secure the market to himself. Throwing himself, therefore, among the Indians, he opened his packs of merchandise and displayed the most tempting wares: bright cloths, and scarlet blankets, and glittering ornaments, and everything gay and glorious in the eyes of warrior or squaw; all, however, was in vain. The Hudson's Bay trader was a perfect master of his business, thoroughly acquainted with the Indians he had to deal with, and held such control over them that none dared to act openly in opposition to his wishes; nay, more – he came nigh turning the tables upon the captain, and shaking the allegiance of some of his free trappers, by distributing liquors among them. The latter, therefore, was glad to give up a competition, where the war was likely to be carried into his own camp ... Shortly after Captain Bonneville's*

ineffectual attempt to participate in the trade of the associated camp, the supplies of the Hudson's Bay Company arrived; and the resident trader was enabled to monopolize the market.[138]

Bonneville found himself severely out-traded by Ermatinger. Historian Bernard DeVoto was convinced the Hudson's Bay man who trounced Bonneville was Francois Payette.[139] Indeed, Payette was in the area with the Nez Perce and slated to meet with them; likely both Ermatinger and Payette were involved. Payette may have been waiting to receive trade goods from Ermatinger, or Payette may have been delivering fresh supplies to Ermatinger. When Ermatinger later read Irving's account of the incident, however, he was convinced that the author referred to him.[140]

Although Wyeth recorded no such encounter between Bonneville and an HBC trader, he had known for four weeks that Payette was not far behind their camp. A letter Wyeth wrote to Ermatinger later that summer intimates that he and the two HBC men were together at some point.[141]

One last tidbit revealed in Wyeth's unsent correspondence was that Wyeth was hoping to bring the West home with him. He planned to send a young boy named Baptiste to Cambridge for Elizabeth to raise. Baptiste was the thirteen-year-old son of Francois Payette and his Flathead wife. Wyeth had apparently agreed to take the lad east to further the boy's education.

Not mentioned in these letters was a twenty-year-old Nez Perce man who would appear later in Wyeth's journals. Nor is there evidence that Wyeth informed his wife that she would soon be responsible for two more people, though he may simply have not kept a record of this correspondence.

July 7, 1833   *Henry's Fork*

7th. This morning our camp forked in three directions   Mr. Hodgkin for a trapping excursion with the Nez Perces, Mr. Ermatinger with the Ponderays to go to Flathead river, ourselves East 18 miles to Henrys fork here wooded with narrow leafed cotton wood   our route over a very dry plain passing at about half the distance some low hills of pure sand with not the least appearance of vegetation.   The party is 26 all told.

When Bonneville and his trapping brigades had split up the preceding spring, they arranged to meet at the annual summer rendezvous at the Green River Valley's Horse Creek, near present Pinedale, Wyoming. That date was rapidly approaching. Wyeth, too, would have been eager to attend, in order to connect with another eastbound company for safe passage to St. Louis. As Bonneville was packing, the Flathead, Nez Perce and Pend Oreille Indians in camp tried their best to convince the army officer to accompany them "to their country; which, they assured him, abounded in beaver." Bonneville refused, citing his other obligations. The free trappers in his party, in contrast, suddenly changed course, declining to continue with him. These men insisted there was no need to risk "mountain passes infested with Blackfeet" when good trapping ground was nearer at hand.[142]

On the brink of departure, Bonneville fitted them out and appointed Hodgkiss to once again ride herd on these independents whose "will and whim were apt to be law." This brigade would skip rendezvous and acquire any needed supplies in the fall. After fixing a meeting time and place for winter camp, twenty-one trappers, along with nearly half a dozen camp keepers, set out.[143]

As this transpired, Ermatinger was stuffing merchandise back into the panniers, loading his pack animals, and preparing to head out with the Flatheads. HBC had assigned his brigade to follow the main band all season, trading for the tribe's furs rather than trapping. Ermatinger evidently gave some thought to attending the rendezvous instead, but ultimately opted to comply with his earlier orders. Bonneville was able to convince the HBC men to travel at least part of the way with Hodgkiss, to better protect his brigade against roving bands of Blackfoot.

Ermatinger had already gone much farther south than he had planned or been authorized. The HBC man was east of the Continental Divide. On Wyeth's behalf, Ermatinger had also convinced the Flathead to travel beyond their normal spring trip to the buffalo ground. All this, Chief Factor John McLoughlin asserted, was "in order to facilitate my friend Mr. Wyeth's getting to the American Rendezvous."[144]

Meanwhile, Wyeth and his two men, plus Bonneville and his remaining crew, making up a party of twenty-six men by the New Englander's count, set their compass heading east toward rendezvous.[145] Irving described the scene as they raised camp:

The scene was wild and picturesque; the long line of traders,
trappers, and Indians, with their rugged and fantastic dresses and
accoutrements; their varied weapons, their innumerable horses, some
under the saddle, some burdened with packages, others following
in droves; all stretching in lengthening cavalcades across the vast
landscape, making for different points of the plains and mountains.[146]

Halfway through the day's march, they passed to the south of nearly 11,000 acres of mounded sand, about eight miles west of modern
St. Anthony, Idaho. Ferris had crossed these dunes the year before, and
indicated their location on the map he drew of the Fur Country.[147] The
combined party of Wyeth and Bonneville reached Henry's Fork of Snake
River later that afternoon. This stream was named for Andrew Henry, former partner with Manuel Lisa in the St. Louis Missouri Fur Company.
Henry had built a trading post along the river in 1810, and in 1822, he
had teamed up with William Ashley to bring one hundred "enterprising
young men" into the Rocky Mountains to trap and make their fortune.[148]
    Wyeth noted narrow-leafed cottonwood trees along the banks of
Henry's Fork. He understood the significance of this important winter
feed for the livestock. The narrow-leaf variety was often referred to as
sweet cottonwood, in contrast to the round-leafed, bitter type. Trappers, including Zenas Leonard, were keenly aware of the distinction
between the two:

About the 1st of December [1831] finding our horses getting very
poor, we thought it necessary to commence feeding [them] on
Cottonwood bark; for which purpose each man turned out and peeled
and collected a quantity of this bark, from the grove in which we were
encamped for his horses; but to our utter surprise and discomfiture, on
presenting it to them they would not eat it, and upon examining it by
tasting, we found it to be the bitter, instead of the sweet Cottonwood.
Immediately upon finding we were deceived, men were despatched up
and down the valley, on search of Sweet Cottonwood. [149]

Shortly after arriving at Henry's Fork, all hands came to a halt and
watched, as amid a clatter of hooves a solitary Nez Perce woman galloped into camp and dismounted. She walked boldly into the center of

MAP 8   *Pierre's Hole to Green River Rendezvous to Yellowstone River, 1833*

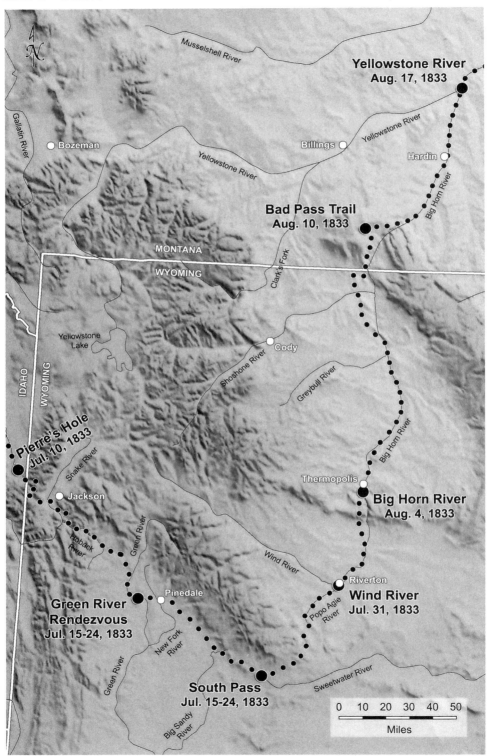

the men, and seated herself silently on the ground, still clutching the rope halter looped under the lower jaw of her mustang. The resolute demeanor of this woman roused the curiosity of the gathering trappers. Bonneville strode up to interrogate the calm, self-possessed female who answered simply "I love the whites – I will go with them." She was "forthwith invited to a lodge, of which she readily took possession, and from that time forward was considered one of the camp."[150]

As they traveled east, Bonneville instituted a military order to the procession. He sent scouting parties to patrol the outer edges of the route. At night, the horses were brought in and picketed for safety. In the mornings, a reconnaissance team scoured the neighborhood for half a mile around before the stock was let loose to graze.

July 8, 1833   *Henry's Fork*

8th. Followed up the river where we were much annoyed by mosquitos about 8 miles N.N.E. there forded it about belly deep going E. by S. 5 mils to a large river which must be Lewis fork here we found Buffaloe these two rivers form a junction about 15 miles from this point as I believe near two butes but some say not until you get as low as Three Butes on this river are not many mosquitoes.

The party crossed Henry's Fork near today's Parker, Idaho. Traveling southeast, they struck the Teton River, which Wyeth thought surely was the Lewis, or Snake, River. The Teton flowed into the Henry's Fork due west of their location, then a few more miles downriver, the combined streams met the Snake near the Menan Buttes. Menan was the Shoshone word for "many waters," an apt description of that confluence. These "two butes," as Wyeth called them, were a landmark to early travelers.[151]

July 9, 1833   *Teton River*

9th.   Made this day 22 1/2 miles due East toward the Trois Tetons   at 8 miles struck a small creek with cut rock banks running N.W. and to the river last crossed, which is not Lewis fork.   At 20 miles cut a mountain which rises and is wooded to the S W. and diminishes to the plain to the N.E.   We entered Pierre's Hole and camped on the N.W. side of it.   Here we found Buffaloe.

The "small creek" in this entry was named Canyon Creek by Ferdinand V. Hayden of the 1872 U.S. Geological Survey. Its major feature is a deep gorge that intersects with the Teton River Canyon.[152] Near the end of the day, the travelers cut over what is now known as the Rexburg Bench. The wooded area Wyeth noted to the southwest was the Big Hole Mountain Range. They entered Pierre's Hole, crossed the Teton River (known then as Pierre's River), and made camp. The group had roughly paralleled today's Idaho Highway 33, traversing the rolling hills that would later become dry farms. As Wyeth and Bonneville wound up their first full year in the Rocky Mountains, both leaders were in familiar territory. They had come through this area on their westbound treks.

July 10, 1833   *Teton Valley*

10th.   Moved 12 miles S.E. crossing a difficult swamp and camped about 2 miles from the battle ground of last year with the Gros Ventres   Day warm and a great quantity of grasshoppers for several days past   so much so as to discolor the ground in many places.

The southward trail crossed the entire length of present-day Teton Basin. Revisiting the site of the Battle of Pierre's Hole no doubt gave Wyeth the opportunity to dramatically recount the event to Bonneville. When Irving eventually wrote up the conflict in *The Adventures of Captain Bonneville*, his prose was surely flavored by Wyeth's first-hand information.

Even today in this area, a seeming plague of grasshoppers occurs in mid to late summer each year.

> **July 11, 1833**   *Snake River*
>
> *11th.   Started early and made 3 miles E.S.E. to the foot of the mountains then 8 miles E.S.E. to the summit then 6 miles E. to Lewis fork and 1 mile E. across it at the same place we crossed last year   found it very high for fording but succeeded at last.   Wind strong N.W.   clear and moderately warm.   Horses troubled with horse flies on the mountains but not in this plain   found buffaloe in the bottom   also mosquitoes   The river is here much choked up with islands and heaps of drift wood and a great quantity of mud   in coming over the mountains lost one mule and sent a man back for it   he has not returned yet [at] sundown   got a wet jacket in the river trying to find a ford.   There is the trail of about 8 men who have passed through this defile before us as I think about 14 days   they marked a name on the trees and we suppose that they are men of Dripps & Fontenelle.   We as yet see no appearance of the Blkft. except very old forts and lodges.   Lewis fork here runs S.E. about 9 miles then turns S.*

From their overnight stay near the site of modern Victor, Idaho, Wyeth and Bonneville pushed their men to the mouth of Moose Creek, then up and over the Teton Range, likely following the passage William Sublette had shown Wyeth in 1832. The trail took them into present-day Wyoming, down to the Snake River in the southern end of Jackson Hole. After some difficulty, they were able to ford at the same place Sublette had guided them across, as greenhorns, on their way to Pierre's Hole the year before. At that time, Wyeth had been forced to cache goods in order to free up horses for his sick men to ride over the pass. Interestingly, Wyeth made no mention of retrieving these goods as he passed by the same spot.

Without describing all the clues he found on the trail, Wyeth deduced that American Fur Company men preceded them. A trapper customarily placed a marker, such as the one Wyeth noted, on his way to rendezvous as a signal to other members of the same brigade coming along behind. The trapper in question may in fact have been Robert Campbell. After reaching rendezvous at the Green River and Horse Creek, he had led a small contingent back out on July 8 to make a quick run to Pierre's Hole in order to retrieve ten packs of beaver secretly cached there. Passing that way just a few days before Wyeth, one of Campbell's new recruits may have left his mark.[153]

July 12, 1833   *Hoback Canyon*

12th.   This morning my man came back having been out all night   he found the mule at our last camp.   Made this day 9 miles S.E. along the river then 3 miles E.S.E. to a small creek running into the river.   At this place 9 men under Capt. Stevens were attacked by about 30 Blkft. a little later than this time last year and several of them killed.   Mr. Bonneville informs me that when he passed last year in August their bones were laying about the valley.   I am apprehensive that More, a sick man whom I left in charge of Stevens, must be one of them.   6 miles more over a hilly broken limestone country S.E. to a considerable fork of Lewis river   this stream is strongly impregnated with sulphur.   This camp is almost without grass.   In the first place this morning we moved 3 miles and crossed a creek putting into the river.   At our camp of to night there is a small branch joining the creek from the S.E.

The man Wyeth sent back for the lost mule ended up going all the way across the pass to the previous camp to retrieve the animal – a lot of trouble for a mule. Following the Snake River for nine miles, Wyeth and Bonneville took Game Creek over the ridge and dropped onto the Hoback River.

George More had been one of the sick men who rode horseback over Teton Pass the previous summer. More had stayed in Pierre's Hole when Wyeth and his remnant crew continued west after the 1832 rendezvous. Now, Wyeth learned More's fate from Bonneville as they passed through Hoback Canyon.[154]

Alfred Stephens had recruited to his trapping brigade More, Mississippian John Foy of the Bean-Sinclair party, "two grandsons of the celebrated Daniel Boone," and two others who were not identified.[155] As the trappers descended a hill into the canyon, they were ambushed by a party of Gros Ventres. More, who was in front, was within about twenty yards of the Indians when they sprang up and fired. His horse wheeled in fright, dumping the young Bostonian to the ground. The greenhorn tried to scramble across the side of the hill, but with a screaming horde of two dozen warriors bearing down on him, he froze, paralyzed in fear. John Wyeth later reported:

> As the Indians knew that More could not get away from them, they passed him, and about twenty Indians were coming up the hill where they were. Eight or ten Indians followed up while only five trappers had gained the hill. They were considering how to save George More, when one of them shot him through the head, which was a better fate than if they had taken him alive, as they would have tortured him to death.[156]

More's comrades fled back up the hill but two of them, Foy and Stephens, seeing the danger More was in, turned back and dismounted to go to his aid. Foy was instantly shot and killed. Stephens was severely wounded in the thigh but managed to get back on his horse. One of the party's extra mules was also killed. Stephens and the others hightailed it out of Hoback Canyon, leaving the bodies of More and Foy where they lay. From John Wyeth's wording, it was not clear just who shot More, perhaps an Indian, perhaps one of his own companions. The five survivors returned to Pierre's Hole on the evening of July 27, bearing tidings of the disaster. Stephens succumbed to his wound several days later.[157]

While going through the Hoback Canyon in early August 1832, Warren Ferris reported that hunters from his party saw the bones of two men and supposed them to be those of More and Foy.[158] Confusing the matter, when Ferris's brigade passed back through the canyon on August 15, they collected the remains of the two men and deposited them in a small stream.[159] Bonneville had come through the Hoback Canyon from his fort on the Green River about the first of September that year, on his way to Teton Pass. For him to have seen "the bones of these unfortunate young men bleaching among the rocks; and ... caused them to be decently interred," meant he removed the skeletal remains from the creek where they had been placed just a week or so before by Ferris.[160]

> **July 13, 1833**   *Hoback Canyon*
>
> *13th.   East 5 miles   N.E. 1/2 mile through bad cut rocks on the N. side of the river   there is also a trail on the S. side   then 1/2 mile E.   then 1/4 mile S.E.   then following a left hand fork of the river a few rods N.E.   crossed it and made E. 3 miles to the right hand fork again which we followed E. 2 miles then S.E. 4 miles to camp   crossing it several times   a good trail most of the way   one horse of the Indians killed by falling from the cut rock trail down to the river   in the first of the cut rocks there is a handsome cave rock lime & sand   a few boulders of granite seen today as also on the E. side of the mountains of Pierres hole.   The river which we followed this day is rapid and too deep below the branches to ford   during the last of the route several small forks from each side.*

Entering into the steepest segment of Hoback Canyon, they traveled up the river of the same name, crossing and re-crossing it several times, sometimes scrambling up the rugged hillside when the banks closed in on the river. At one point, possibly along the sandstone cliffs some called the "Red Ledges," one of the Indian horses fell to its death from the trail, which at that point ran high above the river. The long day of rugged road ended in what trappers called Jackson's Little Hole, near today's Bondurant, Wyoming.[161]

Wyeth did not mention parting from Bonneville, but that probably occurred the night before or early on this date. According to Irving, Bonneville arrived at his fort in the Green River Valley on July 13. Twenty-five miles, just one long day in the saddle, separated Jackson's Little Hole from Fort Bonneville near the confluence of the Green River and Horse Creek. Irving reported that on Bonneville's arrival he found the valley strewn with buffalo carcasses. Fearing the presence of hostile Indians, he sent out scouts to investigate as soon as it was dark.

July 14, 1833   *Green River*

14th.   Made 9 miles S.E. to the height of land between this river and Green river then 5 miles S.S.E. to a creek running into Green river.   there are good trails all the way and to the divide much timber   The creek on which we camped last night just above the camp divided into three forks.   We followed the most southwardly for awhile then mounted the hill on the left side of it.   There has been for two days a high range of Mts. on our left about 10 miles distant apparently of sand stone and limestone   these E.S.E. & N.N.W. and on the divide between this and Wind river   also on our right there have been a range of Mts. of same composition about 15 mils distant.   Both ranges have snow in patches   Many alarms today but still no enemys   killed plenty of Buffaloe.

Climbing up to the Hoback Rim, Wyeth found a good trail down to Beaver Creek. Wyeth's view to the east (his left) took in both the Gros Ventre and Wind River ranges. The Wind River and its range were so named by Native Americans who noted the prevailing strong wind currents coming down the stream from the mountains.[162] The view to the west (Wyeth's right) took in the Wyoming Range. Year-round snow was not unusual in any of these segments of the Rocky Mountain chain.

11.
Rendezvous at Green River: 1833

When Bonneville's spies returned to Fort Bonneville from their reconnaissance in the early morning, they were accompanied by three of his trappers from another brigade, who told him the rest of the company was expecting him at the rendezvous grounds. He learned that the buffalo slaughter had been the work of friendly Shoshones attending rendezvous. Following a quick debriefing, the trio of "worthies" brandished a "small keg of 'alcohol,' which they had brought with them to enliven this merry meeting."[1] For Bonneville, rendezvous had begun.

July 15, 1833   *Green River Rendezvous*

15th.   Made E.S.E. 12 miles to Green river and to Mr. Bonnevilles fort   day clear and fine.   Found here collected Capt. Walker, Bonneville, Cerry, of one Co.   Dripps & Fontenelle of the Am. Fur co.   Mr. Campbell just from St. Louis, Mess. Fitzpatric, Gervais, Milton Sublette of the Rocky Mountain Fur Co. and in all the Cos. about 300 whites and a small village of Snakes   here I got letters from home.   During the last year among all the Cos there has been in all about 25 men killed two of my original party with them, viz Mr More & O'Neil.

Some have questioned the location, appearance, or even the existence of a fort built by Bonneville. Yet the mileages and directions listed in Wyeth's journal brought him awfully close to the purported site of "Fort Nonsense."[2] Here, the New Englander found ensconced in the storehouse not only Bonneville, but his lieutenants Michel Cerré and Joseph Walker. Like Cerré, Walker had prior experience in the Santa Fe trade. Historians have speculated that these two men had convinced Bonneville to take wagons to the Rocky Mountains the year before.[3]

Walker had returned from his brigade's trapping foray into what is now Montana in the fall of 1832. He would lead an expedition of forty men all the way to California at Bonneville's behest after the close of this summer's rendezvous.[4]

At Bonneville's log structure Wyeth found other acquaintances – American Fur Company partisans Andrew Drips and Lucien Fontenelle; Rocky Mountain Fur Company partners Tom Fitzpatrick and Milton Sublette, Wyeth's mentor and guide. Another familiar face might have been Jean Baptiste Gervais. He had become a partner in the Rocky Mountain Fur Company when Fitzpatrick, Milton Sublette, Jim Bridger, Henry Fraeb and Gervais bought that firm during the 1832 rendezvous in Pierre's Hole, so Wyeth could have met him then. Gervais had joined the Northwest Company at the age of seventeen, transferred to the Hudson's Bay Company at the time of the merger, and had been a member of the first Snake Country brigade led by Peter Skene Ogden. In 1829, he appeared on the Popo Agie River, trapping in the employ of Smith, Jackson and Sublette. Jean Baptiste may have been the younger brother of Joseph Gervais, one of the earliest settlers on French Prairie.[5]

Earlier that morning, Robert Campbell had returned from his quick jaunt to Pierre's Hole. He and William Sublette had recently established a new business arrangement; Campbell was now a full partner with Sublette in a venture without a formal name or title. Together, the two planned to compete head-to-head against Drips's and Fontenelle's American Fur Company. Conspicuously absent from the rendezvous, Sublette was then on the upper Missouri building several forts to support the business plan he and Campbell were developing.

With so many prominent fur trade chieftains in the same room, high-level dealing as well as friendly bonding must have created a heady atmosphere for the eager Wyeth, still a relative newcomer, though he did not record any of it in his journal. One result of this executive session may have been an agreement to divvy up the trapping grounds for the coming year. American Fur Company would work the Flathead, Snake River and Great Salt Lake regions while the RMFC men would trap the Green, Three Forks and Yellowstone watersheds.[6]

A detail Wyeth did choose to record was the number of deaths among the companies for the prior trapping season. The twenty-five trappers who had gone under from unspecified causes included two members of his own Pacific Trading Company. The unfortunate story of George More has been related. Since no one on Wyeth's roster was listed as "O'Neil," Young may have mistranscribed Wyeth's handwriting from the original journal. This second death probably referred to William Nudd, who had abandoned Wyeth in Pierre's Hole, signed on as a trapper with William Sublette, and been killed by Blackfeet in the mountains during the winter.[7]

Campbell had left Lexington, Missouri, with a company of forty to fifty men in early May and had pulled into rendezvous on July 5. Fontenelle had arrived three days later. Campbell brought a wide assortment of goods, and his companions were a varied lot of characters as well. The wealthy Scotsman William Drummond Stewart aimed to slake his thirst for adventure by hunting trophy specimens of several Rocky Mountain game animals.

> *The sight of Captain Stewart, garbed as he was in all the accouterments of a Scottish nobleman hunting the stag in the glens of Perthshire, all but overwhelmed the tatterdemalion men in buckskin. But since he rode [with] Robert Campbell, they withheld the uninhibited comments they would otherwise have made.*[8]

A former military man who had seen action at the Battle of Waterloo, Stewart was likely intrigued, when Bonneville arrived at rendezvous, to meet a bona fide officer of the United States Army.

Another of Campbell's cohorts was Edmund Christy, a St. Louis businessman who hoped to make his fortune in the valuable hides that could be acquired in western waters. Doctor Benjamin Harrison, son of the soon-to-be ninth president of the United States, William H. Harrison, had been sent west by his father in hopes of finding a cure for his alcoholism. Apparently the elder Harrison was misinformed about the realities of rendezvous. And Charles Larpenteur, who would spend the next forty years as a trader on the upper Missouri, was just then embarking on his new career.[9]

Other attendees, though not mentioned in Wyeth's journal, would have been recognized by today's students of the fur trade. These included trappers Warren Ferris, Zenas Leonard, Robert Newell, George Holmes, Joe Meek and his brother Stephen, Louis Vasquez, Jim Bridger,

Moses "Black" Harris, John Gray, Jean Baptiste Charbonneau and William O'Fallon.[10] Joe Meek misremembered artist Alfred Jacob Miller at this event (Miller's first and only rendezvous, in company with a returning William Drummond Stewart, would come in 1837).[11]

Campbell, fresh from the States, delivered letters to Wyeth from friends and family at home. Other trappers also received long-awaited news from loved ones. Historian Bernard DeVoto explained:

> *There were newspapers only two months old. For a few there were letters, for everyone there was talk with men who had read papers through the winter and spring and had lived in daily touch with the trivia of civilization ... The West now learned, for example, that Jackson had vetoed the recharter of the Second Bank of the United States, that the democracy had returned him to the White House with a landslide vote, that South Carolina had declared the new tariff nullified within its borders only to have Old Hickory bare his teeth and settle that question for a generation, that a business recession had been setting in when Campbell left the settlements.*[12]

Wyeth would comment on several of these issues in the letters he would write from this rendezvous. The news would certainly play into his plans for the coming year.

July 16-17, 1833   *Green River Rendezvous*

16th.   Same camp.

17th.   Moved 10 miles down the river S.E.   it is here a large and rapid stream and to be forded only in a few places.   Here we were followed by the Snake village   we encamped with the Rocky Mountain Fur Co.

The 1833 rendezvous was in full swing. The Green River Valley was populated by 250 to 300 Euro-Americans, plus hundreds more Native Americans, Shoshone the most prevalent. Camps were spread out for ten miles along the river in order to accommodate the enormous quantity of livestock. Bonneville kept his brigades at his stockade to the north. Fontenelle had set up the American Fur Company five miles down the Green, near its confluence with Horse Creek.

The RMFC trappers were another five miles below AFC. Wyeth threw in with Milton Sublette and the men with whom he had traveled the previous summer. Larpenteur would write that at their camp, they built a fur press to compact the beaver skins for easier packing.[13]

Jim Beckwourth would claim that his brigade named Horse Creek "in honor of a wild horse we found on its banks," but this version is corroborated only by Beckwourth himself.[14] Irving wrote that Jedediah Smith and Tom Fitzpatrick were robbed of their horses in Green River Valley and "the place where the robbery took place still bears the name of Horse Creek."[15] In 1847, Fitzpatrick recalled that event of June 1824 to newspaper reporter John S. Robb, who wrote under the pseudonym of "Solitaire," that a party of Shoshone had run off with every horse and mule of their brigade while they were working the tributaries of Green River.[16] Trapper James Clyman recalled further details:

> We left to trap on the branches of the stream as soon as the ice gave way ... We found a small family of diggers or Shoshone Indians on our trapping ground whom we feed with the overplus of Beaver ... the snow disapearing our diggar friends moved off without our knowledge of when or where and when they had gone our horses runing loose on[e] night they all disapeared and we were unable to find them or in what direction they had gone we continued trapping on foot with fair success for about six weeks when the 10th of June was drawing close and we had promised all who were alive to meet at our cash on Sweet Water accordingly we cashed traps & furs hung our saddle & horse equipments on trees & set out for Sweet water the same day about noon on turning the point of a ridge we met face to face with five & six indians mounted on some of our horses preparing to take posesion of as many horses each on[e] taking hold of a lariet and ordering our friens to dismount but after a short consultation we decided to go with them to their camp about one mile up a steep mountain where we found six lodges 18 men with a large supply of squaws & children & our old acquaintences that we had fed with the fat of Beaver while the earth was thickly covered with snow ... all our horses wer given up but one and we concluded

this one was hid in the mountain so we caught one of the men tied him fast told them we intended to kill him if our horse was not given back which soon brought him we gave them a few presents and left for our old camp dug up our cashe cut down our saddles and again started for Sweet water.[17]

Competition between the companies in the trapping fields had been fierce over the fall and spring hunts – a rivalry that culminated in the death of AFC leader William Henry Vanderburgh. However, on the verdant benches of the Green River, men from all sides

engaged in contests of skill at running, jumping, wrestling, shooting with the rifle, and running horses. And then their rough hunters' feastings and carousels. They drank together, they sang, they laughed, they whooped; they tried to out-brag and out-lie each other in stories of their adventures and achievements. Here the free trappers were in all their glory; they considered themselves the "cocks of the walk," and always carried the highest crests. Now and then familiarity was pushed too far, and would effervesce into a brawl, and a "rough and tumble" fight; but it all ended in cordial reconciliation and maudlin endearment.[18]

A tent had been rigged into a saloon and Campbell's man, Redmond, pulled the bungs on the liquor kegs and started selling whiskey as fast as he could pour it. So much drinking, yelling and shooting went on that soon, even Redmond was as polluted as the rest. The head men, too, drank their share – Campbell had been seen "flat on his belly in the green grass, pouring out what he could not hold in." The only sober man to be found in camp was Charles Larpenteur, who was consequently put in charge of the store. He reported that for several days, nothing sold except whiskey and though there was fighting and quarreling outside, everyone was civil to him because he was the bartender.[19]

When the bales of goods were torn into and the contents displayed for those eager to spend their hard-earned beaver, trappers lined up to buy their necessary supplies plus the extra gewgaws that replenished their dwindling trading stock. After a year in the mountains, and facing the coming year without a friendly neighborhood grocer, the men needed gunpowder and lead for hunting and war – "rifles, hunting knives, traps, scarlet cloth, red blankets, garish beads, and glittering trinkets, were bought at any price, and scores run up without any thought how they were ever to be rubbed off."[20]

> **July 18-24, 1833**   *Green River Rendezvous*
>
> *18th to the 24   remained at the same camp during which time the weather was pleasant and warm   for several nights we were anoyed by mad dogs or wolves which I cannot say but believe the latter as one was killed.   I think one animal did the whole mischief as when men were bitten at one camp none were at the other   about nine persons were bitten at Dripps & Fontenelles camp and three at ours.   D. & Fs. camp is 4 miles above us on the same side of the river   we hope he was not mad as no simtons have yet appeared.*

During this season of folly and frolic, a rumor of mad wolves in the two lower camps buzzed through the rendezvous. For three nights in a row, it was said, one or more of the rabid animals had entered the camps. They had bitten several people and some of the cattle Campbell had brought from the East to supply his new forts. Though Wyeth reported soon after the attacks that no symptoms of rabies were yet apparent, Bonneville told a different story about

> *an Indian, who was a universal favorite in the lower camp. He had been bitten by one of these animals. Being out with a party shortly afterwards, he grew silent and gloomy, and lagged behind the rest as if he wished to leave them. They halted and urged him to move faster, but he entreated them not to approach him, and, leaping from his horse, began to roll frantically on the earth, gnashing his teeth and foaming at the mouth. Still he retained his senses, and warned his companions not to come near him, as he should not be able to restrain himself from biting them. They hurried off to obtain relief; but on their return he was nowhere to be found. His horse and his accoutrements remained upon the spot. Three or four days afterwards a solitary Indian, believed to be the same,* was

observed crossing a valley, and pursued; but he darted away into the fastnesses of the mountains, and was seen no more.

Another instance we have from a different person who was present in the encampment. One of the men of the Rocky Mountain Fur Company had been bitten. He set out shortly afterwards in company with two white men on his return to the settlements. In the course of a few days he showed symptoms of hydrophobia, and became raving toward night. At length, breaking away from his companions, he rushed into a thicket of willows, where they left him to his fate! [21]

Campbell lamented about the cattle:

One night a mad wolf came into our three camps and bit ten or twelve men. He rushed into my camp and bit two of the animals. One of them went mad, and three or four weeks afterwards died. It was a bull I had taken up from Lexington, Lafayette county, Mo., from the blue bunch grass pastures of that county.

The heifer that was bitten by the wolf at the same time, had a calf, and to anticipate my story, I will add here, that she died at the mouth of the Yellowstone, eight or nine months afterwards. I had driven these cattle from Missouri to the Green river. [22]

Larpenteur also told of the incident:

we learned that a mad wolf had got into Mr. Fontenelle's camp about five miles from us, and had bitten some of his men and horses. My messmates, who were old hands, had heard of the like before, when men had gone mad. It was very warm, toward the latter end of July; we were in the habit of sleeping in the open air, and never took the trouble to put up the tent, except in bad weather; but when evening came the boys set up the tent. Some of the other messes asked, "What is that for?" The reply was, "Oh, mad wolf come — he bite me." When the time came to retire the pack saddles were brought up to barricade the entrance of our tent; the only one up in camp, excepting that of the boss. After all

*hands had retired nothing was heard in the camp except, now and
then, the cry of "All's well," and some loud snoring, till the sudden
cry of, "Oh, I'm bitten!" then immediately another, and another.
Three of our men were bitten that night, all of them in the face. One
poor fellow, by the name of George Holmes, was badly bitten on
the right ear and face. All hands got up with their guns in pursuit
of the animal, but he made his escape. When daylight came men
were mounted to go in search, but nothing could be seen of him. It
was then thought that he had gone and was not likely to return,
and no further precaution was taken than the night before. But it
seems that Mr. Wolf, who was thought far away, had hidden near
camp; for about midnight the cry of "mad wolf" was heard again.
This time the animal was among the cattle and bit our largest bull,
which went mad afterward ... The wolf could have been shot, but
orders were not to shoot in camp, for fear of accidentally killing
some one, and so Mr. Wolf again escaped. But we learned afterward
that he had been killed by some of Mr. Fontenelle's men.*[23]

Despite the fact that alcohol was selling for $5.00 a pint, Joe Meek
admitted to being "powerful drunk" at times.[24] He was sober enough,
however, to have known about the mad wolves:

*while at this rendezvous, there occurred one of those incidents of
wilderness life which make the blood creep with horror. Twelve of
the men were bitten by a mad wolf, which hung about the camp
for two or three nights. Two of these were seized with madness in
camp, sometime afterwards, and ran off into the mountains, where
they perished. One was attacked by the paroxysm while on a hunt;
when, throwing himself off his horse, he struggled and foamed
at the mouth, gnashing his teeth, and barking like a wolf. Yet he
retained consciousness enough to warn away his companions, who
hastened in search of assistance; but when they returned he was
nowhere to be found. It was thought that he was seen a day or two
afterwards, but no one could come up with him, and of course, he
too, perished. Another died on his journey to St. Louis; and several
died at different times within the next two years.*

At the time, however, immediately following the visit of the wolf to camp, Captain Stuart was admonishing Meek on the folly of his ways, telling him that the wolf might easily have bitten him, he was so drunk. "It would have killed him, – sure, if it hadn't cured him!" said Meek, – alluding to the belief that alcohol is a remedy for the poison of hydrophobia.[25]

William Drummond Stewart left an account of a somewhat more personal nature:

I was with Campbell's camp, we had moved to the spot but a day or two before, and George Holmes, a young mountaineer, had aided me in constructing a bower of birch and willow, over which to throw a blanket in case of rain, and in which to contain our couch ... the best looking of the young squaws of the neighbouring camp, came over in groups to wonder at the riches of the white man, as well as to tempt him to dispense them ... On an evening of one of these days, I had for some cause, which appeared to me at the time sufficiently reasonable, begged my friend Holmes to take his blanket, and make himself a welcome in some other hut, as I wished to have our shanty for the night at my disposal; he consented, but as I afterwards found out he had laid himself down on the ground to sleep by a brake of fragrant rushes close by ... The night came, and deepened on towards the middle watch, when I was roused by confused sounds, shouts, and the discharge of firearms ... when there came a sharp cry close to the bower and in a voice I well knew ... Poor Holmes was seated on the ground, the side of his head and his ear bleeding; a mad wolf was ravaging the camp ... Poor Holmes changed from that hour.[26]

Regrettably, Holmes, whom the trappers had nicknamed "Beauty," would suffer greatly and later disappear, causing Stewart to lament "There never has quitted my breast a reproachful remorse for the part I played him on that sad night."[27]

While all this was going on around him, Wyeth was dutifully writing letters. On July 18, he sent a note to his financiers regarding a draft against Bonneville for $366.66 that Cerré would be delivering. Wyeth,

now bound for Boston, had sold his pack animals and tack to Bonneville after the business deal between them had failed to materialize.[28]

Wyeth inked a letter to John Ball, whom Wyeth assumed was still
on the Columbia River. Wyeth's Boston agents had sent two trunks
and some other correspondence to Ball at Fort Vancouver via Hawaii.
At this time, however, Ball had taken up farming on the Willamette –
briefly, as it would turn out.

Significantly, Wyeth had been considering his own homeward
route; he informed Ball he would be heading east by way of the Yellowstone and Missouri rivers. This letter shows that Wyeth had already
planned to attach himself to the main fur trade caravan returning east by
that more northerly trail, not back the way he had come, via the Sweetwater and the Platte.[29]

Wyeth also wrote to Francis Ermatinger. Wyeth imparted State-side
news that he thought might interest his friend, but took most of the
page to bring the HBC man up to date concerning the fur trade on the
American side of the Continental Divide. Interestingly, Wyeth's report
was relentlessly gloomy, noting that Sublette and Campbell had built
competing trading posts up the Missouri near each AFC establishment.
Bonneville had lost an entire trapping party's horses and peltry to the
Crow. The Arikara had stolen livestock and attacked Bridger and Fraeb,
as well as a party under Moses Harris.

Wyeth closed by congratulating Ermatinger for having chosen
not to attend the rendezvous, assuring him that "you would have been
Robbed of your goods and Beaver if you had come here although it is
the west side of the Mts." Wyeth closed with the infamous lines: "There
is here a great majority of Scoundrels. I should much doubt the personal
safety of any one from your side of the house." Wyeth emphasized that
his was an "honest opinion which you can communicate to the Co."[30]

It was of course in Wyeth's interest to dissuade HBC from sending a brigade to the American rendezvous. In his proposal to Simpson,
Wyeth had insisted he could go places east of the Divide from which
the British were then excluded. Had Ermatinger or some other Company brigade succeeded in the area, his claim would have been proven
false. Speculation about what might have happened to Ermatinger had
he decided to attend rendezvous was meant to warn HBC just how dangerous it could be to compete with American companies, and to shore

up Wyeth's scheme to be the sole Pacific Coast supplier in the Rocky Mountains.[31]

At the bottom of the sheet of paper Wyeth listed the American enterprises at rendezvous and their take in beaver:

Drips and Fontenelle arrd July 8th 160 men a good supply of animals Obtained 51 packs of 100 lbs ea. Beaver.

Rocky Mtn. Fur Co. 55 packs 55 men well supplied one party not in Beaver sent home by Mr. Campbell.

Mess. Bonneville & Co. 22 ½ packs. Few goods few horses and poor Capt. Cerry goes home B. remains.

Harris party now in hand 7 packs Beaver are on foot.[32]

No doubt Wyeth passed this data on to Ermatinger to demonstrate his loyalty to the Company, and to increase the chances that HBC might accept his proposal. Apparently, Wyeth thought business was good enough to refer to these same figures in later correspondence with his financial backers.[33]

On July 20, the Rocky Mountain Fur Company was dissolved and a new organization was chartered to replace it: the Rocky Mountain Fur Company and Christy. Adding Edmund Christy's ready cash to the partnership rolls would fuel the outfit for one year. Christy was to be paid in beaver the next summer at the rate of $3.25 per pound.[34]

Wyeth did not mention in his journal what he told Ermatinger about his friend Milton's business having generated sixty-two packs of beaver. In St. Louis, these one-hundred-pound fur bundles would be worth nearly $21,000. Still, Wyeth's colleagues would not be breaking even. Transportation costs of 50¢ per pound would cut the profit by more than $3,000. RMFC still owed supplier William Sublette $5,400, even after the sale of the 1832 catch – an amount then accruing an additional eight percent interest. Supplies for this year's rendezvous had totaled almost $15,000 and RMFC owed its men a year's pay. Despite a reasonable take in peltry, RMFC would remain in debt to the tune of nearly $3,000.[35] Wyeth viewed the death grip that William Sublette and Robert Campbell held on his associates as an opportunity for him-self. His profit-motivated mind was concocting a way to horn in on that monopoly.

Also on July 20, Warren Ferris and Robert Newell departed "at the head of an equipment destined for the Flat-head trade" with elev-en armed men and the requisite pack animals. Wyeth likely sent his letter to Ermatinger with one of these AFC traders; the HBC man remained stationed with the Flathead. Ferris jotted in his diary that he met Ermatinger near the Bitterroot in November. That autumn, all three men would travel north together as far as Flathead Post, where Ermatinger would cache his trade goods in one of the falling-down log buildings.[36]

Jean Baptiste Gervais left the rendezvous two days later with thirty RMFC men to trap in the "root digger country," the region Wyeth had thoroughly traversed last year on the way to the Columbia.[37] Andrew Drips and the AFC brigade hit the trail up the Green, bound for the Snake River drainage.

Benjamin Bonneville put Joe Walker in charge and watched his bri-gade pull out for California on July 24.[38] Apparently what Bonneville had refused to do in partnership with Wyeth, he was prepared to carry out on his own. Perhaps Wyeth's proposal had sounded too lucrative to share.

About that time, Larpenteur responded to a summons from his bourgeois, Robert Campbell:

> On entering his tent I was presented with a good cup of coffee and a large-sized biscuit; this was a great treat, for I believe that it was the first coffee I had drunk since I left Lexington. Then he remarked, "Charles, I suppose you have heard that I sold out our interest in the mountains; but I have reserved all your mess, ten mules, and the cattle (we had four cows and two bulls, intended for the Yellowstone). I have 30 packs of beaver, which Fitz is to assist me with as far as the Big Horn River, where I intend to make skin boats and take my beaver down to the mouth of the Yellowstone. There I expect to meet [William] Sublette, who is to take the packs on to St. Louis ... The beaver was all packed and pressed ready for the march; so the next day the order came to catch up the animals, receive our packs, and move camp.[39]

The summer trade fair broke up in general on July 24. One mountaineer touted the rendezvous of 1833 as the last "good year, for with
1834 came the spoilers – the idlers, the missionaries, the hard seekers
of money."[40]

July 24, 1833   *Boulder Creek*

*24th.   Moved E. 12 miles cutting a small divide   came to a
wide valley parallel with Wind river Mts. in which we crossed 3
large creeks and camped on the 4th.   Which has much pine
timber on it and is called Pine fork   they all come into one
quite soon by appearance and are not near as large as the
main fork on which we first found the whites and which we have
now crossed.   In coming here it passed to our left that is up
stream.   Found plenty of Antelope and Bulls.*

Wyeth left the main rendezvous on July 24 in company with Milton
Sublette, Fitzpatrick, Campbell and their small crew transporting the
beaver east. The company crossed the Pinedale Anticline, known locally
as the Mesa (Wyeth's "small divide") by going up Tyler Draw. The plan
was to cross South Pass, then, rather than follow the Platte River trail,
head for the Bighorn and ultimately the Yellowstone and Missouri rivers. During a day of predominantly eastbound travel, the men forded
New Fork, Pine Creek and Pole Creek before arriving on the fourth
stream – Boulder Creek – a conifer-lined watercourse that flows from a
lake of the same name a few miles to the north. Wyeth apparently confused the names of the creeks, because from the mileages he recorded,
the group would have encountered Pine Creek early in the day and continued on. After Pole Creek, the route for the next few days followed the
well-worn foothill trail used for centuries between the north end of the
valley and South Pass. The travelers likely knew to head due east from
the Green River until they hit the old foothill trail leading south.

Wyeth could have returned via the familiar Platte River trail he
took on his way west, but perhaps he could find no one to accompany
him in that direction. In addition, traveling to St. Louis via the Big
Horn, Yellowstone and Missouri rivers would give Wyeth an opportunity to see more of the West, as well as a chance to witness a few

American trading posts in operation and compare them with HBC's. The detour would also provide more time with Milton Sublette, Tom Fitzpatrick and Robert Campbell, to pick their brains about fur trade business. The route was not the customary one for bringing furs to St. Louis, but Campbell had compelling reasons for choosing it.

The cattle Campbell drove were destined for William Sublette's new fort near the confluence of the Missouri and Yellowstone. Sublette would meet him there with a keel boat bound for St. Louis, the cattle would be dropped off, and the furs loaded for river transport.

The travel plan was not without precedent. William Ashley had taken the same route with furs from the 1825 rendezvous. Rather than taking bull boats all the way to St. Louis, Ashley had made arrangements with the U.S. Army and was met by General Henry Atkinson at the mouth of the Yellowstone. Atkinson traveled in specially designed keelboats equipped with manually operated wheel mechanisms.[41]

July 25, 1833   *East Fork River*

25th. Crossed the stream and moved E.S.E. 3 miles to a creek   the same on which I made a cash last year and crossed at a good ford just below two stony hills   then on 7 1/2 mile E.S.E. following a branch of the same creek and camped to noon.   Buffaloe throwing the dust in the air in every direction and Antelope always in sight.   This day a Mr. Worthington in running a bull fell from his horse, the Bull furious ran at the horse and passed him within 3 feet then turned again and passed him   he having got up from the ground ran and escaped   he killed the bull and found he had but one eye owing to which circumstance he escaped.   Afternoon made S.E. 13 miles leaving the last creek of what is called New fork to which all the waters we have passed since leaving rendesvous belong   the one we camped on last night heads in a lake about 1 1/2 miles over and not far from where we slept.   We now struck the west fork of Sandy and camped at an old camp of last year at a place where Ball left his rifle[?]   Country covered with Buffaloe.

There are no streams three miles' travel from Boulder Creek; the transcriber possibly misread the number eight. Eight miles from his previous camp would have brought Wyeth to the East Fork River, a tributary of the Green. He had made no record at the time of having cached goods on his way to Pierre's Hole the previous summer, yet Wyeth now mentioned such a cache somewhere along the present-day East Fork, probably close to a "good ford," south of Fremont Butte. Again, Wyeth did not record retrieving the items he had deposited.

The East Fork loops north of Fremont Butte, a prominent landscape feature. Wyeth crossed the fork and rode southeast below the "stony hills" for a handful of miles, to rejoin the bank of the same creek before stopping for a break a bit farther downstream.

The practice of "nooning" was common in mountain travel. Artist Alfred Jacob Miller, who would be in this same area four years later, painted a colorful picture of trappers napping along the trail:

> Every day at 12 o'clock the caravan halts, the horses are permitted to rest and feed, men receive their dinner, and then take a siesta ... The time however to me was too valuable to indulge in the luxury, – so immediately after our halt, I would mount the wagon, get out my port-folio, and go to work. Our Captain [Stewart], who took great interest in the matter, came up to me one day while so engaged, & said "you should sketch this and that thing" and so on. "Well!" I answered (possibly with a slight asperity)," if I had half a dozen pair of hands, it should be done!"
>
> Capt. (Smiling) "That would be a great misfortune."
>
> "Why?" Capt. (Smiling still more.) "It would be very expensive in the matter of kid gloves."
>
> The absurdity required no answer ... A guard is stationed of course, on the bluff to prevent surprise, and also to look after the horses.[42]

Leaving the last tributaries of the New Fork River and moving on southeast, they camped that evening on what Wyeth called "west fork of Sandy," however, there is no such fork. The mileage would have brought them to the Big Sandy River, and a ford that came to be known as Buckskin Crossing. The historical marker at that location reads in part,

> *The place where this road crosses the Big Sandy River ... is known as Buckskin Crossing ... First noted in 1812 by Robert Stuart's Astorian party returning from the Pacific Coast, the site was heavily used by the mountain men, including Jim Bridger, Jed Smith, and William Sublette, as they pursued the beaver trade in the 1820s and 1830s. Supply trains crossed here enroute to Rendezvous held near today's Daniel, Wyoming. These caravans brought the area's first tourist, William Drummond Stewart, its first artist, Alfred Jacob Miller, and the West's first white women, Eliza Spaulding and Narcissa Whitman ... In his first trip exploring the West in 1842, John Charles Fremont, guided by mountain man Kit Carson, "nooned" here the week before climbing Fremont Peak ... According to local legend, the crossing was named in the late 1800s for a hunter and trapper called "Buckskin Joe," who lived in a cabin near here with his wife and daughter.*[43]

Wyeth's eastbound party spent the night at a spot where he had camped on the westbound journey the previous year. At the time, neither John Wyeth, Nathaniel Wyeth, nor John Ball himself mentioned in their journals that Ball had left a gun at the site. Wyeth would later invite Missourian James Worthington to join his second expedition west; it is possible that James was the buffalo hunter in Wyeth's dramatic account, or may have been a relative of this man.[44]

Following closely on the group's heels were Bonneville and Cerré, who on this date packed up their beaver and left the rendezvous grounds just a day behind Wyeth. Bonneville's party would soon catch up, taking advantage of the protection of the larger group. From the trail, Bonneville wrote a lengthy letter to Colonel Roger Jones, then Adjutant General of the U.S. Army. Bonneville included an amazing amount of information about the West, much of it obtained from other sources, and from Wyeth in particular, though Bonneville did not credit his informants. Bonneville would later split off to take up trapping in the Crow country while Cerré traveled on with Wyeth and the others.[45]

July 26, 1833   *Sweetwater River*

26th.   Made S.E. 9 miles and camped on another fork of Sandy   then S.E. by E. 15 miles to Sweet water   all the country is granite from rendezvous so far   Buffaloe quite plenty also Antelope   Today shot a cow with a very young calf   the calf ran after our mules for a long way until it found the difference.

Taking their noon break on the Little Sandy, Wyeth and his party continued southeast along Lander Creek until coming to the Sweetwater River. Though Wyeth made no mention of it, they had crossed South Pass and were now on the waters of the Missouri drainage.

Orphaned buffalo calves after the hunt were not unusual. In fact, trappers occasionally kept these young creatures as pets for short periods. John Townsend, who would come west with Wyeth in 1834, left this account:

The young buffalo calf is also very often taken, and if removed from the mother, and out of sight of the herd, he will follow the camp as steadily as a dog; but his propensity for keeping close to the horse's heels often gets him into trouble, as he meets with more kicks than caresses from them. He is considered an interloper, and treated accordingly. The bull calf of a month or two old, is sometimes rather difficult to manage; he shows no inclination to follow the camp like the younger ones, and requires to be dragged along by main force. At such times, he watches for a good opportunity, and before his captor is aware of what is going on, he receives a butt from the clumsy head of the intractable little brute, which, in most cases, lays him sprawling upon the ground.[46]

Townsend also told of keeping a young antelope as a pet and described a few abortive attempts to tame grizzly cubs which were ultimately found to be "cross and snappish" to handle.

July 27-28, 1833   *Sweetwater River*

*27th.   Made down the creek 1 1/2 miles E.S.E.   then E. 8
miles to another branch of Sweet water then 6 miles E. by N. to
another branch of same then down this branch S.E. 2 miles and
camped.   Saw one band of Elk and many Antelope   plenty of
Buffaloe.*

*28th.   Made E. 2 mils to another Creek running S. by E.
crossed   made E. 6 miles E. by N. 4 miles   at the creek a sort
of slate prevailed but soon ran into a red sandstone   passed
at 11 mils a small pond to our right   few Buffaloe today   last
night Capt. Stewart had some sport with a bear near our
camp in the willows which he wounded but did not kill   He
represented him as large as a mule.   In the afternoon made E.
by N. 6 miles to Sweet water river then N. E. 3 miles up it and
camped.   I came ahead and found a white bear in a thickett
and after firing a pistol and throwing stones into it started him
out   he came as though he meant to fight us but I gave him
the shot of my rifle through the body   He then rushed on us
and I ran as fast as I could   Mr. Kamel snapped at him   Mr
Sublette ran also being on a mule   the bear followed us no
great distance and turned and ran up creek   some horsemen
followed and killed him after putting 4 more balls into him.*

Crossing over the southern segment of the Wind River Mountains,
the party had its share of run-ins with grizzly bears. William Drummond Stewart had come to the West for such hunting and probably
relished the exhilaration of the chase. Wyeth, however, got a bit more
than he may have bargained for by throwing rocks, a real greenhorn
thing to do, and then firing his pistol to spook the bear out of the thicket. As the enraged and wounded bruin advanced, Campbell pulled the
trigger, but his percussion cap "snapped," failing to fire. Milton Sublette
gigged his mule clear as the bear charged. The attack was short-lived
and the wounded silver-tip was brought down by other hunters. Meriwether Lewis aptly described his experiences with grizzlies in 1805:
"these bear being so hard to die reather intimedates us all; I must con-
fess that I do not like the gentlemen and had reather fight two Indians
than one bear."[47]

July 29-30, 1833   *Little Popo Agie River*

29th.   Same camp, rained all day   two men went out to hunt and at night one returned alone the other in the morning being still absent.

30th.   Started out to hunt the man and in about 8 miles came to the place   hunted the whole country and found nothing but a white bear the largest and the whitest I have yet seen   run him about a mile and fired one shot but could not kill him.   After a long ride returned to camp   found the party had moved on   followed them N.N.W.   in 6 miles struck Popoise [Popo Agie] in a small rapid thread running through sandstone banks   this we followed N. W. 3 miles then N. by E. 9 miles more   thousands of Buffaloe in sight and the red bottom of the streams deep and muddy with recent rains and found camp a little after sundown.   The afternoon of the 29th we found lime rock almost entirely   today sand stone and a kind of glassy stone resembling Carnelian   a course kind of which I think it is.

Given the number of bear encounters in the previous days, it was no wonder Wyeth expressed some worry about a hunter not coming in. After fruitlessly pursuing the largest grizzly he had seen so far, Wyeth turned back, only to find the camp had moved on.

The Little Popo Agie River, Irving explained, "takes its rise in the Wind River Mountains. Its name, like most Indian names, is characteristic. "Popo," in the Crow language, signifies head; and "Agie," river."[48] Wyeth's odd spelling of the river's name was an attempt to render phonetically the pronunciation of this Indian term. Other examples are Zenas Leonard's "Popoasia," Osborne Russell's "Po po azia," and Charles Larpenteur's "Pappah-ah-je."[49]

During the group's time along the Popo Agie, Dr. Harrison visited the oil spring, a regional phenomenon first recorded in a letter Daniel Potts wrote in 1827: "There is an oil spring in this valley, which discharges 60 or 70 gallons of pure oil per day. The oil has very much the appearance, taste and smell of British oil."[50] British oil is "a rubefacient liniment composed of oil of turpentine, linseed oil, oil of amber, oil of juniper, Barbados petroleum and crude petroleum." Trappers in the

Rockies used the medicinal properties of this free-flowing goo as a salve to soothe a myriad of wounds.[51] Stephen Meek went so far as to identify the Popo Agie as the "Tar River."[52] Bonneville had also searched for this "great Tar Spring,"

> *one of the wonders of the mountains; the medicinal properties of which, he had heard extravagantly lauded by the trappers. After a toilsome search, he found it at the foot of a sand-bluff, a little east of the Wind River Mountains; where it exuded in a small stream of the color and consistency of tar. The men immediately hastened to collect a quantity of it, to use as an ointment for the galled backs of their horses, and as a balsam for their own pains and aches. From the description given of it, it is evidently the bituminous oil, called petrolium or naphtha, which forms a principal ingredient in the potent medicine called British Oil. It is found in various parts of Europe and Asia, in several of the West India islands, and in some places of the United States. In the state of New York, it is called Seneca Oil, from being found near the Seneca lake.[53]*

Zenas Leonard wrote that his brigade arrived

> *on Popoasia creek, where we found an oil spring, rising out of the earth similar to that of any other spring. After emptying into the creek, the oil can be seen floating on the surface for a considerable distance. The oil is of a dark hue when in the fountain, almost like tar, but is as thin as water. If this spring was in the States, I have no doubt the chemist might make a valuable use of it. A Mr. Bergen, belonging to our company, & who had been severely afflicted with the rheumatism, procured a phial of it, which he used and afterwards said afforded him entire relief.[54]*

But not all of the trappers used the solvent for beneficial purposes, according to Osborne Russell:

> *this spring produces about one Gallon per hour of pure Oil of Coal or rather Coal Tar the scent of which often carried on the wind 5 or 6 mls. The Oil issues from the ground within 30 feet of the stream*

and runs off slowly into the water Camp stopped here eight days We set fire to the spring when there was 2 or 3 Bbls. of oil on the ground about it, it burnt very quick and clear but produced a dense column of thick black smoke the oil above ground being consumed the fire soon went out.[55]

Taking advantage of the obvious, the first modern oil wells to be drilled in the present state of Wyoming were sunk in this vicinity – now known as the Dallas Dome – in the 1880s. Bonneville indicated the oil spring on the map he prepared for Irving's book. An 1841 map of the Oregon Territory, drawn by Charles Wilkes, and showing the apparent influence of Jedediah Smith, included the location of this seep.[56]

> **July 31, 1833**   *Wind River*
>
> *31st   N.N.W. 8 miles through a muddy Bottom and little grass to some large willows   found a party of 4 whites who have lost their horses and one of them wounded in the head with a Ball and in the body with an arrow very badly   they suppose the Snakes did it but I think not.   Little grass.   In the afternoon moved N. 9 miles to the junction of Great Popoise river which comes from the S.W.   then N. by E. 4 miles to the junction of Wind river which comes from the W. turning around as I suppose and running along Wind River Mountains which run N.W.   Altogether they form a large and muddy river but fordable now which is after a heavy rain.*

Riding through the wet bottomlands of the Little Popo Agie, the party's scout ran onto a small group of trappers from Fraeb's RMFC brigade, who had been sent to meet up with Fitzpatrick and Campbell. This four-man team had been attacked by Indians. Wyeth, with Blackfoot on his mind, doubted the assailants could have been Shoshone.

It was a simple matter to follow the Little Popo Agie to the main branch, near today's Hudson, Wyoming, then on to its confluence with the Wind River, at present Riverton. Deep into summer, snowmelt had decreased and even with recent heavy rains, fording the Wind was manageable.

August 1, 1833   *Wind River*

Aug. 1st.   Same camp   find Mr. Bonneville camped a few miles above us.   On farther inquiry I changed my opinion expressed above in regard to the Indians who stole the horses   I think they were 15 Snakes who left our camp at Green river a few days before we left that place.   The case was this.   Mr. Bridger sent 4 men to this river to look for us viz Mr. Smith, Thomson, Charboneau a half breed and Evans.   Two days before it happened 15 Inds came to them (Snakes) and after smoking departed   the second day after they were gone Thompson having been out hunting [hobbled?] his horse to the others and thought he would sit down by them until it was time to water them and having been on guard much of the time previous fell asleep   he was waked by a noise among the horses which he supposed to [be] his comrades come to water them   raising his head and opening his eyes the first thing that presented itself to his sight was the muzzle of a gun in the hands of an Indian   it was immediately discharged and so near his head that the front piece of his cap alone saved his eyes from being put out by the powder   the Ball entered the head outside of the eye and breaking the cheek bone passing downward and lodged behind the ear in the neck   this stunned him and while insensible an arrow was shot into him on the top of the shoulder downward which entered about 6 inches, the Inds. got 7 horses   all there were.   Charboneau pursued them on foot but wet his gun in crossing a little stream and only snapped twice.

Whoever attacked the RMFC trappers was well disguised in hats made of bushes, Larpenteur wrote, and snuck so near that "the powder burned the vizzer of his cap."[57] Philip Thomson was badly injured, having been shot after presumably falling asleep on horse guard. Larpenteur said the ball had entered the wounded man's head at the upper part of his cheek, and exited under the lower back part of the ear. Thomson was hit by three arrows, one arrow-point still embedded in his shoulder blade. Dr. Harrison extracted the arrowhead and tended to the man's wounds.[58]

Staying in the same camp an extra day gave Dr. Harrison a chance to check up on his patient. It also allowed Wyeth time to interview the wounded man's companions: Jefferson Smith; Robert Evans; and Jean Baptiste Charbonneau, Wyeth's "half-breed." The latter was the son of Lewis and Clark's interpreter, Toussaint Charbonneau, with the Shoshone woman, Sacagawea.[59] Robert Evans would play a significant role in Wyeth's second expedition to the mountains; this may have been the place the two first met. Evans was an Ashley man who had gone to California with Jedediah Smith in 1826. He had crossed the Great Basin with Smith on his eastward journey the next year. Evans left the fur trade following the 1827 rendezvous, but in 1832 had come back to the mountains under William Sublette.[60]

In 1860 at Fort Berthold, Larpenteur would meet up with Jefferson Smith again, running with Henry Boller. Smith was described by Boller as a "veteran of over thirty years experience," and was known to the Gros Ventre people as "Kee-re-pe-tee-ah," or Big-Bull.[61] Of Thomson, nothing else is known.

Wyeth said the four trappers had been sent by Bridger, but Larpenteur reported them as dispatched by Fraeb. Both Fraeb and Bridger were RMFC partners, and either may have directed the small party to overtake Fitzpatrick's band. Irving said these four men "were reconnoitering the country in advance of the main body."[62] It is also possible that Wyeth, Campbell and company had gotten turned around on their way to the Big Horn and the four men had been sent to guide them. In any case, Larpenteur's account is considered the more reliable.

Bonneville, tagging along behind, learned that Wyeth's contingent was camped only a few miles ahead. He had seen

> *a long line of horsemen descending the slope of hills on the opposite side of the Popo Agie. His first idea was that they were Indians; he soon discovered, however, that they were white men, and, by the long line of pack-horses, ascertained them to be the convoy of Campbell.[63]*

From his position on the river, Bonneville sent scouts to look for a place to ford so he could cross and join Wyeth and his escorts but, unlike the Wind River, the Popo Agie was too swollen.

August 2-4, 1833   *Wind River*

2nd.   Found the river unfordable and assended to west crossing Popoise & Wind river 5 miles up and made thence 20 miles N.E. by N. to a little creek going to Wind now on our right.

3rd.   11 miles N.N.E. to the summit of the mountains which are called little Wind River Mts. and run E. & W.   then N. 5 miles to the river.

4th.   2 miles N. along the river to a clump of sweet cotton wood.

Possibly due to weather high in the mountains, the water level of the Wind River had risen to the point that fording was not safe. The group proceeded up the east bank to about where today's Haymaker Creek enters the Wind and crossed there. Traveling now on the Wind's west bank, they covered twenty miles of relatively easy riding before coming to about where today's Muddy Creek runs into the Boysen Reservoir on the now-dammed Wind River.

The camp of August 2 was close to the mouth of Wind River Canyon, a gap between the Owl Creek and Bridger mountains. The next day, rather than try to stay on the river through the steep-walled gorge, the party traveled into Wyeth's "little Wind River Mts.," the Owl Creeks. Bonneville labeled this range on his 1837 map as the "Little Horn Mountains." Wyeth's party reached the vicinity of today's Thermopolis, Wyoming, by the end of the day.

Two more miles on August 4 brought them to a spot a little north of Kirby Creek, near present Lucerne, Wyoming. Bonneville caught up with Wyeth's caravan, both groups having "passed through the gap" of the canyon. The two parties now formed a large company of over one hundred men who traveled together over the next few days.[64]

Where the Wind River enters the southern end of the twelve-mile long canyon, its name changes to the Big Horn. This anomaly appears to have posed problems from the start, and no satisfactory explanation for the river's split personality has ever come to light. General William F. Raynolds led an exploration of that country in the late 1850s and tried to clarify the situation:

Here I desire to state a fact of some importance with reference to the nomenclature of the Big Horn and its branches. The river which last summer we descended under the name of the Big Horn is formed by the junction of the Popo-Agie and the Wind River at this point, and should properly be called the Big Horn below the site of our present camp. By the trappers, however, it is always spoken of as the Wind River until it enters the cañon some 30 miles below here. There is no good reason for this arbitrary distinction, whereby the same stream passes into the mountains under one name and emerges with another, and it is necessary that these facts be known to avoid confusion.[65]

Some sources indicate the name change does not occur in the canyon, but at the "Wedding of the Waters," an otherwise indistinguishable spot a few river miles south of Thermopolis. Others say that when the Popo Agie merges with the Wind River, the Big Horn begins.[66] Whatever the case, the Big Horn was named for the species of sheep that was once so prevalent along its banks, particularly at the mouth. Lewis and Clark interpreted the Indian word "Ar-Sar-Ta" to mean Bighorn; Francis Antoine Laroque called the stream by that name in 1805. *Grosse Corne* also appeared in some instances, being the French term for the name.[67]

August 5, 1833   *Big Horn River*

5th.   7 miles N. by W. to the River which between makes a considerable bend to the eastward   camped in good grass and some large cotton wood trees   this morning past beautiful camps   afternoon N. by E. 12 miles   3 horses found this day and yesterday probably left by some party of Inds. who have passed this way   saw the tracks of several more   we think that when the Crows stole horses of the Snakes last winter they came this route and left their animals on account of giving out for want of food in the snow.   Few Buffaloe and those running indicates Indians near.

Between the modern Wyoming towns of Kirby and Winchester, the Big Horn River makes a decided eastward bend. Cutting overland, the combined parties went northwest seven miles before hitting the river again, having shaved a few miles off their day's travel. Continuing along the east bank another dozen miles, the evening camp was near today's Worland, Wyoming.

Writing in the 1850s, Edwin Denig explained the Indian practice of leaving horses behind during travel. Denig told of a February 1856 Blackfoot raid on a Crow village, in which seventy horses were driven off through deep snow by the intruders. The Crow gave chase, each man mounted on a fast steed and leading another. Riding hard, they would leave a tired animal and saddle a second to continue pursuit with little rest. At the end of the second day, when these reserve horses gave out, they too were discarded along the trail, and the Crow went ahead on foot.[68]

August 6, 1833   *Big Horn River*

6th.   N 10 miles to the River again to noon   found little grass   day cool   afternoon 10 miles N.N.E. to the main river again.   Since crossing the last Mts. we crossed a creek the second forenoon   afternoon one   yesterday 2   today 2   all small and I suppose sometimes dry

---

The Big Horn bottoms are several miles wide in this area with the main channel hugging the bluffs along the western bank. The party rode through the valley, returning to the stream banks to noon and again for evening camp. Several small creeks feed the Big Horn from both sides of the basin. The ones mentioned in this journal entry cannot be identified.

August 7, 1833   *Big Horn River*

7th.   12 miles N.N.W and camped on Grey Bull River   here I found a piece of about 5 lbs of Bituminous coal which burned freely   It had in it some substance which I took to be Amber   also an impression of wood   It looked like and as good as Liverpool Coal.   Its fracture was too perfect to have come far.   20 miles above and on the E. side comes in the River   Travelled[?] in afternoon 6 miles N.N.W. and again struck Wind river.   Shell river comes in 3 miles below Grey Bull on the E. side and from the Mts. in the direction E. by N.   Grey Bull is from the S.W. and much the largest stream on this side since Wind river.   For three days have found no Buffaloe and from the nature of the country think it is not often found in abundance along here except in the winter   no antelope   a few Elk and deer.

The Greybull River was said to have been named for an albino buffalo that once roamed the area and was held sacred by the local Native Americans. Pictographs on a cliff overhanging the river show a bison with an arrow through its body. A local historical group contended that the term came from a Crow chieftain of the same name. Indeed, there was an Indian leader called Gray Bull but the earliest references to such a chief date only to about 1859. Wyeth's earlier reference supports the white buffalo legend. While the town may have been named for the chief, it is doubtful the river was.[69]

Wyeth's "20 miles above on the E. side comes in the River" is obscure. At that distance upstream, in other words, going back in the direction from which he had come, Nowood Creek enters the Big Horn. The stream received its name when a cavalry detachment spent a wet, cold night camped there and could not find wood to build a warming fire.[70]

Since Wyeth said he camped at the Greybull, yet moved on six more miles and "again struck the Wind river," the caravan apparently took its noon rest at the Wind River's mouth. Generally Wyeth made clear that he moved on in the second half of the day. It is also noteworthy that Wyeth continued to call the river the "Wind" instead of the Big Horn. Flowing into the Big Horn below Greybull was Shell Creek, named for the numerous fossil shells found along its banks. Bonneville included it in the 1837 map he produced for Irving.[71]

The scarcity of buffalo over several days was likely continuing evidence that Indians had recently hunted them. Larpenteur reported that game had been scarce for some time and that they had been forced to "live for two days on such berries and roots as we could find."[72]

August 8, 1833   *Big Horn River*

8th.   W.N.W. 3 miles then 21 miles N.E. toward the right of two considerable Mts. where Wind river passes.   We camped West of these hills on a river larger than Grey Bull called Stinking River coming from the S.W.   This days travel was made between parrallel ridges of broken lime and sand rock   some of it appeared calcined and much like fine caked salt.   This day picked up some shell   they are very numerous   also found a round concretion which are found also on Cannon Ball River from which the name also a concretion of much the same substance but long   pointed at one end with a core in the middle   a hole at big end.   During this space there was no water   to our right there is a range of Mts. running N.W. about 9 miles distant and the other side of Wind River.

Rather than struggle through the defile that the Big Horn River makes as it cuts through Sheep and Little Sheep mountains, the caravan opted to go around Sheep Mountain to camp on its west side. The rocky, treeless terrain presented a long, dry march. The travelers ended their trek on the banks of what is today known as the Shoshone River, originally known as the "Stinking Water," a few miles downstream from today's Lovell, Wyoming. On this watercourse, though much farther upstream, near present-day Cody, Wyoming, John Colter claimed to have seen steaming fumaroles and smelled the rotten-egg odor of boiling sulphur springs. That thermal area became known to trappers as Colter's Hell.[73] The range on the east side of the main river, which Wyeth described as running northwest, was the upper end of the Big Horn Range.

A concretion is a geologic formation in sedimentary rock in which mineral cement fills spaces between the granules, creating an ovoid or spherical shape. The Cannon Ball River, in today's southwestern North Dakota, was named for these orbs of stone found in abundance along the river bed. Wyeth had not yet seen North Dakota, but someone else in the party may have. Alternatively, Wyeth may have read about the Cannon Ball River in the Lewis and Clark journals, where it is mentioned several times.

August 9, 1833   *Big Horn River*

*9th.   10 miles N. striking a small stream of water   This days
travel and yesterday was over ground naked of vegetables
in which the animals sank near six inches deep at every
step   perfectly dry and resembling, but of different color, lime in
the operation of slacking   full of holes down which the waters
at the wet season sink   the rock is sand and lime stone.*

Ten miles overland brought the company to Gypsum Creek at the
base of Big Pryor Mountain, just south of today's Montana/Wyoming
state border. Gypsum deposits are common in the northwestern portion
of the Big Horn Basin, hence the creek's name. Early settlers once operated a furnace near here to manufacture plaster from the local gypsum.
Wyeth's "slacking" should be understood as "slaking." Slaked lime was created by burning the raw material in a kiln, then adding water to form a
thick putty. During this process, its color was whitish-gray or dirty white.[74]

August 10, 1833   *Bad Pass Trail*

*10th.   N. 15 miles   passing near but not exactly on the river
and through rocky hills of no great height.   The river here looks
tranquil but flows between two perpendicular banks of stone
of perhaps 5 to 800 feet high   the chasm even at the top of
no great width   the rock of lime and sand   this days march
saw Plaster of Paris   found for first time this year ripe Service
berrys.   Killed one mountain sheep which was all the meat killed
this day for 48 men   short commons.   hard rains last night.*

Traveling close to the west bank, the caravan dropped into the val-
ley on a portion of the Bad Pass Trail. This path, used for centuries by
Paleo-Indians, wound its way along the rugged western edge of Big
Horn Canyon. Marked by rock cairns, the trail led from the plains of
what is now Wyoming to the buffalo country farther north, in present
Montana.[75] This day ended at the confluence of the north fork of Trail
Creek and Big Horn River.

Plaster of Paris does not occur naturally, so Wyeth undoubtedly found more gypsum. To be on "short commons," as Wyeth described, meant to be low on rations. "Common doings" was contemporary slang for plain or simple food as opposed to delicacies.[76]

Wyeth counted forty-eight men at this camp he shared with Robert Campbell, Milton Sublette, Tom Fitzpatrick and the RMFC employees. Wyeth was not counting the company aligned with Bonneville, although they traveled together; Bonneville's was a separate concern. Bonneville, worried that Fitzpatrick and his trappers would beat him to streams he planned to hunt that fall, had already "secretly detached" a small party to the waters west of the Big Horn, so while the number of men in Bonneville's brigade is not known, it was probably fewer than fifty.[77]

About this time, the bull that had been bitten by the rabid wolf during the Horse Creek rendezvous began to exhibit "symptoms of hydrophobia by bellowing at a great rate and pawing the ground." This understandably frightened George Holmes, still with the party, who had also been attacked that fateful night. Larpenteur had come to know Holmes fairly well during their journey. He reported that

> *The poor fellow now and then asked me if I thought he would go mad; although thinking within myself he would, being so badly bitten, I did all I could to make him believe otherwise. When he said to me, "Larpenteur, don't you hear the bull — he is going mad — I am getting scared," I do believe I felt worse than he did, and scarcely knew how to answer him.*[78]

Larpenteur told the story of his friend's ensuing madness in the weeks ahead, after the parties separated. Holmes had stayed with Fitzpatrick's trapping brigade, and often could not bear to cross the small streams which they struck from time to time. Eventually, the men had to cover him with a blanket to get him over the simplest of creeks. Before long, they began to leave Holmes with two men until his fit ended; ultimately, his guardians would stay only briefly before leaving him on his own. It so upset Holmes's friends that William Drummond Stewart, Black Harris and Dr. Harrison went in search of a mystical stone believed to be the talisman cure for hydrophobia. Finally, during one encampment, after having abandoned Holmes, fellow trappers were sent back after him, but when they arrived at the place he was thought to be, they found only the clothes he had torn off his back. He had run away quite naked, and never was found. "This ended my poor friend Holmes," lamented Larpenteur.[79]

August 11, 1833   *Bad Pass Trail*

11th.   Went out hunting   killed 2 Cows and 4 Bulls   the camp made about a N. course   at six miles crossed a small creek   at 5 more another   probably another branch of the same   at 9 more a creek separate from the others but not large   all these creeks have high perpendicular banks and are very bad to cross   in the course of the day saw 4 Bears   white.   A fine grass country and a great many Buffaloe.

Keeping on the trail that Bonneville referred to as "a rugged and frightful route, emphatically called the 'Bad Pass,'" the group first crossed Deadman's Creek.[80] At the eleventh mile, it met Dry Head Creek (not a branch of Deadman's Creek as Wyeth supposed). During the next leg, the band crossed Spring and Pitchfork creeks far enough upstream to avoid the canyons of "high perpendicular banks." Their final crossing of the day came twenty miles on at Hoodoo Creek.

It was fortunate that there were plenty of bison grazing in this country. They would need a multitude of hides to build the many bull boats they would soon require.

August 12, 1833   *Big Horn River*

12th.   4 miles N.E. to Big Horn River   this day went out to get Bull Hydes for boat   got enough and employed the rest of the day in making a Boat   this day followed down a little stream.

A short day brought the company to a site just upstream from where the Yellow Tail Dam would be built in the 1960s to impound a seventy-mile stretch of the Big Horn River. This same day, Louis Vasquez, Campbell's main clerk, shot an amazingly fat buffalo though it was the hide rather than the meat the hunters needed. Larpenteur described building two "boats of twenty feet in length and eight in breath." He reported three boats were constructed but did not provide dimensions for the third craft. Campbell had thirty 100-pound packs of beaver weighing a total of three thousand pounds. Each hide boat would carry as much as a half ton of the valued cargo.[81]

Though considerably awkward to steer (they could drift as much as a mile downstream during a river crossing), bull boats were unmatched in the rough and ready conditions of the Far West for ferrying heavy loads. The Indian-made, circular-style bull boat could manage cargoes of nearly 700 pounds. Evidently the mountain men's larger, canoe-shaped vessels could be loaded with greater weight.[82]

> **August 13-14, 1833**   *Big Horn River*
>
>   *13th.   Remained at same camp   made a Bull Boat   day fine.*
>
>   *14th.   Same camp   day fine.*

Possibly caught up in the heavy work of constructing bull boats, Wyeth chose not to follow the rabies aftermath in his journal, so did not mention that the largest of the two bulls Campbell had wrangled all the way from the blue bunch-grass pastures around Lexington, Missouri, had succumbed to the ravages of rabies and had to be put down.[83]

About this time, Bonneville dispatched a second brigade, this one comprised of ten men, to catch up with the first party and begin the fall hunt.[84] Meanwhile, Campbell's man Vasquez also left, leading a small contingent of five men, including Larpenteur, who went by land to herd the horses and remaining two cows to the planned reunion with Sublette near the mouth of the Yellowstone.[85]

On August 14, a much more significant event occurred that Wyeth chose to also omit from his daily jottings. Perhaps, as in the letters he wrote from Fort Vancouver, he was reluctant to include business details that someone from the competition might discover.

Here, on the banks of the Big Horn, he secretly made a remarkable arrangement with Milton Sublette and Tom Fitzpatrick, the two Rocky Mountain Fur Company and Christy partners who were present. And this, under the very nose of supplier Robert Campbell, who, with his partner William Sublette, stood to lose a substantial amount of money from their arrangement.[86]

Wyeth had been cogitating on another money-making opportunity. In all likelihood, the seed of Wyeth's idea had taken root in the summer of 1832, from conversations with Milton Sublette during their weeks on the trail. Wyeth now boldly offered to supply the younger Sublette's RMFC at a much lower price than what William Sublette and Campbell were imposing on the company. Wyeth agreed to furnish RMFC goods not to cost more than $3000 in the States, at a far lower markup than Sublette and Campbell, to be delivered at next summer's rendezvous in the Rocky Mountains.

As part of their accord, Milton Sublette would accompany Wyeth eastward to oversee the procurement of supplies. Upon delivery, Wyeth was to be paid the first cost of the merchandise plus $3521, compensated in beaver skins at $4.00 per pound. Wyeth was hoping that if Governor Simpson approved his earlier offer (and he had yet to receive word), he could turn around and sell these furs to the HBC.

Wyeth, sitting on the banks of the Big Horn, was not at all sure he could swing the financing for his deal with Milton Sublette. He needed a way to secure his own release should he find himself unable to buy the supplies. Wyeth proposed, and Milton agreed, that their contract would be null and void if RMFC went out of business before November of that year and notified Wyeth of such demise. Each party bound itself to fulfill the agreement or forfeit $500 in case of default.[87]

Perhaps more competition in the Rocky Mountain supply system could make a difference. In the four years that RMFC had been tied to William Sublette, he had personally managed to deliver only one caravan of goods to rendezvous. In 1831, Fitzpatrick had been forced to go east to St. Louis, then to Santa Fe to procure the needed goods for company trappers, though these were purchased through Sublette. With his brother's concentration focused on building new forts to capture the Upper Missouri trade, Milton may have wondered if he could depend on the senior Sublette to bring a timely supply train to the mountains. Wyeth's seemingly sound Yankee proposition would have gotten RMFC's attention. Milton Sublette, Fitzpatrick, and Wyeth signed the contract.[88]

The crux of the plan was establishing a cheaper way to transport supplies to rendezvous. Wyeth had a scheme to send goods, at little financial risk, by ship from New England to the mouth of the Columbia. He reasoned, then, that packing overland across the Rocky Mountains from the Pacific Coast would be more economical than the traditional overland route from St. Louis. By Wyeth's calculations, transporting $3000 in goods from Fort Vancouver to the rendezvous would cost about $1500, while hauling that same merchandise westward from Missouri would cost well over $8000 – regardless of what Sublette and Campbell had charged.[89] All totaled, Wyeth thought he could supply the Rocky Mountain Fur Company for about $6500. The same amount of goods the previous year via William Sublette had come to more than $15,000.[90] Frankly, it would have been foolish not to let Wyeth have a shot.

> **August 15, 1833**   *Big Horn River*
>
> *15th.   Made a start in our Bull Boat   found it to answer the purpose well   large enough   runs well   leaks a little   made 3 miles N.E.   stream rapid   shoals at places 2 feet. Too much liquor to proceed therefore stopped.*

Over the course of the last three days, Wyeth, Campbell, Milton Sublette and Cerré had completed the needed bull boats. They were ready to load their precious beaver skins and paddle their way toward St. Louis. Despite, or perhaps due to, having conducted a momentous business transaction the evening before, the New Englander approached floating the Big Horn River with alacrity. His crew was the first to complete a boat and they were soon paddling around the bend.[91]

The seams of bull boats were sealed with an elk tallow and ash mixture. Wyeth may not have done a thorough job caulking the stitching where the hides were joined. Soon, the other boats were ready and they too pushed off downstream. After just three miles floating and bouncing down the Big Horn, Wyeth decided he was too hung over to continue. Even with such a short start, he remained ahead of the other boats.

August 16, 1833   *Big Horn River*

16th.   Made a start in our boat   found travelling quite pleasant but requires much caution on account of some snaggs and bars.   We frequently took one half of the river which dividing again gave too little water for our boat which draws 1 1/2 feet   it is quite too much   the [boat] ought to have been flatter   We grounded about 6 times this forenoon   it is surprising how hard a thump these bull Boats will stand   ours is made of three skins   is 18 feet long and about 5 1/2 wide sharp at both ends   Round bottom.   Have seen on the banks of the river this forenoon 3 grisly bears and some Bulls in the river and on the banks   they stare and wonder much   the direction of this march was as near as I can judge N. by E.   we went from 5 to 11 as I think about 6 miles per hour   the indirection I suppose to be not more than 1/4.   All feel badly today from a severe bout of drinking last night.   Afternoon made 4 hours at a good 6 mile rate   grounded three times   saw a few elk and much Beaver sign all day   there is here the best trapping that I have ever found on so large a river   it is about 100 yards wide when all together but is much cut into slews which makes the navigation very difficult.   The musquitoes have anoyed me much today   they affect me almost as bad as a rattle snake   this afternoons course about N.N.W.   at 6 miles from our noon camp passed a place where we supposed the Little Horn River came in from the S.E.   at least there is a considerable river at that place   but it is difficult to tell a returning slew from a river   this afternoon a severe thunderstorm which compelled us to put ashore until it was over

At the previous day's camp, Bonneville's band had assembled three hide vessels; the Captain put Cerré in charge of their loading and navigation. With all the pelts and a party of thirty-six men, these crude boats must have been filled to near capacity. Campbell took charge of his own trio of crafts and soon the improvised flotilla was gliding along with the current of the Big Horn, dodging snags and watching for sandbars.[92]

Now Bonneville's apprehension – that Fitzpatrick would split off to trap the same western streams to which he had already sent his own men – surely crested. Yet as soon as Campbell had left for St. Louis with all the peltries, Fitzpatrick rounded up the herd of over one hundred horses and struck off with his brigade of twenty men in the opposite direction from Bonneville. Fitzpatrick had planned to head for the tributaries of the Yellowstone all along. William Drummond Stewart and Dr. Harrison, still tagging along with the RMFC brigade, took their adventures with Fitzpatrick.[93]

The crew accompanying Milton Sublette and Wyeth included two mountaineers, described by Irving as "first-rate hunters" and "half-breeds, who claimed to be white men, though a mixture of the French creole and the Shawnee and Potawattomie." The young Nez Perce man and Baptiste Payette, the young Flathead, rounded out the party. Though Wyeth never mentioned them, Irving noted that Wiggin Abbott and John Woodman were also on board.[94]

Wyeth and Sublette were now a day ahead of Campbell and the others. The canoe-shaped boat could have easily carried over one and a half tons of cargo – far more than Wyeth had on board.[95] But their load still drew eighteen inches in the shallow Big Horn; the boat kept scraping and bumping the gravelly river bottom. Adding to their discomfort were the aftereffects of prodigious drinking.

Despite the difficulties, ten hours on the water at Wyeth's estimate of six miles per hour made for sixty miles of float in a mainly northeasterly direction. Wyeth correctly identified the Little Big Horn. That river enters the Big Horn near the town of modern Hardin, Montana, and the mileages he quoted match closely.

Irving provided details of Wyeth's downstream float that the Bostonian did not include in his journal or letters. When they stopped for the night, the men would unload the boat and drag it up on shore. There, they built a fire and propped the craft toward the flames so the heat and evening breezes could dry it thoroughly. A bull boat with water-logged hides leaked quickly and sat lower in the water. Even a well-maintained bull boat, however, was short-lived; it usually rotted and fell to pieces in a matter of days or weeks.[96]

To measure the speed of the current, Wyeth may have used a floating object or "drifter," and a timing device. Standing on the shore, timer in hand, he placed the drifter, such as a piece of wood, into the water and measured the amount of time it took to move through a premeasured distance along the bank. He then divided the distance the object traveled by the time it took to travel that distance, which equaled the speed of the current in feet per minute. A mathematical formula could then convert that speed into miles per hour. It appeared as though Wyeth performed this calculation twice a day, before setting out in the morning and following the noon break.[97]

William Clark used a similar method in June 1804 to measure the Missouri River current. He found that "the Current of the River at this place is a Stick will float 48 poles 6 feet in the rapidest part in 23 Seconds." A pole was 16 ½ feet so this calculated to 2.36 miles per hour.[98]

August 17, 1833   *Yellowstone River*

17th.   This day the river made nearly a N. course and we made about 7 1/2 hours at the rate of about 6 miles   the river winding about 1/4 of the distance   we started at 5 ock.   at about 9 ock. saw several persons ahead on the bank of the river which we at first supposed to be whites from the fort but soon found to be Crow Indians   they informed us that the whole nation was behind   we were anxious to avoid them but could not as the river afforded us no hiding place   they showed us that they meant us to land very soon by stepping and swimming into the river   seeing this we chose to land without further trouble   in this way we were obliged to make the shore 6 times   during the day we arrived at the Yellow Stone which was of clear water and did not mix with the waters of the Big Horn which was at this time dirty for some miles   about 3 miles below the mouth of the Big Horn we found Fort Cass one of the Am. F. Co. at which post we traded about 10 packs of Beaver and 150 to 200 pack robes   goods are brough[t] up in boats of about 15 tons burthen   2 of which are now laying here and one of them preparing to descend in two days   we were treated with little or no ceremony by Mr. Tullock, who we found in charge which I attributed to sickness on his part well knowing that a sick man is never disposed to be over civil to others   we therefore pushed on next morning.   Just as we arrived we saw 31 Indians with two American flags come to the other side of the river   they were Gros ventres du Baum   the same we fought with last summer at the Trois Tetons   they came to

MAP 9 *Yellowstone River to Fort Pierre, Missouri River, 1833*

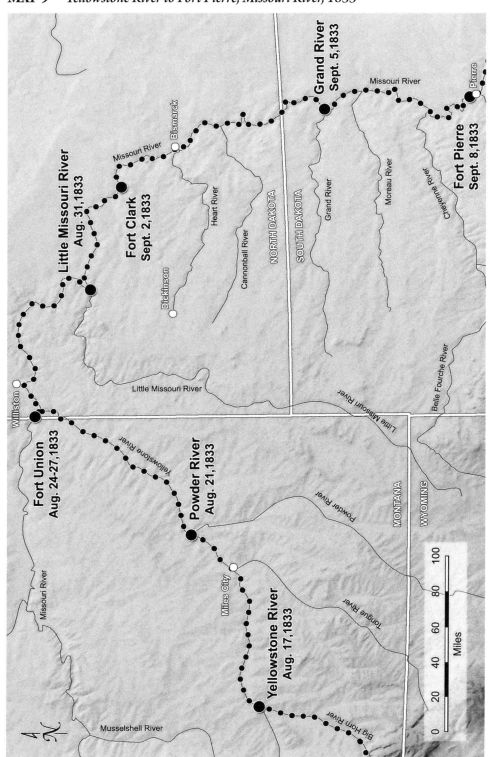

make peace with the Crows   they were treated civilly at the
Fort and before night followed the river up to the Crow village
where I expect their scalps will be taken for the Crows informed
us that not long since a few Blkft. came and made peace with
them   shortly after three Crows went to the Blackfeet two of
which they killed and they were determined to make no more
peace with them.

On this morning, Bonneville, with only four men to marshal forty-six head of horses, set out for his appointed rendezvous with the trapping brigades already in the field back near the Greybull River. He had stayed at the previous day's camp and delayed his departure to make sure Cerré launched without any trouble.[99]

Traveling down the Bighorn River toward its juncture with the Yellowstone, Wyeth and Milton Sublette encountered a Crow woman somewhat apart from the rest of her cohort. The group stopped to confer with her and learned that five bands under several chiefs were just a few miles below them on the Big Horn and coming upriver. This was not good news, but the only option was to forge ahead and trust that the fort was close enough to keep so many Indians at bay.[100]

Irving retold this episode of unwelcome riverside parleys with the Crow in further detail:

Wyeth landed with the best grace in his power and approached the chief of the band. It was Arapooish ... anxious to promote a friendly intercourse between his tribe and the white men. He was a tall, stout man, of good presence, and received the voyagers very graciously. His people, too, thronged around them, and were officiously attentive after the Crow fashion. One took a great fancy to Baptiste the Flathead boy, and a still greater fancy to a ring on his finger, which he transposed to his own with surprising dexterity, and then disappeared with a quick step among the crowd.

Another was no less pleased with the Nez Perce lad, and nothing would do but he must exchange knives with him; drawing a new knife out of the Nez Perce's scabbard, and putting an old one in its place. Another stepped up and replaced this old knife with one still older, and a third helped himself to knife, scabbard and all. It was with much difficulty that Wyeth and his companions extricated themselves from the clutches of these officious Crows before they were entirely plucked.

Falling down the river a little further, they came in sight of the second band, and sheered to the opposite side, with the intention of passing them. The Crows were not to be evaded. Some pointed their guns at the boat, and threatened to fire; others stripped, plunged into the stream, and came swimming across. Making a virtue of necessity, Wyeth threw a cord to the first that came within reach, as if he wished to be drawn to the shore.

In this way he was overhauled by every band, and by the time he and his people came out of the busy hands of the last, they were eased of most of their superfluities. Nothing, in all probability, but the proximity of the American trading post, kept these land pirates from making a good prize of the bull boat and all its contents.[101]

Wyeth and Milton Sublette soon reached the confluence of the Big Horn and Yellowstone rivers. The clear flowing Yellowstone (*Riviére aux Roche Jaune* to early French trappers) was named Elk River by several Indian tribes, including the Crow and the Nez Perce, for the abundance of these animals seen along its banks. A 1796 map drawn by Victor Collot labeled it "Rock or Crow River."[102]

A few miles farther down the Yellowstone, they landed at Fort Cass. This fort had been built in the fall of 1832 by Samuel Tulloch, sometimes referred to as A. J. Tulloch, on behalf of the American Fur Company primarily for trade with the Crow. It stood on the east bank of the river. Although some trappers called it Tulloch's Fort, its official name honored then Secretary of War, Lewis Cass. Beckwourth claimed to have been in charge of building the post (likely an exaggeration).[103]

As Wyeth and his crew beached, they saw on the opposite shore a party of Gros Ventre Indians. For Wyeth and Sublette this evoked memories of the battle following the Pierre's Hole rendezvous the prior summer. Knowing their reputation for unpredictability, Sublette was likely the one responsible for insisting on keeping a low profile. The Gros Ventres had gone on their way by nightfall.

It was a common practice for traders to bestow tribal leaders with special gifts such as a flag or a "chief's coat." Such "rigging" of tribal dignitaries curried much favor as these emblems showed the high regard in which the chief was held by the trader and the influence that particular man had with the company. Prince Maximilian, while on his way to Fort McKenzie earlier this same year, also recorded an American flag hoisted on a pole in front of a Gros Ventre leader's lodge.[104]

While at Fort Cass, Wyeth did a bit of trading, disposing of beaver and buffalo robes though neither Wyeth nor Irving indicate what Wyeth received in return. Wyeth credited Tulloch's lack of hospitality to illness, but more likely, the AFC trader was merely serving the purposes of his company and not caring to assist the competition more than he had to.

Larpenteur showed up at the fort a few days later and described Tulloch as

a man possessed of good common sense, very reliable, and brave withal. He was called the 'Crane' by all the Indians, on account of the extreme length and slenderness for which he was remarkable – almost a curiosity.[105]

August 18, 1833   *Yellowstone River*

18th. Started down the river made 3 hours with a hard wind about 4 miles an hour and put up to noon seeing some elk which we were in hopes to get to eat course about N. afternoon the river tended more Eastwardly and at last came to E.N.E. We made at the rate of 5 miles an hour for 3 1/2 hours and camped to fish and hunt having no meat on hand there is along this river pretty bottoms and great quantities of sweet cotton wood which would be fine for winter camps. We saw some large bands of elk but our hunters were more conceited than good which I have generally found to be the case with the hunters in this country they are not willing that a new hand should even try, and are far from good shots themselves and commonly have miserable flint guns which snap continually and afford an excuse for not killing. The river sometimes cuts blufs which are mostly of sand stone but the river brings down granite and porphry. Fort Cass is scituated on the E. bank of the Yellow stone river is about 130 feet square made of sapling cotton wood pickets with two bastions at the extreme corners and was erected in the fall of 1832. The Yellow stone comes from the S.W. til it meets the Big Horn then the two go about N. until they bend to the eastward.

Wyeth provided a good description of the post in this journal entry. Beckwourth said the fort's "stipulated dimensions were one hundred and twenty yards for each front, the building to be square, with a block house at opposite corners." He added that Fort Cass was built of hewn cottonwood pickets planted perpendicularly in the ground with eighteen-foot-high walls. The dimensions provided by Beckwourth are significantly greater than those given by Wyeth. Beckwourth may have meant feet rather than yards, which would make the size relatively close. Historian Chittenden accepted Wyeth's measurements as correct.[106]

According to Irving, Wyeth's party launched its bull boats in the morning but fought a headwind that slowed them down considerably. In the course of the day, movement on the bank drew their attention and, thinking it might be game, they edged toward the shore. In the nick of time, they saw that it was Indians lurking in the brush. Wyeth figured them to be remnants of the Gros Ventre band seen the previous day at Fort Cass since they had come from the same direction.[107]

Paddling hard to the opposite side of the Yellowstone, they proceeded downstream until stopping for the night, probably six or so miles below present Hysham, Montana. Wyeth had chosen percussion guns to arm his Pacific Trading Company, and while these weapons had their own issues, as described earlier, it is not surprising the Bostonian continued to favor this style of firing mechanism.

August 19, 1833   *Yellowstone River*

19th.   Made 5 1/2 hours in a calm fine day   I should think about 6 miles the hour the river going E.N.E.   stopped early to try a band of Buffaloe that we see on the left of us, at first we were careful to see if they were really Buffaloe for yesterday we were near approaching a band of Indians which I suppose were the residue of the Blackfeet which I saw at the fort as they appeared coming down from that way.   Nooned in a fine cool place under the shade of a large Cotton wood in a large green bottom   the musquitoes take much from the pleasure of the trip which is otherwise fine but I believe for a party like ours rather dangerous   in afternoon 2 1/2 hours about 6 per H.   River E.   stopped on hearing the bellowing of Buffaloe on shore to get meat.   Our hunters as usual having failed went myself and killed a cow   got a good ducking from a shower and returned loaded with meat much fatigued.   About 4 miles before we stopped we passed the mouth of Rose Bud   a river coming from S.S.W.

About an hour before they halted for the day, Wyeth and his crew aboard the bull boat floated past Rosebud Creek. The Crow called this stream "Bichkapaashe," which translated as "Rosehip River."[108] Around 1835, Fort Cass would be abandoned and a new trading post, Fort Van Buren, constructed in this vicinity. Samuel Tulloch, then working for Pratte, Chouteau and Company, would be chief builder and trader at the fort, named in honor of Vice-President Martin Van Buren.[109]

At least a day behind Wyeth, Robert Campbell ran into a bit of trouble. On this day, the boat in which Campbell rode was sucked under a fallen tree and swamped.[110] With some difficulty, Campbell managed to extricate himself:

Thrice I went under and but for an all wise and all merciful God I should never have seen the termination of the Year. I got safe to shore and succeeded in recovering all but about 4 packs of Beaver and our arms. Besides I lost my saddle bags &c.[111]

Most of the floating skins were picked up by other boats, but several packs may have been lost. Some of the beaver was later found by a couple of American Fur Company trappers and sold at Fort Union.[112]

August 20, 1833   *Yellowstone River*

20th.   Started early and made this forenoon 6 hours at the rate of about 5 1/2 miles.   River about E.N.E.   last night a smart rain which wet our clothes much   caught just at dusk last night plenty of Blue Catfish and a small one which resembles an Ale wife   soon after starting this morning found an immense herd of Buffaloe close to the river   stopped and killed 2 fat cows and could have killed any number more but this was enough   they keep up a continued grunting night and day now that we have fairly got into them   in the afternoon made 5 1/2 hours   current about 6 miles and E.N.E.   at 5 hours found bad rapids but at this low stage of the water it is said to be better passing on account of the chanell being more visible   we had a good joke on the old hands as they call them selves in distinction to those who have been a short time in the country   two bald headed Eagles being perched on a tree on a point and ranged to the other side of the river   our motion made them appear moving   the old one cried out Les Savvages   others of them said on horseback with white scarfs   I looked long but not supposing that they meant the eagles I said I saw nothing but the eagles   they soon found out their mistake and we had a good laugh at them and a pleasant one as all the Indians we meet here we expect to fight.   This day and yesterday whenever the river makes perpendicular banks we saw veins of poor bituminous coal in 5 to 7 veins horizontal from 3 ft. to 6 inches thick and 10 to 15 feet above each other   rock sandstone.

The anglers caught plenty of catfish and goldeye, a native Montana species that looks a lot like a herring. Wyeth's comparison of the fish to "an Ale wife" was an apt reference to a type of herring common in New England. Meriwether Lewis caught a few of these on the Marias River in 1805 and described them as resembling the "Hickory Shad or oldwife" except for their large eyes and long teeth.[113]

In his own inimitable style, Irving retold the embarrassing faux pas of Wyeth's two mountaineers:

As the boat was gliding swiftly round a low promontory, thinly covered with trees, one of them gave the alarm of Indians. The boat was instantly shoved from shore and every one caught up his rifle. "Where are they?" cried Wyeth.

"There — there! riding on horseback!" cried one of the hunters.

"Yes; with white scarfs on!" cried the other.

Wyeth looked in the direction they pointed, but descried nothing but two bald eagles, perched on a low dry branch beyond the thickets, and seeming, from the rapid motion of the boat, to be moving swiftly in an opposite direction. The detection of this blunder in the two veterans, who prided themselves on the sureness and quickness of their sight, produced a hearty laugh at their expense, and put an end to their vauntings.[114]

At the end of this day's float, the company put to shore near present day Saugus, Montana.

August 21, 1833   *Yellowstone River*

21st.   Made 5 hours   river about E.N.E.   passed the mouth of Powder River at 4 hours and half an hour below a bad and rocky rapid but without accident   the coal still continues and thousands of Buffaloe   day fine   stopped to noon a little below the rapids   in the afternoon made 5 hours   current about 5 miles per hour in about E.N.E. direction   no rapids of consequence   the blufs have ceased   these blufs are a part of the Black hills as I am informed   the Black Hills I am also informed make the Falls of Missouri   at the Three Forks just on leaving the blufs the coal veins appeared thicker   day fine.   buffaloe plenty.

The boats passed the mouth of Powder River fairly early in the day. The river's name was a translation of the Sioux word "yela," meaning powdery, to describe the consistency of the stream bottom. Prince Maximilian called it *La Riviére a la Poudre* in his diary of 1832-34.[115]

Wyeth identified the bluffs along the Powder River as part of the Black Hills, but in this period, it was customary to call any of the foothills of the Rocky Mountains "black hills," not just the ones in present South Dakota.[116] Wyeth's bluffs may have been the badlands around today's Makoshika State Park. The evening camp would have been in the neighborhood of modern Glendive, Montana.

A colorful riverside event, caused by swarming bison, befell Wyeth and his fellow travelers at this camp. The scene seemed made for Irving's dramatic pen:

> *It was the lot of the voyagers, one night, to encamp at one of these buffalo landing places, and exactly on the trail. They had not been long asleep, when they were awakened by a great bellowing, and tramping, and the rush, and splash, and snorting of animals in the river. They had just time to ascertain that a buffalo army was entering the river on the opposite side, and making toward the landing place. With all haste they moved their boat and shifted their camp, by which time the head of the column had reached the shore, and came pressing up the bank.*

> *It was a singular spectacle, by the uncertain moonlight, to behold this countless throng making their way across the river, blowing, and bellowing, and splashing. Sometimes they pass in such dense and continuous column as to form a temporary dam across the river, the waters of which rise and rush over their backs, or between their squadrons. The roaring and rushing sound of one of these vast herds crossing a river, may sometimes in a still night be heard for miles.*

> *The voyagers now had game in profusion. They could kill as many buffaloes as they pleased, and, occasionally, were wanton in their havoc; especially among scattered herds, that came swimming near the boat. On one occasion, an old buffalo bull approached so near that the half-breeds must fain try to noose him as they would a*

*wild horse. The noose was successfully thrown around his head, and
secured him by the horns, and they now promised themselves ample
sport. The buffalo made prodigious turmoil in the water, bellowing,
and blowing, and floundering; and they all floated down the stream
together. At length he found foothold on a sandbar, and taking to
his heels, whirled the boat after him like a whale when harpooned;
so that the hunters were obliged to cast off their rope, with which
strange head-gear the venerable bull made off to the prairies.*[117]

August 22, 1883   *Yellowstone River*

*22nd.   Made at 5 1/2 per hour 6 hours   in forenoon using a
sail which we found of little advantage and but a little   course
of the river N.N.E. and from the junction on the E. side of first
Rose Bud then Tongue and then Powder River it is of about
the color of the Missouri   altho the Yellow stone above is of
clear water quite so above the junction of the Big Horn.   Our
boat getting quite rotten   in afternoon made 5 hours same
course   5 miles per hour   river better not so [many] bars and
country not mountainous   the coal appears to have given out.*

The men rigged up a sail, possibly from tent canvas or pack covers, and hoisted it when the winds seemed favorable, but overall, it
was to no avail. Wyeth noted that the waters of the Yellowstone River
were gradually growing turbid, assuming the yellow-clay-color of the
Missouri as they drifted closer and closer to the Big Muddy. When the
Corps of Discovery had reached this same confluence in early August
1806, William Clark pointed out

*The Colour of the [Yellowstone's] Water differs from that of the
Missouri it being of a yellowish brown, whilst that of the Missouri is
of a deep drab Colour containing a greater portion of mud than the
Rochejhone.*[118]

Wyeth's observation concerning the decaying condition of the bull
boat suggests that such a craft's lifespan was about one week of heavy use.

August 23, 1883   *Yellowstone River*

23rd.   Made in forenoon 4 hours at the [rate] of 5 [miles] per hour   river about N.E.   Day fine and hot   plenty of Elks in herds   afternoon made 4 hours N. then 2 1/2 hours E.N.E.   current about 4 miles per hour   saw but little game only 2 Elk   river broad and shoal.

By "shoal," Wyeth meant the river was becoming shallower. The party crossed the present border between the states of Montana and North Dakota during this day's float.

August 24, 1833   *Missouri River*

24th   Made N.N.E. 2 hours with a heavy head wind about 4 miles per hour   then the river turned Westwardly and when it enters the Missouri is running W. by S.   this made one hour more when we found the Missouri which we assended N.W. about 5 miles to Fort Union where we arrived about noon and were met with all possible hospitality and politeness by Mr. McKensie the Am. F. Co. agent in this country.

As he entered the Missouri River, Wyeth was forced, for the first time since launching his fragile bull boat, to paddle against the current. Yet it took only an hour to propel his craft the final six upriver miles. Wyeth and the accompanying flotilla had reached Fort Union – a key player in the Upper Missouri trading system. Construction of the post had begun in the fall of 1829 and was completed in 1830. Nearly 53,000 square feet of ground were enclosed within its stockade, making it the largest trade house on the upper Missouri at the time. In June 1832, the first steamboat to reach that far up the Missouri, the *Yellow Stone*, had docked at Fort Union.[119]

The fort's location on the Missouri, upriver from the mouth of the Yellowstone, might have been inconvenient for travelers on the latter waterway, but the site was favorable in many other respects. For one thing, the local Assiniboine recommended it; and the high gravel bank upon which the fort was built kept it safe from flooding. With the river flowing just below the building site, cargo could be easily unloaded even during the busiest times. The fort's surroundings provided ample timber as well as a plain large enough to accommodate populous Indian encampments.[120]

12.
Fort Union and the Missouri River

F ort Union was the brainchild of the senior partner in the Upper
Missouri Outfit of the American Fur Company, Kenneth McKenzie. Though John Jacob Astor pulled the strings from corporate headquarters in New York, McKenzie ruled the Missouri River.[1] McKenzie
chose to move his headquarters from Fort Tecumseh, near modern
Pierre, South Dakota, to the mouth of the Yellowstone River, near
today's Williston, North Dakota, in a bid to expand his command to the
farthest reaches of the Missouri. Originally from Scotland, McKenzie
had worked for the Northwest Company, but upon its merger with
HBC, he had relocated to St. Louis, applied for American citizenship,
and entered the fur trade as a partner in Joseph Renville's newly formed
Columbia Fur Company. Said to be ruthless, ambitious and proud,
McKenzie had the necessary boldness to accomplish the goals he set.[2]

August 27, 1833   *Fort Union*

*27th.   This day at 1/2 past 10 oclock we took leave [of]
our hospitable entertainers and on the experience of a few
days with prepossessions highly in their favor we found Mr.
McKensie a most polite host   I was particularly pleased with
a Mr. Hamilton and I am perhaps presumptious in saying
that I felt able to appreciate his refined politeness   he is a
man of superior education and an Englishman.   I was here
supplied with a peroque traded from the Blackfeet.   A Mr.
Patten shewed me a powder flask which he traded from
the Blkft.   I immediately knew it to be one of mine and on
examination found No. 4 H.G.O.M. graven with a point on
it.   It was Mores flask who was killed in Little Jackson Hole
last year on his return home after rendezvous.   Fort Union is
pleasantly scituated on the N. bank of the Missouri   6 miles
above the junction of Yellow stone   there is no timber on a*

high bank above the fort I am told that there is not enough moisture here to raise vegetables potatoes grass ect, Some corn is traded from the Inds. lower down the fort is of usual construction about 220 feet square and is better furnished inside than any British fort I have ever seen at Table we have flour Bread Bacon Cheese Butter they live well I here saw a small sturgeon but they are very rare Cat fish are good and plenty they have cows and bulls milk etc. I saw lime burning also coal here they are beginning to distil spirits from corn traded from the Inds. below. This owing to some restrictions on the introduction of the article into the country. Above this we have met plumbs, grapes, cherrys, Currants, ash, elm. The river being already well laid down shall no longer give the course we left the fort and went 2 hours and stopped for Mr. Sublette who remained behind to finish some business he came accompanied by the gentlemen of the fort after leaving us we made 4 hours then supped and made one hour more and found Mr. Wm. L. Sublette at anchor with a large Bull boat this gentleman we had expected to have found on our arrival at the Missouri he is come to trade furs in opposition to the Am. F. Co. he treated us with much politeness his brother preferred to remain and come to the states with him we are therefore left without any one who has decended the Missouri but I can go down stream.

Wyeth spent three days at Fort Union, where he renewed his acquaintance with Kenneth McKenzie, whom he had met on his way through St. Louis the year before. From this lengthy diary entry, it was evident that he got the full VIP tour, met the primary staff and enjoyed all the comforts the post had to offer. McKenzie was generous in providing for Wyeth, both while at Fort Union and providing supplies for the New Englander's return to the States. He answered all manner of questions Wyeth put to him, explaining the particulars of how trade was carried on and describing the kinds of profit that the AFC stood to gain from it.[3]

Here, Wyeth was introduced to James Archdale Hamilton, an English nobleman whose real name was Archibald Palmer. Little is known of his early life, though Hamilton spent some months downriver at AFC's Fort Tecumseh in 1830 before coming to Fort Union as

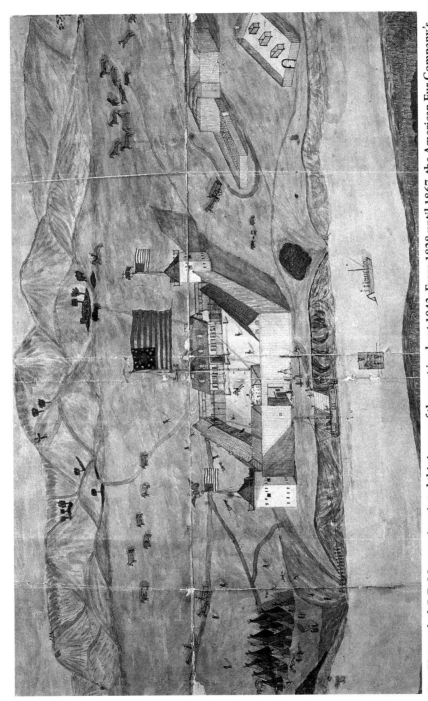

Fort Union clerk J. B. Moncravie painted this image of the post in about 1843. From 1828 until 1867, the American Fur Company's Fort Union was one of the most important fur trading posts on the upper Missouri River. MIDWEST JESUIT ARCHIVES, MISSOURI PROVINCE COLLECTION,

McKenzie's bookkeeper. He was often put in charge of the post in McKenzie's absence. Artist George Catlin reported in 1832 that Hamilton's "intellectual and polished society" enhanced his visit to the isolated post. Hamilton suffered from gout, which often made him crabby. He wore clean, ruffled shirts and a gold chain around his neck, and was always well-scented and oiled because he bathed every day.[4]

Wyeth also crossed trails with Edwin L. Patton, who had been a clerk at Fort McKenzie, up the Missouri from Fort Union near the mouth of the Marias River. Built in 1832 and named after the King of the Missouri, this trading center focused on the Blackfoot nations.[5] Patton would leave Fort Union with Kenneth McKenzie in September to visit his brother in Alabama. Edwin was likely the same Patton whom William Sublette would put in charge of the construction of Fort William (later to become Fort Laramie) in 1834.[6]

Patton had reached Fort Union from Fort McKenzie a few days prior to Wyeth. His departure from that post was recorded by Maximilian, visiting at the time, who wrote that on August 14, Patton had left "with eleven *engagés,* in a strong *pirogue,* to return to Fort Union, and thence to Fort St. Louis."[7] Since he planned to continue on down the Missouri in company with Kenneth McKenzie, Patton no longer needed the Blackfoot dugout canoe in which he had arrived. Patton's surplus vessel was offered to Wyeth, whose hide boat was rotting away.

The upriver trader showed Wyeth a powder flask that he may have received in exchange from the very warrior who had taken it from its American owner. Wyeth recognized the flask right away as an item from his own expedition inventory, container #4, which had been signed out to George More. The man's initials had been scratched onto it. After the Gros Ventres had attacked the Stephens party in Hoback Canyon following the 1832 rendezvous in Pierre's Hole, the Indians had apparently brought the captured plunder to their local trader. Even if the Indians had told Patton how they obtained the powder flask, neither Patton nor the Blackfeet, as Patton identified him, would have connected the item to Wyeth. It was an odd coincidence for Patton to come across Wyeth at Fort Union, and perhaps more odd that he still had the flask in his possession.

In his exploration of Fort Union, Wyeth noted various industries that helped make the fort self-sufficient. Fort Union produced its own charcoal, primarily for use in the blacksmith shop, and ran a lime kiln

Nicknamed "King of the Missouri," Kenneth McKenzie (1797-1861) headed the AFC's Upper Missouri outfit, creating a virtual monopoly over the fur trade of the northern plains. MONTANA HISTORICAL SOCIETY RESEARCH CENTER - PHOTOGRAPH ARCHIVES, HELENA, MT

to make mortar for masonry projects. Wyeth was understandably impressed with the distillery with which McKenzie bypassed Federal regulations against the entry of liquor into Indian Country. Corn for this still came from tribes lower down the Missouri who regularly cultivated it. Wyeth may not have known, or chosen to admit knowing, about the more stringent laws the government had passed the previous year with regard to alcohol and the Native trade; a complete prohibition of alcohol had been imposed in July 1832, well after Wyeth had left St. Louis.[8]

Wyeth found all the comforts of home at the fort and was astounded by how well a person could live so far from civilization. He was especially impressed with the supply of breads and dairy products. McKenzie lived in style; he spread his dining table with a white table cloth, his clerks wore coats to meals and sat according to rank, and he was known to serve his guests Madeira and port wines from bottles set in a pail of ice.[9] Since leaving Cambridge, Wyeth had seen numerous forts, both British and American, but Fort Union was unsurpassed. Months ago, when he left Fort Vancouver, he could never have imagined that this place would prove superior to that exceptional wilderness outpost.

Nor would Wyeth have dreamed that in a few months his name would be embroiled in a leak to government officials that McKenzie was distilling spirits at the mouth of the Yellowstone. Special Indian Commissioner Henry L. Ellsworth, stationed at Fort Leavenworth, arrived August 3, 1833, and then set out in early September to visit local Indian Agencies. When Wyeth visited the post in late September, Ellsworth was still away; he would not return until the first of November.[10]

Ellsworth somehow got wind of Fort Union's liquor manufacturing and informed his superior, Elbert Herring, in Washington. In a letter dated November 8, 1833, Ellsworth reported "a mountain trapper on his way down the Missouri" told him that McKenzie had "a distillery of whiskey." Ellsworth also said "Mr. Sublitz of St. Louis just from there, says he tasted the whiskey made there, and found it of an excellent quality."[11]

When government officials asked AFC headman Pierre Chouteau for details, he sidestepped by saying the rumor was exaggerated, if not wholly unfounded. Such behavior would not be authorized by the Company. In reality, Chouteau knew all about it and had warned his staff to be extra careful. With the new laws and enforcement attempts in the news, all eyes would be upon them.

In self-defense, McKenzie wrote to Chouteau blaming the whole affair on Wyeth and a trapper he identified as L. Cere. Bonneville's Lieutenant Michel Sylvester Cerré, often called Lami, had arrived at the post shortly after Wyeth. In 1830, when the AFC had bought out the French Fur Company, Michel's older brother Gabriel was offered employment but the younger Cerré had been rejected.[12] At Fort Union, McKenzie told Chouteau, he had turned down Wyeth's and Cerré's requests to purchase liquor, offering wine instead. The rebuffed customers

> appeared mortified & displeased. Independent whereof, the character of the former [Wyeth] & the wounded self-love of the latter [Cerré] in being deemed unworthy of an engagement for the Am. F. C. would in my mind account for their unwarranted proceeding.[13]

Two days later, McKenzie followed up with a second defensive salvo, claiming Wyeth was "beastly drunk" during his downriver trip and that a man with such "dissipated habits" should never be taken seriously.[14]

Wyeth might have let the cat out of the bag when he reached Fort Leavenworth, but it is worth noting that Sublette and his keel boat left Fort Union nearly one month behind Wyeth's pirogue, on September 20. The keelboat *Gallant*, carrying William and Milton Sublette, had arrived at Fort Leavenworth by November 2, possibly a day or two earlier.[15] That left an approximate thirty-day window for many a "mountain trapper" to have visited Ellsworth apart from Wyeth and Cerré. Indeed, the jilted Cerré was not the only one with incentive for undermining McKenzie's alcohol trade. Milton and William Sublette directly competed against the AFC – William with a new post right at Fort Union's back door. The two brothers traveled together, so either could have been the "Mr. Sublitz" to whom Ellsworth referred. In fact, Ellsworth wrote that William told him "the law does not forbid *making* whiskey – it only precludes its *introduction*."[16]

Like McKenzie, Larpenteur suspected it was Wyeth who ratted them out, but he may have only been parroting McKenzie. Larpenteur took pains in his narrative to

> *explain how it happened that the distillery was given up. A certain*
> *gentleman from the Eastern States, by the name of Capt. Wheitte,*
> *who had been on a tour to the Columbia, and returned by way of*
> *the Big Horn and the Yellowstone in 1833, reaching Fort Union*
> *about 10 days before we did, thought proper to have better means*
> *of going down the Missouri, and called on Mr. McKenzie to make*
> *the necessary preparations for this journey. Mr. McKenzie, who was*
> *a perfect gentleman, not suspecting the captain, who I cannot say*
> *was a spy, did all he could to make his stay pleasant, showed all the*
> *arrangements of the fort, explained how trade was carried on, what*
> *immense profit was derived, and also showed him the distillery. Capt.*
> *Wheitte appeared to be delighted to see this fine establishment, and*
> *probably would not have done what he did, had he not found, when*
> *everything was in readiness for his departure and he came to settle*
> *his bill, that the charges were exorbitant. He said nothing, settled,*
> *and started; but made it his business, as soon as he arrived, to report*
> *Mr. McKenzie. A dispatch was sent up that winter for the distillery to*
> *be destroyed. This was the last distillery in the Indian country.*[17]

In contrast, Wyeth uttered nothing but praise for McKenzie throughout existing documents. He could have betrayed McKenzie to curry favor with the Sublette brothers. But his motives were not the strongest, and he would not directly benefit. As it turned out, Wyeth appears to have remained unaffected and may not have been aware of the aftermath of his Fort Union visit. He certainly did not appear to have been aware of a provision in the laws pertaining to alcohol in Indian Territory that would cause the operator of an illegal still to pay a $5,000 penalty, a share of which would go to the person who turned in the unlawful operator. Wyeth was certainly in a position to have benefitted from a little extra cash.[18]

As Wyeth noted in his journal entry, by mid-morning of August 27, 1833, he and his small crew of Milton Sublette, Baptiste Payette and the Nez Perce youth, Wiggin Abbott and the two "half-breed" hunters had the twenty-foot-long pirogue loaded for the 2,200 mile journey to St. Louis. John Woodman decided to stay at Fort Union with some trappers there and catch up with Wyeth on his expected return expedition from Boston. Milton Sublette was detained briefly by last-minute business and joined the boat a few hours into its voyage.

Everyone had expected to find the elder Sublette at Fort Union when they arrived, but Milton Sublette and Wyeth met William seven hours down the river. With the meanderings of the river and the minimum of landmarks Wyeth identified, it is difficult to estimate how many miles the pirogue made in an hour. It seemed to average between two and three miles per hour on most days, which would put Sublette about fifteen miles downriver. The site of Fort William, to which Sublette was then headed, was two to three miles below Fort Union, so Sublette would have had a few more miles to push upriver the next day.

Sublette's keel boat, the *Gallant*, was anchored on the north bank, near the site of what would become his latest fur trading post.[19] Though Wyeth's journal reads "Bull" boat, the *Gallant* was a keel boat. This is another instance in which having the original journal to compare transcriptions would be helpful since "keel" might easily be read as "Bull." Irving interpreted Wyeth's statement about Sublette's "politeness" as a convivial gathering onboard the keel boat "talking over past scenes and adventures, and especially the memorable fight at Pierre's Hole."[20]

During this evening of wilderness hospitality, Milton Sublette decided to stay with his older brother, returning to St. Louis with William. Wiggin Abbott also chose to accompany the Sublette brothers. Milton was suffering from a foot injury, and historians have supposed that he chose to ride more comfortably on William's keel boat rather than crew the pirogue. It has also been postulated that Milton's injury needed medical attention and that is why he left the mountains to begin with.[21] William, who was not in the best of health himself, would get sicker in the days to come, and be but "barely recovered" when he finally shoved off on September 20.[22]

Left to man the pirogue were Wyeth, the young Nez Perce man and Baptiste, the Flathead boy. The two hunters likely stuck with the New Englander; Irving places them on board.[23] This was a small crew, but it was a small boat. Milton's departure left Nathaniel with no one in the party who had yet descended the Missouri. Wyeth reckoned that it would be difficult for him to get lost between Fort Union and St. Louis.

August 28, 1833   *Missouri River*

28th.   Pulled one hour   put by from wind and to regulate then pulled 6 hours and stopped to supper   the banks continually falling in   after supper we floated through the night   11 hours   Calm

By "regulate" Wyeth probably meant to adjust the weight and balance of cargo in the pirogue, before rowing for six more hours and stopping for the evening meal. In nautical terms, "pull" is to heave on the oars. Pirogues were typically rowed or poled, occasionally sailed. In order to avoid the full force of the current, these smallish craft kept close to the shore in shallow water. A sixteen- to twenty-foot pole could be planted in the riverbed, then pushed against, forcing the boat along.[24]

The men saw the river's bank eroding before their eyes as the edges repeatedly calved, a not uncommon sight. For example, while traveling up the Missouri River with Wilson Price Hunt in 1810, John Bradbury reported that "the perpendicular banks, both above and below us, began to fall into the river in such vast masses, as nearly to sink our boat by the swell they occasioned."[25] Drifting past the modern town site of Williston, North Dakota, Wyeth's crew would have entered the upper section of today's Lake Sakakawea Reservoir, formed by the completion of Garrison Dam on the Missouri River in 1953.

Wyeth would often float through the dark as he did on this night. Irving again asserts that the nighttime strategy protected them as they approached the country of more hostile tribes, such as the Arikara.[26] It also allowed them to cover a few extra miles.

When Washington Irving wrote his tale of Benjamin Bonneville's excursion to the Rocky Mountains, he had access to Wyeth's journal

– the identical pages presented here. Still, Irving's addition of some interesting tidbits indicates that he must have had further communication with Wyeth while preparing the manuscript – or that he was demonstrating what a fine novelist he truly was. Assuming that Irving enjoyed direct contact with Wyeth, the following information illuminates an unusual aspect of the Bostonian's river float:

> Whenever they could they encamped on islands for the greater security. If on the mainland, and in a dangerous neighborhood, they would shift their camp after dark, leaving their fire burning, dropping down the river some distance, and making no fire at their second encampment. Sometimes they would float all night with the current; one keeping watch and steering while the rest slept: in such case, they would haul their boat on shore, at noon of the following day to dry; for notwithstanding every precaution, she was gradually getting water-soaked and rotten.
>
> There was something pleasingly solemn and mysterious in thus floating down these wild rivers at night. The purity of the atmosphere in these elevated regions gave additional splendor to the stars, and heightened the magnificence of the firmament. The occasional rush and laving of the waters; the vague sounds from the surrounding wilderness; the dreary howl, or rather whine of wolves from the plains; the low grunting and bellowing of the buffalo, and the shrill neighing of the elk, struck the ear with an effect unknown in the daytime.[27]

Navigating the Missouri was not as simple as Wyeth had first anticipated. It was not a matter of passively allowing the current to pull the boat downstream. River travel was unpredictable and routinely dangerous. The average speed of the current was three miles an hour, but picked up in troughs and chutes. Reflected moonlight at night and fog in the morning made the river difficult to read. These and other conditions could slow, if not halt, even the best boatman.[28]

Obstacles were frequent. Trees fell into the river, creating underwater snags or "sawyers" that bobbed just below the surface. Sand or gravel bars could appear with hardly any notice, abruptly reducing the water's depth. Sudden storms brought torrents of rain and harsh, gale-force winds. Hypothermia was a constant threat to those exposed in a small, open pirogue.

In modern times, the myriad of meanders and bends through most of this portion of the Missouri have largely been streamlined, and river miles decreased, with the construction of a deep-water channel and a series of dams and reservoirs between St. Louis and Fort Union.

Campbell, still making his way down the Yellowstone River on his way to the Fort William construction site, finally arrived at the Missouri on this date. Wyeth's journal entry did not mention him, thus the Bostonian's dugout had probably already slipped into the Missouri current by the time Campbell arrived.[29]

Vasquez, Larpenteur and the cattle were still trailing overland but were greatly slowed by frequent encounters with the same tribal groups Wyeth had met. The small party of trappers-turned-cowpunchers constantly anticipated danger, and erected a large pen for the animals every night. To the apprehensive crew, even a distant herd of elk bore a striking resemblance to a mounted war party. Although the presence of livestock brought dietary benefits, the rocky trail created its own impediments, as Larpenteur explained:

> *Our two cows added a great deal to our good living; as we had no coffee, milk was a great relish. We made but slow progress, on account of the cattle, whose feet became very tender, and finally got so bad that we were obliged to make shoes of raw buffalo hide.*[30]

August 29, 1833　　　　　　　　　　　*Missouri River*

29　While breakfast was preparing went out to hunt　killed one deer and found a severe time in the thick swamp and mosqutoes　pulled 8 1/2 hours and drifted 11 hours through the night which exposed me to much rain and wind from two thunder showers.　I had much difficulty to keep the boat from bars and snaggs　ran several times on to Bars　all hands being asleep had to jump over board to get off　In the night elk keep up a continual squeling it being now the commencement of their rutting season.

Wyeth had become less meticulous about giving distances and landmarks, perhaps because, as he stated earlier, the Missouri was well mapped by this time. On this date, Wyeth was drifting through the upper end of today's Lake Sakakawea, a bit beyond Hofflund Bay.

August 30, 1833   *Missouri River*

30th   Day pulled 9 hours   Saw three white Bears this day and some Elk and a herd of Buffaloe   night floated 8 1/2 hours and were stopped by a gale from the S.E.   not thinking it expedient to pull with a head wind and in the dark.

About the three grizzlies, Irving relayed a more elaborate story that must have come from Wyeth, though unremarked in his journal. The bears had been observed individually and at different times along the bank; the last grizzly was working its way down the steep embankment, heading for water. Spurred into action, the two half-breed hunters were

eager to repeat the [August 21] manoeuvre of the noose; promising to entrap Bruin, and have rare sport in strangling and drowning him. Their only fear was, that he might take fright and return to land before they could get between him and the shore. Holding back, therefore, until he was fairly committed in the centre of the stream, they then pulled forward with might and main, so as to cut off his retreat, and take him in the rear. One of the worthies stationed himself in the bow, with the cord and slip-noose, the other, with the Nez Perce, managed the paddles. There was nothing further from the thoughts of honest Bruin, however, than to beat a retreat. Just as the canoe was drawing near, he turned suddenly round and made for it, with a horrible snarl and a tremendous show of teeth. The affrighted hunter called to his comrades to paddle off. Scarce had they turned the boat when the bear laid his enormous claws on the gunwale, and attempted to get on board. The canoe was nearly overturned, and a deluge of water came pouring over the gunwale. All was clamor, terror, and confusion. Every one bawled out – the bear roared and snarled – one caught up a gun; but water had

*rendered it useless. Others handled their paddles more effectually,
and beating old Bruin about the head and claws, obliged him to
relinquish his hold. They now plied their paddles with might and
main, the bear made the best of his way to shore, and so ended the
second exploit of the noose; the hunters determined to have no more
naval contests with grizzly bears.*[31]

August 31, 1833   *Missouri River*

*31st   Blowing a gale.   Made about 4 hours about the rate of
2 mils per hour and finding it too bad laid by at a considerable
river coming from the S. entering by 2 mouths   this I took to be
the little Missouri as laid down in the maps.   In this vicinity we
find primitive pebles and bolders   much petryfied wood   other
aluvial productions   stopped all night on acc. of wind and rain
which made our scituation uncomfortable in the extreme   the
weather had heretofore been very warm   average as much as
90°   this day cold like an Eastwardly storm.*

With severe weather, the boat put in at the mouth of the Little Missouri River, the first landmark Wyeth has mentioned since leaving Fort Union and the first indication that he might have maps or charts of the river. This delta is now under the waters of Lake Sakakawea.

September 1, 1833   *Missouri River*

*1st.   At seven the weather having abated a little made a
start.   At 3 o'clock found some of Sublettes men cutting
timber for a fort and learned from them that the upper Mandan
was 9 miles ahead   we made it at 6   this day made only
about 3 per hour   this village was about 1 1/2 miles from the
river   taking my Indian and a man   with me I went to it and
was well received by Mr. Dorherty, Mr. Subletes clerk and the
Inds.   Stopped about one hour with him and then pulled three
hours more   passing three villages of Mandans and not seeing
the fort and being afraid of passing it stopped for the night.*

When the weather turned more cooperative, Wyeth made it to the next downriver trading post under construction by Sublette and Campbell. That partnership built at least thirteen of these stations, most of which consisted of one man working out of a hastily built cabin.[32] Maximilian would visit this post on November 7, 1833, a mere two months after Wyeth had passed, and said it was among the "Manitari," a name often used for the Hidatsa. Based on the distance from the river that Wyeth reported it to be, the village probably belonged to the Hidatsa, rather than the Mandan as the Bostonian presumed.[33]

Somehow, Wyeth knew Fort Clark was nearby, either from conversations at Fort Union or from a map he may have had. Stopping short, Wyeth visited with the trader at Sublette's post. He has been identified by historians as John Dougherty, but this was not possible. John Dougherty had recently been made a government Indian Agent at Fort Leavenworth. At this time, Dougherty was wrapping up treaty negotiations with the Iowa nation some eight hundred miles down the Missouri. Furthermore, John Dougherty never worked for the Sublette and Campbell firm.[34]

More likely, this was Hannibal Dougherty, John's brother. Hannibal had accompanied the Stephen H. Long expedition in 1820 as a hunter; he was proficient in the Otoe language and was familiar with many Missouri River tribes. Maximilian would meet him at this same post a few months later. Toussaint Charbonneau was Dougherty's interpreter.[35] When Sublette visited on his way downriver, he was satisfied with Hannibal Dougherty's efforts. He replaced two of his other agents along the Missouri.

September 2, 1833   *Fort Clark*

2nd.   Pulled 1/2 hour   arrived first on a high point at the village then immediately round the point found the fort and was well received by Mr. Kipp.   the Am. F. Co. agent for the Mandans   Stopped 2 hours   took breakfast   the[y] presented me some dry corn and some roasting ears.   All these villages cultivate corn peas beans pumpkins ect.   at 1/2 past 7 ock pulled a short distance when we had a good breeze and sailed until 5 ock then stopped to supper   then floated from 6 until 12 ock   then stopped owing to fog with head wind.

James Kipp constructed Fort Clark in the summer of 1831 for the American Fur Company.[36] Named in honor of William Clark, then Superintendent of Indian Affairs, the fort was built primarily for the Mandan trade, and became one of the primary posts on the Missouri River.

Born near Montreal about 1788, Kipp had entered the fur trade by the age of twenty and was working on the Missouri by 1818. In 1823, Kipp built the Columbia Fur Company trading post known as Tilton's Fort on the south side of the Missouri, above the future site of Fort Clark. Kipp was commissioned by AFC's McKenzie in October 1828 to build Fort Union, completed in 1830. Kipp also built the first American Fur Company trading post for the Blackfeet in 1831. He is said to have been the only white man to master the Mandan language.[37]

After breakfast, Kipp loaded up the travelers with ears of corn for the voyage ahead. More stationary tribes, such as the Mandan, cultivated relatively large garden plots. Jacob Halsey, when working for Columbia Fur Company in 1826 at this village, reported that the Mandan raised "corn, beans and pumpkins in great abundance."[38]

Before stopping due to fog and headwind, Wyeth and his men had floated into what is now South Dakota.

September 3, 1833   *Missouri River*

3rd.   Floated 2 hours and stopped to Breakfast   having found no game have lived much upon the stores we have taken from the forts above   At the last place we were presented with some green corn which we are now roasting   Makes us think of Old Lang Sine.   We have had for four days rainy cloudy & foggy weather   our bed clothes are wet and musty in consequence   after Breakfast pulled 6 hours when I thought best to go on shore to cook   I sent a man out to hunt in the meantime   as soon as he assended the high bank he perceived horses on the other side   we after counted 21 lodges and from the number of horses I have no doubt there might have been from 75 to 100.   I immediately had the boat put into a little thicket and fortifyed as well as I could then went to fishing and spent the afternoon   caught but two large catfish   as soon as it was dark we proceeded forward with a

*high wind and a cloudy sky and no Moon   all went well until
we were just opposite the village when we perceived lodges
and fires on our side also   On seeing this I stered the boat
to the middle of the river but unluckly took ground on a sand
bar   here we worked for some time to get off and had the
Indians seen or heard us her[e] we were in distance for shot
from both sides and could have made little resistance but they
did not and after some time we got off and glad we were.   We
proceed in all 4 hours pulled, then stopped for the night   these
were probably the Aricarey and would have scalped us.   I
feared much for my Nez Perce for we could not speak to any
Indian on the river and all would without explanation have made
some fuss and perhaps have killed him.*

The Robert Burns song, "Auld Lang Syne," includes the verse, "We two have paddled in the stream, from morning sun till dine." The roasting ears brought the lyric to mind though nothing in the words of the song seem to mention corn.

There was a good chance that Wyeth correctly identified the Indians whose village he floated through as Arikaras. Traditionally, their villages were in the vicinity of the Grand River's mouth, near present Mobridge, South Dakota, though Wyeth was not yet that far south. Irving averred that the dogs started barking on the bank but that, fortunately, the people

took no heed of their clamor. Wyeth instantly sheered his boat out into the stream; when, unluckily it struck upon a sand-bar, and stuck fast. It was a perilous and trying situation; for he was fixed between the two camps, and within rifle range of both. All hands jumped out into the water, and tried to get the boat off; but as no one dared to give the word, they could not pull together, and their labor was in vain. In this way they labored for a long time; until Wyeth thought of giving a signal for a general heave, by lifting his hat. The expedient succeeded. They launched their canoe again into deep water, and getting in, had the delight of seeing the camp fires of the savages soon fading in the distance.[39]

In 1823, the Arikara had attacked William Ashley's fur brigades as they traveled up the Missouri. Colonel Henry Leavenworth's U.S. Army troops had come to Ashley's aid. It was one of the first conflicts between western tribes and American forces. The incident resulted in the Arikara leaving their besieged village in the middle of the night; American trappers burned the log and earthen lodges the next day. The Arikara abandoned their customary settlements and took up a more nomadic lifestyle for several years.[40]

George Catlin found the Arikara on the Grand River in 1832 and they were relatively hospitable. However, the bulk of the Rees, as trappers often called them, relocated south in about 1833, taking up with the Pawnee on the Loup River in what is now Nebraska. Like Wyeth, Maximilian did not find them at the Grand when he passed there two months after the New Englander.[41]

September 4-5, 1833   *Missouri River*

4th.   With almost a gale of wind from the W. pulled 6 hours and then stopped to eat having twice nearly upset in carrying sail and wet all our things   after drying and eating started on   still blowing fresh and pulled 3 hours   then floated through the night 11 hours   It was a beautiful still night   the stillness interrupted only by the neighing of the Elk   the continual low of the Buffaloe which we came to soon after starting   the hooting of large owls and the screeching of small ones and occasionally the nearer noise of a beaver gnawing a tree or splashing into the water and even the gong like sound of the swan   it was really poetical but sleep at last laid in his claim and I gave the helm to a man.   Oak is now plenty in the Bottoms and for a few days past has been seen   The upland along the river is here pretty good   plumbs we occasionally see and have since we first took water on the Big Horn   frequent squalls of rain yesterday.

5th.   Pulled 7 hours   stopped to eat   pulled one more   came to a deserted village on the S. bank   fired two guns to see if there was any one in it but had no answer   pulled one hour more then floated 7 hours more   then pulled 3 to Breakfast   saw in morning a band of Elk playing like children in

> *the water   failed of killing any of them owing to the impatience of one of the men who fired too soon   pulled through a dreadful rain 7 hours and camped wet and cold   rained all night   strong east wind.*

The deserted village was likely the ruins of the long-established Arikara town at the mouth of the Grand River, mentioned earlier. This entry, describing the longest day on the river thus far, accounts for a twenty-four hour period of travel, nearly a third of it through rainy, windy conditions.

> **September 6-7, 1833**   ***Missouri River***
>
> *6.   In the morning made 8 hours pulling   seeing an Elk on the sand Bar   stopped and killed him   very aceptable as we have had nothing to eat since yesterday noon and saved his horns for my best of friends Mr. F. Tudor of Boston   pulled 2 hours more and the night being dark and appearance of a storm did not run.*
>
> *7th.   Last night about 11 ock was awakened by the water making a breach over the boat   got her off the shore but was obliged to make the shore again on account of some of the men who were so frightened that if I had not they would have jumped overboard   laid the rest of the night on a lee shore   thundering in a loud strain and raining at no allowance   spent a most uncomfortable night an rose in the morning benumbed with cold and all hands as dead as loggs   started after eating at 8 ock and pulled until 2 ock when we had a fine breeze which gradualy increased to a gale before which we scudded at a good rate almost despairing of seeing Fort Piere which we began to think we had passed   at about sundown we saw people on the hills which we supposed to be Inds.   therefore kept on   they fired but we did not choose to hear   about an hour after sundown we smelt the flavor of coal and landed and found people who had just burned a kiln who informed us that the fort was 3 mils ahead   we though[t] to go to sleep at the fort but soon found that night and a gale of*

> *wind was a poor time for travelling and also that 3 miles was in fact 3 leagues   after being near filled by the surf and running afoul of several sand bars and getting overboard to push off we concluded to stop for the night which we did cold and tired and wet   we spent the night as we best could   one comfort plenty of elk meat   stopped at 10 ock.*

At dusk on September 7, Wyeth feigned not hearing the shots and ignored the invitation. He probably thought the people were Arikara, and he was right to be cautious. Having recently been at Fort Cass, Wyeth, like Maximilian, may have heard about what happened to Johnson Gardner that past winter. Gardner and about twenty men

> *were seated about several fires, the Indians suddenly appeared, addressed them in the Manitari language, surrounded the fire, and dried their shoes. Gardner, being well acquainted with the character of the Indians, immediately took some precautions, which was the more necessary, as a Manitari woman, who was with his party, told him that the strangers were Arikaras.*[42]

Gardner spread the word amongst his men, sending a few trappers into the woods to construct a fortification of tree trunks. Gardner watched his enemy closely, looking for a sign of impending attack. Upon realizing that some of his horses were already missing, Gardner seized two Arikara as hostages, demanding the return of his mounts. Gardner noted that one of them had Hugh Glass's knife and rifle. When the hostages attempted to escape, both were killed and scalped. Gardner put out his campfires and returned to Fort Cass. William Clark was later told that the two Arikara were scalped and burned alive when they could not explain why they had Glass's weapons. Edmund Flagg, a newspaper reporter who in 1836-37 traveled throughout the regions of Missouri and Illinois, related that "not long afterwards Gardiner himself fell into the hands of the Erickeraws, who inflicted upon him the same dreadful death."[43]

In 1824, Hugh Glass had made a similar mistake, with different results, while descending the Platte River. He and four companions beached their bull boat and discovered a large body of Indians whom they mistook for Pawnees but proved to be Arikara. The two nations speak nearly the same language. During a meal, Glass overheard a few words that revealed the truth. Leaning to a comrade, he whispered "'these are Pickarees' – The Chief understanding him, replied, 'No, Pawnees we' – Glass ran & the rest followed him."[44]

A league was a unit of measurement originally intended to represent the distance a person could walk in an hour, typically equal to three miles. Thus, Fort Pierre was another nine miles away.

September 8-9, 1833   *Fort Pierre*

8.   Made by sailing 3 miles and found Fort Piere pleasantly scituated on the right bank   rather low but withall romantic were received with all hospitality imaginable by Mr. Laidlow who is in charge of the Am. F. Co. post here.   was much pleased by the order and regularity apparent about the place   we stopped here for the day and visited Mr. and Mrs. Sublette who is scituated about one mile below   we here saw melons of two kinds   corn   pork   cows   horses and stacks of hay.

9th.   Remained at the fort until about 1 ock. when we made by pulling 2 hours an Island 9 miles below the fort on which the Co. have about 15 acres of ground under cultivation   here I remained all this day eating and drinking of the good things afforded by the earth and the cellars of the Co.   Found cucumbers   water & musk melons   beets   carrots   potatoes   onions   corn and a good cabin and the Company of Mr. Laidlow and Doct.

Two years previous, spring runoff had badly eroded the bank in front of AFC's Fort Tecumseh, across the river from today's Pierre, South Dakota. Recognizing that it would only be a matter of time before the fort was undermined, in the fall of 1831, the company began construction on a new trading post on higher ground two miles upstream. Officially christened Fort Pierre Chouteau after the company's manager, the new post opened for business in July 1832. The stockade walls enclosed over one hundred thousand square feet, making it larger than Fort Union. It was the AFC's primary depot for the Sioux trade.[45]

Map 10 *Fort Pierre to Fort Leavenworth, Missouri River, 1833*

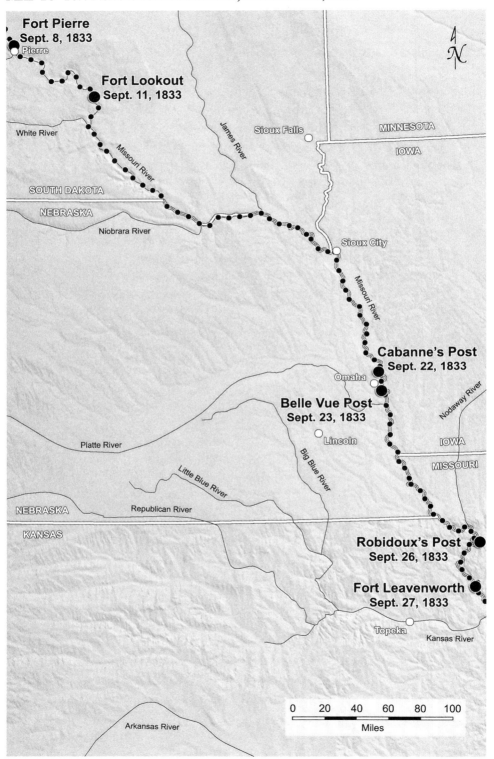

In charge at the post was William Laidlaw, a Scot who had worked with McKenzie and Kipp in the Columbia Fur Company. When that firm merged with the AFC, Laidlaw transferred. He had been at the helm of Fort Tecumseh, overseeing trade downriver as far as the confluence with the Platte. Noted historian Hiram Chittenden described him as one of the "ablest of the fur traders who came to the Missouri."[46]

Wyeth's "Mr. and Mrs. Sublette" was a facetious reference to the string of posts Sublette and Campbell were building along the Missouri River. Earlier that summer of 1833, the partners had installed a trader near the mouth of Bad River, not far from the site of the former Fort Tecumseh, intending to compete with Fort Pierre for the Sioux business.[47] Each of Sublette and Campbell's posts was built practically on top of a neighboring American Fur Company fort.

In the early afternoon of September 9, having spent the night at Fort Pierre, Wyeth floated nine miles down to Farm Island. This was where the gardens for the post were located, planted and tilled in relative safety. The surrounding water helped keep at bay prairie fires and those who might steal the produce.[48] Here, Wyeth found a good cabin and plenty of vegetables. Maximilian, who was showing symptoms of scurvy due to poor diet, described a similar abundance when he stopped at Fort Pierre on his return to St. Louis in April, 1834:

> superior provisions in the fort, which we enjoyed at Mr. Laidlow's table, after having long been deprived of them: one of these luxuries was new wheaten bread, and there were also potatoes, cabbages, carrots, several kinds of preserves and pickles, as well as coffee, sugar, tea &c.[49]

The "good things afforded by ... the cellars of the company" would have pleased Wyeth. He must have gotten along well with Laidlaw in that regard; Larpenteur, the teetotaler, characterized the Fort's chief as an "old tyrant" and one of the "greater drunkards" at Fort Union in the early 1840s.[50] Maximilian even accused the trader of draining his personal barrel of liquor, notwithstanding that "the brandy, had, however, been almost exhausted." To cover his tracks, Laidlaw had filled the prince's keg with water.[51]

Wyeth mentioned an unnamed doctor participating in his revel. Dr. Benjamn Harrison had not remained with Wyeth, but had accompanied

Fitzpatrick when the group split up on the Big Horn. He was now experiencing the life of a Rocky Mountain trapper. More likely, this "Doct." was Dr. Thomas McKenny, son of Indian agent Thomas L. McKenny. Young McKenny was a guest at Fort Pierre that summer, hoping to take a liking to the primitive lifestyle at a trading post and learn the trade. He would travel from Fort Pierre up to Fort Union in company with Kenneth McKenzie in November 1833. Having made that journey with McKenny, McKenzie suspected that the young doctor would "find his own expectations were raised too high," for

> *I fear it is beyond my power to convert him into a good Indian trader ... our trade ... is made up of so many trifling transactions as to disgust all who are not at a comparatively young age initiated into its mysteries ... and the drudgery of an inferior clerk would ill comport with his character ... in his medical capacity such has been hitherto the salubrity of this climate, no one post could furnish him on the average a patient a month: salts, castor oil, & essence of peppermint are our usual specifics and it requires but little skill in administering them: in cases arising from amatory passions the remedies are equally simple.*[52]

September 10, 1833   *Missouri River*

10th.   At 8 ock. began pulling   the water has within two days risen about 2 feet in consequence of the rains which so anoyed me above and the surface of the water is covered with all manner of drift rubbish and the water as muddy as possible.   Wind ahead all day but current much improved   stopped at 6 ock. at the commencement of the great Bend and remained all night.

Wyeth camped near the huge meander called the Great Bend, or Grand Detour, which had been a well-known Missouri River landmark for many years. When the Corps of Discovery arrived at its lower bend on September 19, 1805, Captain Clark dispatched George Drouillard and John Shields across the neck, or "gouge," to hunt while the rest of the party proceeded around the bend. Clark wrote that "We Sent a man to step off the Distance across the gouge. He made it 2000 yds. The distance around is 30 miles."[53]

September 11, 1833   *Fort Lookout*

11th.   Commenced pulling at 1/2 past 6 after having sent a hunter across the foot of the Bend and after 6 hours got past the Bend and found our hunters who had hid themselves in the brush being alarmed by seeing Inds. whom we also saw and gave some ammunition to   took them in and in two hours more came to the agency for the Sioux & Poncas   Mr. Bean agent but not at the post   we found it a miserable concern only three or four men but poorly fed and buildings out of order though new and shabbily built at best   we were hospitably received by the young man in charge.

Like Clark, nearly thirty years earlier, Wyeth sent hunters across the neck to take advantage of the time. In July 1810, naturalist John Bradbury had maximized this stretch of the river in similar fashion by collecting specimens. Bradbury was returning to St. Louis after having briefly accompanied Wilson Price Hunt's westbound Astorians upriver. The naturalist's description captures a bucolic setting:

> *Before we entirely passed the Great Bend ... I determined not to lose this opportunity to add a few species to my collection ... the track of land which is inclosed in the Bend probably contains about forty square miles, nearly level, and the soil excellent. It was at this time covered with fine grass and scattered groves of trees, betwixt which many herds of buffaloes were quietly grazing.*[54]

A few more hours brought the pirogue to the Sioux Agency at Fort Lookout, on the west bank of the river about a dozen miles upstream from modern Chamberlain, South Dakota. Jonathan L. Bean, originally from Pennsylvania, had been appointed Indian sub-agent there in 1827. Bean was not fond of the American Fur Company and the feelings were mutual. Laidlaw was known to complain of "Father Bean's assistance to our opponents."[55] Bean was absent upon Wyeth's arrival.

Maximilian described the agency's buildings as surrounded by high pickets of squared logs, about sixty paces to each of its four sides. The dwellings consisted of three blockhouses and several apartments, all built close to the palisades. He concurred with Wyeth that the agency was "shabbily built." Characteristically close to the fort, a bit to the north, Sublette and Campbell had also built a "dwelling-house, with a store."[56]

September 12-14, 1833   *Missouri River*

12. *Pulled against a severe head wind 9 hours in hopes of finding White River but camped without seeing it   got plenty of good plumbs which were an object to stop for as we are about out of food and the vicinity almost destitute of game.*

13th   *Pulled against a severe head wind 3 1/2 hours   finding we did not make much headway laid by for the day.*

14th.   *Blowing still fresh ahead   we started and made 15 hours night and day continuing until 12 ock at night   it was dark and we were nearly upset by a snag but our fears of starvation impelled us to haste   did not see an animal all day   during the latter part of the night it rained in torrents and wet all our things and persons.*

The White River, named for the water's whitish-gray color due to the eroded sand, clay, and volcanic ash it carried, would have been a significant milepost along the Missouri and an easy target for Wyeth on a typical day of rowing.[57] The pirogue would have drifted past the White River's mouth the morning of September 13.

Rowing and poling for fifteen hours, right up until midnight on September 14, must have exhausted the entire party.

September 15-16, 1833   *Missouri River*

15th.   *Commenced pulling at 7 ock.   Still blowing fresh ahead and raining a little   about 3 ock cleared off and stopped to cook   during meal time killed a fawn which was very good*

> *luck   after supper pulled 5 hours more and found a keel boat*
> *of the Am. F. Co. alongside of which we stopped for the night*
> *in the morning of*
>
> *16th.   Put ahead with a fine wind not having been asked*
> *on board of her and immediately passed the Ponca village*
> *but I believe not in its usual place   saw and delivered a*
> *message to Mr. Sublettes agt. here and gave the Chief some*
> *tobacco.   Made with a wind which as usual soon died away*
> *and pulling 13 hours when we ran on a sand bar and was*
> *unable in the dark to extricate her and slept all night on it   the*
> *musquitoes almost murder us   rained most of the night.*

It appeared as though Wyeth wrote both of these entries on the evening of September 16 if the transcription was correct. Docking alongside an American Fur Company keel boat provided an added measure of safety for a lone pirogue transiting Sioux country, but evidently no socializing occurred. Wyeth had not mentioned an AFC vessel passing him going downstream, therefore this boat was presumably headed to one of the company's upriver posts.

The Ponca were primarily horticulturists who lived in earth-lodge villages but made seasonal hunting trips far out onto the plains. The tribe did not encounter Lewis and Clark in early September 1804 because it was on such an excursion.[58] A Ponca presence this far north was out of the ordinary, as Wyeth pointed out. Traditionally, the Ponca village was located on any of the creeks in the vicinity of the Niobrara River, such as Bazille, L'Eau qui Court, or Ponca creeks.[59] It was not surprising to find that Sublette and Campbell had staffed this region. The message Wyeth delivered was likely to have come from one of the traders at a post he had visited on the way downstream rather than from Sublette or Campbell themselves.

The Missouri River route of the next few days straddled the present states of Nebraska and South Dakota.

September 17, 1833   *Missouri River*

17. Started at 5 ock. Pulled this day 10 hours rained some in the course of the day saw Powquet the first since leaving the states also mulberry trees Bass wood.

Wyeth's "Powquet" (his spelling of the archaic word "Paroquet") is a parakeet, the only truly indigenous species of parrot in the United States. The first reference to a Carolina parakeet (*Conuropsis carolinensis*) west of the Mississippi came from William Clark on June 26, 1804, at the mouth of Kansas River when he wrote, "I observed a great number of *Parrot queets.*" This bird, bright green with a yellow head and about the size of a mourning dove, moved about in flocks numbering into the hundreds.

John Townsend would collect several specimens of Carolina parakeets while accompanying Wyeth in 1834; one of these may still be seen at the United States National Museum in Washington D.C. Townsend noted in his diary that these birds

> *flew around us in flocks, keeping a constant and loud screaming, as though they would chide us for invading their territory; and the splendid green and red of their plumage glancing in the sunshine, as they whirled and circled within a few feet of us, had a most magnificent appearance. They seem entirely unsuspicious of danger, and after being fired at, only huddle closer together, as if to obtain protection from each other, and as their companions are falling around them, they curve down their necks, and look at them fluttering upon the ground, as though perfectly at a loss to account for so unusual an occurrence.*[60]

Townsend proved prescient. The species is now extinct, the last living Carolina parakeet having died in the Cincinnati Zoo in 1918.[61]

September 18-19, 1833   *Missouri River*

18th.   Started early after a rainy night and pulled 10 hours   saw wild Turkeys this evening but killed none   nearly out of all kinds of provisions   saw this day a herd of Elk   tryed hard to get some but failed.

19th.   Made with a strong and fine wind 12 hours and camped without meat   supped on a little flour boiled in water   Saw during the day 3 deer   looked with folly at them and fired two shots and they ran off.

Wyeth never hinted at how much gunpowder and ammunition the men had on board, but they were frequently firing at game, often with no success. Besides suffering hunger, the thought must have crossed Wyeth's mind that he could run out of one of his most important supplies.

The small crew lived off the land but experienced a "feast or famine" existence in an environment that was once game rich. When Lewis and Clark passed through this vicinity in the first five days of September 1804, they reported grouse, ducks, large flocks of geese, turkey, wild goats, deer, "fat" elk, buffalo, beaver, catfish, plums, hackberries and grapes. Thirty years later, Wyeth expressed a distinct lack of food sources.[62]

The prodigious appetites of fur men and their ability to consume massive quantities of food are well known. At Fort Clark, just up the river from Wyeth's current location, game was normally plentiful, yet 25 percent of the journal entries made by head man Francis Chardon over a four-year period reflect his concern about obtaining meat.[63]

Trapper Warren Ferris described how his brigade faced down starvation:

We were consequently reduced to the necessity of living on whatever came to hand. Famished wolves, ravens, magpies, and even raw hide made tender by two days boiling, were greedily devoured. We lived or rather starved in this manner ten or twelve days, daily expecting the arrival of our hunters with meat, but they came not.[64]

As trading posts multiplied along the Missouri River in the three decades after the Corps of Discovery, game dramatically reduced near its banks. Euro-American settlements pushing upriver amplified food competition with Native American villages. Even with provisions from traders and hospitable tribes, Wyeth's food supply dwindled to a pasty gruel.

September 20, 1833   *Missouri River*

20th. Stopped until 1/2 past 6 to hunt   caught one goose which we eat for breakfast   afterward put ashore the hunters for game   they were fortunate enough to kill a fat doe in which we feasted right merryly and having lost so much time we concluded to run until the moon went down altho we were before informed that it was not safe   a few hours we got along well enough but at last went over a snagg with limbs above which taking our mast and the boat swinging broadside she was taking in water at a jolly rate and in a little she would have gone with the suck under the rock   I immediately had the mast cut away just in time to save her   escaped from this I determined to try more   we ran a little and were driven head foremost on a large tree lying across the river   We stopped about midway and lay swinging like a pendulum   with much danger and difficulty we extricated her   not being yet discouraged we ran on but soon were driven into a large drift   we narrowly escaped being carried under and half full of water and our oar broke we made the shore as soon as possible   resolved to run no more nights, after making 10 1/2 hours.

Friday, September 20, 1833, was a day Wyeth would likely remember for a while. Reminiscent of his earlier experience with log rafts, such occasions raise the question of how a slow learner ever survived in the West. Irving elaborated on this scenario, adding that the pirogue

then drove down the stream, but left one of the unlucky half-breeds clinging to the snag, like a monkey to a pole. It was necessary to run in shore, toil up, laboriously, along the eddies and to attain some distance above the snag, when they launched forth again into the stream and floated down with it to his rescue.[65]

September 21, 1833   *Council Bluffs*

21st.   Made 9 hours with a head wind and camped at the old post of Council Bluffs   it is now grown up with high weeds a memento of much money spent to little purpose   it is a beautiful situation   the magazine and three or four chimneys only remain.

The "old post of Council Bluffs" was the 1819-20 winter quarters for the Stephen H. Long Expedition. The specially designed shallow-draft steamboat, *Western Engineer*, was the first steamboat to ascend the Missouri as far as the Council Bluffs. Long's expedition camped here where limestone and timber were readily available for construction of their post. Maximilian saw the ruins on his excursion:

saw the ruins of the former cantonment, or fort, at Council Bluffs ... the barracks formed a quadrangle, with a bastion or blockhouse, in two of the angles. At present there were only the stone chimneys, and, in the centre, a brick storehouse under roof.[66]

The site was in the Ponca Hills about four miles north of present-day Omaha, Nebraska.[67]

September 22, 1833   *Cabanné's Post*

22nd.   After 5 hours in a dead current we arrived at a trading post of the Am. F. Co.   Mr. Josh Pilcher agent by whom we were entertained with the utmost hospitality   I had met Mr. P. at St. Louis on my way out   on this account I had much pleasure in stopping   we found a good assortment of vegetables and a supply of such things as we wanted.   dined with him and made three hours more and stopped to hunt   Killed a fat deer and camped for the night.

Making a short stop at this AFC post, Wyeth and Joshua Pilcher renewed their brief acquaintance from the spring of 1832 when Wyeth's

Pacific Trading Company had first arrived in St. Louis. Pilcher, a Virginian, started in the fur trade as a partner with Manuel Lisa in 1819. He would be named Upper Missouri Indian Agent in 1834 and would succeed William Clark as Superintendent of Indian Affairs in 1838.[68]

Cabanné's Post was built by Jean Pierre Cabanné in the early 1820s for Berthold, Chouteau and Pratte, who later joined the American Fur Company. Pilcher replaced Cabanné a few months before Wyeth arrived, remodeling the post to suit his own tastes.[69] Maximilian also left an account of these white-washed structures:

> *The trading post consists of a row of buildings of various sizes, stores, and the houses of the engages, married to Indian women, among which was that of Mr. Cabanné, which is two stories high ... From the balcony of his house was a fine view over the river ... between the buildings runs a small stream.*[70]

An extensive garden raised corn, potatoes and a variety of other crops, from which Pilcher fed Wyeth and his men an ample meal. Upon departure, the trader supplied them with flour, sugar, pepper and salt from the storeroom.[71]

September 23, 1833   *Belle Vue*

23rd.   Made 2 hours pulling and passed an agency 1/2 mile farther   a trading post of Mess. Dripps & Fontenelle.   Made in all 13 hours and camped   during the day killed one deer from the Boat   from Council Bluffs to this have found the Hicory   Shagbark   Sicamore and Coffee Bean   trees not seen above   also Night Shade Brier.   Ducks   Gese and Pelicans have been very numerous but shy for about 8 days   stopped at the above trading post   found only an old negro at home   the rest out cutting wood.

A few miles downriver was the site of Belle Vue (French for "beautiful view"), a trading post that had been built by the Missouri Fur Company around 1822 for trade with the Omaha, Otoe and Pawnee tribes. When George Catlin and Karl Bodmer painted it, in 1832 and 1833,

Belle Vue on the Missouri River in 1833, engraved by Lucas Weber from a painting by Karl Bodmer. The first permanent community of settlers in Nebraska was established as a fur-trading post in the 1820s, then became the headquarters of John Dougherty's Indian Agency and a post for the American Fur Company. LIBRARY OF CONGRESS

respectively, they referred to it as the agency of Major Dougherty. In 1830 Warren Ferris, like Wyeth, had identified the post as being that of "Messrs. Fontenelle & Drips."[72]

When the steamboat *Yellow Stone* had stopped at Belle Vue on its way upriver in May 1833, Indian Agent John Dougherty disembarked. Maximilian, also on board, mentioned meeting sub-agent R. P. Beauchampe, as well as a blacksmith and some "servants of the company," one of whom may have been the black man Wyeth found.

September 24-26, 1833   *Robidoux's Post*

24th.   Made this day 10 1/2 hours   Killed one goose   saw plenty of deer

25th.   Made 11 hours   Killed one Turkey from the boat   saw this day the first Pawpau fruit and trees   wounded one deer from boat and stopped to search for him but without success

> *26th.   Made 11 hours   at 8 hours came to a trading house of*
> *the Am. F. Co. called Rubideau Fort at the Black Snake hills*
> *and on the N. bank of the river on a little rise of ground in the*
> *rear of a beautiful bottom.   Today saw the Black Locust for*
> *the first time   the lands are here quite fine and the hills as far*
> *back as we can see clothed with timber and verdure of the most*
> *luxuriant appearance   the country is one of the most pleasant I*
> *have ever seen*

After two long yet uneventful days in the Missouri current, Wyeth crossed into modern Kansas, passed the mouth of the Nodaway River, and soon reached the AFC post of Joseph Robidoux on the north bank (east side) of the river. In just a few years, this trade house would become the hub of the present town of St. Joseph, Missouri. The Robidoux name was well represented in the fur trade by a long history of family traders, the founder of this post being the third in a succession of Josephs. Built around 1825, this post was sometimes called the Blacksnake Hills Post. The store operated as an independent outfit after Robidoux bought out the Western Department of the American Fur Company.[73]

September 27, 1833   *Fort Leavenworth*

> *27th.   After 7 hours pulling arrived at the Cantonment*
> *Leavenworth   on the route we saw several Indian canoes with*
> *Squaws children ect.   I had no letters of introduction at the*
> *fort and therefore could not expect any great extension of the*
> *laws of hospitality but was received with all the politeness that*
> *expected   was offered all the stores which I might require by*
> *Leiut. Richardson   the officer of the day.   My boy Baptiste and*
> *the Indian wer vacinated by Doct. Fellows.   It was amusing to*
> *observe the actions of Baptiste and the Indian when I went from*
> *the boat towards the Barracks   the Boy followed me until I was*
> *hailed by the sentry   at view of one so strangely attired and*
> *with a knife on the end of his gun he broke like a quarter Nag*
> *crying Pegoni   and the Indian was only prevented from taking*
> *the run also by being assured that he would not be harmed.   I*

> *took the two to Doct Fellows quarters to be vaccinated   the Docts wife and another lady happened to be present   they were really beautiful women but the eyes of the two were riveted on the White Squaws   Baptiste who speaks a little English told the other Boys when he returned to the boat that he had seen a white squaw white as snow and so pretty.*

Cantonment Leavenworth was established in 1827 by Colonel Henry Leavenworth, Third U.S. Infantry, for whom the post was named. Built on the west side of the Missouri River to protect the Santa Fe Trail, the Army required all boats going upriver into Indian country to stop here for inspection, the primary search being for contraband liquor.[74]

At the post's landing, Wyeth was met by the sentry whose uniform and glittering bayonet unnerved young Baptiste Payette. The youth alerted his small brigade to the presence of what he took to be Peigan Blackfoot, and tried to flee. Once Wyeth reassured both Baptiste and the Nez Perce, they were escorted before First Lieutenant Asa Richardson of Company E, the officer of the day. In November 1833, Richardson would sign as a witness to an Indian Peace Council treaty.[75]

Dr. Benjamin F. Fellowes, assistant surgeon and post medical officer, had been commissioned in March of 1833 and had traveled to Fort Leavenworth on the steamboat *Yellow Stone* along with Maximilian on his May 1833 upriver journey. Fellowes served at the fort for seven years.[76]

Like Maximilian before him, Wyeth was offered whatever supplies he needed, the post quartermaster "taking care, however, to be well paid for them."[77]

September 28, 1833   *Liberty, Missouri*

28th.   Made about 45 miles to Liberty where I found Mr. E. M. Samuel an old acquaintance who received me with all hospitality   supplyed me w[it]h money and all that I wanted.

After a month on the Missouri River, starting from Fort Union, Wyeth had finally reached the bastions of civilization. Once in Liberty, Missouri, Wyeth immediately began writing letters and making plans for his future. One of the first things he did was to inquire with merchant Edward M. Samuel about the possibility of financial support for an expedition the coming spring. Wyeth explained to Samuel his intention of returning "across the mountains to the Columbia." In essence Wyeth recruited an agent to assist him in equipping a second trip West, including "horses harnesses and men." He estimated costs at between "3 to 4000$," a figure which did not appear to keep Samuel from taking on the task.[78]

Wyeth also negotiated a small advance from Samuel so he would have some spending money, and asked Samuel to keep an eye out for Wiggin Abbott, who would be arriving on the *Gallant* with William and Milton Sublette in several weeks. He asked Samuel to supply Abbott with money and clothing, and to pay his travel expenses to Boston. Wyeth left a similar message for Abbott, so the hired man would know who to look up once he got to the settlements.[79]

September 29-30, 1833   *Liberty, Missouri*

29th.   Rained all day   did not start

30.   Went to the landing after breakfast   a boat arrived going to the Garrison and joined her as I shall arrive at St Louis as soon by this means as any other and more comfortably

---

The steamboat *John Nelson* was headed back upriver to Fort Leavenworth, then down again, to St. Louis. This recently-built steamer had been named in honor of Captain John Nelson, the first to pilot a paddle-wheeler up the Missouri, having gone as far as Franklin, Missouri, in 1819.[80] For Wyeth, it would be easier and no more time-consuming to ride the steamboat for its entire loop than to keep going in the pirogue. Thus, on September 30, 1833, Wyeth and his two Indian charges left the dugout behind and boarded the *John Nelson* at Liberty Landing.

September 30, 1833, was Nathaniel Wyeth's final journal entry for his 1832-33 expedition. He made one last notation:

> *Shall close memorandum here with Boat   I after returned to Leavenworth and was treated with great politeness by the officers of the garrison   especially a Capt. Nichols who invited me to dinner.*

Connecticut-born John Nicholls had joined the U.S. Army in 1818 as a cadet in the Military Academy, from which he graduated in 1823. He had been assigned to Fort Atkinson and Jefferson Barracks before fighting in the Black Hawk War of 1832. He may have treated Wyeth with "great politeness," but he was dismissed in May 1835 for "unofficer-like conduct."[81]

Backtracking the fifty river miles from Liberty to Fort Leavenworth aboard the steamboat, Wyeth paid Dr. Fellowes, most likely for vaccinating his two young charges. He had given a draft against Samuel earlier but now had money to pay that medical bill.[82]

The last page of writing in Wyeth's journal was a summation of distances supplied by Francis Ermatinger, probably early in their joint travels. Ermatinger started his tally at Boat Encampment, an important HBC depot on the Columbia at its northernmost bend, at the mouth of the Canoe River. Wyeth probably recorded the mileage in the back of his diary, and Young transcribed the data as the final page of the document:

> *Memo of distances on the Columbia according to the estimates of the English Traders.*
>
> | | From | Boat encampment to Colville | 309 | miles |
> |---|---|---|---|---|
> | | " | Colville to Oakenagen | 150 | " |
> | | " | Oakenagen to Walla Walla | 207 | " |
> | | " | Walla Walla to Vancouver | 203 | " |
> | | " | Vancouver to Cape Disappointment | 80 | " |
> | | | | 949 | " |
>
> *From Ermatinger.*

Thus concludes all that Wyeth wrote in the journal of his first expedition. The next few months are pieced together primarily from letters Wyeth wrote to family members and business associates. The details of Wyeth's return itinerary from St. Louis are not fully known.

From Fort Leavenworth, Wyeth was headed east again onboard the *John Nelson* on or about October 3. The next day, while steaming downstream, Wyeth penned letters to his Boston financiers Tucker and Williams and Henry Hall, and to Frederic Tudor, to inform them all of his anticipated arrival in New England in November. He also sent a message to Samuel regarding a counterfeit note, though the details of that issue were vague.[83]

Aboard the steamboat *John Nelson*, Wyeth retraced the voyage downstream nearly 320 miles, arriving in St. Louis on October 9, 1833.[84] He wasted no time mailing a letter to Milton Sublette, whom he expected to reach St. Louis by early November, reassuring the RMFC partisan that he could depend on the contract they had entered. He left a note at the Towns Hotel informing Sublette that a letter awaited him at the post office. The next day, Wyeth headed on to Louisville, Kentucky.[85]

From Louisville, Wyeth's next destination was Cincinnati, Ohio, where he arrived on October 17. Here, he posted a letter to William Harrison, informing the future president that he had met Harrison's son, Benjamin, in the mountains. Wyeth enclosed a note from son to father that Benjamin had given him on the Big Horn before the younger man had left to trap with Fitzpatrick's brigade.[86]

Four days later, in Baltimore, Maryland, Wyeth inked a letter to HBC Governor George Simpson, pressing him about the proposal he had dispatched from Fort Colvile to London back in March. Wyeth admitted to Simpson that he had arrived in New England too late to proceed to the Columbia District, even by ship, that year. Ignoring Simpson's profound silence on the subject, Wyeth was eager to add a new wrinkle to his proposition. He told Simpson about his contract with the Rocky Mountain Fur Company, and pledged to deliver RMFC's fur to Fort Vancouver or Walla Walla in lieu of the $1000 security in his earlier offer.[87]

Wyeth spent several days in Baltimore. He asked brother Leonard to visit Alfred Seton, one of Bonneville's backers, to see if that businessman would cover a draft for a little over $400. Bank drafts were not like promissory notes but were instructions to a bank authorizing a payment from a person's account – provided funds were available.[88] Wyeth wanted Seton to pay Bonneville's bill. Seton, a former Astorian, was now a prominent insurance man in New York and also owned a fur store.[89] Wyeth sought to collect the cash from his sale of pack animals and tack to Bonneville back on the Green River. He knew that Bonneville's lieutenant Michel Cerré was bringing the party's furs down to St. Louis and would soon make good on any claims.[90]

From Baltimore, Wyeth put his two Native protégés on board the brig *Calo,* along with "one trunk one rifle pair Elk Horns pacage of papers small bundle of cloths." He also mailed a note to uncle Jonas Wyeth requesting all cargo be delivered safely to his house in Cambridge.[91] Scheduled to sail November 1, the *Calo* was a packet ship that cruised regularly between Boston and Baltimore under Captain Franklin Percival of Cape Cod.[92] There is no evidence that Wyeth notified his wife of her approaching guests, Baptiste and the Nez Perce.

Nathaniel Wyeth arrived safely in Cambridge, Massachusetts on November 6, 1833, after more than eighteen months and thousands of miles far outside his comfort zone – and he immediately set about making preparations to go back.

Though Wyeth's initial foray into the Rocky Mountains had cost him, the Boston ice merchant had purchased experience and information. It remained to be seen if he could put all that he had learned to good effect. No doubt Wyeth sorted through his prospects during the lengthy trip home. He had plenty of ideas about how to make a profit from the salmon fishery along the shores of the Columbia River. He had first-hand knowledge of the principal routes, main rivers and their tributaries, and primary trapping grounds in the West. He had picked up new talents, including trapping and the use of bull boats, and had honed the outdoor survival skills he already possessed. In hand, Wyeth had a contract with Rocky Mountain Fur Company to provide trade goods at the 1834 rendezvous, and a pending proposal to partner with the Hudson's Bay Company.

Add to all this his scrutiny of several fur trade forts – some of the most active bastions of trade in the Rockies – plus what he had gleaned from key personnel with the Hudson's Bay Company, American Fur Company, Rocky Mountain Fur Company and independents like Benjamin Bonneville, William Sublette and Robert Campbell. Nathaniel

Wyeth thus occupied a prime position from which to embark on a successful financial endeavor.

History has labeled Wyeth's first expedition a failure. Yet he had trade goods and hides cached at numerous locations throughout the West – enough, if recovered, to pay the expenses of his first excursion. On the down side, he started his journey burdened by a lack of sufficient capital, and had repeatedly lost merchandise, from his abandoned amphibious boats to capsized rafts at river crossings. The wreck of the *Sultana* had left him without replacement supplies at a critical juncture. For a host of reasons, all the members of the Pacific Trading Company had turned their backs on him. Nevertheless, these lessons provided the basis for a better plan in the coming year.

Epilogue

In the summer of 1832, after the battle at Pierre's Hole, the men who broke from the Pacific Trading Company chose to either pursue the fur trade independently or head back home. R. C. Wakefield, William Nudd, and Lane enlisted as trappers with William Sublette for the coming year. These three men stayed in the mountains. John Wyeth, Dr. Jacob Wyeth, Hamilton Law, Theophilus Bache, and Walter Palmer chose to return to the East. As Nathaniel Wyeth was preparing to continue west to the Columbia, the latter five set out from the 1832 Rendezvous with St. Louis-bound William Sublette and his caravan of pelt-laden pack animals.[1] Either Law or Bache may have been known by the nickname "Styles," as this name sometimes appeared in accounts where one or the other did not. Once home, seventeen-year-old John Wyeth would chronicle his entire western journey.

According to the young Wyeth, ten days out of Pierre's Hole, a large body of Blackfoot appeared. Sublette, armed and alert, was freighting his entire stock of furs, worth eighty thousand dollars in St. Louis. The Indians rode up and completely surrounded the fur men. Sublette advanced to the chief, and expressed his hope for peace, at which the Blackfoot replied that peace would cost twenty-five pounds of tobacco. Sublette complied and the Indian army left. Sublette pushed ahead with speed, lest the warriors should repent their bargain.

After this dramatic encounter, "nothing occurred worth relating until we arrived at the town of Independence," about the middle of September.[2] Indeed, compared with the events that would follow, John Wyeth's pack trip with William Sublette would have seemed quite tranquil. The returning PTC members were somewhat familiar with Independence, having passed through on their westbound journey the previous spring. Anxious to keep moving but tired of riding horseback, Dr. Jacob Wyeth, Walter Palmer, Styles, and John Wyeth pooled their money and bought a canoe. The expense left John with only a six-cent piece to get him through St. Louis and home to Boston. As the men prepared to launch into the Missouri River, a thick, obscuring fog rolled in, preventing an early departure. To pass the time, John strolled around Independence and got lost.

Meanwhile, the fog had cleared. John's companions waited for an hour, then pushed off, deserting him. They left word that they would wait for him at the next river town, about twenty miles downstream. John raced along the bank for about five miles but at last decided he would never overtake them on foot. The young man plopped down on the shore in despair. He spied a small skiff complete with oars, and without thinking it through, "jumped into the boat, cast off her painter, and pulled away for dear life down the stream."[3]

The owner of the boat soon discovered John's theft. Grabbing another man, the owner got into a canoe and rowed after the impetuous Wyeth, who had proceeded downriver only a quarter of a mile. John laid into the oars with all his strength, and managed to stay ahead of his pursuers.

John Wyeth reached the settlement with only enough distance between himself and the owner of the boat to allow him to dash into the first barn that he saw. Shortly, the neighbors were alerted and guards placed around the barn. Burrowing into the hay, John managed to elude capture, though more than once he was nearly stepped on. As he lay huddled in the barn, John contemplated his situation. Poverty laws at that time obliged those who could not afford the fines "to atone for their poverty by stripes [i.e., a whipping], ... reckoned to be worth a dollar a stripe in that cheap country."[4]

A few nights later, hunger forced John Wyeth from hiding. He went into the tavern, and found Jacob Wyeth, Palmer, and Styles. He ate supper, then returned to the barn for the night, apparently unable or unwilling to rejoin the others.

The next morning, John returned to the tavern and found himself face-to-face with the boat owner. John was turned over to the constable. While the crowds were standing thick around the bar, however, John crept unobserved out the back door and into a large cornfield, which enabled him to return unseen to the barn, regaining his hideout.

The next morning before dawn, John ventured out again and ran down to the river. Finding yet another boat, he jumped in and paddled across to the opposite bank, confident that authorities would be searching for him "on the right bank of the river, while I marched on the left." He had made his escape.[5]

Near St. Louis by early October, John talked a ferryman into accepting his six-cent piece in lieu of the twelve-cent full fare; at last the youth made it to the city. His companions had arrived the day before "in the steam-boat, like gentlemen, while I, the youngest in the whole Oregon company, like a runaway."[6] Although destitute, John convinced a tavern landlord to let him sleep in the barn.

In his published account, the younger Wyeth plainly expressed his resentment toward the other members of his party:

> Should any one enquire how I came to leave my old companions, and they me, I need only say that I had a very serious quarrel with one of them, even to blows; and with that one too who ought to have been the last to treat me with neglect.[7]

But John Wyeth's struggle to return home, independent of his elder companions, had just begun. It would be nearly three more months before he saw Boston again. Dr. Jacob Wyeth left for New Orleans before John could meet up with him, and Palmer accepted work on a monthly rate aboard a steamboat plying the Missouri between St. Louis and Independence. Styles was not mentioned again. With no one to depend on but himself, the next morning the lone New Englander went in search of work, but nobody would hire him,

> for in truth I was so ragged and dirty, that I had nothing to recommend me; and I suffered more ... during the following six days of my sojourn at St. Louis, than in any part of my route. The steam-boats refused me and ... I was left alone ... without employ, victuals, or decent clothing. I could not bear to go to people's doors to beg; but I went on board steam-boats and begged for food ... My dress was buck-skin moccasins, and pantaloons; the remains of a shirt I put on in the Rocky Mountains, the remnants of a kersey waistcoat which I had worn ever since I left Cambridge, and a hat I had worn all the time from Boston.[8]

At length, John approached Captain Tufts of the steamboat *Constitution* from Charlestown, Massachusetts. He told Tufts who he was, detailed his sufferings, and implored the opportunity to work for passage home. Tufts consented, gave the lad a fresh shirt and pants, and set him toiling as one of twelve firemen who fed the steam boilers.

From St. Louis, the *Constitution* was bound for New Orleans with 240 passengers on board. On the downriver voyage, soon after leaving Natchez, Mississippi, cholera broke out among the travelers, eighty of whom died before reaching New Orleans. On arriving at their destination, Captain Tufts offered Wyeth twenty dollars a month to hire on and return to St. Louis with him. But the younger Wyeth was determined to get home. With cholera raging, he soon secured fulltime work as a grave digger, making two dollars a day.

In the first three days, the twenty-five-man crew dug a separate grave for each person. The men soon found they could not keep up with the bodies brought in. At one point, John counted eighty-seven unburied bodies left on the ground. The next plan was to dig a trench fifty-seven feet long, eight feet wide, and four feet deep, in which they laid the bodies as compactly as possible, filling in vacant spaces with children. John reported as many as three hundred bodies were buried in this trench.

Before long, John himself was attacked with symptoms of yellow fever, including violent pain in his head, back, and stomach. At the time, he was living with a French family. The man of the house,

> *among his various occupations, pretended to skill in physic. He fed*
> *me on castor oil. I took in one day four wine glasses of it, which*
> *required as much resolution as I was master of: but my doctor*
> *assured me that he had repeatedly scared away the yellow fever at the*
> *beginning of it, by large and often repeated doses of that medicine. Its*
> *operation was not one way, but every way. I thought I should have*
> *no insides left to go home with. Yet it is a fact, and I record it with*
> *pleasure, that it carried off all my dreadful symptoms, and in a very*
> *few days, I had nothing to complain of but weakness, which a good*
> *appetite soon cured.*[9]

Sometime around Christmas 1832, John booked passage from New Orleans on the *Henry Thomson,* and arrived in Boston on January 2, 1833, after an absence of ten months. Later that year, with the assistance of Dr. Benjamin Waterhouse, Wyeth released his account of the expedition, severely criticizing his older cousin, Nathaniel. The work's acrimonious tone comes as no surprise, given that Waterhouse considered it a

*sacred cause of humanity ... to disabuse the people of dwelling on
these Atlantic shores respecting the Oregon paradise, lest our farmers'
sons and young mechanics should ... stray from home, and go they
know not whither, – to seek they know not what.*[10]

Dr. Jacob Wyeth returned to Boston without writing publicly about
his adventures, and later relocated to Galena, Illinois. He married and
opened a medical practice. Jacob and Nathaniel corresponded intermit-
tently, but the tension that had developed between them during the
journey created a rift that never closed.[11]

John Ball, who remained in the Pacific Northwest through most of
1833, weathered a mixture of difficulties as well. His farming venture
began to sour during the autumn of that year, about the same time
that Nathaniel Wyeth was navigating the Missouri River to St. Louis.
Ball and fellow farmer John Sinclair, another former PTC member,
both became quite ill. Discouraged, Ball sold what produce he had
gleaned to the staff at Fort Vancouver and was ready to go home. On
September 20, 1833, Ball wrote in his journal,

*I left my farm with something of regret, but on the whole glad,
seeing there was no prospect of any settlers and no society. Sick and
discouraged I started down the river to the falls ... The proceeds
of my farm enabled me to buy my passage in the forecastle of the
brig "Dryad," commanded by Captain Kipling, bound for the
Sandwich Islands.*[12]

Ball and Sinclair boarded HBC's ship, the *Dryad,* at Fort Vancouver and sailed down the Columbia. Two other former members of the
Pacific Trading Company – Stephen Burdett and Whittier – were also
on the ship bound for Hawaii. Wyeth's four former shareholders arrived
at Fort George near the Columbia's mouth on October 6. The following
day, HBC trader Duncan Finlayson and botanist David Douglas, whom
Ball had met during his stay at Fort Vancouver, appeared at the dock to
book passage on the same ship. Apparently happy to see Ball, Finlayson
invited the New Englander to share their more comfortable and spa-
cious cabin for the voyage.

October 14 saw the *Dryad* still anchored in Baker's Bay, waiting to pass the bar of the Columbia whenever the wind and sea swells calmed enough to allow the ship to cross into open seas. Ball was sick with another attack of ague, the chills lasting all day.[13] It was not until four days later that the *Dryad* finally cleared the mouth of the Columbia, sailing for Hawaii via San Francisco. Ball had been confined to his berth for several days, suffering from a combination of seasickness during the tumultuous Columbia bar crossing, and his recurring ague, a symptom of malaria.[14]

On November 4, Ball and his companions sailed into San Francisco Bay. They spent several weeks touring the mission, the presidio and the surrounding countryside, watching the caballeros and generally sampling California life. But they were anxious to get home and had become impatient waiting for the *Dryad* to again set sail. A whaling ship, the *Helvetius*, had entered the bay at the same time as the *Dryad*; Captain George S. Brewster of New London, Connecticut, was now ready to set out for his home port. Rather than suffer more delays with the HBC ship, Sinclair, Whittier and Burdett booked passage with the whaler and sailed off on November 27, leaving Ball in San Francisco. Two days later, the *Dryad* embarked for Hawaii and Ball was again on his way home.[15]

The *Dryad* took three weeks to reach Honolulu, arriving on December 22, 1833. Ball was invited to Christmas dinner by an American merchant named William S. Hinckley. King Kamehameha III and some of his cabinet were present at the banquet as well. While in Hawaii, Ball did some sightseeing, including climbing up the Punch Bowl. He was also pleased to intercept at that port a trunk addressed to him, which had been shipped from Boston and was then on its way to the Columbia River. The chest, one of two Wyeth mentioned in his July 18, 1833, letter to Ball from Rendezvous, contained clothes and miscellaneous items. Ball was especially pleased by its assortment of newspapers, which, though months old, he read avidly.[16] Ball probably never received Wyeth's letter from the Green River.

On January 6, 1834, Ball obtained passage on the whaler *Nautillus*, bound for New Bedford, Massachusetts. He bade farewell to his Hudson's Bay friends and Oahu, but once again, he was soon stricken with seasickness that continued for weeks, leaving him fragile and emaciated. Being onboard a whaler, Ball watched the crew catch half a dozen of the immense mammals, whose rendered blubber topped off the load of oil being taken to New England.[17]

The *Nautillus* stopped in Tahiti for supplies on March 7. While there, Ball visited the site where the *Bounty* had moored to collect breadfruit in 1787. The story of the crew's mutiny, primarily due to the sailors' interest in Tahiti's bounteous beauties, intrigued and amused Ball.[18]

At sea once more, Ball remarked in his journal that he had never seen wind and waves like those the ship met as it rounded Cape Horn. One night, a tremendous wind hit the ship, sweeping away everything on deck, including all but one life boat. Days later, Ball wrote:

> *I was in my berth and the captain in his near by and the ship went down so far and we being on the lee side it rolled us over onto the side of the ship, and while righting the captain sprang and climbed up to get out and ... going on deck the ship's rigging, spars and sails, seemed mostly gone. The main yard snapped in the middle, and these spars and most of the sails overboard.*[19]

The *Nautillus* limped into Rio de Janeiro on June 3. Here, Ball found several United States men-of-war. One of the ships was under the command of Lieutenant David G. Farragut, who would later become well known for saying "Damn the torpedoes!" during the Civil War battle of Mobile Bay in which the Union captured New Orleans. Five days after landing in Rio, Ball transferred to the schooner *Boxer* as Farragut's clerk.[20]

Farragut headed for his home port at the naval base in Hampton Roads, Virginia, where they anchored July 16, 1834. Ball next found passage on a steamer bound for Baltimore. Sailing up Chesapeake Bay and into the Patapsco River, the steamer entered Baltimore Harbor. Here, Ball had finally reached "terra cognita, a place I had often visited before, and which I last left two years and four months ago."

From Baltimore, Ball traveled by railroad to Philadelphia and New York. He expressed amazement that trains now ran from city to city and were driven by locomotives instead of horses – remarkable changes in rail travel since his first experience on the B&O in the spring of 1832 with the newly-formed Pacific Trading Company. Ball went by steamer up to Hudson, New York, then by stagecoach to Lansingburgh. On July 22, 1834, he returned home at last.[21] As will be seen in Volume 2, Wyeth would be deep into his second expedition on this date.

Ball opened a law office in Grand Rapids, Michigan, in 1837 and became a stalwart member of that community, where he spent the rest of his life. He was elected to the state legislature in 1838 and married Mary Webster on New Year's Eve, 1850. John Ball Park and John Ball Zoo, in Grand Rapids, were built on land he donated to that city. He died on February 3, 1884, at the age of 89.[22]

The fate of other members of the Pacific Trading Company can be sketched only in thumbnail form. G. Sargent, who had persevered with Nathaniel Wyeth until Fort Vancouver, then secured employment with Hudson's Bay Company, died in 1836 of "dissipation," implying intemperate living and excessive drinking.[23] Bache, who left Pierre's Hole with John Wyeth, disappeared from the younger Wyeth's account before reaching Independence, Missouri. John reported "We had one man wounded in the thigh by an arrow; he was obliged to ford a river in his hasty retreat, and probably took a chill, which occasioned a mortification, of which he died." This account suggests someone wounded in the mountains but does not relay the timeframe; the man may have been Bache, or John might have been describing Alfred Stephens, the Gantt and Blackwell trapper wounded in Hoback Canyon following the 1832 Rendezvous.[24]

Nathaniel Wyeth's venture brought a fruitful outcome for two members of the Pacific Trading Company, Solomon Smith and Calvin Tibbetts. The men stayed in Oregon and successfully farmed, becoming the first American emigrants to settle permanently in the territory. In that regard, Nathaniel Wyeth had accomplished Hall J. Kelley's original goal of inspiring Americans to start new lives in Oregon country. Smith and Tibbetts became firm friends during their overland journey and were afterward never far apart. Smith took over teaching duties for John Ball in early 1833 and taught for several years. He became romantically involved with Celiast, daughter of Clatsop chieftain Kobaway and then-wife of the Fort Vancouver baker Basile Poirier. Smith married her in 1837. Tibbetts was part of the Willamette Cattle Company, which drove the first cattle from California to Oregon in 1837; he voted for the establishment of provisional government in 1843, and became a

Clatsop County judge two years later.[25] The strong friendship between the two men was sundered by Tibbetts's untimely death in 1849.

By the time Nathaniel Wyeth returned home on November 6, 1833, the Pacific Trading Company was defunct. Wyeth's western adventure, however, continues in Volume Two of this work, with some PTC members from his first expedition, notably Wiggin Abbott, still playing a role. Though he had returned to Cambridge, Wyeth's mind remained focused on profits in the West; just two days after his homecoming, he wrote a multi-page letter to his financiers – a letter that described a business plan reinforced with obstinate hope.

Endnotes

Notes to the Introduction

1   Farnham, *Travels in the Great Western Prairie*, 2:95.

2   A relative value of $542,000 was derived from a calculator that adjusts for changes in the Consumer Price Index between 1832 and 2011, found online at http://www.measuringworth.com/uscompare/relativevalue.php (accessed 5-10-12).

3   Nuttall, "A Catalogue of a Collection of Plants," 5-60.

4   Schoolcraft, *Indian Tribes of the United States*, 1:204-228.

5   Wyeth, "Mr. Wyeth's Memoir," 6-22.

6   Letter, Mary J. Fish to Frederic G. Young, June 20, 1898, Oregon Historical Society, Portland, OR.

7   Young, *Journals of Captain Wyeth,* 155.

8   John Wyeth, "Oregon," 19-106; Ball, *Born to Wander.*

9   Townsend, "Narrative of a Journey," 107-369; Russell, *Journal of a Trapper*; Marsh, *Four Years in the Rockies*; Lee and Frost, *Ten Years in Oregon*; Mudge, *Memoir of Cyrus Shepard.*

10 Anderson, *Journals*; Irving, *Captain Bonneville.*

11 Young, *Journals of Captain Wyeth,* vi.

12 *Boston Evening Transcript*, September 2, 1856.

13 John A. Wyeth, "Nathaniel J. Wyeth and the Struggle for Oregon," *Harper's New Monthly Magazine* 85, no. 510 (November 1892): 835-847; Mary Fish, *Morning Oregonian*, June 30, 1902; Dr. John A. Wyeth to C. J. Brosnan, November 5, 1917, Cornelius J. Brosnan Papers, University of Idaho Library, Special Collections and Archives, Moscow, ID, Manuscript Group 18, Series I.

14 Bancroft, *History of the Northwest Coast*, 2:598.

Notes to Chapter 1: The Early Years

1   Pelletreau, *Historic Homes*, 2:160.

2   Gilman, "Background," 28-29; Michaelis, *N. C. Wyeth*, 6; Paige, *History of Cambridge*, 702.

3   Gilman, "Background," 30.

4   Ibid.

5   Ibid.

6   Ibid.; McFeeters and Zimmerman, "Mount Auburn Cemetery Reception House."

7   Sinclair, *Fresh Pond*, 20; McFeeters and Zimmerman, "Mount Auburn Cemetery Reception House."

8   Michaelis, *N. C. Wyeth,* 6.

9   Paige, *History of Cambridge*, 704; Pelletreau, *Historic Homes*, 2:160.

10 Paige, *History of Cambridge*, 705.

11 Brosnan, *History of the State of Idaho*, 79.

12 Gilman, "Background," 31; Sharples, "Nathaniel Jarvis Wyeth," 36.

13 Sinclair, *Fresh Pond*, 21.

14 Ibid., 22.

15 Gilman, "Background," 30-31; Sinclair, *Fresh Pond*, 30-31.

16 Class of 1829, Commencement. August 26, 1829, reported by May, *Proceedings*, 12-14.

17 Sampson, "Wyeth," 5:381.

18 Paige, *History of Cambridge*, 705; Pelletreau, *Historic Homes*, 160-161.

19 Paige, *History of Cambridge*, 705; Sampson, "Wyeth," 5:381.

20 Gilman, "Background," 32.

21 Sampson, "Wyeth," 5:382-383.

22 Seaburg and Paterson, *The Ice King*, 122.

23 Gilman, "Background," 31.

24 Ibid.

25 Seaburg and Paterson, *The Ice King*, 122.

26 Weightman, *Frozen Water Trade*, 79.

27 Seaburg and Paterson, *The Ice King*, 130.

28 Ibid.

29 Ibid.

30 Ibid., 128-137; Sampson, "Wyeth," 5:382.

31 Seaburg and Paterson, *The Ice King*, 137-138.

32 Ibid., 138.

33 Ibid., 139-143.

Notes to Chapter 2: Oregon Beckons

1 Powell, *Hall J. Kelley*, ix.

2 Powell, "Hall Jackson Kelley," 1:25, 44.

3 For a concise discussion of Joint Occupation and its effects on the fur trade, see Reid, *Contested Empire*, 3-6.

4 Sampson, "Wyeth," 5:383.

5 Seaburg and Paterson, *The Ice King*, 143.

6 John Wyeth, "Oregon," 25.

7 Letter, Nathaniel Wyeth to Hall J. Kelley, August 30, 1831, Young, *Journals of Captain Wyeth*. Letters in the journals are chronological and can easily be located by date rather than page number.

8 Letter, Nathaniel Wyeth to Charles Wyeth, October 5, 1831, Young, *Journals of Captain Wyeth*.

9 Powell, *Hall J. Kelley*, 343.

10 Letter, Nathaniel Wyeth to Jacob Wyeth, October 5, 1831, Young, *Journals of Captain Wyeth*.

11 Powell, *Hall J. Kelley*, xii.

12 Tudor's diary recorded this information on September 19, 1831, and January 6, 1832, as found in Sinclair, *Fresh Pond*, 165n9.

13 Letter, Nathaniel Wyeth to Charles Wyeth, December 4, 1831, Young, *Journals of Captain Wyeth*; Powell, *Hall J. Kelley*, 91, 98.

14 Letter, Nathaniel Wyeth to Jacob Wyeth, December 8, 1831, Young, *Journals of Captain Wyeth*.

15 Ibid., Nathaniel Wyeth to Leonard Wyeth, December 5, 1831.

16   Ibid., Nathaniel Wyeth to Theophilus Bache, January 18, 1832.

17   Ibid.

18   Ibid., Nathaniel Wyeth to Hon. E. Everett, December 19, 1831.

19   Graustein, *Thomas Nuttall, Naturalist*, 238, 278.

20   Letter, Nathaniel Wyeth to Hon. E. Everett, January 6, 1832, Young, *Journals of Captain Wyeth.*

21   Ibid., Nathaniel Wyeth to Solomon K. Livermore, February 6, 1832.

22   Quaife, "Letters of John Ball," 450-451.

23   Letter, Hall J. Kelley to John Ball, November 1, 1831; Letter, Hall J. Kelley to John Ball, February 4, 1832, John Ball Collection #044, Series I Correspondence, Box 9, Folder 246, "H.J. Kelley 1831." Grand Rapids History and Special Collections, Archives, Grand Rapids Public Library, Grand Rapids, Michigan.

24   Ball, *Born to Wander,* 34.

25   Letter, John Ball to T. C. Brinsmade, April 29, 1832, in Quaife, "Letters of John Ball," 452.

26   John Ball, *Born to Wander*, 34.

27   Letter, Nathaniel Wyeth to Solomon K. Livermore, January 3, 1832, Young, *Journals of Captain Wyeth.*

28   Ibid., Nathaniel Wyeth to Leonard Jarvis, February 6, 1832.

29   Seaburg and Paterson, *The Ice King,* 145.

30   Letter, Nathaniel Wyeth to Charles Wyeth, January 23, 1832, Young, *Journals of Captain Wyeth.*

31   Moulton, *Journals of Lewis & Clark*, 2:72.

32   Letter, Nathaniel Wyeth to Solomon K. Livermore, January 23, 1832, Young, *Journals of Captain Wyeth.*

33   Ibid., Nathaniel Wyeth to I. P. Hughes, January 27, 1832.

34   Ibid., Nathaniel Wyeth to Charles Wyeth, December 4, 1831.

35   Ibid., Nathaniel Wyeth to Leonard Wyeth, January 28, 1832.

36   Ibid., Nathaniel Wyeth to Charles Wyeth, January 27, 1832.

37   Ibid., Nathaniel Wyeth to Robert H. Gardner, January 31, 1832.

38   Morrison, "Columbia River Salmon Trade," 115.

39   Mackenzie, *Voyages from Montreal*, 493.

40   Letter, Albert Gallatin to Thomas Jefferson, April 13, 1803, in Jackson, *Letters of the Lewis and Clark Expedition*, 1:32-33. See also, Ronda, "Names of the Nations," 12.

41   Letter, Meriwether Lewis to Thomas Jefferson, September 23, 1806, in Jackson, *Letters of the Lewis and Clark Expedition*, 1:321-322.

42   Letter, John Jacob Astor to DeWitt Clinton, January 25, 1808, Clinton Papers, Columbia University Library as quoted in Phillips, *The Fur Trade*, 2:270.

43   Irving, *Astoria*, 32.

44   A modern treatment of this topic can be found in Ronda, *Astoria & Empire*, 1-64.

45   Pistono, *Nathaniel Jarvis Wyeth*, 9.

46   Letter, Nathaniel Wyeth to Seymour Whiting, February 5, 1832, Young, *Journals of Captain Wyeth.*

47   Ibid., Nathaniel Wyeth to Hall J. Kelley, February 13, 1832.

48   Powell, *Hall J. Kelley*, xiii.

49   See various letters between Wyeth and his benefactors in Young, *Journals of Captain Wyeth,* up to and through March, 1832.

50   Letter, Nathaniel Wyeth to Leonard Wyeth, March 15, 1832, Young, *Journals of Captain Wyeth.*

51   John Wyeth, "Oregon," 31.

52   For more on Ashley, see Clokey, *William H. Ashley.*

53   Ball, *Born to Wander*, 37.

54   Ibid.

55   Ibid., 36-38.

56   Ball, *Born to Wander*, 38.

57   Letter, Nathaniel Wyeth to Leonard Wyeth, March 15, 1832, Young, *Journals of Captain Wyeth.*

58   Victor, "Flotsam and Jetsam," 41.

59   Morrison, "Columbia River Salmon Trade," 116, 132.

60   Letter, Nathaniel Wyeth to Leonard Wyeth, March 15, 1832, Young, *Journals of Captain Wyeth.*

61   Ibid., Nathaniel Wyeth to an unknown addressee, 56. The removal of a leaf from the letter book resulted in a fragmentary portion of correspondence and perhaps the loss of other letters. This letter was written sometime between January 16 and March 12, 1833, likely on the latter of those two dates.

Notes to Chapter 3: Departure for the West

1   A concise biography of what little is known about these men is found in Overmeyer, "Members of First Wyeth Expedition," 95-101.

2   John Wyeth, "Oregon," 31; Overmeyer, "Members of First Wyeth Expedition," 97, 98.

3   Robertson, *Fort Hall*, 71.

4   Letter, John Ball to T. C. Brinsmade, April 29, 1832, in Quaife, "Letters of John Ball," 452; Ball, *Born to Wander*, 38.

5   John Wyeth, "Oregon," 30.

6   Ibid., 33.

7   Ibid.

8   Eliot, "All Aboard the 'Natwyethum'!" 41.

9   John Wyeth, "Oregon," 31.

10   Ibid., 32.

11   Ibid., 31.

12   Ibid., 32.

13   Ibid.

14   Letter, Nathaniel Wyeth to Leonard Jarvis, November 31, 1833, Young, *Journals of Captain Wyeth.*

15   Neil, "Mystery of the Phoenix Buttons," 4-5; Sprague, "The Literature and Locations of the Phoenix Button," 56-77.

16   State Street Trust, *Some Events of Boston*, 9-13.

17   Letter, Nathaniel Wyeth to Hall J. Kelley, March 3, 1832, Young, *Journals of Captain Wyeth.*

18   John Wyeth, "Oregon," 34.

19   Letter, Nathaniel Wyeth to Leonard Jarvis, November 31, 1833, Young, *Journals of Captain Wyeth.*

20 Ibid.

21 Ibid., Nathaniel Wyeth to Leonard Wyeth, March 15, 1832.

22 Ball, "Across the Continent Seventy Years Ago," 84. This article was compiled from the diary Ball kept, whereas his autobiography *Born to Wander* was collected from various diaries he kept throughout his life, as well as letters and stories written from memory. Thus, there are occasional details that differ between the two accounts.

23 The Friday, April 6, 1832, *Rhode-Island American* of Providence, RI, reprinted the article from the Saturday, March 31, 1832, *Frederick Herald.* Online at www.genealogybank.com/gbnk/newspapers (accessed October 11, 2012).

24 Ball, *Born to Wander,* 38.

25 John Wyeth, "Oregon," 35.

26 Ibid., 36.

27 Ibid., 36-37.

28 Ball, "Across the Continent Seventy Years Ago," 84.

29 Letter, Nathaniel Wyeth to Hall J. Kelley, April 8, 1832, Young, *Journals of Captain Wyeth.*

30 Jeffery, *Converting the West,* 27, 64-65.

31 Ball, *Born to Wander,* 39.

32 Ball, "Across the Continent Seventy Years Ago," 84.

33 "Druggist Circular," 621.

34 Ball says it was April 12; Ball, "Across the Continent Seventy Years Ago," 84.

35 John Wyeth, "Oregon," 41.

36 Ibid.,

37 Ibid., 42.

38 Ball, *Born to Wander,* 39.

39 John Wyeth, "Oregon," 45.

40 Ball, *Born to Wander,* 39.

41 Cass, "Abstract of Licenses Issued."

42 Ball, "Across the Continent Seventy Years Ago," 85.

43 Letter, John Ball to Dr. T. C. Brinsmade, April 29, 1832, Quaife, "Letters of John Ball," 452.

44 Ball, *Born to Wander,* 41.

45 John Wyeth, "Oregon," 47.

46 Ibid., 47; Ball, *Born to Wander,* 42; Hafen, *Broken Hand,* 107.

47 Sunder, *Bill Sublette,* 103-104.

48 Letter, Nathaniel Wyeth to Leonard Jarvis, November 31, 1833, Young, *Journals of Captain Wyeth.*

49 Letter, William Sublette to William Ashley, May 12, 1832, Sublette County Fur Trade Papers, #2010.551.0094, Museum of the Mountain Man, Pinedale, WY.

50 Letter, Nathaniel Wyeth to Leonard Jarvis, November 31, 1833, Young, *Journals of Captain Wyeth.*

51 Ibid., Nathaniel Wyeth to John G. Palfrey, December 13, 1847.

52 Ibid.

53 John Wyeth, "Oregon," 48.

54 Letter, Nathaniel Wyeth to Leonard Jarvis, November 31, 1833, Young, *Journals of Captain Wyeth.*

55   Porter and Romig, "The Prairie Branch," 19.

56   Ball, *Born to Wander*, 43.

57   Skinner, "Sweet Encounters," 50-55.

58   Ball, *Born to Wander*, 49.

59   Letter, Nathaniel Wyeth to Leonard Jarvis, November 31, 1833, Young, *Journals of Captain Wyeth*.

60   Ball "Across the Continent Seventy Years Ago," 87.

61   Hansen, "A Tragedy of the Oregon Trail," 17:113.

62   Goetzman, *Exploration and Empire*, 147-150.

63   Williams, "Wheels to Rendezvous," 108-125. Bonneville's adventures were put to paper in Irving, *Captain Bonneville*.

64   Urbanek, *Wyoming Place Names*, 151.

Notes to Chapter 4: Westward to the Continental Divide

1   Ball, *Born to Wander*, 43-44; Ball, "Across the Continent Seventy Years Ago," 86.

2   Ball, "Across the Continent Seventy Years Ago," 86.

3   Letter, Henry Harmon Spalding to Brother Leavitt, July 11, 1836, in Drury, *Henry Harmon Spalding*, 137.

4   John Wyeth, "Oregon," 51;

5   Blevins, *Dictionary of the American West*, 213; Larpenteur, *Forty Years a Fur Trader*, 21.

6   John Wyeth, "Oregon," 50.

7   Ball, *Born to Wander*, 44.

8   Ibid.

9   Ibid.

10   John Wyeth, "Oregon," 50.

11   Ruxton, *Life in the Far West*, 98.

12   Sage, *Rocky Mountain Life*, 187.

13   Ibid., 347.

14   Ball, *Born to Wander*, 44.

15   Ibid.

16   John Wyeth, "Oregon," 52.

17   Anderson, *Journals*, 102.

18   Bonney and Bonney, *Guide to the Wyoming Mountains*, 343.

19   Robert Campbell to Hugh Campbell, July 18, 1832, in Campbell, *Rocky Mountain Letters*, 8.

20   Urbanek, *Wyoming Place Names*, 125.

21   Ball, *Born to Wander*, 45.

22   Leonard, *Narrative*, 12-13, 45-46. These events are summarized in Carter, "John Gantt," 5:104-107. The events of Fitzpatrick's perilous ride are chronicled in Hafen, *Broken Hand*, 106-120.

23   Ball, *Born to Wander*, 45.

24   John Wyeth, "Oregon," 53.

25   Ibid., 52.

26   Ball, *Born to Wander*, 45.

27 Jackson and Spence, *The Expeditions of John Charles Fremont,* 1:239.

28 Urbanek, *Wyoming Place Names,* 204.

29 Urbanek, *Wyoming Place Names,* 107; Ferris, *Life in the Rocky Mountains,* 109-110; Anderson, *Journals,* 119-120; John Wyeth, "Oregon," 53; Ball, *Born to Wander,* 46.

30 John Wyeth, "Oregon," 53.

31 Ibid., 54-56.

32 Ibid., 53.

33 Rocky Mountain Fur Company Account, William Sublette Papers, B. 1/f. 5, January - July 1832, Missouri History Museum, St. Louis, MO.

34 John Wyeth, "Oregon," 56.

35 Ibid., 54, 56.

36 John Wyeth, "Oregon," 58; Ball, "Across the Continent Seventy Years Ago," 89.

37 Ball, *Born to Wander,* 46.

38 John Wyeth, "Oregon," 56-58.

39 Ibid., 58.

40 William L. Sublette to William H. Ashley, September 21, 1832, Sublette Family Papers, Missouri History Museum, St. Louis, MO, as quoted in Sunder, *Bill Sublette,* 106-107.

41 Ball, *Born to Wander,* 47.

42 Nathaniel Wyeth to Charles Wyeth, July 14, 1832, in a private collection; Nathaniel Wyeth to Elizabeth Wyeth, July 14, 1832, Sublette County Fur Trade Papers #2010.551.0096, Museum of the Mountain Man, Pinedale, WY.

43 Telephone and e-mail correspondence between Terry Brockie, Gros Ventre historian, and the author, Sept. 2009. Information here and in the next two paragraphs appeared originally in Hardee, *Pierre's Hole,* 187, 325n2.

44 Chittenden, *History of the American Fur Trade,* 2:851-853.

45 Wishart, *Encyclopedia of the Great Plains Indians,* 76.

46 Lowie, *Indians of the Plains,* 7.

47 Letter, John Ball to Benjamin Silliman, November 7, 1834, in Ball, *Born to Wander,* 47, 152. This lengthy letter was printed in *The American Journal of Science and Arts,* 25 (January 1834) and is reproduced in the appendix of Ball, *Born to Wander,* 151-156.

48 Ball, "Across the Continent Seventy Years Ago," 90.

49 For the geology of the Tetons, see Fryxell, *The Tetons.*

50 Negretti and Zambra, *A Treatise on Meteorological Instruments,* 94-99.

51 Ball, *Born to Wander,* 47.

52 Hunt, *Overland Diary,* 32.

53 Ferris, *Life in the Rocky Mountains,* 225.

54 John Wyeth, "Oregon," 59-60.

55 Ibid., 59.

Notes to Chapter 5: Rendezvous at Pierre's Hole

1   Merrill J. Mattes, *Jackson Hole*, 16.

2   John Wyeth, "Oregon," 60.

3   Ibid., 61.

4   Ibid., 62.

5   Peterson, *Edible Wild Plants*, 164.

5   Ball, "Across the Continent Seventy Years Ago," 90.

6   Much has been written about the fur trade rendezvous. A thorough examination of the 1832 event in Pierre's Hole is found in Hardee, *Pierre's Hole!*, which contains all known primary accounts of this rendezvous. For an overall view of these summer trade fairs, see Gowans, *Rocky Mountain Rendezvous*.

7   Primary accounts from John Ball, John Wyeth, Warren Ferris, Zenas Leonard, Joseph Meek, Robert Newell, and George Nidever will be used only to frame and clarify Wyeth's viewpoint, which is the focus of this book. Washington Irving's account, based on Benjamin Bonneville's diaries, is also referenced, although Bonneville did not attend the 1832 rendezvous.

8   John Wyeth, "Oregon," 64.

9   Ball, *Born to Wander*, 48.

10   Letter, John Ball to Nathaniel Ball, July 13, 1832, in Quaife, "Letters of John Ball," 457.

11   John Wyeth, "Oregon," 64-66.

12   Ibid., 67.

13   John Wyeth, "Oregon," 72-73; Overmeyer, "Members of the First Wyeth Expedition," 95-101.

14   Ball, *Born to Wander*, 48.

15   Ibid., 49.

16   Robert Campbell's letter to Hugh Campbell is reproduced in Hardee, *Pierre's Hole*, 203-208.

17   Letter, Nathaniel Wyeth to Leonard Wyeth, July 19, 1832, Sublette County Fur Trade Papers #2010.550.0007, Museum of the Mountain Man, Pinedale, WY.

18   Primary accounts of the battle come from John Ball, Benjamin Bonneville, Robert Campbell, Warren Ferris, Zenas Leonard, Joseph Meek, Robert Newell, George Nidever, Samuel Parker, Louis Rivet, William Sublette, John Wyeth and Nathaniel Wyeth. All thirteen accounts are compiled and thoroughly analyzed in Hardee, *Pierre's Hole*, 187-284.

19   Ball, *Born to Wander*, 50.

20   Ibid.

21   Reid et al., "Another Roll of the Dice."

22   Victor, *The River of the West*, 115.

23   Ball, *Born to Wander*, 50.

24   John Wyeth, "Oregon," 71, 72.

25   Irving identifies this man as Joseph More. Washington Irving, *Captain Bonneville*, 65.

26   John Wyeth, "Oregon," 73-74.

Notes to Chapter 6: Crossing the Snake River Plain

1   Ball, *Born to Wander*, 52.

2   Russell, *Journal of a Trapper*, 40.

3   Boone, *Idaho Place Names*, 132.

4   Ball, "Across the Continent Seventy Years Ago," 93.

5   Boone, *Idaho Place Names*, 163.

6   Russell, *Journal of a Trapper*, 14, 40, 96, 109-110, 112, 158n39; Ferris, *Life in the Rocky Mountains*, 157, 159, 160, 187n5, 194, 214, 251n3, 263.

7   Ball, *Born to Wander*, 50.

8   Ibid., 52.

9   Russell, *Journal of a Trapper*, 109.

10   Dary, *The Buffalo Book*, 6-7, 44-50.

11   Irving, *Captain Bonneville*, 361-362.

12   Correspondence with Dr. Kenneth Zontek. See also Lott, *American Bison*, 67-68.

13   Kurz, *On the Upper Missouri*, 126-127.

14   Russell, *Journal of a Trapper*, 109-110, 140-141.

15   Ball, *Born to Wander, 51.*

16   Ibid., 51.

17   Ibid., 50.

18   Russell, *Firearms, Traps and Tools*, 145-156.

19   Gowans, *Rocky Mountain Rendezvous*, 78.

20   Ball, *Born to Wander*, 52.

21   Boone, *Idaho Place Names*, 37.

22   Ball, *Born to Wander,* 51.

23   Ball, "Across the Continent Seventy Years Ago," 93.

24   Ogden, *1824-26 Journals*, 228n1; Ferris, *Life in the Rocky Mountains*, 208.

25   Ball, "Across the Continent Seventy Years Ago," 93.

26   Wyeth, "Indian Tribes of the South Pass," 210.

27   Nidever, *Life and Adventures*, 30.

28   Ball, *Born to Wander*, 52.

29   Ball, "Across the Continent Seventy Years Ago," 93.

30   Hunt, *Overland Diary*, 37; Irving, *Astoria*, 275.

31   Stuart, *Robert Stuart's Narratives*, 116.

32   Palmer, "Journal of Travels," 30, 90n68.

33   Boone, *Idaho Place Names*, 7.

34   Irving, *Captain Bonneville,* 220.

35   Boone, *Idaho Place Names*, 69.

36   Ferris, *Life in the Rocky Mountains*, 135; Russell, *Journal of a Trapper,* 93.

37   Lee, "The Diary of Reverend Jason Lee," 244.

38   Ogden, *1824-26 Journals*, 356.

39   Stuart, *Robert Stuart's Narratives*, 115.

40   Irving, *Captain Bonneville*, 220.

41   Work, *Snake Country Expedition of 1830-1831*, 106.

42   Miller, "The Yankee Pedlar," 85-92.

43   Wyeth, "Indian Tribes of the South Pass," 210.

44   Ferris, *Life in the Rocky Mountains*, 345; Ogden, *1824-26 Journals*, 42.

45   Victor, *River of the West*, 121.

46   Ibid., 120.

47   Work, *Snake Country Expedition of 1830-1831*, 105.

48   Ball, "Across the Continent Seventy Years Ago," 94.

49   Ogden, *1824-26 Journals*, 164; Boone, *Idaho Place Names,* 158.

50   A concise discussion of trappers in the City of Rocks/Goose Creek region may be found in "Exploration of City of Rocks," 189.

51   Reid, *Contested Empire*, 42-43.

52   Ball, *Born to Wander*, vii, 156.

53   For a concise discussion of the Shoshone name, see Hardee, *Pierre's Hole*, 15-16.

54   Ball, "Across the Continent Seventy Years Ago," 94.

55   Madsen, *The Northern Shoshoni,* 18.

56   Ball, "Across the Continent Seventy Years Ago," 94.

57   In the few edits Young provided in the original publication, he indicated Wyeth's dates were off from August 17 until September 4. No confusion is apparent in the entries of August 17-22, though Wyeth does appear to lose his bearing again at the first of September; the initial entry for the month is dated the 2nd.

58   Conrad, *Uncle Dick Wooten*, 55-56.

59   Ogden, *1824-26 Journals*, 168-67; Morgan, *Jedediah Smith*, 186, 410n19.

60   Wyeth, "Indian Tribes of the South Pass," 206.

61   "The Oregon History Project." See also Smoak, *Ghost Dances and Identity*, 16.

62   Russell, *Journal of a Trapper*, 144; Ferris, *Life in the Rocky Mountains*, 171; Irving, *Captain Bonneville*, 224-228, 283, 352.

63   Trenholm and Carley, *The Shoshonis*, 5, 7, 15, 17-40, 113, 204.

64   Wyeth, "Indian Tribes of the South Pass," 213.

65   Ibid., 207.

66   Ball, *Born to Wander*, 152-153.

67   Ibid., 52. In this same passage, Ball mentions that "the sixteen free trappers left us on the Humboldt," which, in addition to his August 28 date, must be in error since the party had not reached that river.

68   Victor, *River of the West*, 119.

69   Ball, "Across the Continent Seventy Years Ago," 95.

70   Wyeth, "Indian Tribes of the South Pass," 210.

71   Victor, *River of the West*, 122.

72   Wyeth, "Mr. Wyeth's Memoir," 14.

73   Ball, *Born to Wander*, 53.

74   Ibid., 153.

75   Ibid.

76   Moulton, *Journals of Lewis & Clark*, 5:81.

77   Ball, *Born to Wander*, 52.

78   Idaho State Department of Fish and Game, "Idaho Record Fish – Other Species."

Notes to Chapter 7: On the Columbia

1   Nevada State Library and Archives web site, search term "Jarbidge." Article by Guy Rocha, "Myth 52, There is No Bridge in Jarbidge."

2   Lysne, *Freshwater Mollusks*, 37, 38.

3   Woodward, *Jarbidge Resource Management Plan*, 75, 76.

4   Ball, *Born to Wander*, 53.

5   Ibid.

6   Boone, *Idaho Place Names*, 51, 52; "Exploration of the Bruneau Country," Idaho State Historical Society, 1.

7   Stuart, *Robert Stuart's Narratives,* 107, 117.

8   Ogden, *1824-26 Journals*, 133, 168, 170, 171, 173, 174, 175. The Kittson map showing the route of Ogden's Snake Country Expedition is contained in the end pocket of that volume. Work, *Snake Country Expedition of 1830-1831*, 118.

9   Wheat, *Mapping the Transmississippi West*, 2:158, 159; Irving, *The Rocky Mountains*.

10   Davidson, et al., *Bruneau Subbasin Summary*, 13, 54.

11   Ball, *Born to Wander,* 53.

12   Wyeth, "Indian Tribes of the South Pass," 209.

13   Ball, *Born to Wander*, 53.

14   The Engages, "Fish Hooks," 9.

15   Wyeth, "Indian Tribes of the South Pass," 212.

16   Hoffman, "Poisoned Arrows," 70.

17   Ibid.

18   Russell, *Journal of a Trapper*, 144.

19   Moulton, *Journals of Lewis & Clark*, 8:14, 17.

20   Irving, *Captain Bonneville*, 260.

21   Ryser, *Birds of the Great Basin*, 345.

22   Wyeth, "Indian Tribes of the South Pass," 210.

23   Boone, *Idaho Place Names,* 186.

24   Tekiela, *Birds of Idaho*, 47.

25   Wyeth, "Indian Tribes of the South Pass," 216.

26   Ibid., 215.

27   Ibid., 206.

28   Ibid., 374-375.

29   Ronayne, Patla, and Saxton, *Idaho's Amphibians and Reptiles*, 8.

30   Ball, *Born to Wander*, 54.

31   Ibid.

32   Stuart, *Robert Stuart's Narratives*, 107.

33   Madsen, *The Northern Shoshoni*, 13, 18-19; Hodge, *Indians North of Mexico*, 1:168.

34   Wyeth, "Indian Tribes of the South Pass," 213.

35   Frazer, *Amateur Rodmaking*, 129.

36   Ball, *Born to Wander*, 54.

37   Wyeth, "Indian Tribes of the South Pass," 213.

38   Ball, "Across the Continent Seventy Years Ago," 95.

39   Stuart, *Robert Stuart's Narratives,* 86. Rollins has combined information from two Stuart sources, his published narrative and his field notes, or "traveling memoranda." The portion of this quote contained within brackets is from the field notes.

40   Boone, *Idaho Place Names,* 343.

41   Jones, "Utter Party Massacre," 1. For the complete emigrant diary see Judson, *Diary of 1862.*

42   Ogden, *1827-29 Journals,* 26, 27.

43   Letter, Henry Harmon Spalding to Brother Leavitt, July 11, 1836, found in Drury, *Henry Harmon Spalding,* 137.

44   Hunter, *Encyclopaedic Dictionary,* 6:387.

45   Wyeth, "Indian Tribes of the South Pass," 214.

46   Stuart, *Robert Stuart's Narratives,* 85, 103. Rollins referred to the sand flies as midges.

47   Information regarding salt grass may be obtained on the United States Forest Service web page, found online at: http://www.fs.fed.us/database/feis/plants/graminoid/disspi/all.html (accessed 10-9-11).

48   Timbrook, *Chumash Ethnobotany,* 77.

49   Sage, *Rocky Mountain Life,* 148.

50   Hipol, "Hawaiians in the American Fur Trade," 77, 80-81.

51   Hanson, "Fur Trade Fishhooks," 4, 8; discussion with Paul W. Jones, owner/operator of Historic Angling Enterprises, Arp, TX.

52   Moulton, "Memorandum by Clark of a baling invoice of sundries, being necessary for Stores" found in the Lewis and Clark Journals, online version, located at http://lewisandclarkjournals.unl.edu/read/?_xmlsrc=1804-1805.winter.part6&_xslsrc=LCstyles.xsl (accessed 10-9-11).

53   Ball, *Born to Wander,* 54.

54   Ibid., 44; Ball, "Across the Continent Seventy Years Ago," 86.

55   Work, *Snake Country Expedition of 1830-1831,* 109.

56   Ogden, *1824-26 Journals,* 128.

57   Holman, "History of the Counties of Oregon," 61.

58   Wheat, *Mapping the Transmississippi West,* 2:155-158.

59   Boone, *Idaho Place Names,* 289; Holmes, "Francois Payette," 6:328, 331.

60   Ball, *Born to Wander,* 55.

61   Victor, *River of the West,* 119-121.

62   Boone, *Idaho Place Names,* 43.

63   Victor, *River of the West,* 129.

64   Hunt, *Overland Diary,* 51.

65   Stuart, *Robert Stuart's Narratives,* 80, 96.

66   Fremont, *Report of the Exploring Expedition -1843-1844,* 174.

67   McArthur, *Oregon Geographic Names,* 68.

68   For Hunt, see Irving, *Astoria,* 365; for Stuart, see Stuart, *Robert Stuart's Narratives,* 79, 95n83; for Ogden, see Ogden, *1824-26 Journals,* 92-93.

69   Work, *Snake Country Expedition of 1830-1831,* 9-11.

70   Thompson, "Journal of David Thompson," 56.

71   Cox, *The Columbia River,* 87.

72   Work, *Snake Country Expedition of 1830-1831,* 3-10.

73   Youngblood et al., *Old-growth Ponderosa Pine Forests.*

74   Ball, "Across the Continent Seventy Years Ago," 96.

75   Irving, *Astoria*, 307; Stuart, *Robert Stuart's Narratives,*79.

76   Irving, *Astoria*, 307.

77   Ogden, *1827-28 Journals*, 7.

78   McArthur, *Oregon Geographic Names,* 285.

79   Stuart, *Robert Stuart's Narratives*, 76.

80   Ogden, *1827-28 Journals*, 5.

81   Irving, *Captain Bonneville,* 244; Holman, "History of the Counties of Oregon," 59; McArthur, *Oregon Geographic Names,* 270-271; Baird, *In Nez Perce Country,* 74n3.

82   Ball, "Across the Continent Seventy Years Ago," 96.

83   Ball, *Born to Wander*, 55; Ball, "Across the Continent Seventy Years Ago," 96.

84   Moulton, *Journals of Lewis & Clark*, 5:222.

85   Fremont, *Report of the Exploring Expedition – 1842*, 180.

86   McArthur, *Oregon Geographic Names*, 364.

87   Moulton, *Journals of Lewis & Clark*, 7:173,177n1.

88   Ross, *Fur Hunters*, 126; Stuart, *Robert Stuart's Narratives*, 61, 73n87, 303.

89   Ball, "Across the Continent Seventy Years Ago," 96; Ball, *Born to Wander*, 55.

90   McArthur, *Oregon Geographic Names*, 373.

91   Moulton, *Journals of Lewis & Clark*, 6:454, 468.

92   Stuart, *Robert Stuart's Narratives*, 61-62.

93   Ross, *Fur Hunters*, 120.

94   Ball, "Across the Continent Seventy Years Ago," 97.

95   Drury, *First White Women Over the Rockies*, 94-95.

96   Holmes, "Pierre Chrysologue Pambrun," 3:239- 247. The entire Character Book may be found in Williams, "The 'Character Book' of George Simpson," 151-236.

97   Merk, *Fur Trade and Empire*, 54-55.

98   Losey, *Let Them Be Remembered*, 466-473.

99   Ibid.

100   Irving, *Captain Bonneville*, 261.

101   Losey, *Let Them Be Remembered*, 471.

102   Ball, "Across the Continent Seventy Years Ago," 96; Ball, *Born to Wander*, 55.

103   Ball, "Across the Continent Seventy Years Ago," 153.

104   Ball, *Born to Wander*, 55.

105   Ball, "Across the Continent Seventy Years Ago," 97; Ball, *Born to Wander*, 55.

106   Ibid.

107   Gibson, *Lifeline of the Oregon Country*, 101-104. For a discussion of York boats, see Johnson, *York Boats.*

108   Gibson, *Lifeline of the Oregon Country*, 102-103.

109   Franchére, *Adventure at Astoria*, 108.

110   Ball, "Across the Continent Seventy Years Ago," 97.

111 Ibid.

112 Grauer, *Mount Hood*, 9.

113 Moulton, *Journals of Lewis & Clark*, 5:301n9.

114 Ball, "Across the Continent Seventy Years Ago," 97-98; Ball, *Born to Wander*, 57.

115 Nelson, *Pelicans, Cormorants and Their Relatives*, 162–163.

116 Ammer, *Dictionary of Clichés*, 221.

117 Patton, *Lewis & Clark, Doctors in the Wilderness*, 52-53.

118 Moulton, *Journals of Lewis & Clark*, 5:311.

119 Ball, *Born to Wander*, 59.

120 Irving, *Astoria*, 138-139; McArthur, *Oregon Geographic Names*, 327. For a full account of Day's experience, see Ross, *Adventures of the First Settlers*, 204-208.

121 Moulton, *Journals of Lewis & Clark*, 1: Atlas Map 77; Ogden, *1824-26 Journals*, 98.

122 Wilkes, *Exploring Expedition*, 4:349.

123 Gibson, *Lifeline of the Oregon Country*, 125-126.

124 Moulton, *Journals of Lewis & Clark*, 5:322.

125 Stuart, *Robert Stuart's Narratives*, 64-66.

126 Grose, *Dictionary of the Vulgar Tongue*, 278.

127 Moulton, *Journals of Lewis & Clark*, 5:320-328; Hunt, *Overland Diary*, 57; Stuart, *Robert Stuart's Narratives*, 54; Elliott, "The Journal of John Work," (1915), 29.

128 Gibson, *Lifeline of the Oregon Country*, 125-126.

129 Franchére, *Adventure at Astoria*, 125.

130 Ball, *Born to Wander*, 57.

131 Gibson, *Lifeline of the Oregon Country*, 126.

132 Douglas, *Journals of David Douglas*, 1:41.

133 Gibson, *Lifeline of the Oregon Country*, 126.

134 Ross, *Adventures of the First Settlers*, 129.

135 Boyd, *People of the Dalles*, 85.

136 Parker, *Journal of an Exploring Tour*, 132, 209, 307.

137 Townsend, "Narrative of a Journey," 346.

138 Galbraith, *The Hudson's Bay Company as an Imperial Factor*, 100; McLoughlin, *Letters of John McLoughlin*, 57, 62, 89, 92, 298; Boyd, *People of the Dalles*, 14.

139 Irving, *Astoria*, 99-100; Franchére, *Adventure at Astoria*, 47-48; Ross, *Adventures of the First Settlers*, 113-114.

140 Moulton, *Journals of Lewis & Clark*, 5:349, 352, 353n5.

141 Wright, "Economic Development and Native American Women in the Early Nineteenth Century," 525-536.

142 Cox, *The Columbia River*, 79.

143 Ball, *Born to Wander*, 57.

144 Ruby and Brown, *The Chinook Indians*, 185-200.

145 Moulton, *Journals of Lewis & Clark*, 7:39; Bright, *Native American Place Names*, 550.

146 Cox, *The Columbia River*, 77.

147 Ross, *Adventures of the First Settlers*, 119.

148 Ball, "Across the Continent Seventy Years Ago," 98.

149 McLoughlin, *Letters of John McLoughlin*, 260, 285.

150 Ball, *Born to Wander*, 59.

151 Hipol, "Hawaiians in the Fur Trade," 75.

152 Ball, "Across the Continent Seventy Years Ago," 98; Irving, *Astoria*, 236-237; Jones, *Annals of Astoria*, 94n29, 228; Ronda, *Astoria & Empire*, 120.

Notes to Chapter 8: Fort Vancouver

1 Hussey, *History of Fort Vancouver*, 1.

2 Robertson, *Competitive Struggle*, 241-242.

3 Ball, "Across the Continent Seventy Years Ago," 98.

4 Much has been written about Chief Factor McLoughlin. For a concise biography, see Holmes, "John McLoughlin," 8:235-245. For more in-depth works, see Holman, *Dr. John McLoughlin, the Father of Oregon* or Morrison, *Outpost, John McLoughlin and the Far Northwest*.

5 Letter, John McLoughlin to the Governor, Deputy Governor and Committee, Honorable Hudson's Bay Company, October 29, 1832, found in McLoughlin, *Letters of John McLoughlin*, 108-109.

6 Ball, "Across the Continent Seventy Years Ago," 98.

7 Letter, John McLoughlin to the Governor, Deputy Governor and Committee, Honorable Hudson's Bay Company, October 28, 1832, found in McLoughlin, *Letters of John McLoughlin*, 100-106.

8 For Archibald McDonald, see Lewis, "Archibald McDonald," 93-102; for Thomas McKay, see Bird, *Thomas McKay*. George Allan is much more elusive. He left a collection of letters from the 1860s and wrote a few articles that have been published. Of these, Allan, "Reminiscences of Fort Vancouver," 75-80, is most useful. For the story of the *Tonquin*, see Franchére, *Adventure at Astoria*.

9 Letter, John McLoughlin to the Governor, Deputy Governor and Committee, Honorable Hudson's Bay Company, October 28, 1832, found in McLoughlin, *Letters of John McLoughlin*, 100-106.

10 Erigero, *Fort Vancouver, Cultural Landscape Report*.

11 John Ball, "John Ball's 3rd Letter," *Zion's Herald*, January 6, 1834.

12 Allan, "Reminiscences of Fort Vancouver," 75.

13 Erigero, *Fort Vancouver, Cultural Landscape Report*.

14 Letter, John McLoughlin to the Governor, Deputy Governor and Committee, Honorable Hudson's Bay Company, June 16, 1832, found in McLoughlin, *Letters of John McLoughlin*, 98-100.

15 "Certificate of the Vancouver," in Barker, *Letters of John McLoughlin*, 112.

16 Letter, John McLoughlin to the Governor, Deputy Governor and Committee, Honorable Hudson's Bay Company, October 28, 1832, found in McLoughlin, *Letters of John McLoughlin*, 100-106.

17 McArthur, *Oregon Geographic Names*, 433-434, 654-655; Clark, *History of the Willamette Valley*, 28-29.

18 Letter, John McLoughlin to the Governor, Deputy Governor and Committee, Honorable Hudson's Bay Company, November 16, 1836, found in McLoughlin, *Letters of John McLoughlin*, 165-178.

19   Ibid.

20   Munnick, "Etienne Lucier," 6:253-254; Dobbs, *Men of Champoeg*, 15-16.

21   Powell, *Hall J. Kelley*, 99.

22   Holman, *Dr. John McLoughlin, the Father of Oregon*, 101-114.

23   Ball, "Across the Continent Seventy Years Ago," 99.

24   Moulton, *Journals of Lewis & Clark*, 6:267.

25   Woodger and Toropov, *Encyclopedia of Lewis and Clark*, 355.

26   McArthur, *Oregon Geographic Names*, 605-606, 673.

27   Ibid., 673.

28   Ball, "Across the Continent Seventy Years Ago," 102.

29   Ball, *Born to Wander*, 60.

30   Moulton, *Journals of Lewis & Clark*, 6:262-272.

31   Ibid., 6:41-42.

32   Bancroft, *History of the Northwest Coast*, 2:276n10.

33   Ball, "Across the Continent Seventy Years Ago," 99.

34   Ibid., 99-100.

35   Montgomery, *The White-Headed Eagle*, 161-162.

36   Gray, *Life and Letters of Mrs. Jason Lee*, 153.

37   Ball, "Across the Continent Seventy Years Ago," 100, 103.

38   Letter, Nathaniel Wyeth to Jacob Wyeth, March 18, 1834, Young, *Journals of Captain Wyeth*.

39   Letter, John McLoughlin to John McLeod, from Fort Vancouver, March 1, 1833, in Dye, "Documents," 167-168.

40   Victor, "Flotsam and Jetsam," 36-54.

41   Ibid., 42-52. The information in the next several paragraphs is a condensed version of Lemont's remarkable tale of survival.

42   *Niles Weekly Register*, September 15, 1832, 42.

43   Letters, Nathaniel Wyeth to William H. Boardman, July 4, 1833, Nathaniel Wyeth to Joseph Baker & Son, July 4, 1833, in Young, *Journals of Captain Wyeth*.

44   Bancroft, *History of the Northwest Coast*, 2:566-567.

45   Letter, Nathaniel Wyeth to "Parents," January 16, 1833, Young, *Journals of Captain Wyeth*.

46   Crampton, "The San Buenaventura – Mythical River of the West," 163-171.

47   Clark, *History of the Willamette Valley*, 280-281.

48   Kenneth L. Holmes, "Joseph Gervais," 7:131-145

49   Ball, "Across the Continent Seventy Years Ago," 100.

50   Bird, *Thomas McKay*, 12; Holmes, "James Douglas," 9:142; Morrison, *Outpost, John McLoughlin and the Far Northwest*, 236; Barker, *Letters of John McLoughlin*, 315; and Lavender, "Thomas McKay," 6:273.

51   Montgomery, *The White-Headed Eagle*, 177.

Notes for Chapter 9: A New Year and the Return East

1   Wyeth, "Mr. Wyeth's Memoir," 7.

2   Parker, *Journal of an Exploring Tour*, 179.

3   Moulton, *Journals of Lewis & Clark*, 10:207.

4   Parker, *Journal of an Exploring Tour*, 179-180.

5   Jones, *Annals of Astoria*, 58, 131.

6   Allan, "Reminiscences of Fort Vancouver," 79. See also Danisi, *The Truth about Meriwether Lewis*, 179-185.

7   McLoughlin, *Letters of John McLoughlin*, 100, 100n4.

8   Parker, *Journal of an Exploring Tour*, 147.

9   Ibid., 151-152.

10   *Dictionary of Canadian Biography Online*, "Sir James Douglas" and "Duncan Finlayson."

11   United States Department of the Interior, Bureau of Reclamation, "Report on Proposed Columbia River Project" (Denver, 1932), 1719.

12   Letter, Nathaniel Wyeth, probably to Frederick Tudor, undated, in Young, *Journals of Captain Wyeth*. According to editor Young, the letter opens without date or superscription. The letters in the letter book are numbered sequentially and the letter before this was written at Cincinnati, Ohio. It appears as if the letter book was not used again until Fort Vancouver. The words "Probably to F. Tudor, Esq." are written on the page in Wyeth's hand. The next five letters are dated January 16, 1833, so it is likely this undated letter was written between January 14 and 16, probably the latter.

13   Munnick, "The Ermatinger Brothers," 8:157-173; see also McDonald, *Letters of Francis Ermatinger*.

14   Carter, "William H. Vanderburgh," 7:315-320; also, Phillips, "William Henry Vanderburgh: Fur Trader," 377-394. The idea of Ermatinger's possible trespass on American soil is explored in McDonald, *Letters of Francis Ermatinger*, 164n35.

15   Ibid. See also, Victor, *River of the West*; 130-132; Ferris, *Life in the Rocky Mountains*, 242-243.

16   Letter, Nathaniel Wyeth, probably to Frederick Tudor, undated, in Young, *Journals of Captain Wyeth*. Wyeth used similar wording in all five of the letters he wrote on January 16, 1833. Also see Nathaniel Wyeth to Leonard Jarvis, January 16, 1833, and Nathaniel Wyeth to Mess. Tucker & Williams, January 16, 1833, in Young, *Journals of Captain Wyeth*.

17   Ball, *Born to Wander*, 61; Ball, "Across the Continent Seventy Years Ago," 101.

18   Letters, Nathaniel Wyeth, to "Parents," January 16, 1833, Nathaniel Wyeth to Leonard Wyeth, January 16, 1833, in Young, *Journals of Captain Wyeth*.

19   Ibid., Nathaniel Wyeth to Charles Wyeth, January 16, 1833.

20   Ibid., Nathaniel Wyeth to Leonard Jarvis, January 16, 1833, Nathaniel Wyeth to Charles Wyeth, January 16, 1833.

21   Ibid., Nathaniel Wyeth, probably to Frederick Tudor, undated.

22   English, *Dictionary of Canadian Biography Online*, "David Douglas."

23   Bancroft, *California Pioneer Register*, 388; Nisbet, *The Collector*, 201.

24   Letter, John Jacob Astor to Thomas Jefferson, March 14, 1812, in Porter, *John Jacob Astor*, 1:508-09.

25   Mackie, *Trading Beyond the Mountains*, 127-131; British Columbia Geographical Names, online.

26   *Dictionary of Canadian Biography Online*, "Donald Manson"; Munnick, "Donald Manson," 7:217-225; Mackie, *Trading Beyond the Mountains*, 132.

27 Letter, George Simpson to John McLoughlin, July 10, 1826, in Merk, *Fur Trade and Empire*, xxiii.

28 McArthur, *Oregon Geographic Names*, 617.

29 McArthur, *Oregon Geographic Names*, 344; Bright, *Native American Placenames*, 228.

30 Nunis, "Michel Laframboise," 5:145-178. For information on Laframboise and his exploits in California, see Dillon, *Siskiyou Trail*.

31 Moulton, *Journals of Lewis & Clark*, 2:511-512.

32 Barry, "Astorians Who Became Permanent Settlers," 288-290.

33 Morgan, *Jedediah Smith*, 256-79.

34 Letter, John McLoughlin to John McLeod, from Fort Vancouver, March 1, 1833, in Dye, "Documents,"167-168.

35 Gibson, *Lifeline of the Oregon Country*, 157, provides a chart of departure dates for the inbound brigades for most of the years 1825-47.

36 McDonald, *Letters of Francis Ermatinger*, 166.

37 Gibson, *Lifeline of the Oregon Country*, 5, 79.

38 Cox, *The Columbia River*, 269.

39 Fremont, *Narrative of the Exploring Expedition to the Rockies*, 174.

40 Ball, "Across the Continent Seventy Years Ago," 100; Overmeyer, "Members of the First Wyeth Expedition," 98-101.

41 Moulton, *Journals of Lewis & Clark*, 6:8.

42 Clemans, "The Dalles Dam Visitor Center to Host Eagle Watch."

43 Moulton, *Journals of Lewis & Clark*, 5:362, 7:78.

44 Ross, *Adventures of the First Settlers*, 117; Parker, *Journal of an Exploring Tour*, 136-137.

45 Rowlett, *How Many?*, 305.

46 Ross, *Adventures of the First Settlers*, 121.

47 Ibid.; James P. Ronda, *Lewis and Clark Among the Indians*, 215-217.

48 Macdonell, "The Diary of John Macdonell," 77.

49 McGillivray, *Journal of Duncan McGillivray*, lii.

50 Moulton, *Journals of Lewis & Clark*, 5:356.

51 McArthur, *Oregon Geographic Names*, 668.

52 Stuart, *Robert Stuart's Narratives*, 55, 67n31.

53 Moulton, *Journals of Lewis & Clark*, 6:72.

54 Kane, "Wanderings of an Artist," 92; Russell, "Duncan McDougall," 5:223-224.

55 Kane, "Wanderings of an Artist," 91-92; and Baker, "Chinook Leader Buried in Hudson's Bay Co. Cemetery."

56 Gibson, *Lifeline of the Oregon Country*, 160.

57 Work, "The Journal of John Work, 1826," 30.

58 Simpson, *An Overland Journey Around the World*, 102.

59 Bagley, *Early Catholic Missions*, 1:40.

60 McArthur, *Oregon Geographic Names*, 182.

61 Wislizenus, *A Journey to the Rocky Mountains*, 19.

62 Moulton, *Journals of Lewis & Clark*, 5:265.

63 Ibid., 7:180.

64 Lewis and Meyers, "John Work's Journal," 111.

65   Douglas, *Journal Kept by David Douglas*, 188.

66   Kane, "Wanderings of an Artist," 114.

67   Ermatinger, "Edward Ermatinger's York Factory Express Journal," 72.

68   Work, "The Journal of John Work," (1915), 30; Work, *The Journal of John Work* (1923), 74.

69   Meany, "Washington Geographic Names," (October 1917): 287.

70   Wilkes, *Narrative*, 4:388, 390.

71   Cox, *The Columbia River*, 86.

72   Ibid.

73   Merk, *Fur Trade and Empire*, 128.

74   Losey, *Let Them Be Remembered*, 468-469; Merk, *Fur Trade and Empire*, 54; and Stern, *Chiefs & Chief Traders*, 144.

75   Stern, *Chiefs & Chief Traders*, 151.

76   Ibid., 145. Several examples of horse trades were recorded by McGillivray and are included in Stern's book.

77   Ibid.

78   Moulton, *Journals of Lewis & Clark*, 7:187-205.

79   Aoki, *Nez Perce Dictionary*, 803.

80   Wyeth's report of covering 22.5 miles is incorrect if this itinerary is on course. He has occasionally hedged an estimate and has certainly done so here, with "say four miles." The original journal would need to be examined to confirm whether it was transcribed correctly.

81   Moulton, *Journals of Lewis & Clark*, 5:268; Irving, *Astoria*, 433-434; Ross, *Adventures of the First Settlers*, 226; Work, "*The Journal of John Work*," (1914): 88; and Kane, *Wanderings of an Artist*, 114-115.

82   Durham, *History of the City of Spokane*, 1:629.

83   Hardee, *Pierre's Hole*, 11.

84   McCaslin, "Little Known Lyons Ferry Played Historic Role Here," 3.

85   Mullan, *Report on the Construction of a Military Road*, 29.

86   Stelling and Tucker, *Floods, Faults and Fire*, 238.

87   Moulton, *Journals of Lewis & Clark*, 5:268-275, 9:238, 11:354.

88   Josephy, *The Nez Perce Indians*, 74.

89   Lyman, "The Holocene History of Pronghorn," 104.

90   Robertson, *Competitive Struggle*, 99.

91   Merk, *Fur Trade and Empire*, 134, 139.

92   Weaver, "A Study of the Vegetation of Southeastern Washington and Adjacent Idaho," 11.

93   Meany, *Washington Geographic Names*, (October 1917): 292.

94   Moulton, *Journals of Lewis & Clark*, 6:480; White, *David Thompson's Journals*, 186, 196; Cox, *The Columbia River*, 91; and Ruby and Brown, *The Spokane Indians*, 8. See also, Meany, *Washington Geographic Names*, 212-213.

95   Boone, *Idaho Place Names*, 85; Cox, *The Columbia River*, 262.

96   Losey, *Let Them Be Remembered*, 426-433.

97   Additional information regarding Spokane House is available on the Friends of Spokane House website, found online at http://www.friendsofspokanehouse.com (accessed 12-09-11).

98   McDonald, *Letters of Francis Ermatinger*, 166.

99   McLoughlin, *Letters of John McLoughlin*, xcix; Williams, "Character Book," 194-195.

100   McDonald, *Letters of Francis Ermatinger*, 156.

101   Letter, Nathaniel Wyeth to John McLoughlin, March 12, 1833, Young, *Journals of Captain Wyeth*.

102   The "two foregoing letters" refers to the one written to George Simpson, the second to John McLoughlin. In the letter book, there is a leaf missing between letter LXXI and LXXII, resulting in both of those letters being fragmentary. LXXI contains the addressee; however, LXXII begins in midsentence. Based on the wording in that letter, it is clear that Wyeth sent a copy of his proposal to McLoughlin.

103   Letter, Nathaniel Wyeth to George Simpson, March 12, 1833, Young, *Journals of Captain Wyeth*.

104   Sunder, *Joshua Pilcher*, 70. Pilcher's original letter to Simpson has not been found in the HBC archives, thus the plan is inferred by Sunder based on Simpson's response.

105   Merk, *Fur Trade and Empire*, 307-308.

106   McLoughlin, *Letters of John McLoughlin*, lxxvi-lxxvii.

107   Merk, *Fur Trade and Empire*, 317-318.

108   Pistono, *Nathaniel Jarvis Wyeth*, 35-36.

109   Walker, "Warren Ferris, the Hudson's Bay Company and the Rendezvous of 1834," 80-107.

110   Letter, John McLoughlin to John McLeod, from Fort Vancouver, March 1, 1833, in Dye, "Documents,"167-168.

111   Ball, "Across the Continent Seventy Years Ago," 103.

112   Ball, *Born to Wander*, 61.

113   Ibid.

114   Durham, *History of the City of Spokane*, 53; Meany, *Washington Geographic Names*, 118. Some sources indicate the lake was named for Etienne Eduard Laliberte. Durham said Louis Laliberte was probably the ancestor of the Liberty family, thus both sources are potentially correct.

115   Cox, *The Columbia River*, 215.

116   E-mail correspondence with Northern Idaho archeologist Kathryn Arneson (12-12-11). Arneson, who works frequently in this area, reported running into similar problems when walking transects by compass, forcing her to turn to more expensive GPS units which compensate for these anomalies. Even the GPS sometimes had difficulty in V-shaped ravines lined with talus. Also, E-mail correspondence with Russ Burmester, Geology Department, Western Washington University, Bellingham, Washington (12-15-11).

117   Moulton, *Journals of Lewis & Clark*, 1:10-11, 2:26, 7:216.

118   Cox, *The Columbia River*, 274.

119   Boone, *Idaho Place Names*, 291; Coues, *New Light on the Early History of the Greater Northwest*, 2:711.

Notes to Chapter 10: The Road to the Buffalo

1   Moulton, *Journals of Lewis & Clark*, 8:85; Nisbet, *Sources of the River*, 144; Haywood, *Sometimes Only Horses to Eat*, 113.

2   Point, *Wilderness Kingdom*, 43.

3   Ferris, *Life in the Rocky Mountains*, 316-317.

4   Nisbet, *Sources of the River*, 144; Robertson, *Competitive Struggle*, 141; Conley, *Idaho for the Curious*, 581-582; Work Progress Administration, *Idaho, a Guide in Word and Picture*, 231.

5   Boone, *Idaho Place Names*, 80.

6   Cox, *The Columbia River*, 110.

7   Teit, "The Salishan Tribes," 295; Ferris, *Life in the Rocky Mountains*, 162.

8   Geranios, "Small Submarines Test Silent, Test Deep in Mysterious Idaho Lake," *Los Angeles Times*, August 23, 1998.

9   Gunter, "Wasunka: The Mother of Twins," *Bonner County Daily Bee*, March 5, 2011.

10   Wickstrom and Barco, *Albeni Falls Dam Flexible Winter Power Operation*.

11   Stewart, *Cedar: Tree of Life*, 21-26.

12   Idaho State Department of Fish and Game, "Idaho Record Fish – Trout Family."

13   Robertson, *Competitive Struggle*, 108, 110. See also Archives of Manitoba, "Flathead Post Report"; Morgan, *Jedediah Smith*, 133.

14   Gray, *Journey East*, 24. For more on the locations of Flathead Post, see Smith, "The Location of Flathead Post," 47-54.

15   Moulton, *Journals of Lewis & Clark*, 9:98; Munnick, "Francois Rivet," 7:237-240.

16   Barker, *Letters of John McLoughlin*, 263-264.

17   Ferris, *Life in the Rocky Mountains*, 332n34; Walker, "Warren Ferris, the Hudson's Bay Company and the Rendezvous of 1834," 88-91.

18   Moulton, *Journals of Lewis & Clark*, 6:313.

19   De Smet, *Life, Letters and Travels*, 3:991.

20   Johnson, *Flathead and Kootenay*, 199.

21   Ewers, *The Blackfeet*, 128.

22   Irving, *Captain Bonneville*, 100-101.

23   Ferris, *Life in the Rocky Mountains*, 181.

24   Nisbet, *Sources of the River*, 151; White, *David Thompson's Journals*, cxlii.

25   For example, see White, *David Thompson's Journals*, 49; Elliott, "The Journal of John Work," 42; Mullan, *Report on the Construction of a Military Road*, 148.

26   Mullan, *Report on the Construction of a Military Road*, 148.

27   De Smet, *Life, Letters and Travels*, 1:348.

28   Johnson, *Flathead and Kootenay*, 157.

29   Ewers, *The Horse in Blackfoot Indian Culture*, 174; Teit, "The Salishan Tribes," 127-128, 361-365.

30   White, *David Thompson's Journals*, 50.

31   Ferris, *Life in the Rocky Mountains*, 303.

32   De Smet, *Life, Letters and Travels*, 1:347.

33   Ewers, *The Horse in Blackfoot Indian Culture*, 172.

34   Woody, "A Sketch of the Early History of Western Montana," 95.

35   Ogden, *1824-26 Journals*, 9, 211.

36   Ferris, *Life in the Rocky Mountains*, 247.

37   Wyeth, "Indian Tribes of the South Pass," 208.

38   Cox, *The Columbia River*, 84-85; Watson, *Lives Lived West of the Divide*, 2:548; McDonald, *Letters of Francis Ermatinger*, 116.

39   Ferris, *Life in the Rocky Mountains*, 303.

40 Work, *The Journal of John Work*, 64n136. In the index to Ferris's book, editor Leroy Hafen lists "Wild Horse Creek see Jocko" and "Jocko (Wild Horse) Creek," Ferris, *Life in the Rocky Mountains*, 437, 443.

41 Salish-Pend d'Oreille Culture Committee, *The Salish People*, 41.

42 Watson, *Lives Lived West of the Divide*, 1:289; Stone, *Following Old Trails*, 27-30.

43 Clark, *Indian Tales from the Northern Rockies*, 89-90.

44 Salish-Pend d'Oreille Culture Committee, *The Salish People*, 61.

45 Moulton, *Journals of Lewis & Clark*, 5:193-201, 8:65-83.

46 Ferris, *Life in the Rocky Mountains*, 161.

47 Moulton, *Journals of Lewis & Clark*, 5:79; Gray, *Journey East*, 30.

48 Nuttall, "A Catalogue of a Collection," 213; Ross, *Fur Hunters*, 213.

49 Hart, *Montana Native Plants*, 96-97.

50 Moulton, *Journals of Lewis & Clark*, 5:143.

51 Ibid., 5:246.

52 Newell, *Robert Newell's Memoranda*, 33.

53 Schoolcraft, *Historical and Statistical Information*, 204-228.

54 Ferris, *Life in the Rocky Mountains*, 166-168; Teit, "The Salishan Tribes," 260-261.

55 Ferris, *Life in the Rocky Mountains*, 162.

56 Cox, *The Columbia River*, 135.

57 Merriam, *Ethnomusicology of the Flathead Indians*, 114-115.

58 Wyeth, "Indian Tribes of the South Pass," 213.

59 Cox, *The Columbia River*, 135.

60 De Smet, *Life, Letters and Travels*, 3:1012.

61 Featherman, *Social History of the Races*, 365.

62 Russell, *Journal of a Trapper*, 148. For a discussion of various menses-related taboos, see Niethammer, *Daughters of the Earth*, 37-55.

63 Moulton, *Journals of Lewis & Clark*, 7:206.

64 Ferris, *Life in the Rocky Mountains*, 332n32.

65 Salish-Pend d'Oreille Culture Committee, *The Salish People*, 63-65.

66 Spier, *The Prophet Dance*, 20.

67 Teit, "The Salishan Tribes," 152, 376.

68 Birdsall, "The Second Great Awakening," 345-364.

69 Letter, Nathaniel Wyeth to Perry Clark, written from the brig *Ida* in early March 1832, Young, *Journals of Captain Wyeth*.

70 Ibid.

71 Moulton, *Journals of Lewis & Clark*, 5:185-186.

72 Salish-Pend d'Oreille Culture Committee, *The Salish People*, 66.

73 Ferris, *Life in the Rocky Mountains*, 182, 402, 403-404, 410, 412, 413, 418-419; Gray, *Journey East*, 30.

74 Aarstad, et. al., *Montana Place Names*, 244.

75 Lieber, *A Popular Dictionary of Arts*, 5:383.

76 Ferris, *Life in the Rocky Mountains*, 403.

77 Irving, *Captain Bonneville*, 343-344.

78   Josephy, *The Nez Perce Indians* 124; Ewers, "Iroquois Indians in the Far West," 7-8.

79   Moulton, *Journals of Lewis & Clark*, 5:26-27; Zwickel and Schroeder, "Grouse of the Lewis and Clark Expedition," 5-6.

80   Salish-Pend d'Oreille Culture Committee, *The Salish People,* 71.

81   Ferris, *Life in the Rocky Mountains*, 301-302.

82   Ross, *The Fur Hunters*, 217.

83   Clark, *Indian Legends*, 78-79.

84   Ross, *The Fur Hunters*, 218.

85   Moulton, *Journals of Lewis & Clark*, 5:189.

86   Ross, *The Fur Hunters*, 225.

87   Salish-Pend d'Oreille Culture Committee, *The Salish People,* 35, 76.

88   Teit, "The Salishan Tribes," 90, 92, 482. See also, Kuhnlein and Turner, *Traditional Plant Foods*.

89   Josephy, *The Nez Perce Indians*, 577-589.

90   Ross, *The Fur Hunters*, 234.

91   Salish-Pend d'Oreille Culture Committee, *The Salish People*, 78; Moulton, *Journals of Lewis & Clark*, 5:54.

92   Merriam, *Ethnomusicology of the Flathead Indians*, 117.

93   Teit, "The Salishan Tribes," 58.

94   Holman, *Dr. John McLoughlin,* 31-32.

95   Barker, *Letters of John McLoughlin*, 112, 290-291.

96   Grose, *Dictionary of the Vulgar Tongue,* 365, 368; Bartlett, *Glossary of Words and Phrases*, 246.

97   Maximilian, "Travels in the Interior of North America," 23:42. For more information on temporary brush shelters, see Ewers, "The Blackfoot War Lodge," 182-192.

98   Teit, "The Salishan Tribes," 88-89, 432; Kuhnlein and Turner, *Traditional Plant Foods*.

99   Nuttall, "Catalog of a Collection of Plants," 27.

100   Grose, *Dictionary of the Vulgar Tongue*, 44.

101   Ferris, *Life in the Rocky Mountains*, 287-288.

102   Anderson, *Journals*, 132-133. A short biography of Insula may be found in this same source, 329-333.

103   Ibid., 134-135.

104   Ibid., 333-334.

105   Work, *Journal of John Work,* 143.

106   Ferris, *Life in the Rocky Mountains*, 169, 188n14, 257.

107   Anderson, *Journals*, 255; Irving, *Captain Bonneville*, 132, 138, 145-146. Irving's editor, Edgeley Todd, identified this clerk as E. Hodgkiss.

108   Irving, *Captain Bonneville,* 140-141.

109   Ewers, "The Blackfoot War Lodge," 185.

110   Ross, *Fur Hunters*, 248.

111   Haines, "Antoine Godin," 2:175-178.

112   Boone, *Idaho Place Names*, 227-228.

113   Ferris, *Life in the Rocky Mountains*, 200.

114 For a discussion of the confusion between the Buttes and the modern Tetons, see Hardee, *Pierre's Hole*, 10-14.

115 Irving, *Astoria*, 257.

116 *Commercial Atlas of America – Idaho*, 482-483. This map can be found online at http://www.davidrumsey.com (accessed 1-7-12).

117 Holmes, "Francois Payette," 6:325-352.

118 Hanson, "Michel Sylvestre Cerré," 8:61-67; Irving, *Captain Bonneville*, 17, 79.

119 Johnson, *Flathead and Kootenay*, 96.

120 Sage, *Rocky Mountain Life*, 153.

121 Irving, *Captain Bonneville*, 277.

122 Teit, "The Salishan Tribes," 354.

123 Ferris, *Life in the Rocky Mountains*, 217.

124 Ibid., 113.

125 Letter, Nathaniel Wyeth to Captain Bonneville, June 22, 1833, Young, *Journals of Captain Wyeth*.

126 Ibid., Nathaniel Wyeth to Joseph Baker & Sons, July 4, 1833.

127 DeVoto, *Across the Wide Missouri*, 108.

128 Pistono, *Nathaniel Jarvis Wyeth*, 38.

129 Letters, Nathaniel Wyeth to Tucker & Williams and Henry Hall, July 4, 1833, Nathaniel Wyeth to Leonard Jarvis, July 4, 1833, in Young, *Journals of Captain Wyeth*.

130 Ibid., Nathaniel Wyeth to John McLoughlin, July 5, 1833.

131 Moulton, *Journals of Lewis & Clark*, 10:231.

132 Aarstad, et. al. *Montana Place Names* 265-266; John Willard, *Adventure Trails in Montana*, 10, 52; for variants of Madison River, see Library of Congress web page, found online at http://id.loc.gov/authorities/subjects/sh86003620.html (accessed 1-8-12).

133 Urbanek, *Wyoming Place Names*, 92. There are many variants of the spelling of Sisk-a-dee.

134 Letters, Nathaniel Wyeth to Joseph Baker & Son, July 4, 1833, Nathaniel Wyeth to William H. Boardman, July 4, 1833, Nathaniel Wyeth to Frederic Tudor, July 4, 1833, Nathaniel Wyeth to Mess. Tucker & Williams and Henry Hall, Esq., July 4, 1833, Nathaniel Wyeth to Leonard Wyeth, July 4, 1833, Nathaniel Wyeth to Charles Wyeth, July 4, 1833, Nathaniel Wyeth to Leonard Jarvis, July 4, 1833, and Nathaniel Wyeth to Thomas Nuttall, July 4, 1833, in Young, *Journals of Captain Wyeth*.

135 Ibid., Nathaniel Wyeth to John McLoughlin, July 5, 1833.

136 DeVoto, *Across the Wide Missouri*, 108.

137 Irving, *Captain Bonneville*, xx, 53.

138 Ibid., 142-143.

139 DeVoto, *Across the Wide Missouri*, 94.

140 McDonald, *Letters of Francis Ermatinger*, 168.

141 Letter, Nathaniel Wyeth to Francis Ermatinger, July 18, 1833, Young, *Journals of Captain Wyeth*.

142 Irving, *Captain Bonneville*, 144-145.

143 Ibid.

144 McLoughlin, *Letters of John McLoughlin III*, 270.

145 Irving, *Captain Bonneville*, 145-146.

146 Ibid., 146.

147 Ferris, *Life in the Rocky Mountains*, 218, 227, 289-290, 326.

148 Clements, "Andrew Henry," 6:173-184.

149 Leonard, *Narrative*, 19-20.

150 Irving, *Captain Bonneville*, 148.

151 Boone, *Idaho Place Names*, 251.

152 Ibid., 65.

153 Larpenteur, *Forty Years a Fur Trader*, 32.

154 This and the following three paragraphs appeared previously in Hardee, *Pierre's Hole*, 272-273.

155 Irving, *Captain Bonneville*, 65.

156 John Wyeth, *Oregon*, 73-74.

157 Ferris, *Life in the Rocky Mountains*, 223.

158 Ibid., 224-225.

159 Ibid., 226.

160 Irving, *Captain Bonneville*, 77.

161 Mattes, *Jackson Hole, Crossroads*, 14.

162 Urbanek, *Wyoming Place Names*, 227.

Notes to Chapter 11: Rendezvous at Green River, 1833

1 Irving, *Captain Bonneville*, 149.

2 Eddins, "Was Fort Bonneville Simply Nonsense?" 21-33.

3 Williams, "Wheels to Rendezvous," 115.

4 Walker, "Joseph R. Walker," 5:361-380.

5 Munnick, "Jean Baptiste Gervais," 7:122-129.

6 Nester, *From Mountain Man to Millionaire*, 72. Nester likely referred to information provided in Fayell, *Narrative of Colonel Robert Campbell*, 44-45.

7 For the death of Nudd, see letters, Nathaniel Wyeth to Francis Ermatinger, July 18, 1833, and Nathaniel Wyeth to Jacob Wyeth, November 10, 1833, in *Young, Journals of Captain Wyeth*.

8 Porter and Davenport, *Scotsman in Buckskin*, 49.

9 Gowans, *Rocky Mountain Rendezvous*, 80-81.

10 Irving, *Captain Bonneville*, 154n1; Ferris, *Life in the Rocky Mountains*, 274.

11 Gowans, *Rocky Mountain Rendezvous*, 89.

12 De Voto, *Across the Wide Missouri*, 97.

13 Larpenteur, *Original Journal*, 5; Fayell, *Narrative of Colonel Robert Campbell*, 43.

14 Beckwourth, *Life and Adventures*, 62.

15 Irving, *Captain Bonneville*, 167.

16 Hafen, *Broken Hand*, 340. Robb's article appeared in the *Weekly Reveille* of St. Louis on March 1, 1847.

17 Clyman, *James Clyman*, 25-26.

18 Irving, *Captain Bonneville*, 155-156.

19 Larpenteur, *Forty Years a Fur Trader*, 27, 33-34.

20 Ibid., 156.

21   Ibid., 157.

22   Fayell, *Narrative of Colonel Robert Campbell*, 43.

23   Larpenteur, *Forty Years a Fur Trader*, 36-38.

24   Ibid., 33.

25   Victor, *River of the West*, 143.

26   Stewart, *Edward Warren*, 428-429n48.

27   Ibid.

28   Letter, Nathaniel Wyeth to Von Phul & McGill, July 18, 1833, Young, *Journals of Captain Wyeth*.

29   Ibid., Nathaniel Wyeth to John Ball, July 18, 1833.

30   Ibid., Nathaniel Wyeth to Francis Ermatinger, July 18, 1833.

31   Pistono, *Nathaniel Jarvis Wyeth*, 40-41.

32   Letter, Nathaniel Wyeth to Francis Ermatinger, July 18, 1833, Young, *Journals of Captain Wyeth*.

33   Ibid., Nathaniel Wyeth to Henry Hall and Tucker & Williams, November 8, 1833.

34   Gowans, *Rocky Mountain Rendezvous*, 96-97.

35   Ibid., 97. See also, Berry, *A Majority of Scoundrels*, 273-275, 320-321, 416-419.

36   Newell, *Robert Newell's Memoranda*, 33; Ferris, *Life in the Rocky Mountains*, 283, 302.

37   Larpenteur, *Forty Years a Fur Trader*, 37n3.

38   Carter, "Andrew Drips," 8:149; Leonard, *Narrative*, 105.

39   Larpenteur, *Forty Years a Fur Trader*, 35-36.

40   Stewart, *Edward Warren*, 274, quoted in Gowans, *Rocky Mountain Rendezvous*, 96.

41   Jensen and Hutchins, *Wheelboats on the Missouri*, 30, 155-156, 162-162, 172-174. For Ashley's 1824 visit to Fort Atkinson, see Dale, *The Ashley-Smith Explorations*, 114-116. See also Beckwourth, *Life and Adventures*, 81-84.

42   Ross, *The West of Alfred Jacob Miller*, 139.

43   The marker was placed by the Sublette County Historical Society in conjunction with the United States Department of the Interior, Bureau of Land Management.

44   Letter, Nathaniel Wyeth to James Worthington, December 9, 1833, Young, *Journals of Captain Wyeth*.

45   Irving, *Captain Bonneville*, 171-178; Letter, Benjamin Bonneville to Roger Jones, July 29, 1833, in Barry and Abel-Henderson, "Documents," 210-219.

46   Townsend, *Narrative of a Journey*, 206.

47   Moulton, *Journals of Lewis & Clark*, 4:141.

48   Irving, *Captain Bonneville*, 172.

49   Leonard, *Narrative*, 221, 225, 261; Russell, *Journal of a Trapper*, 57, 90; Larpenteur, *Forty Years a Fur Trader*, 40.

50   Larpenteur, *Forty Years a Fur Trader*, 40; Letter, Daniel Potts to Robert Potts, July 16, 1826, original in the archives of Yellowstone National Park.

51   Whitney and Smith, *The Century Dictionary*, 5:4096.

52   Meek, *Autobiography*, 5.

53   Irving, *Captain Bonneville*, 172-173.

54   Leonard, *Narrative*, 225.

55   Russell, *Journal of a Trapper*, 57-58.

56 Woodruff, *The Lander and Salt Creek Oil Fields*, 31-32; Morgan and Wheat, *Jedediah Smith and His Maps*, 23-25. A full-size reproduction of the Wilkes map was included with this publication. Bonneville's "Map of the Sources of the Colorado & Big Salt Lake," was one of two maps published in Irving, *The Rocky Mountains*.

57 Larpenteur, *Forty Years a Fur Trader*, 40; Larpenteur, *Original Journal*, 4.

58 Larpenteur, *Forty Years a Fur Trader*, 40.

59 Hafen, "Jean Baptiste Charbonneau," 1:205-224.

60 Thrapp, *Encyclopedia of Frontier Biography*, 4:164-165.

61 Larpenteur, *Forty Years a Fur Trader*, 309-310. Larpenteur chronicled a rather regrettable trading partnership with Smith (see pages 310-329).

62 Alter, *Jim Bridger,* 138; Irving, *Captain Bonneville*, 176.

63 Irving, *Captain Bonneville*, 174.

64 Ibid., 174, 176.

65 Raynolds, *Report on the Exploration of the Yellowstone River*, 82.

66 Urbanek, *Wyoming Place Names*, 227.

67 Moulton, *Journals of Lewis & Clark*, 3:365; LaRoque, *Journals of Francois Antoine Laroque*, 16; Urbanek, *Wyoming Place Names*, 23.

68 Denig, *Of the Crow Nation*, 26.

69 Urbanek, *Wyoming Place Names*, 93; Hoxie, *Parading Through History,* 160.

70 Urbanek, *Wyoming Place Names*, 151.

71 Irving, *Captain Bonneville*, 184.

72 Larpenteur, *Forty Years a Fur Trader*, 40.

73 Mattes, "Behind the Legend of Colter's Hell," 251-282.

74 Appleton, *Appleton's Dictionary of Machines,* 2:222-230.

75 The National Park Service oversees a National Recreation Area in the Big Horn Canyon. Its web pages are quite informative regarding the region as well as the cultural and natural history of the canyon. It is found on line at: http://www.nps.gov/bica/index.htm (accessed 1-15-12).

76 Bartlett, *Glossary of Words and Phrases,* 93.

77 Irving, *Captain Bonneville*, 177-178.

78 Larpenteur, *Forty Years a Fur Trader*, 41.

79 Ibid.

80 Irving, *Captain Bonneville*, 177.

81 Larpenteur, *Original Journal*, 4; Larpenteur, *Forty Years a Fur Trader*, 42. In his *Original Journal*, Larpenteur reported only two bull boats were built.

82 Baldwin, *The Keelboat Age*, 40.

83 Fayell, *Narrative of Colonel Robert Campbell*, 43.

84 Irving, *Captain Bonneville*, 177.

85 Larpenteur, *Original Journal*, 4; Larpenteur, *Forty Years a Fur Trader*, 42-43.

86 Hafen, *Broken Hand*, 132-133; Sunder, *Bill Sublette*, 127-128. The original document is cited as Wyeth-Fitzpatrick-M. Sublette Agreement, August 14, 1833, Sublette Family Papers, 1819-1860, Missouri History Museum, St. Louis, MO.

87 Ibid.

88 Pistono, *Nathaniel Jarvis Wyeth*, 42-43.

89   Letter, Nathaniel Wyeth to Henry Hall and Mess. Tucker & Williams, November 8, 1833, Young, *Journals of Captain Wyeth*.

90   Berry, *A Majority of Scoundrels*, 326-327, 416-418.

91   Irving, *Captain Bonneville*, 177.

92   Ibid.,178.

93   Ibid.

94   Ibid., 303-304.

95   Leland, *The Keelboat Age*, 40-41, says a canoe-shaped bull boat, thirty feet long and twelve feet wide, could carry three tons of cargo. Wyeth's boat, as eighteen feet long and five and a half feet wide, is roughly thirty percent that size.

96   Leland, *The Keelboat Age*, 40; Irving, *Captain Bonneville*, 304-305.

97   Unites Stated Department of Commerce, National Oceanic and Atmospheric Administration web site, found on line at http://oceanservice.noaa.gov/education/kits/currents/07measure1.html (accessed 1-16-12).

98   Moulton, *Journals of Lewis & Clark*, 2:305, 307n2.

99   Irving, *Captain Bonneville*, 178.

100 Ibid., 305-306.

101 Ibid., 306-307. It must be presumed that Irving had additional correspondence with Wyeth to obtain these details that were not contained in the New Englander's journal – or that Irving had a grand imagination. These same bands of Crow would rob Fitzpatrick and harass Bonneville later in the year.

102 Chittenden, *The Yellowstone National Park*, 3-8.

103 Robertson, *Competitive Struggle*, 89; Beckwourth, *Life and Adventures*, 212; De Land, "Old Fort Pierre," 1:356-357; and Chittenden, *History of the American Fur Trade*, 2:964-965. The actual distance from the mouth of the Yellowstone to the post was stated by Wyeth to be three miles. Larpenteur stated it was only two miles while Beckwourth about a mile below where there was a better location to land the boats (Larpenteur, *Forty Years a Fur Trader*, 47; Beckwourth, *Life and Adventures*, 212).

104 Fowler, *Shared Customs*, 35; Maximilian, "Travels in the Interior of North America," 23:71, 126-127.

105 Larpenteur, *Forty Years a Fur Trader*, 46.

106 Irving, *Captain Bonneville*, 310.

107 Beckwourth, *Life and Adventures*, 212-213; Chittenden, *History of the American Fur Trade*, 2:964.

108 Aarstad, et. al., *Montana Place Names*, 230.

109 Robertson, *Competitive Struggle*, 89, 236, 272n13. Compare Chittenden, *History of the American Fur Trade*, 2:965 and Sunder, *Fur Trade on the Upper Missouri*, 59.

110 Fayell, *Narrative of Colonel Robert Campbell*, 43.

111 Campbell, "Private Journal," 34.

112 Campbell, "Private Journal," 22; Larpenteur, *Forty Years a Fur Trader*, 49.

113 Moulton, *Journals of Lewis & Clark*, 4:278.

114 Irving, *Captain Bonneville*, 312.

115 Aarstad, et. al., *Montana Place Names*, 211; Maximilian, "Travels in the Interior of North America," 22:374.

116 Irving, *Captain Bonneville*, 36n2.

117   Ibid., 313-314.

118   Moulton, *Journals of Lewis & Clark*, 8:277.

119   Thompson, *Fort Union Trading Post*, 11, 15, 18-19.

120   Barbour, *Fort Union*, 39; Matzko, *Reconstructing Fort Union*, 11.

Notes to Chapter 12: Fort Union on the Missouri River

1   Larpenteur, *Forty Years a Fur Trader*, 65.

2   Thompson, *Fort Union Trading Post*, 3-6.

3   Larpenteur, *Forty Years a Fur Trader*, 74-75.

4   Mattison, "James A. Hamilton (Palmer)," 3:163-166; Chittenden, *History of the American Fur Trade*, 1:389.

5   Robertson, *Competitive Struggle*, 170-171.

6   Anderson, *Journals,* 110-111, 340-341.

7   Maximilian, "Travels in the Interior of North America," 23:135-136.

8   Martin, "The Greatest Evil," 35-53.

9   Mattison, "Kenneth McKenzie," 2:222.

10   Barry, *Beginning of the West*, 239-242, 246, 248, 250-252.

11   Letter, Henry L. Ellsworth to Elbert Herring, November 8, 1833, copy in Indian Collection, Missouri History Museum, St. Louis, MO.

12   Hanson, "Michel Sylvestre Cerré," 8:62-65.

13   Letter, Kenneth McKenzie to Pierre Chouteau, March 18, 1834, Fort Union letter book, Chouteau Collection, Missouri History Museum, St. Louis, MO, Box 2. The full text of the letter is printed in Barbour, *Fort Union*, 168-169.

14   Letter, Kenneth McKenzie to Pierre Chouteau, March 20, 1834, Fort Union letter book, Chouteau Collection, Missouri History Museum, St. Louis, MO. Barbour's evaluation of this Wyeth-McKenzie affair is contained in Barbour, *Fort Union*, 166-169.

15   Barry, *Beginning of the West*, 250.

16   Barbour, *Fort Union*, 167.

17   Larpenteur, *Forty Years a Fur Trader*, 75-76.

18   Clubb, *The Maine Liquor Law,* 414-415. Section 20 of "An Act to Fix the Compensations And Increase The Responsibility Of The Collectors Of The Direct Tax And Internal Duties, And For Other Purposes Connected With The Collection Thereof" was approved on March 3, 1815.

19   Campbell, "Private Journal," 5.

20   Irving, *Captain Bonneville*, 315.

21   See Sunder, *Bill Sublette*, 129; Berry, *A Majority of Scoundrels*, 333; and Robertson, *Competitive Struggle*, 230.

22   Campbell, "Private Journal," 34. Some writers portray Sublette as near death: see Sunder, *Bill Sublette*, 130; Nester, *From Mountain Man to Millionaire*, 76; and Berry, *A Majority of Scoundrels*, 332.

23   DeVoto made an intriguing comment but gave no source, "Wyeth stepped into his bull boat and started down the Missouri, leaving one of his two remaining charter members at the mouth of the Yellowstone," (DeVoto, *Across the Wide Missouri*, 122). Since Abbott returned with Wyeth in 1834, DeVoto can only mean Woodman, though whether DeVoto thought he stayed at Fort Union or with Sublette is unknown. The two hunters are mentioned in Irving, *Captain Bonneville*, 316.

24   Baldwin, *The Keelboat Age*, 41, 62-63.

25   Bradbury, *Travels in the Interior of America*, 200.

26   Irving, *Captain Bonneville*, 317.

27   Ibid., 311-312. This interesting bit information does not pertain to any certain journal entry but more to the entire float on the Big Horn and Yellowstone rivers.

28   Larsen and Cottrell, *Steamboats West*, 24-31.

29   The date that Campbell met up with Sublette is somewhat vague. Campbell reported he arrived a day after Sublette, so based on Wyeth's journals, Campbell floated in on August 28, 1833, (Fayell, *Narrative of Colonel Robert Campbell*, 44). But in a lengthy journal entry for December 31, 1833, that recapped the entire year, Campbell said he arrived on August 30 (Campbell, "Private Journal," 34). Larpenteur said he and Vasquez arrived on September 3 and "Mr. William Sublette arrived there eight days before and Mr. Campbell three." (Larpenteur, *Forty Years a Fur Trader*, 48-49). Given the discrepancies, Sublette's biographer hedged his bets and reported William did not arrive at the appointed place until "a day or two before August 29, and settled down to wait for Campbell" (Sunder, *Bill Sublette*, 127).

30   Larpenteur, *Forty Years a Fur Trader*, 47-48.

31   Irving, *Captain Bonneville*, 316-317.

32   Nester, *From Mountain Man to Millionaire*, 76.

33   Wood et al., *Fort Clark and Its Indian Neighbors*, 156.

34   Information regarding Dougherty came from conversations with Mark Kelly from Leavenworth, Kansas, whose soon-to-be-published manuscript on John Dougherty contains many revealing facts about the man.

35   Thwaites, *Early Western Travels*, 23:217-218n167. Sublette had written a letter to Campbell naming "Dougherty," but giving no first name, cited in Sunder, *Bill Sublette*, 130, as Letter, William Sublette to Robert Campbell, September 25, 1833, Robert Campbell papers, 1832-1842, William H. Semsrott, St. Louis, MO. Thwaites identified this man as Joseph Dougherty, another brother of John, but he did not accompany Long.

36   An earlier version of the fort, called by the same name, was built by the Columbia Fur Company near this same location; see Wood, "James Kipp," 2-35.

37   Hardee, "An 1824-1825 Columbia Fur Company Ledger," 126.

38   Wood et al., *Fort Clark and Its Indian Neighbors*, 106-107.

39   Irving, *Captain Bonneville*, 318.

40   Much has been written about the Arikara War of 1823. For a full treatment, see Nester, *The Arikara War*.

41   Wood et al., *Fort Clark and Its Indian Neighbors*, 54.

42   Maximilian, "Travels in the Interior of North America," 24:103.

43   Ibid., 24:103-104; Haines, "Johnson Gardner," 159.

44   Yount, *Chronicles of the West*, 203.

45   Robertson, *Competitive Struggle*, 203-204.

46   Mattison, "William Laidlaw," 3:167-172.

47   Robertson, *Competitive Struggle*, 222-223.

48   Ehrensperger, *South Dakota Place Names*, 4:48.

49   Maximilian, "Travels in the Interior of North America," 24:89.

50   Larpenteur, *Forty Years a Fur Trader*, 160-162.

51   Maximilian, "Travels in the Interior of North America," 24:89.

52   Abel, *Chardon's Journal*, 368.

53   Moulton, *Journals of Lewis & Clark*, 3:88-99.

54   Bradbury, *"Travels in the Interior of America,"* 5:184-185.

55   Maximilian, "Travels in the Interior of North America," 22:235n171; Abel, *Chardon's Journal*, 234n101.

56   Maximilian, "Travels in the Interior of North America," 22:303-304.

57   Benke and Cushing, *Rivers of North America*, 445.

58   Moulton, *Journals of Lewis & Clark*, 3:48-51.

59   An interesting and concise history of the Ponca Nation, including the various areas in which they were known to have lived from 1785 through 1856, may be found in "The Ponca Tribe."

60   Townsend, *Narrative of a Journey*, 134.

61   Moulton, *Journals of Lewis & Clark*, 2:324; Cutright, *Lewis and Clark, Pioneering Naturalists*, 58; Means, *John Kirk Townsend*, 43, 46, 48, 288.

62   Moulton, *Journals of Lewis & Clark*, 3:37-51.

63   Wood, et al., *Fort Clark*, 104.

64   Ferris, *Life in the Rocky Mountains*, 145.

65   Irving, *Captain Bonneville*, 319.

66   Maximilian, "Travels in the Interior of North America," 22:275.

67   Carlson, Bozell, and Pepperl, *The Search for Engineer Cantonment*, 2-6.

68   Mattison, "Joshua Pilcher," 4:251-260.

69   Jensen, *Trading Posts*, 22-24; Sunder, *Joshua Pilcher*, 100-104.

70   Maximilian, "Travels in the Interior of North America," 22:271-272.

71   Letter, Joshua Pilcher to Pierre Chouteau, Jr., September 23, 1833, Chouteau Family Papers, Missouri History Museum, St. Louis, MO.

72   Jensen, *Trading Posts*, 12-13; Ferris, *Life in the Rocky Mountains*, 91.

73   Mattes, "Joseph Robidoux," 8:287-314.

74   Robertson, *Competitive Struggle*, 148; Maximilian, "Travels in the Interior of North America," 22:253-254.

75   Heitman, *Historical Register*, 828.

76   Ibid., 416; Maximilian, "Travels in the Interior of North America," 24:114-115.

77   Maximilian, "Travels in the Interior of North America," 24:113.

78   Letter, Nathaniel Wyeth to E. M. Samuel, September 29, 1833, Young, *Journals of Captain Wyeth*.

79   Ibid., Nathaniel Wyeth to Wiggin Abbot, September 29, 1833.

80   Giffen, *"Walks in Water,"* 17-18.

81   Heitman, *Historical Register*, 747.

82   Letter, Nathaniel Wyeth to Edward M. Samuel, October 4, 1833, Young, *Journals of Captain Wyeth*.

83   Ibid., Nathaniel Wyeth to Edward M. Samuel, October 4, 1833, Nathaniel Wyeth to Frederic Tudor, October 4, 1833, Nathaniel Wyeth to Tucker & Williams and Henry Hall, October 4, 1833, in Young, *Journals of Captain Wyeth*.

84   Barry, "Kansas Before 1854," 336.

85   Letter, Nathaniel Wyeth to Milton G. Sublette, October 9, 1833, Young, *Journals of Captain Wyeth*.

86   Ibid., Nathaniel Wyeth to William Harrison, October, 17, 1833.

87   Ibid., Nathaniel Wyeth to George Simpson, October 21, 1833.

88   Conant, *Principles of Money and Banking,* 188.

89   Irving, *Captain Bonneville,* xxvi, li n3.

90   Letter, Nathaniel Wyeth to Leonard Wyeth, October 26, 1833, Young, *Journals of Captain Wyeth.*

91   Ibid., Nathaniel Wyeth to Jonas Wyeth, October 28, 1833.

92   Letter, Francis W. Ryder to Prof. S. F. Baird, February 16, 1834, in Baird, *Bulletin of the United States Fish Commission,* 384.

Notes to Epilogue

1   The return trip for John Wyeth is condensed from John Wyeth, "Oregon," 78-95.

2   Ibid., 88; Sunder, *Bill Sublette,* 113.

3   Ibid., 89.

4   Ibid.

5   Ibid., 90.

6   Ibid., 90-91.

7   Ibid., 91.

8   Ibid., 91-92.

9   Ibid., 95.

10   John Wyeth, "Oregon," 104-105.

11   Overmeyer, "Members of the First Wyeth Expedition," 98.

12   Ball, "Across the Continent Seventy Years Ago," 105.

13   Ball, "Across the Continent Seventy Years Ago," 105; Ball, *Born to Wander,* 63.

14   Ball, *Born to Wander,* 63. Dobson, *Contours of Death,* 338.

15   Ball, "Across the Continent Seventy Years Ago," 105-106.

16   Ball, *Born to Wander,* 67-69.

17   Ibid., 71-73.

18   Ball, *Born to Wander,* 71; Pacific Union College, Pitcairn Islands Study Center, "History of Pitcairn Island," http://library.puc.edu/pitcairn/pitcairn/history.shtml (accessed 1-2-13).

19   Ball, *Born to Wander,* 75.

20   Ibid., 77-79.

21   Ibid., 80-81, 156.

22   Ball, *Born to Wander,* 148; Overmeyer, "Members of the First Wyeth Expedition," 99.

23   Overmeyer, "Members of the First Wyeth Expedition," 99; Bancroft, *History of Oregon,* 1:75.

24   John Wyeth, "Oregon," 76.

25   Hussey, *Champoeg,* 67-68; Overmeyer, "Members of the First Wyeth Expedition," 100-101; Watson, *Lives Lived West of the Divide,* 785-786.

Bibliography

Aarstad, Rich, Ellie Arguimbau, Ellen Baumler, Charlene Porsild and Brian Shovers. *Montana Place Names from Alzada to Zortman*. Helena, MT: Montana Historical Society Press, 2009.

Abel, Anne Heloise, ed. *Chardon's Journal at Fort Clark, 1834-1839*. Pierre, SD: Department of History, State of South Dakota, 1932.

Allan, George T. "Reminiscences of Fort Vancouver on Columbia River, Oregon, as It Stood in 1832." *Transactions of the Ninth-Annual Reunion of the Oregon Pioneer Association for 1881*. Salem, OR: E. M. Waite Steam Printer and Bookbinder, 1882.

Alter, J. Cecil. *Jim Bridger*. Norman, OK: University of Oklahoma Press, 1950.

Ammer, Christine. *The Facts on File Dictionary of Clichés*. New York, NY: Facts on File, Inc., 2006.

Anderson, William M. *The Rocky Mountain Journals of William Marshall Anderson – The West in 1834*. Edited by Eleanor T. Harris and Dale L. Morgan. San Marino, CA: The Huntington Library, 1967.

Aoki, Haruo. *Nez Perce Dictionary*. Berkeley, CA: University of California Press, 1994.

Appleton, D. *Appleton's Dictionary of Machines, Mechanics, Engine-work and Engineering*. New York, NY: D. Appleton & Company, 1869.

Bagley, Clarence B., ed. *Early Catholic Missions in Old Oregon*. Seattle, WA: Lowman and Hanford Company, 1932.

Baird, Lynn and Dennis Baird, comps. *In Nez Perce Country: Accounts of the Bitterroots and the Clearwater After Lewis and Clark*. Moscow, ID: University of Idaho Press, 2003.

Baird, Spencer F. *Bulletin of the United State Fish Commission*. Washington, DC: Government Printing Office, 1882.

Baker, Dean. "Chinook Leader Buried in Hudson's Bay Co. Cemetery." *Columbian*. (Vancouver, WA) May 9, 2005.

Baldwin, Leland D. *The Keelboat Age on Western Waters*. Pittsburgh, PA: University of Pittsburgh Press, 1941.

Ball, John. "Across the Continent Seventy Years Ago." Compiled by Kate Ball Powers. *The Quarterly of the Oregon Historical Society* 3, no. 1 (March 1902): 82-106.

_____. *Born to Wander, Autobiography of John Ball*. Compiled by Kate Ball Powers, Flora Ball Hopkins and Lucy Ball. Grand Rapids, MI: The Grand Rapids Historical Commission, 1925.

_____. "John Ball's 3rd Letter, Part 1, From Beyond the Rocky Mountains," *Zion's Herald*, January 6, 1834, Mss. 195, Oregon Historical Society, Portland, OR.

Bancroft, Hubert Howe. *California Pioneer Register and Index 1542-1848*. Baltimore, MD: Regional Publishing, 1964.

_____. *History of Oregon*. Vol. 1. San Francisco, CA: The History Company, Publishers, 1886.

_____. *History of the Northwest Coast 1800-1846*. San Francisco, CA: A. L. Bancroft & Company, Publishers, 1884.

Barbour, Barton H. *Fort Union and the Upper Missouri Fur Trade*. Norman, OK: University of Oklahoma Press, 2001.

Barry, J. Nielson. "Astorians Who Became Permanent Settlers." *Washington Historical Quarterly* 24, no. 4 (October 1933): 288-90.

Barry, J. Neilson and Anne H. Abel-Henderson. "Documents." *The Washington Historical Quarterly* 18, no. 3 (July 1927): 210-219.

Barry, Louise. *The Beginning of the West, Annals of the Kansas Gateway to the American West, 1540-1854*. Topeka, KS: The Kansas State Historical Society, 1972.

_____. "Kansas Before 1854: A Revised Annals, Part Seven, 1833-1834." *Kansas Historical Quarterly* 28, no. 3 (Autumn 1962): 317-369.

Bartlett, John Russell. *A Glossary of Words and Phrases Usually Regarded as Peculiar to the United States*. Boston, MA: Little, Brown and Company, 1859.

Beckwourth, James P. *The Life and Adventures of James P. Beckwourth as Told to Thomas D. Bonner*. Edited by Delmont R. Oswald. Lincoln, NE: University of Nebraska Press, 1972.

Benke, Arthur C. and Colbert E. Cushing, eds. *Rivers of North America*. Burlington, MA: Elsevier Academic Press, 2005.

Berry, Don. *A Majority of Scoundrels*. New York, NY: Harper & Brothers, 1961.

Bird, Annie L. *Thomas McKay*. Caldwell, ID: The Caxton Printers, Ltd., 1972.

Birdsall, Richard D. "The Second Great Awakening and the New England Social Order," *Church History* 39, no. 3 (September 1970): 345-364.

Blevins, Winfred. *Dictionary of the American West*. New York, NY: Facts on File, 1993.

Bonney, Orrin H. and Lorraine Bonney. *Guide to the Wyoming Mountains and Wilderness Area*. Denver, CO: Sage Books, 1960.

Boone, Lalia. *Idaho Place Names, A Geographical Dictionary*. Moscow, ID: University of Idaho Press, 1988.

Boyd, Robert. *People of the Dalles, The Indians of Wascopam Mission*. Lincoln, NE: University of Nebraska Press, 1996.

Bradbury, John. *Travels in the Interior of America in the Years 1809, 1810, and 1811*. London: Sherwood, Neely, and Jones, 1817.

_____. "Travels in the Interior of America in the Years 1809, 1810, and 1811." *Early Western Travels 1748- 1846*. Vol. 5. Edited by Reuben G. Thwaites. New York, NY: AMS Press, Inc., 1966.

Bright, William. *Native American Place Names of the United States*. Norman, OK: University of Oklahoma Press, 2004.

British Columbia Geographical Names. Victoria, BC: Geographical Names Office, 2010.

Brosnan, Cornelius J. *History of the State of Idaho*. New York, NY: Charles Scribner's Sons, 1918.

Campbell, Robert. "The Private Journal of Robert Campbell." Edited by George R. Brooks. Reprinted from *The Bulletin of the Missouri Historical Society*. October 1963 and January 1964.

_____. *The Rocky Mountain Letters of Robert Campbell*. New York, NY: Frederick W. Beinecke, 1955.

Carlson, Gayle F., John R. Bozell and Robert Pepperl. *The Search for Engineer Cantonment*. Omaha, NE: Nebraska State Historical Society, 2004.

Carter, Harvey L. "Andrew Drips." *The Mountain Men and the Fur Trade of the Far West*. Vol. 8. Edited by Leroy R. Hafen. Glendale, CA: The Arthur H. Clark Company, 1971.

_____. "John Gantt." *The Mountain Men and the Fur Trade of the Far West*. Vol. 5. Edited by Leroy R. Hafen. Glendale, CA: The Arthur H. Clark Company, 1968.

_____. "William H. Vanderburgh." *The Mountain Men and the Fur Trade of the Far West*. Vol. 7. Edited by Leroy R. Hafen. Glendale, CA: The Arthur H. Clark Company, 1969.

Cass, Lewis. "Abstract of Licenses Issued to Persons to Trade with the Indians During the Year Ending 30th Sept., 1832." House Document 104, 22nd Congress, 2nd Session.

Chittenden, Hiram M. *A History of the American Fur Trade of the Far West*. Stanford, CA: Academic Reprints, 1954.

_____. *The Yellowstone National Park*. Edited by Richard A. Bartlett. Norman, OK: University of Oklahoma Press, 1964.

Clark, Ella E. *Indian Tales from the Northern Rockies*. Norman, OK: University of Oklahoma Press, 1966.

Clark, Robert C. *History of the Willamette Valley, Oregon*. Chicago, IL: The S. J. Clarke Publishing Company, 1927.

Clemans, Scott. "The Dalles Dam Visitor Center to Host Eagle Watch," News Release. #11- 005, US Army Corps of Engineer. Portland District, Portland, OR. Online at http://www.nwp.usace.army.mil/pa/news/shownews.asp?rn=11-005 (accessed November 21, 2011).

Clements, Louis J. "Andrew Henry." *The Mountain Men and the Fur Trade of the Far West*. Vol. 6. Edited by Leroy R. Hafen., Glendale, CA: The Arthur H. Clark Company, 1968.

Clokey, Richard M. *William H. Ashley, Enterprise and Politics in the Trans-Mississippi West*. Norman, OK: University of Oklahoma Press, 1980.

Clubb, Henry Stephen. *The Maine Liquor Law: Its Origin, History and Results*. New York, NY: Fowler and Wells, 1856.

Clyman, James. *James Clyman, Frontiersman.* Edited by Charles L. Camp. Portland, OR: The Champoeg Press, 1960.

Commercial Atlas of America – Idaho. Chicago, IL: Rand McNally and Company, 1924.

Conant, Charles A. *The Principles of Money and Banking.* New York, NY: Harper & Brothers, 1908.

Conley, Cort. *Idaho for the Curious.* Cambridge, ID: Backeddy Books, 1982.

Conrad, Howard L. *Uncle Dick Wooten.* Chicago, IL: Lakeside Press, R. R. Donnelley & Sons Co., 1957.

Coues, Elliott, ed. *New Light on the Early History of the Greater Northwest. The Manuscript Journals of Alexander Henry, Fur Trader of the Northwest Company, and David Thompson, Official Geographer of the Same Company.* Minneapolis, MN: Ross & Haines, Inc., 1965.

Cox, Ross. *The Columbia River.* Edited by Edgar I. Stewart and Jane R. Stewart. Norman, OK: University of Oklahoma Press, 1957.

Crampton, C. Gregory. "The San Buenaventura – Mythical River of the West." Pacific Historical Review 25, no. 2 (May 1956): 163-171.

Cutright, Paul Russell. *Lewis and Clark, Pioneering Naturalists.* Urbana, IL: University of Illinois Press, 1969.

Dale, Harrison Clifford. *The Ashley-Smith Explorations and the Discovery of a Central Route to the Pacific, 1822-1829.* Cleveland, OH: The Arthur H. Clark Company, 1918.

Danisi, Thomas C. *Uncovering the Truth about Meriwether Lewis.* Amherst, NY: Prometheus Books, 2012.

Dary, David A. *The Buffalo Book.* Chicago, IL: Sage Books, 1974.

Davidson, Anne, Carol Perugini, Craig Rabeg and Darian Saul. Bruneau Subbasin Summary – Draft (prepared for the Northwest Power Planning Council, May 17, 2002.) Online at http://www.cbfwa.org/FWProgram/ReviewCycle/fy2003is/workplan/020517Bruneau.pdf (accessed 10-6-11).

De Land, Charles E. "Editorial Notes on Old Fort Pierre and Its Neighbors." *South Dakota Historical Collections.* Compiled by Doane Robinson. Pierre, SD: South Dakota State Historical Society, 1906.

Denig, Edwin T., *Of the Crow Nation*. Washington, DC: Government Printing Office, 1953. Anthropological Papers, No. 33. Bureau of Ethnology Bulletin, No. 151.

De Smet, Pierre-Jean. *Life, Letters and Travels of Father Pierre-Jean De Smet, S. J., 1801-1873*. New York, NY: Francis P. Harper, 1905.

De Voto, Bernard. *Across the Wide Missouri*. Boston, MA: Houghton Mifflin Company, 1947.

Dictionary of Canadian Biography Online. Edited by John English. http://www.biographi.ca/index-e.html (accessed November 1, 2011).

Dillon, Richard. *Siskiyou Trail, The Hudson's Bay Company Route to California*. New York, NY: McGraw-Hill Book Company, 1975.

Dobbs, Caroline C. *Men of Champoeg*. Portland, OR: Metropolitan Press, Publishers, 1932.

Dobson, Mary J. *Contours of Death in Early Modern England*. Cambridge, UK: Cambridge University Press, 1997.

Douglas, David. *The Oregon Journals of David Douglas*. Edited by David Lavender. Ashland, OR: The Oregon Book Society, 1972.

_____. *Journal Kept by David Douglas During His Travels in North America 1823-1827*. London: William Wesley & Son, 1914.

Drury, Clifford M. *First White Women Over the Rockies*. Glendale, CA: The Arthur H. Clark Company, 1963.

_____. *Henry Harmon Spalding*. Caldwell, ID: The Caxton Printers, Ltd., 1936.

Durham, Nelson W. *History of the City of Spokane and Spokane County, Washington*. Spokane, WA: The S. J. Clarke Publishing Company, 1912.

Dye, Eva E. "Old Letters from Hudson's Bay Company Officials and Employees from 1829 to 1840." *Washington Historical Quarterly* 2, no. 1 (October 1907): 40-43.

Eddins, O. Ned. "Was Fort Bonneville Simply Nonsense?" *The Rocky Mountain Fur Trade Journal* 5 (2011): 21-33.

Ehrensperger, E. C., comp. *South Dakota Place Names*. Vermillion, SD: University of South Dakota, 1940. Workers of the Writers' Program of the Work Projects Administration in the State of South Dakota.

Eliot, Samuel Atkins. "All Aboard the 'Natwyethum'!" *Cambridge Historical Society Publications, Proceedings, 1906-1907.* Cambridge, MA: Cambridge Historical Society, 1907.

Engages, The. "Fish Hooks." *The Museum of the Fur Trade Quarterly* 16, no. 4 (Winter 1980); 9-10.

Erigero, Patricia C. Fort Vancouver, Cultural Landscape Report. Vol. 2. Seattle, WA: National Park Service, 1992. Online at http://www.cr.nps.gov/history/online_books/fova/clr2-2b2a.htm (accessed October 25, 2011).

Ermatinger, Edward. "Edward Ermatinger's York Factory Express Journal, Being a Record of Journeys Made Between Fort Vancouver and Hudson Bay in the Years 1827-1828." *Proceedings and Transactions of the Royal Society of Canada,* Edited by C. O. Ermatinger. Ottawa, ON: James Hope & Son; London: The Copp-Clark Co., Ltd.; London: Bernard Quaritch, 1913. Third Series, Vol. 4, Transactions, Section 2.

Ewers, John C. *The Blackfeet, Raiders on the Northwestern Plains.* Norman, OK: University of Oklahoma Press, 1958.

_____. "The Blackfoot War Lodge: Its Construction and Use." *American Anthropologist* 46, no. 2 (April, June 1944): 182-192.

_____. *The Horse in Blackfoot Indian Culture.* Washington, DC: Government Printing Office, 1955. Smithsonian Institution Bureau of American Ethnology, Bulletin 159.

_____. "Iroquois Indians in the Far West," *Montana the Magazine of Western History* 13, no. 2 (April 1963): 2-10.

"Exploration of the Bruneau Country," Idaho State Historical Society Reference Series, (Boise, ID), No. 502, 1973.

"Exploration of City of Rocks and Granite Pass," Idaho State Historical Society Reference Series, (Boise, ID), No. 189, August 1995.

Farnham, Thomas J. *Travels in the Great Western Prairie, the Anahuac and Rocky Mountains, and in the Oregon Territory.* London: Richard Bentley, 1843.

Fayell, William. *A Narrative of Colonel Robert Campbell's Experiences in the Rocky Mountain Fur Trade from 1825 to 1835.* Edited by Drew Alan Holloway. Fairfield, WA: Ye Galleon Press, 1991.

Featherman, Americus. *Social History of the Races of Mankind.* London: Trubner & Co., 1889.

Ferris, Warren A. *Life in the Rocky Mountains.* Edited by Leroy R. Hafen. Denver, CO: The Old West Publishing Company, 1983.

Fowler, Loretta. *Shared Customs, Contested Meaning: Gros Ventre Culture and History, 1798-1984.* Ithaca, NY: Cornell University Press, 1987.

Franchére, Gabriel. *Adventure at Astoria, 1810-1814.* Edited and translated by Hoyt C. Franchére. Norman, OK: University of Oklahoma Press, 1967.

Frazer, Perry D. *Amateur Rodmaking.* New York, NY: Outing Publishing Company, 1914.

Fremont, John C. *Narrative of the Exploring Expedition to the Rockies, Oregon and California.* Washington, DC: Taylor, Wilde & Co., 1845.

_____. *Report of the Exploring Expedition to the Rocky Mountains in the Year 1842.* Washington, DC: Blair and Rives, Printers, 1845.

_____. *Report of the Exploring Expedition to the Rocky Mountains in the Years 1843-44.* Washington, DC: Gales and Seaton, Printers, 1845.

Galbraith, John S. *The Hudson's Bay Company as an Imperial Factor.* Berkeley, CA: The University of California Press, 1957.

Geranios, Nicholas K. "Small Submarines Test Silent, Test Deep in Mysterious Idaho Lake," *Los Angeles Times.* August 23, 1998.

Gibson, James R. *The Lifeline of the Oregon Country, The Fraser –Columbia Brigade System, 1811-47.* Vancouver, BC: University of British Columbia Press, 1997.

Giffen, Lawrence Everett. *"Walks in Water,"* *The Impact of Steamboating on the Lower Missouri River.* Jefferson City, MO: Giffen Enterprises, 2001.

Gilman, Roger. "The Wyeth Background." *Cambridge Historical Society Publications, Proceedings for the Year 1942.* Cambridge, MA: Cambridge Historical Society, 1943.

Goetzman, William H. *Exploration and Empire.* New York, NY: Alfred A. Knopf, 1967.

Gowans, Fred R. *Rocky Mountain Rendezvous.* Layton, UT: Gibbs M. Smith, Inc., 1985.

Grauer, Jack. *Mount Hood, a Complete History.* Gresham, OR: the Author, 1975.

Graustein, Jeanette E. *Thomas Nuttall, Naturalist – Explorations in America, 1808-1841.* Cambridge, MA: Harvard University Press, 1967.

Gray, Theressa. *Life and Letters of Mrs. Jason Lee.* Portland, OR: Metropolitan Press, 1935.

Gray, William H. *Journal of his Journey East, 1836-1837.* Edited by Donald R. Johnson. Fairfield, WA: Ye Galleon Press, 1980.

Grose, Francis. *A Classical Dictionary of the Vulgar Tongue.* Edited by Eric Partridge. New York, NY: Dorset Press, 1992.

Gunter, Bob. "Wasunka: The Mother of Twins." *Bonner County Daily Bee.* March 5, 2011.

Hafen, Ann W. "Jean Baptiste Charbonneau." *The Mountain Men and the Fur Trade of the Far West.* Vol. 1. Edited by Leroy R. Hafen. Glendale, CA: The Arthur H. Clark Company, 1965.

Hafen, Leroy R. *Broken Hand, the Life of Thomas Fitzpatrick, Mountain Man, Guide and Indian Agent.* Denver, CO: Old West Publishing Company, 1973.

Haines, Aubrey L. "Antoine Godin." *The Mountain Men and the Fur Trade of the Far West.* Vol. 2. Edited by Leroy R. Hafen. Glendale, CA: The Arthur H. Clark Company, 1965.

_____. "Johnson Gardner." The Mountain Men and the Fur Trade of the Far West. Vol. 2. Edited by Leroy R. Hafen. Glendale, CA: The Arthur H. Clark Company, 1965.

Hanson, Charles E., Jr. "Michel Sylvestre Cerré," *The Mountain Men and the Fur Trade of the Far West.* Vol. 8. Edited by Leroy R. Hafen. Glendale, CA: The Arthur H. Clark Company, 1971.

Hansen, George W. "A Tragedy on the Oregon Trail." Edited by Albert Watkins. *Nebraska State Historical Society Collections,* Vol. 17. Lincoln, NE: Nebraska State Historical Society, 1913.

Hanson, James A. "Some More Fur Trade Fishhooks." *Museum of the Fur Trade Quarterly* 34, no. 4 (Winter 1998): 4-9.

Hardee, Jim. *Pierre's Hole! The Fur Trade History of Teton Valley, Idaho.* Pinedale, WY: The Museum of the Mountain Man, 2010.

_____. "An 1824-1825 Columbia Fur Company Ledger." *Rocky Mountain Fur Trade Journal* 5 (2011): 119-149.

Hart, Jeff. *Montana Native Plants and Early People.* Helena, MT: Montana Historical Society Press, 1967.

Haywood, Carl W. *Sometimes Only Horses to Eat.* Stevensville, MT: Stoneydale Press Publishing Co., 2008.

Heitman, Francis B. *Historical Register and Dictionary of the United States Army.* Washington, DC: Government Printing Office, 1903.

Hipol, Keith "Moki." "Hawaiians in the American Fur Trade." *The Rocky Mountain Fur Trade Journal* 1 (2007): 75-84.

Hodge, Frederick Webb., ed. *Handbook of American Indians North of Mexico.* Washington, DC: Government Printing Office, 1907. Smithsonian Institution Bureau of American Ethnology, Bulletin 30: 1-168.

Hoffman, W. J. "Poisoned Arrows." *American Anthropologist* 4, no.1 (January 1891): 67-71.

Holman, Frederick V. *Dr. John McLoughlin, the Father of Oregon.* Cleveland, OH: The Arthur H. Clark Company, 1907.

_____. "History of the Counties of Oregon." *The Quarterly of the Oregon Historical Society* 11, no. 1 (March 1910): 1-81.

_____. "James Douglas." *The Mountain Men and the Fur Trade of the Far West.* Vol. 9. Edited by Leroy R. Hafen. Glendale, CA: The Arthur H. Clark Company, 1972.

_____. "Joseph Gervais." *The Mountains Men and the Fur Trade of the Far West.* Vol. 7. Edited by Leroy R. Hafen. Glendale, CA: The Arthur H. Clark Company, 1969.

_____. "John McLoughlin." *The Mountain Men and the Fur Trade of the Far West.* Vol. 8, Edited by Leroy R. Hafen. Glendale, CA: The Arthur H. Clark Company, 1971.

_____. "Pierre Chrysologue Pambrun." *The Mountain Men and the Fur Trade of the Far West.* Vol. 3. Edited by Leroy R. Hafen. Glendale, CA: The Arthur H. Clark Company, 1966.

_____. "Francois Payette." *The Mountain Men and the Fur Trade of the Far West.* Vol. 6. Edited by Leroy R. Hafen. Glendale, CA: The Arthur H. Clark Company, 1968.

Hoxie, Frederick E. *Parading Through History; the Making of the Crow Nation in America, 1805-1935.* Cambridge, MA: Cambridge University Press, 1995.

Hunt, Wilson Price. *The Overland Diary of Wilson Price Hunt.* Edited by Hoyt C. Franchére. Ashland, OR: The Oregon Book Society, 1973.

Hunter, Robert, comp. *The Encyclopaedic Dictionary: A New and Original Work of Reference to All the Words in the English Language.* London: Cassell & Company, Ltd., 1887.

Hussey, John A. *Champoeg: Place of Transition.* Portland, OR: Oregon Historical Society, 1967.

_____. *The History of Fort Vancouver and its Physical Structure.* Portland, OR: Abbott, Kerns & Bell Company, 1957.

Idaho State Department of Fish and Game, "Idaho Record Fish – Other Species," found online at http://fishandgame.idaho.gov/public/fish/?getPage=82 (accessed December 16, 2011).

Irving, Washington. *Astoria or Anecdotes of an Enterprise Beyond the Rocky Mountains,* Edited by Edgeley W. Todd. Norman, OK: University of Oklahoma Press, 1964. First published Philadelphia, PA: Carey, Lea and Blanchard, 1836.

_____. *The Adventures of Captain Bonneville, USA.* Edited by Edgeley W. Todd. Norman, OK: University of Oklahoma Press, 1961.

_____. *The Rocky Mountains; or, Scenes, Incidents, and Adventures in the Far West.* Philadelphia, PA: Carey, Lea & Blanchard, 1837.

Jackson, Donald, ed. *Letters of the Lewis and Clark Expedition with Related Documents, 1783-1854.* Urbana, IL: University of Illinois Press, 1978.

Jeffery, Julie R. *Converting the West, A Biography of Narcissa Whitman.* Norman, OK: University of Oklahoma Press, 1991.

Jensen, Richard E. *The Fontenelle & Cabanné Trading Posts.* Omaha, NE: Nebraska State Historical Society, 1998.

Jensen, Richard E. and James S. Hutchins. *Wheelboats on the Missouri, the Journals of the Atkinson-O'Fallon Expedition, 1824-26.* Helena, MT: The Montana Historical Society Press, 2001.

Johnson, Dennis F. *York Boats of the Hudson's Bay Company, Canada's Inland Armada.* Calgary, AB: Fifth House Ltd., 2006.

Johnson, Olga Weydemeyer. *Flathead and Kootenay – The Rivers, the Tribes, and the Region's Traders.* Glendale, CA: The Arthur H. Clark Company, 1969.

Jones, Larry. "Site of the Utter Party Massacre." *Idaho State Historical Society Reference Series.* Boise, ID. No. 233, June 1993.

Jones, Robert F. *Annals of Astoria, the Headquarters Log of the Pacific Fur Company on the Columbia River, 1811-1813.* New York, NY: Fordham University Press, 1999.

Josephy, Alvin M. *The Nez Perce Indians and the Opening of the West.* New Haven, CT: Yale University Press, 1965.

Judson, Henry M. *Diary of 1862, Omaha to Oregon.* MS 953. Nebraska State Historical Society, Lincoln, NE.

Kane, Paul. "Wanderings of an Artist among the Indians of North America from Canada to Vancouver's Island and Oregon through the Hudson's Bay Company's Territory and Back Again," *Paul Kane's Frontier.* Edited by J. Russell Harper. Austin, TX: University of Texas Press, 1971.

Kuhnlein, Harriet V. and Nancy J. Turner. Traditional Plant Foods of Canadian Indigenous Peoples; Nutrition, Botany and Use. Amsterdam: Gordon and Breach Publishers, 1991. Online at http://www.fao.org/wairdocs/other/ai215e/AI215E06. htm#fg6 (accessed 12-26-11).

Kurz, Rudolph Friedrich. *On the Upper Missouri, the Journal of Rudolph Friedrich Kurz, 1852-1852.* Edited by Carla Kelly. Norman, OK: University of Oklahoma Press, 2005.

LaRocque, Francois Antoine. "The Journals of Francois Antoine Larocque from the Assiniboine River to the Yellowstone – 1805." Translated and edited by Ruth Hazlitt. *The Frontier and Midland, A Magazine of the Northwest* 14 (1934):241-247, 332-339; 15 (1934): 67-75, 88.

Larpenteur, Charles. *Forty Years a Fur Trader on the Upper Missouri, the Personal Narrative of Charles Larpenteur, 1833-1872.* Edited by Elliott Coues. Minneapolis, MN: Ross & Haines, Inc., 1962.

_____. *The Original Journal of Charles Larpenteur: My Travels to the Rocky Mountains between 1833 and 1872.* Edited by Michael M. Casler. Chadron, NE: The Museum Association of the American Frontier, 2007.

Larsen, Lawrence H. and Barbara J. Cottrell. *Steamboats West, the 1859 American Fur Company Missouri River Expedition.* Norman, OK: The Arthur H. Clark Company, 2010.

Lavender, David. "Thomas McKay." *The Mountain Men and the Fur Trade of the Far West.* Vol. 6. Edited by Leroy R. Hafen. Glendale, CA: The Arthur H. Clark Company, 1968.

Lee, Daniel and J. H. Frost, *Ten Years in Oregon.* New York, NY: the Authors, 1844.

Lee, Jason. "The Diary of Reverend Jason Lee." *Oregon Historical Society Quarterly* 17, nos. 1, 2, 3 (June, September, December 1916): 116-146, 240-266, 397-430.

Leonard, Zenas. *Narrative of the Adventures of Zenas Leonard.* Edited by Milo M. Quaife. Chicago, IL: R. R. Donnelly & Sons Co., 1934.

Lieber, Francis, ed. *A Popular Dictionary of Arts, Sciences, Literature, History, Politics and Biography.* Philadelphia, PA: Lea & Blanchard, 1844.

Lewis, William S. "Archibald McDonald: Biography and Genealogy." *The Washington Historical Quarterly* 9, no. 2 (July 1918): 93-102.

Lewis, William S. and Jacob A. Meyers. "John Work's Journal of a Trip from Fort Colville to Fort Vancouver and Return in 1828." *The Washington Historical Quarterly* 11, no. 2 (April 1920): 104-114.

Losey, Elizabeth B. *Let Them Be Remembered, The Story of the Fur Trade Forts.* New York, NY: Vantage Press, Inc., 1999.

Lott, Dale F. *American Bison, a Natural History.* Berkeley, CA: University of California Press, 2002.

Lowie, Robert H. *The Crow Indians.* Lincoln, NE: University of Nebraska Press, 1963.

Lyman, R. Lee. "The Holocene History of Pronghorn (Antilocapra Americana) in Eastern Washington State." *Northwest Science* 81, no. 2 (2007): 104-111.

Lysne, Steve. *A Guide to Southern Idaho's Freshwater Mollusks.* Boise, ID: US Fish and Wildlife Service, Idaho Fish and Wildlife Office, 2010.

Macdonell, John. "The Diary of John Macdonell." *Five Fur Traders of the Northwest.* Edited by Charles M. Gates. St. Paul, MN: Minnesota Historical Society, 1965.

Mackenzie, Alexander. *Voyages from Montreal on the River St. Laurence, through the Continent of North America to the Frozen and Pacific Oceans in the Years 1789 and 1793.* London: T. Cadell, Jr. & W. Davies, 1801.

Mackie, Richard Somerset. *Trading Beyond the Mountains, the British Fur Trade on the Pacific, 1793-1843.* Vancouver, BC: University of British Columbia Press, 1997.

Madsen, Brigham D. *The Northern Shoshoni.* Caldwell, ID: Caxton Printers, Ltd., 1980.

Manitoba, Archives of. "Flathead Post Report," (Winnipeg, MB). Online at http://pam.minisisinc.com/scripts/mwimain.dll/351/AUTHORITY_LINK/NAME/Flathead~20Post?JUMP (accessed 12-17-11).

Marsh, James B. *Four Years in the Rockies; or the Adventures of Isaac P. Rose.* New Castle, PA: W. B. Thomas, 1884.

Martin, Jill E. "'The Greatest Evil': Interpretations of Indian Prohibition Laws, 1832-1953." *Great Plains Quarterly* 23, no. 1 (Winter 2003): 35-53.

Mattes, Merrill J. *Jackson Hole, Crossroads of the Western Fur Trade 1807-1840.* Jackson, WY: Jackson Hole Museum and Teton County Historical Society, 1994.

_____. "Behind the Legend of Colter's Hell: the Early Exploration of Yellowstone National Park." *The Mississippi Valley Historical Review* 36, no. 2 (September 1949): 251-282.

_____. "Joseph Robidoux." *The Mountain Men and the Fur Trade of the Far West.* Vol. 8. Edited by Leroy R. Hafen. Glendale, CA: The Arthur H. Clark Company, 1971.

Mattison, Ray H. "James A. Hamilton (Palmer)." *The Mountain Men and the Fur Trade of the Far West.* Vol. 3. Edited by Leroy R. Hafen. Glendale, CA: The Arthur H. Clark Company, 1966.

_____. "William Laidlaw." *The Mountain Men and the Fur Trade of the Far West.* Vol. 3. Edited by Leroy R. Hafen. Glendale, CA: The Arthur H. Clark Company, 1966.

_____. "Kenneth McKenzie." *The Mountain Men and the Fur Trade of the Far West.* Vol. 2. Edited by Leroy R. Hafen. Glendale, CA: The Arthur H. Clark Company, 1965.

_____. "Joshua Pilcher." *The Mountain Men and the Fur Trade of the Far West*. Vol. 4. Edited by Leroy R. Hafen. Glendale, CA: The Arthur H. Clark Company, 1966.

Matzko, John. *Reconstructing Fort Union*. Lincoln, NE: University of Nebraska Press, 2001.

May, Samuel. "Class of 1829, Commencement. August 26, 1829." *Proceedings of the Cambridge Historical Society*. Cambridge, MA: Cambridge Historical Society, 1829.

Maximilian, Phillip. "Travels in the Interior of North America." *Early Western Travels 1748-1846*. Vols. 22-24. Edited by Reuben G. Thwaites. New York, NY: AMS Press, Inc., 1966.

McArthur, L. A. *Oregon Geographic Names*. Portland, OR: Oregon Historical Society, 1944.

McCaslin, Gus. "Little Known Lyons Ferry Played Historic Role Here." *Tri-City Herald*. (Pasco, Kennewick & Richland, WA) August 14, 1955.

McDonald, Lois Halliday. *The Fur Trade Letters of Francis Ermatinger*. Glendale, CA: The Arthur H. Clark Company, 1980.

McFeeters, Amy and Sally Zimmerman. *Mount Auburn Cemetery Reception House, Landmark Designation Report*. Cambridge, MA: Cambridge Historical Commission, 1992.

McGillivray, Duncan. *The Journal of Duncan McGillivray of the North West Company*. Edited by Arthur S. Morton. (1929) reprint: Fairfield, WA: Ye Galleon Press, 1989.

McLoughlin, John. *Letters of John McLoughlin*. Edited by Burt B. Barker. Portland, OR: Binfords & Mort, 1948.

_____. *The Letters of John McLoughlin from Fort Vancouver to the Governor and Committee*. First Series, 1825-38. Edited by E. E. Rich. London: The Hudson's Bay Record Society, 1941.

_____. *The Letters of John McLoughlin from Fort Vancouver to the Governor and Committee*. Third Series, 1844-46. Edited by E. E. Rich. London: The Hudson's Bay Record Society, 1944.

Means, Barbara and Richard Means. *John Kirk Townsend, Collector of Audubon's Western Birds and Mammals*. Glascow: the Authors, 2000.

Meany, Edmond S. "Washington Geographic Names." *The Washington Historical Quarterly* 8, no. 4 (October 1917): 265-290; 11, no. 2 (April, 1920): 115-136; 13, no. 3, (July 1922): 122-130; 13, no. 4 (October 1922): 284-292 .

Meek, Stephen Hall. *The Autobiography of a Mountain Man 1805-1889*. Edited by Arthur Woodward. Pasadena, CA: Glen Dawson, 1948.

Merriam, Alan P. *Ethnomusicology of the Flathead Indians*. Piscataway, NJ: Aldine Transactions, 1967.

Merk, Frederick. *Fur Trade and Empire, George Simpson's Journal 1824-25*. Cambridge, MA: The Belknap Press of Harvard University Press, 1968.

Michaelis, David. *N. C. Wyeth – A Biography*. New York, NY: Alfred Knopf, 1998.

Miller, Alex. "The Yankee Pedlar: Introduction of Percussion Lock Firearms into the Far West." *The Rocky Mountain Fur Trade Journal* 1 (2007): 85-92.

Montgomery, Richard G. *The White-Headed Eagle, John McLoughlin: Builder of an Empire*. New York, NY: MacMillan Company, 1934.

Morgan, Dale L. *Jedediah Smith and the Opening of the West*. New York, NY: The Bobbs-Merrill Company, Inc., 1953.

Morgan, Dale L. and Carl I. Wheat. *Jedediah Smith and His Maps of the American West*. San Francisco, CA: The California Historical Society, 1954.

Morrison, Dorothy N. *Outpost, John McLoughlin and the Far Northwest*. Portland, OR: Oregon Historical Society Press, 1999.

Morrison, Samuel E. "New England and the Opening of the Columbia River Salmon Trade, 1830." *The Oregon Historical Quarterly* 28, no. 2 (June 1927): 111-132.

Moulton, Gary E., ed. *The Journals of the Lewis & Clark Expedition*. 12 vols. Lincoln, NE: University of Nebraska Press, 1986-2001. Available online at http://www.lewisandclarkjournals.unl.edu.

Mudge, Zachariah A. *The Missionary Teacher: A Memoir of Cyrus Shepard*. New York, NY: Carlton & Porter, 1848.

Mullan, John. *Report on the Construction of a Military Road from Fort Walla-Walla to Fort Benton*. Washington, DC: Government Printing Office, 1863.

Munnick, Harriet D. "The Ermatinger Brothers, Edward and Francis." *The Mountain Men and the Fur Trade of the Far West.* Vol. 8. Edited by Leroy R. Hafen. Glendale, CA: The Arthur H. Clark Company, 1971.

_____. "Jean Baptiste Gervais." *The Mountain Men and the Fur Trade of the Far West.* Vol. 7. Edited by Leroy R. Hafen. Glendale, CA: The Arthur H. Clark Company, 1969.

_____. "Etienne Lucier." *The Mountain Men and the Fur Trade of the Far West.* Vol. 6. Edited by Leroy R. Hafen. Glendale, CA: The Arthur H. Clark Company, 1968.

_____. "Donald Manson." *The Mountain Men and the Fur Trade of the Far West.* Vol. 7. Edited by Leroy R. Hafen. Glendale, CA: The Arthur H. Clark Company, 1969.

_____. "Francois Rivet." *The Mountain Men and the Fur Trade of the Far West.* Vol. 7. Edited by Leroy R. Hafen. Glendale, CA: The Arthur H. Clark Company, 1969.

Negretti, Henry and Joseph Zambra. *A Treatise on Meteorological Instruments: Their Scientific Principles, Methods of Construction, And Practical Utility.* London: Negretti and Zambra, 1864.

Neil, Wilfred T. "Mystery of the Phoenix Buttons." *Relics, A Link to Our Pioneer Heritage* 2, no. 2 (Fall 1968): 4-5.

Nelson, J. Bryan. *Pelicans, Cormorants and Their Relatives: Pelecanidae, Sulidae, Phalacrocoracidae, Anhingidae, Fregatidae, Phaethontidae.* New York, NY: Oxford University Press, 2005.

Nester, William R. *The Arikara War, the First Plains Indian War, 1823.* Missoula, MT: Montana Press Publishing Company, 2001.

_____. *From Mountain Man to Millionaire, the "Bold and Dashing Life" of Robert Campbell.* Columbia, MO: University of Missouri Press, 2011.

Nevada State Library and Archives web site, found online at: http://nsla. nevadaculture.org/index.php?option=com_content&task=view&id=724& Itemid=418 (accessed October 6, 2011).

Newell, Robert. *Robert Newell's Memoranda.* Edited by Dorothy O. Johansen. Portland, OR: The Champoeg Press, 1959.

Nidever, George. *The Life and Adventures of George Nidever.* Edited by William H. Ellison. Berkeley, CA: University of California Press, 1937.

Niethammer, Carolyn. *Daughters of the Earth*. New York, NY: Collier Books, 1977.

Nisbet, Jack. *Sources of the River, Tracking David Thompson Across Western North America*. Seattle, WA: Sasquatch Books, 1994.

_____. *The Collector, David Douglas and the Natural History of the Northwest*. Seattle, WA: Sasquatch Books, 2009.

Nuttall, Thomas. "A Catalogue of a Collection of Plants made Chiefly in the Valleys of the Rocky Mountains or Northern Andes, Towards the Sources of the Columbia River, by Mr. Nathaniel B. Wyeth, and Described by T. Nuttall." *The Journal of the Academy of Natural Sciences of Philadelphia*, Vol. III, Part I, 1834.

Nunis, Doyce B. "Michel Laframboise." *The Mountain Men and the Fur Trade of the Far West*. Vol. 5. Edited by Leroy R. Hafen. Glendale, CA: The Arthur H. Clark Company, 1968.

Ogden, Peter S. *Peter Skene Ogden's Snake Country Journals, 1824-25 and 1825-26*. Edited by E. E. Rich. London: The Hudson's Bay Record Society, 1950.

_____. *Peter Skene Ogden's Snake Country Journals, 1827-28 and 1828-29*. Edited by Glyndwr Williams. London: The Hudson's Bay Record Society, 1971.

"Oregon History Project," Oregon Historical Society, catalog number: OrHi 45440, found online at: http://www.ohs.org/education/oregonhistory/historical_records/dspDocument.cfm?doc_ID=62F22F79-F524-BDE2-23F017D4416EEFBB (accessed September 13, 2011).

Overmeyer, Philip H. "Members of First Wyeth Expedition." *The Oregon Historical Society Quarterly* 36, no. 1 (March 1935): 95-101.

_____. "Nathaniel Jarvis Wyeth – His First Expedition." *The Washington Historical Quarterly* 24, no. 1 (1933): 28-48.

Paige, Lucius R. *History of Cambridge, 1630-1877*. New York, NY: H. O. Houghton and Company, 1877.

Palmer, Joel. "Journal of Travels over the Rocky Mountains," *Early Western Travels 1748- 1846*. Vol. 30. Edited by Reuben G. Thwaites. New York, NY: AMS Press, Inc., 1966. First published Cleveland, OH: The Arthur H. Clark Company, 1904-1907.

Parker, Samuel. *Journal of an Exploring Tour Beyond the Rocky Mountains*. Minneapolis, MN: Ross & Haines, 1838.

Paterson, Stanley and Carl Seaburg. *The Ice King: Frederic Tudor and His Circle.* Boston, MA: Massachusetts Historical Society and Mystic, CT: Mystic Seaport, 2003.

Patton, Bruce C. *Lewis & Clark, Doctors in the Wilderness.* Golden, CO: Fulcrum Publishing, 2001.

Pelletreau, William S. *Historic Homes and Institutions and Genealogical and Family History of New York.* New York, NY: The Lewis Publishing Company, 1907.

Peterson, Lee Allen. *Edible Wild Plants.* New York, NY: Houghton-Mifflin, 1977.

Phillips, Paul C. *The Fur Trade.* Norman, OK: University of Oklahoma Press, 1961.

_____. "William Henry Vanderburgh: Fur Trader." *The Mississippi Valley Historical Review* 30, no. 3 (December 1943): 377-394.

Pistono, Stephen. *Nathaniel Jarvis Wyeth: Boston Mountain Man in the Pacific Northwest, 1832-1836.* Unpublished thesis. East Lansing, MI: Michigan State University, 1964.

Point, Nicolas. *Wilderness Kingdom, Indian Life in the Rocky Mountains: 1840-1847, The Journals and Paintings of Nicolas Point.* Translated by Joseph P. Donnelly. New York, NY: Holt, Rinehart and Winston, 1967.

"The Ponca Tribe of Indians of Oklahoma vs. The United States of America," Indian Claims Commission case 12 Ind. C1. Corn. 265, Docket 322, July 26, 1963, found on line at http://digital.library.okstate.edu/icc/v12/iccv12ap265.pdf (accessed 1-20-12).

Porter, Kenneth W. *John Jacob Astor: Businessman.* Cambridge, MA: Harvard University Press, 1931.

Porter, Larry C. and Ronald E. Romig. "The Prairie Branch, Jackson County, Missouri: Emergence, Flourishing, and Demise, 1831-1834." *Mormon Historical Studies* 8, nos. 1, 2 (Spring, Fall 2007): 1-38.

Porter, Mae Reed and Odessa Davenport. *Scotsman in Buckskin, Sir William Drummond Stewart and the Rocky Mountain Fur Trade.* New York, NY: Hastings House Publishers, 1963.

Powell, Fred W., ed., *Hall J. Kelley on Oregon.* Princeton, NJ: Princeton University Press, 1932.

_____. "Hall Jackson Kelley – Prophet of Oregon." *The Quarterly of the Oregon Historical Society* 18, nos. 1-4 (March, June, September, December, 1917): 1-53, 93-139, 167-224, 271-270.

Quaife, Milo M. "Letters of John Ball, 1832-1833." *The Mississippi Valley Historical Review* 5, no. 4 (March, 1919): 450-468.

Raynolds, W. F. *Report on the Exploration of the Yellowstone River.* Washington, DC: Government Printing Office, 1868.

Reid, John P. *Contested Empire, Peter Skene Ogden and the Snake River Expeditions.* Norman, OK: University of Oklahoma Press, 2002.

Reid, Kenneth C., Susanne J. Miller and Lori Schiess. "Another Roll of the Dice: The Creekside Meadows Aboriginal Burial (10TE90) in Teton Valley, Eastern Idaho." Archaeology Survey of Idaho Report, 2012.

Robertson, Frank C. *Fort Hall – Gateway to the Oregon Country.* New York: Hastings House Publishers, 1963.

Robertson, R. G. *Competitive Struggle, America's Western Fur Trading Posts, 1746-1865.* Boise, ID: Tamarack Books, Inc., 1999.

Ronayne, Diane, Debra Patla, and Christine Saxton, eds. *Idaho's Amphibians and Reptiles – Description, Habitat & Ecology.* Boise, ID: Endangered Wildlife Program, 1994.

Ronda, James P. *Astoria & Empire.* Lincoln, NE: University of Nebraska Press, 1990.

_____. *Lewis and Clark Among the Indians.* Lincoln, NE: University of Nebraska Press, 1984.

_____. "'The Names of the Nations': Lewis and Clark as Ethnographers." *We Proceeded On* 7, no. 4 (November 1981): 12-17.

Ross, Alexander. *Adventures of the First Settlers on the Oregon or Columbia River.* Edited by Milo M. Quaife. New York, NY: The Citadel Press, 1969.

_____. *The Fur Hunters of the Far West.* Edited by Kenneth A. Spaulding. Norman, OK: University of Oklahoma Press, 1956.

Ross, Marvin C. *The West of Alfred Jacob Miller (1837).* Norman, OK: University of Oklahoma Press, 1968.

Rowlett, Russ. *How Many? A Dictionary of Units of Measurement.* Chapel Hill, NC: University of North Carolina, 2005.

Ruby, Robert H. and John A. Brown. *The Chinook Indians, Traders of the Lower Columbia River.* Norman, OK: University of Oklahoma Press, 1976.

_____. *The Spokane Indians, Children of the Sun.* Norman, OK: University of Oklahoma Press, 2006.

Russell, Carl P. *Firearms, Traps and Tools of the Mountain Man.* New York, NY: Alfred A. Knopf, 1967.

_____. "Duncan McDougall." *The Mountain Men and the Fur Trade of the Far West.* Vol. 5. Edited by Leroy R. Hafen. Glendale, CA: The Arthur H. Clark Company, 1968.

Russell, Osborne. *Journal of a Trapper.* Edited by Aubrey L. Haines. Portland, OR: Oregon Historical Society, 1955.

Ruxton, George. *Life in the Far West.* Edited by Leroy R. Hafen. Norman, OK: University of Oklahoma Press, 1951.

Ryser, Fred A. *Birds of the Great Basin, A Natural History.* Reno, NV: University of Nevada Press, 1985.

Sage, Rufus. *Rocky Mountain Life.* Boston, MA: Worthington & Company, 1857.

Salish-Pend d'Oreille Culture Committee and Elders Cultural Advisory Council, Confederated Salish and Kootenai Tribes. *The Salish People and the Lewis and Clark Expedition.* Lincoln, NE: University of Nebraska Press, 2005.

Sampson, William R. "Nathaniel Jarvis Wyeth." *The Mountain Men and the Fur Trade of the Far West.* Vol. 5. Edited by Leroy R. Hafen. Glendale, CA: The Arthur H. Clark Company, 1968.

Schoolcraft, Henry R. *Historical and Statistical Information Respecting the History, Condition and Prospects of the Indian Tribes of the United States.* Philadelphia, PA: Lippincott, Gambo & Company, 1851.

Sharples, Stephen P. "Nathaniel Jarvis Wyeth." *Cambridge Historical Society Publications, Proceedings, 1906-1907.* Cambridge, MA: Cambridge Historical Society, 1907.

Simpson, George. *An Overland Journey Around the World During the Years 1841 and 1842*. Philadelphia, PA: Lea and Blanchard, 1847.

Sinclair, Jill. *Fresh Pond, The History of a Cambridge Landscape*. Cambridge, MA: The Massachusetts Institute of Technology Press, 2009.

Skinner, G. Gage. "Sweet Encounters: Mountain Men and the Honey Bee on the Fur Trade Frontier." *The Rocky Mountain Fur Trade Journal* 2 (2008): 50-55.

Smith, Allan H. "The Location of Flathead Post." *Pacific Northwest Quarterly* 48, no. 2 (April 1957): 47-54.

Smoak, Gregory E. *Ghost Dances and Identity: Prophetic Religion and American Indian Ethnogenesis in the Nineteenth Century*. Berkeley, CA: University of California Press, 2006.

Spier, Leslie. *The Prophet Dance of the Northwest and Its Derivatives: the Source of the Ghost Dance*. Menasha, WI: George Banta Publishing Company, 1935.

Sprague, Roderick. "The Literature and Locations of the Phoenix Button." *Historical Archaeology* 32, no. 2 (1998): 56-77.

State Street Trust Company. *Some Events of Boston and Its Neighbors*. Boston: Walton Advertising & Printing Company, 1917.

Stelling, Peter and David S. Tucker, eds. *Floods, Faults and Fire: Geologic Fieldtrips in Washington State and Southwest British Columbia*. Boulder, CO: The Geological Society of America, Inc., 2007.

Stern, Theodore. *Chiefs & Chief Traders, Indian Relations at Fort Nez Percés, 1818-1855*. Eugene, OR: University of Oregon Press, 1993.

Stewart, Hilary. *Cedar: Tree of Life to the Northwest Coast Indians*. Vancouver, BC: Douglas and McIntyre, Ltd., 1984.

Stewart, William D. *Edward Warren*. London: Walker, 1854.

Stone, Arthur L. *Following Old Trails*. Missoula, MT: Morton John Elrod, 1913.

Stuart Robert. *The Discovery of the Oregon Trail; Robert Stuart's Narratives*. Edited by Phillip Ashton Rollins. New York, NY: Charles Scribner's Sons, 1935.

Sunder, John E. *Bill Sublette, Mountain Man*. Norman, OK: University of Oklahoma Press, 1959.

_____. *Fur Trade on the Upper Missouri, 1840-1865.* Norman, OK: University of Oklahoma Press, 1965.

_____. *Joshua Pilcher, Fur Trader and Indian Agent.* Norman, OK: University of Oklahoma Press, 1968.

Teit, James A. "The Salishan Tribes of the Western Plateau." *Bureau of American Ethnology.* Washington, DC: Government Printing Office, 1930.

Tekiela, Stan. *Birds of Idaho Field Guide.* Cambridge, MN: Adventure Publications, Inc., 2003.

Thompson, David "The Journal of David Thompson," Edited by T. C. Elliott. *The Quarterly of the Oregon Historical Society* 15, no. 1 (March 1914): 39-63.

Thompson, Erwin N. *Fort Union Trading Post.* Medora, ND: Theodore Roosevelt Nature and History Association, 1986.

Thrapp, Dan L. *Encyclopedia of Frontier Biography.* 4 vols. Spokane, WA: The Arthur H. Clark Company, 1990-1994.

Timbrook, Jan. *Chumash Ethnobotany.* Santa Barbara, CA: Santa Barbara Museum of Natural History, 2007.

Townsend, John Kirk. "Narrative of a Journey Across the Rocky Mountains to the Columbia River." *Early Western Travels 1748-1846.* Vol. 21. Edited by Reuben G. Thwaites. New York, NY: AMS Press, Inc., 1966.

Trenholm, Virginia Cole and Maurine Carley. *The Shoshonis, Sentinels of the Rockies.* Norman, OK: University of Oklahoma Press, 1964.

United States Department of the Interior, Bureau of Reclamation. *Report on Proposed Columbia River Project.* (Denver, 1932).

Urbanek, Mae. *Wyoming Place Names.* Boulder, CO: Johnson Publishing Company, 1974.

Victor, Frances F. "Flotsam and Jetsam of the Pacific – The Voyage of the *Owyhee,* the *Sultana,* and the *May Dacre.*" *The Quarterly of the Oregon Historical Society* 2, no. 5 (March 1901): 36-54.

_____. *River of the West.* Hartford, CN: R. W. Bliss Co., 1870.

Walker, Ardis M. "Joseph R. Walker." *The Mountain Men and the Fur Trade of the Far West.* Vol. 5. Edited by Leroy R. Hafen. Glendale, CA: The Arthur H. Clark Company, 1968.

Walker, Scott. "Warren Ferris, the Hudson's Bay Company and the Rendezvous of 1834." *The Rocky Mountain Fur Trade Journal* 4 (2010): 80-107.

Watson, Bruce McIntyre. *Lives Lived West of the Divide.* Kelowna, BC: University of British Columbia, Okanagon, 2010.

Weaver, John E. "A Study of the Vegetation of Southeastern Washington and Adjacent Idaho." *The University Studies of the University of Nebraska* 17, no. 1 (January 1917): 1- 133.

Weightman, Gavin. *The Frozen Water Trade, How Ice from New England Lakes Kept the World Cool.* London: Harper Collins Publishers, 2001.

Wheat, Carl I. *Mapping the Transmississippi West.* 6 vols. San Francisco, CA: The Institute of Historical Cartography, 1957-1963.

White, M. Catherine. *David Thompson's Journals Relating to Montana and Adjacent Regions, 1808-1812.* Missoula, MT: Montana State University Press, 1950.

Whitney, William Dwight and Benjamin Eli Smith. *The Century Dictionary and Cyclopedia.* New York, NY: The Century Company, 1889.

Wickstrom, Leah and John Barco. *Albeni Falls Dam Flexible Winter Power Operations, Bonner County, Idaho – Final Environmental Assessment.* Seattle, WA: U. S. Army Corps of Engineers-Seattle District and Bonneville Power Administration, 2011.

Wilkes, Charles. *Narrative of the United States Exploring Expedition, 1838-1842.* Philadelphia, PA: Lea and Blanchard, 1845.

Willard, John. *Adventure Trails in Montana.* Helena, MT: State Publishing Company, 1964.

Williams, E. Rick. "Wheels to Rendezvous." *The Rocky Mountain Fur Trade Journal* 4 (2010): 108-125.

Williams, Glyndwr, ed. "The 'Character Book' of George Simpson," *Hudson's Bay Miscellany, 1670-1870.* Winnipeg, MB: Hudson's Bay Record Society, 1975.

Wishart, David J., ed. *Encyclopedia of the Great Plains Indians.* Lincoln, NE: University of Nebraska Press, 2007.

Wislizenus, F. A. *A Journey to the Rocky Mountains in the Year 1839*. Fairfield, WA: Ye Galleon Press, 1989.

Wood, W. Raymund. "James Kipp: Upper Missouri River Fur Trader and Missouri Farmer." *North Dakota History Journal of the Plains* 77, nos. 1, 2 (Winter, Spring 2011): 2-35.

Wood, W. Raymund, William J. Hunt, and Randy H. Williams. *Fort Clark and Its Indian Neighbors; a Trading Post on the Upper Missouri*. Norman, OK: University of Oklahoma Press, 2011.

Woodger, Elin and Brandon Toropov. *Encyclopedia of the Lewis and Clark Expedition*. New York, NY: Facts on File, Inc., 2004.

Woodruff, E. G. *The Lander and Salt Creek Oil Fields, Wyoming*. Department of the Interior, United States Geological Survey, Bulletin 452. Washington, DC: Government Printing Office, 1911.

Woodward, Larry L. *Proposed Jarbidge Resource Management Plan and Final Environmental Impact Statement*. Boise, ID: Department of the Interior, Bureau of Land Management, Boise District, 1985.

Woody, Frank H. "A Sketch of the Early History of Western Montana." *Contributions to the Historical Society of Montana*. Helena, MT: State Publishing Company, 1896.

Work, John. *The Snake Country Expedition of 1830-1831: John Work's Field Journal*. Edited by Francis D. Haines. Norman, OK: University of Oklahoma Press, 1971.

_____. "The Journal of John Work; July 5-September 15, 1826." Edited by T. C. Elliott. *The Washington Historical Quarterly* 6, no. 1 (January 1915): 26-49.

_____. "The Journal of John Work," Edited by T. C. Elliott. *The Washington Historical Quarterly* 5, no. 2 (April 1914): 83-115.

_____. "The Journal of John Work." Edited by T. C. Elliott. *The Washington Historical Quarterly* 5, no. 3 (July 1914): 163-191.

_____. *The Journal of John Work*. Edited by William S. Lewis and Paul C. Phillips. Cleveland, OH: The Arthur H. Clark Company, 1923.

Works Progress Administration. *Idaho, a Guide in Word and Picture*. New York, NY: Oxford University Press, 1950.

Wright, Mary C. "Economic Development and Native American Women in the Early Nineteenth Century." *American Quarterly* 33, no. 5 (Winter 1981): 525-536.

Wyeth, John B. "Oregon; Or a Short History of a Long Journey," *Early Western Travels 1748-1846.* Vol. 21. Edited by Reuben G. Thwaites. New York, NY: AMS Press, Inc., 1966. First published Cleveland, OH: The Arthur H. Clark Company, 1904-1907.

Wyeth, Nathaniel J. "Indian Tribes of the South Pass of the Rocky Mountains; the Salt Lake Basin; the Valley of the Great Säaptin, or Lewis River, and the Pacific Coasts of Oregon." Schoolcraft, Henry R. *Historical and Statistical Information Respecting the History Condition and Prospects of the Indian Tribes of the United States.* Vol. 1. Philadelphia, PA: Lippincott, Gambo & Company, 1851.

Wyeth, Nathaniel J. "Mr. Wyeth's Memoir," Appendix I, 25 Congress, 3 Session, House Reports no. 101. Washington, DC: Government Printing Office, 1839.

Young, Frederic G., ed. "The Correspondence and Journals of Captain Nathaniel J. Wyeth, 1831-6." *Sources of the History of Oregon, Vol. I.* Eugene, OR: Oregon Historical Society, 1899.

Youngblood, Andrew, Timothy Max and Kent Coe. Stand Structure in Eastside Old-growth Ponderosa Pine Forests of Oregon and Northern California. Portland, OR: U. S. Forest Service, Pacific Northwest Research Station, 2004. Online at http://www.arcfuels.org/maggie/AGER%202011.Data/PDF/YoungbloodEt_2004_FEM.pdf (accessed 10-20-11)

Yount, George C. *George C. Yount and His Chronicles of the West.* Edited by Charles L. Camp. Denver, CO: Old West Publishing, 1966.

Zontek, Kenneth. *Buffalo Nation.* Lincoln, NE: University of Nebraska Press, 2007.

Zwickel, Fred C. and Michael A. Schroeder. "Grouse of the Lewis and Clark Expedition, 1803 to 1806." *Northwestern Naturalist* 84 (Spring 2003):1-19.

Index

J